PSALMS, BOOKS 2–3

WISDOM COMMENTARY

Volume 21

Psalms
Books 2-3

Denise Dombkowski Hopkins

Linda M. Maloney
Volume Editor

Barbara E. Reid, OP
General Editor

A Michael Glazier Book

LITURGICAL PRESS

Collegeville, Minnesota

www.litpress.org

A Michael Glazier Book published by Liturgical Press

Cover design by Ann Blattner. *Chapter Letter 'W', Acts of the Apostles, Chapter 4*, Donald Jackson, Copyright 2002, *The Saint John's Bible*, Saint John's University, Collegeville, Minnesota USA. Used by permission. All rights reserved.

1	2	3	4	5	6	7	8	9

Library of Congress Cataloging-in-Publication Data

Names: Hopkins, Denise Dombkowski, author.
Title: Psalms : books 2–3 / Denise Dombkowski Hopkins.
Description: Collegeville, Minnesota : Liturgical Press, 2016. | Series: Wisdom commentary ; Volume 21 | "A Michael Glazier book." | Includes bibliographical references and index.
Identifiers: LCCN 2016030217 (print) | LCCN 2016035650 (ebook) | ISBN 9780814681206 (hardcover : alk. paper) | ISBN 9780814681459 (ebook)
Subjects: LCSH: Bible. Psalms, XLII–LXXXIX—Feminist criticism. | Catholic Church—Doctrines.
Classification: LCC BS1430.52 H67 2016 (print) | LCC BS1430.52 (ebook) | DDC 223/.206—dc23
LC record available at https://lccn.loc.gov/2016030217

*To my mother, Rose Farina Dombkowski (1922–2013),
who raised a feminist even though she was caught
in the web of patriarchy all her life.*

Contents

Abbreviations

ABR	*Australian Biblical Review*
BBR	*Bulletin for Biblical Research*
Bib	*Biblica*
BibInt	*Biblical Interpretation*
BibInt	Biblical Interpretation Series
BRev	*Bible Review*
BSac	*Bibliotheca Sacra*
BZAW	*Beihefte zur Zeitschrift für die alttestamentliche Wissenschaft*
CBQ	*Catholic Biblical Quarterly*
CurTM	*Currents in Theology and Mission*
FAO	Food and Agricultural Organization of the United Nations
FCB	Feminist Companion to the Bible
HBT	*Horizons in Biblical Theology*
HSM	Harvard Semitic Monographs
HTS	Harvard Theological Studies
IFT	Introductions in Feminist Theology
Int	*Interpretation*
JBL	*Journal of Biblical Literature*
JFSR	*Journal of Feminist Studies in Religion*

JPS	Jewish Publication Society
JSem	*Journal of Semitics*
JSOT	*Journal for the Study of the Old Testament*
JSOTSup	Journal for the Study of the Old Testament Supplement Series
JSS	*Journal of Semitic Studies*
JTS	*Journal of Theological Studies*
KJV	King James Version
MT	Masoretic Text
NIB	*New Interpreter's Bible*
NIV	New International Version
NRSV	New Revised Standard Version
OBT	Overtures to Biblical Theology
OLT	Old Testament Library
OtSt	*Oudtestamentische Studiën*
PL	Patrologia Latina
ProEccl	*Pro Ecclesia*
RevExp	*Review and Expositor*
SBL	*Society of Biblical Literature*
SK	*Skrif en kerk*
StBibLit	Studies in Biblical Literature (Lang)
SymS	Symposium Series
USQR	*Union Seminary Quarterly Review*
VT	*Vetus Testamentum*
VTSup	Supplements to Vetus Testamentum
WW	*Word and World*
ZAW	*Zeitschrift für die alttestamentliche Wissenschaft*

Acknowledgments

My thanks to: Barbara Reid for her vision and encouragement; the Contributing Voices to this volume, most of whom are my former students and teaching assistants at Wesley: Amy, Yolanda, Su Jung, Beth, Audrey, Katherine, Lora, Tiffany (SPT); Liturgical Press for its boldness; Wesley Theological Seminary for granting me a one-year sabbatical that allowed me to complete much of this work; Sharon Ringe, my emerita colleague who first suggested that this was something I might want to do; and colleague Michael Koppel for his moral support.

Contributors

Katherine Brown is a doctoral candidate at The Catholic University of America researching the significance of the prophetic texts' materiality as bearing on their message. Brown is an ordained deacon in the United Methodist Church.

The Rev. Dr. Lora F. Hargrove is the executive minister at Mount Calvary Baptist Church in Rockville, Maryland, and is a PhD student in systematic theology at the University of South Africa. She has served as a consultant for Columbia University on sexuality, sexual politics, and the black church and has been a consultant for the Samuel DeWitt Proctor Conference around multiple justice-related issues. Dr. Hargrove is also the former director of Faith-based Outreach for the US Department of Health and Human Services' Office of HIV/AIDS Policy. She is an independent consultant and writer whose focus is connecting faith, scholarship, and public policy.

Rev. Dr. Tiffany Houck-Loomis is a Jungian-oriented psychotherapist in private practice; lecturer in philosophy, religious studies, and pastoral care and counseling; minister of Word and Sacrament within the Reformed Church in America; author of numerous articles at the intersection of Hebrew Bible and depth psychology; yogi; and mother of two. She holds a PhD in psychology and religion and Hebrew Bible from Union Theological Seminary. Of mixed Jewish and Native American descent, she is currently writing for a faith-based educational resource called *Reading Between the Lines* (www.educationalcenter.org).

Amy Beth W. Jones earned her PhD in biblical studies at Drew University and is an ordained deacon in the United Methodist Church. She is currently the director of external relations at Drew Theological School. She has written on the book of Ruth, Genesis 4, and narrative space and identity construction in the book of Judges.

Beth Norcross works in the area of eco-theology. Beth is the founder and director of the Center for Spirituality in Nature, which offers experiences in nature designed to deepen spirituality and encourage loving relationships with all earth's creatures (www.centerforspiritualityinnature .org). She is also the cofounder of the national Green Seminary Initiative (www.greenseminaries.org), which encourages seminaries to integrate care and engagement with creation into all aspects of theological education.

Rev. Yolanda M. Norton is a PhD candidate at Vanderbilt University in Hebrew Bible and ancient Israel whose research interests include womanist biblical interpretation and literary criticism. Her publications include chapters in *I Found God in Me: A Womanist Biblical Hermeneutics Reader* and *Global Perspectives on the Old Testament*. Yolanda has taught courses at Wesley Theological Seminary and Moravian Theological Seminary. She is an ordained clergywoman in the Christian Church (Disciples of Christ) and has served the church in various capacities, including campus minister, children's pastor, and youth minister.

The Rev. Audrey Coretta Price is an ordained minister in the United Church of Christ and American Baptist Churches USA. She currently works as a director of Christian education in the UCC and is adjunct faculty at Wesley Theological Seminary. She is a PhD candidate at The Catholic University of America studying systematic theology with an emphasis on liberation theology. She brings an advocacy for social justice and womanist interests with a lens on theological aesthetics.

Dr. SuJung Shin is adjunct professor of biblical studies at New Brunswick Theological Seminary in New Jersey. Coming from a religiously diverse Korean cultural context, she offers various perspectives on religion and gender in our multicultural and multi-communicational world. Her research interests in the Hebrew Bible include dialogic hermeneutics of the Bible, Asian feminist readings of the text, interdisciplinary interpretations, and nonstructuralist approaches.

Foreword

"Tell It on the Mountain"—or, "And You Shall Tell Your Daughter [as Well]"

Athalya Brenner-Idan
Universiteit van Amsterdam/Tel Aviv University

What can Wisdom Commentary do to help, and for whom? The commentary genre has always been privileged in biblical studies. Traditionally acclaimed commentary series, such as the International Critical Commentary, Old Testament and New Testament Library, Hermeneia, Anchor Bible, Eerdmans, and Word—to name but several—enjoy nearly automatic prestige; and the number of women authors who participate in those is relatively small by comparison to their growing number in the scholarly guild. There certainly are some volumes written by women in them, especially in recent decades. At this time, however, this does not reflect the situation on the ground. Further, size matters. In that sense, the sheer size of the Wisdom Commentary is essential. This also represents a considerable investment and the possibility of reaching a wider audience than those already "converted."

Expecting women scholars to deal especially or only with what are considered strictly "female" matters seems unwarranted. According to Audre Lorde, "The master's tools will never dismantle the master's house."[1] But this maxim is not relevant to our case. The point of this commentary is not to destroy but to attain greater participation in the interpretive dialogue about biblical texts. Women scholars may bring additional questions to the readerly agenda as well as fresh angles to existing issues. To assume that their questions are designed only to topple a certain male hegemony is not convincing.

At first I did ask myself: is this commentary series an addition to calm raw nerves, an embellishment to make upholding the old hierarchy palatable? Or is it indeed about becoming the Master? On second and third thoughts, however, I understood that becoming the Master is not what this is about. Knowledge is power. Since Foucault at the very least, this cannot be in dispute. Writing commentaries for biblical texts by women for women and for men, of confessional as well as non-confessional convictions, will sabotage (hopefully) the established hierarchy but will not topple it. This is about an attempt to integrate more fully, to introduce another viewpoint, to become. What excites me about the Wisdom Commentary is that it is not offered as just an alternative supplanting or substituting for the dominant discourse.

These commentaries on biblical books will retain nonauthoritative, pluralistic viewpoints. And yes, once again, the weight of a dedicated series, to distinguish from collections of stand-alone volumes, will prove weightier.

That such an approach is especially important in the case of the Hebrew Bible/Old Testament is beyond doubt. Women of Judaism, Christianity, and also Islam have struggled to make it their own for centuries, even more than they have fought for the New Testament and the Qur'an. Every Hebrew Bible/Old Testament volume in this project is evidence that the day has arrived: it is now possible to read *all* the Jewish canonical books as a collection, for a collection they are, with guidance conceived with the needs of women readers (not only men) as an integral inspiration and part thereof.

In my Jewish tradition, the main motivation for reciting the Haggadah, the ritual text recited yearly on Passover, the festival of liberation from

---

1. Audre Lorde, "The Master's Tools Will Never Dismantle the Master's House," in *Sister Outsider: Essays and Speeches* (Berkeley, CA: Crossing Press, 1984, 2007), 110–14. First delivered in the Second Sex Conference in New York, 1979.

bondage, is given as "And you shall tell your son" (from Exod 13:8). The knowledge and experience of past generations is thus transferred to the next, for constructing the present and the future. The ancient maxim is, literally, limited to a male audience. This series remolds the maxim into a new inclusive shape, which is of the utmost consequence: "And you shall tell your son" is extended to "And you shall tell your daughter [as well as your son]." Or, if you want, "Tell it on the mountain," for all to hear.

This is what it's all about.

Editor's Introduction to Wisdom Commentary

"She Is a Breath of the Power of God" (Wis 7:25)

Barbara E. Reid, OP

General Editor

Wisdom Commentary is the first series to offer detailed feminist interpretation of every book of the Bible. The fruit of collaborative work by an ecumenical and interreligious team of scholars, the volumes provide serious, scholarly engagement with the whole biblical text, not only those texts that explicitly mention women. The series is intended for clergy, teachers, ministers, and all serious students of the Bible. Designed to be both accessible and informed by the various approaches of biblical scholarship, it pays particular attention to the world in front of the text, that is, how the text is heard and appropriated. At the same time, this series aims to be faithful to the ancient text and its earliest audiences; thus the volumes also explicate the worlds behind the text and within it. While issues of gender are primary in this project, the volumes also address the intersecting issues of power, authority, ethnicity, race, class, and religious belief and practice. The fifty-eight volumes include the books regarded as canonical by Jews (i.e., the Tanakh); Protestants (the "Hebrew Bible" and the New Testament); and Roman Catholic, Anglican, and Eastern Orthodox Communions (i.e.,

Tobit, Judith, 1 and 2 Maccabees, Wisdom of Solomon, Sirach/Ecclesiasticus, Baruch, including the Letter of Jeremiah, the additions to Esther, and Susanna and Bel and the Dragon in Daniel).

A Symphony of Diverse Voices

Included in the Wisdom Commentary series are voices from scholars of many different religious traditions, of diverse ages, differing sexual identities, and varying cultural, racial, ethnic, and social contexts. Some have been pioneers in feminist biblical interpretation; others are newer contributors from a younger generation. A further distinctive feature of this series is that each volume incorporates voices other than that of the lead author(s). These voices appear alongside the commentary of the lead author(s), in the grayscale inserts. At times, a contributor may offer an alternative interpretation or a critique of the position taken by the lead author(s). At other times, she or he may offer a complementary interpretation from a different cultural context or subject position. Occasionally, portions of previously published material bring in other views. The diverse voices are not intended to be contestants in a debate or a cacophony of discordant notes. The multiple voices reflect that there is no single definitive feminist interpretation of a text. In addition, they show the importance of subject position in the process of interpretation. In this regard, the Wisdom Commentary series takes inspiration from the Talmud and from *The Torah: A Women's Commentary* (ed. Tamara Cohn Eskenazi and Andrea L. Weiss; New York: Women of Reform Judaism, Federation of Temple Sisterhood, 2008), in which many voices, even conflicting ones, are included and not harmonized.

Contributors include biblical scholars, theologians, and readers of Scripture from outside the scholarly and religious guilds. At times, their comments pertain to a particular text. In some instances they address a theme or topic that arises from the text.

Another feature that highlights the collaborative nature of feminist biblical interpretation is that a number of the volumes have two lead authors who have worked in tandem from the inception of the project and whose voices interweave throughout the commentary.

Woman Wisdom

The title, Wisdom Commentary, reflects both the importance to feminists of the figure of Woman Wisdom in the Scriptures and the distinct wisdom that feminist women and men bring to the interpretive process. In the Scriptures, Woman Wisdom appears as "a breath of the power of God, and a pure emanation of the glory of the Almighty" (Wis 7:25), who was present and active in fashioning all that exists (Prov 8:22-31; Wis 8:6). She is a spirit who pervades and penetrates all things (Wis 7:22-23), and she provides guidance and nourishment at her all-inclusive table (Prov 9:1-5). In both postexilic biblical and nonbiblical Jewish sources, Woman Wisdom is often equated with Torah, e.g., Sirach 24:23-34; Baruch 3:9–4:4; 38:2; 46:4-5; 2 Baruch 48:33, 36; 4 Ezra 5:9-10; 13:55; 14:40; 1 Enoch 42.

The New Testament frequently portrays Jesus as Wisdom incarnate. He invites his followers, "take my yoke upon you and learn from me" (Matt 11:29), just as Ben Sira advises, "put your neck under her [Wisdom's] yoke and let your souls receive instruction" (Sir 51:26). Just as Wisdom experiences rejection (Prov 1:23-25; Sir 15:7-8; Wis 10:3; Bar 3:12), so too does Jesus (Mark 8:31; John 1:10-11). Only some accept his invitation to his all-inclusive banquet (Matt 22:1-14; Luke 14:15-24; compare Prov 1:20-21; 9:3-5). Yet, "wisdom is vindicated by her deeds" (Matt 11:19, speaking of Jesus and John the Baptist; in the Lucan parallel at 7:35 they are called "wisdom's children"). There are numerous parallels between what is said of Wisdom and of the *Logos* in the Prologue of the Fourth Gospel (John 1:1-18). These are only a few of many examples. This female embodiment of divine presence and power is an apt image to guide the work of this series.

Feminism

There are many different understandings of the term "feminism." The various meanings, aims, and methods have developed exponentially in recent decades. Feminism is a perspective and a movement that springs from a recognition of inequities toward women, and it advocates for changes in whatever structures prevent full human flourishing. Three waves of feminism in the United States are commonly recognized. The first, arising in the mid-nineteenth century and lasting into the early twentieth, was sparked by women's efforts to be involved in the public sphere and to win the right to vote. In the 1960s and 1970s, the second wave focused on civil rights and equality for women. With the third wave, from the 1980s forward, came global feminism and the emphasis on the contextual nature of interpretation. Now a fourth wave may be emerging, with a stronger emphasis on the intersectionality of women's concerns with those of other marginalized groups and the increased use of the internet as a platform for discussion and activism.[1] As feminism has matured, it has recognized that inequities based on gender are interwoven with power imbalances based on race, class, ethnicity, religion, sexual identity, physical ability, and a host of other social markers.

Feminist Women and Men

Men who choose to identify with and partner with feminist women in the work of deconstructing systems of domination and building structures of equality are rightly regarded as feminists. Some men readily identify with experiences of women who are discriminated against on the basis of sex/gender, having themselves had comparable experiences; others who may not have faced direct discrimination or stereotyping recognize that inequity and problematic characterization still occur, and they seek correction. This series is pleased to include feminist men both as lead authors and as contributing voices.

Feminist Biblical Interpretation

Women interpreting the Bible from the lenses of their own experience is nothing new. Throughout the ages women have recounted the biblical stories, teaching them to their children and others, all the while interpreting them afresh for their time and circumstances.[2] Following is a very brief sketch of select foremothers who laid the groundwork for contemporary feminist biblical interpretation.

One of the earliest known Christian women who challenged patriarchal interpretations of Scripture was a consecrated virgin named Helie, who lived in the second century CE. When she refused to marry, her

---

1. See Martha Rampton, "Four Waves of Feminism" (October 25, 2015), at http://www.pacificu.edu/about-us/news-events/four-waves-feminism; and Ealasaid Munro, "Feminism: A Fourth Wave?," https://www.psa.ac.uk/insight-plus/feminism-fourth-wave.

2. For fuller treatments of this history, see chap. 7, "One Thousand Years of Feminist Bible Criticism," in Gerda Lerner, *Creation of Feminist Consciousness: From the Middle Ages to Eighteen-Seventy* (New York: Oxford University Press, 1993), 138–66; Susanne Scholz, "From the 'Woman's Bible' to the 'Women's Bible,' The History of Feminist Approaches to the Hebrew Bible," in *Introducing the Women's Hebrew Bible*, IFT 13 (New York: T & T Clark, 2007), 12–32; Marion Ann Taylor and Agnes Choi, eds., *Handbook of Women Biblical Interpreters: A Historical and Biographical Guide* (Grand Rapids, MI: Baker Academic, 2012).

parents brought her before a judge, who quoted to her Paul's admonition, "It is better to marry than to be aflame with passion" (1 Cor 7:9). In response, Helie first acknowledges that this is what Scripture says, but then she retorts, "but not for everyone, that is, not for holy virgins."[3] She is one of the first to question the notion that a text has one meaning that is applicable in all situations.

A Jewish woman who also lived in the second century CE, Beruriah, is said to have had "profound knowledge of biblical exegesis and outstanding intelligence."[4] One story preserved in the Talmud (b. Berakot 10a) tells of how she challenged her husband, Rabbi Meir, when he prayed for the destruction of a sinner. Proffering an alternate interpretation, she argued that Psalm 104:35 advocated praying for the destruction of sin, not the sinner.

In medieval times the first written commentaries on Scripture from a critical feminist point of view emerge. While others may have been produced and passed on orally, they are for the most part lost to us now. Among the earliest preserved feminist writings are those of Hildegard of Bingen (1098–1179), German writer, mystic, and abbess of a Benedictine monastery. She reinterpreted the Genesis narratives in a way that presented women and men as complementary and interdependent. She frequently wrote about feminine aspects of the Divine.[5] Along with other women mystics of the time, such as Julian of Norwich (1342–ca. 1416), she spoke authoritatively from her personal experiences of God's revelation in prayer.

In this era, women were also among the scribes who copied biblical manuscripts. Notable among them is Paula Dei Mansi of Verona, from a distinguished family of Jewish scribes. In 1288, she translated from Hebrew into Italian a collection of Bible commentaries written by her father and added her own explanations.[6]

Another pioneer, Christine de Pizan (1365–ca. 1430), was a French court writer and prolific poet. She used allegory and common sense to

3. Madrid, Escorial MS, a II 9, f. 90 v., as cited in Lerner, *Feminist Consciousness*, 140.

4. See Judith R. Baskin, "Women and Post-Biblical Commentary," in *The Torah: A Women's Commentary*, ed. Tamara Cohn Eskenazi and Andrea L. Weiss (New York: Women of Reform Judaism, Federation of Temple Sisterhood, 2008), xlix–lv, at lii.

5. Hildegard of Bingen, *De Operatione Dei*, 1.4.100; PL 197:885bc, as cited in Lerner, *Feminist Consciousness*, 142–43. See also Barbara Newman, *Sister of Wisdom: St. Hildegard's Theology of the Feminine* (Berkeley: University of California Press, 1987).

6. Emily Taitz, Sondra Henry, Cheryl Tallan, eds., *JPS Guide to Jewish Women 600 B.C.E.–1900 C.E.* (Philadelphia: JPS, 2003), 110–11.

subvert misogynist readings of Scripture and celebrated the accomplishments of female biblical figures to argue for women's active roles in building society.[7]

By the seventeenth century, there were women who asserted that the biblical text needs to be understood and interpreted in its historical context. For example, Rachel Speght (1597–ca. 1630), a Calvinist English poet, elaborates on the historical situation in first-century Corinth that prompted Paul to say, "It is well for a man not to touch a woman" (1 Cor 7:1). Her aim was to show that the biblical texts should not be applied in a literal fashion to all times and circumstances. Similarly, Margaret Fell (1614–1702), one of the founders of the Religious Society of Friends (Quakers) in Britain, addressed the Pauline prohibitions against women speaking in church by insisting that they do not have universal validity. Rather, they need to be understood in their historical context, as addressed to a local church in particular time-bound circumstances.[8]

Along with analyzing the historical context of the biblical writings, women in the eighteenth and nineteenth centuries began to attend to misogynistic interpretations based on faulty translations. One of the first to do so was British feminist Mary Astell (1666–1731).[9] In the United States, the Grimké sisters, Sarah (1792–1873) and Angelina (1805–1879), Quaker women from a slaveholding family in South Carolina, learned biblical Greek and Hebrew so that they could interpret the Bible for themselves. They were prompted to do so after men sought to silence them from speaking out against slavery and for women's rights by claiming that the Bible (e.g., 1 Cor 14:34) prevented women from speaking in public.[10] Another prominent abolitionist, Sojourner Truth (ca. 1797–1883), a former slave, quoted the Bible liberally in her speeches[11] and in so doing challenged cultural assumptions and biblical interpretations that undergird gender inequities.

---

7. See further Taylor and Choi, *Handbook of Women Biblical Interpreters*, 127–32.

8. Her major work, *Women's Speaking Justified, Proved and Allowed by the Scriptures*, published in London in 1667, gave a systematic feminist reading of all biblical texts pertaining to women.

9. Mary Astell, *Some Reflections upon Marriage* (New York: Source Book Press, 1970, reprint of the 1730 edition; earliest edition of this work is 1700), 103–4.

10. See further Sarah Grimké, *Letters on the Equality of the Sexes and the Condition of Woman* (Boston: Isaac Knapp, 1838).

11. See, for example, her most famous speech, "Ain't I a Woman?," delivered in 1851 at the Ohio Women's Rights Convention in Akron, OH; http://www.fordham.edu/halsall/mod/sojtruth-woman.asp.

Another monumental work that emerged in nineteenth-century England was that of Jewish theologian Grace Aguilar (1816–1847), *The Women of Israel*,[12] published in 1845. Aguilar's approach was to make connections between the biblical women and contemporary Jewish women's concerns. She aimed to counter the widespread notion that women were degraded in Jewish law and that only in Christianity were women's dignity and value upheld. Her intent was to help Jewish women find strength and encouragement by seeing the evidence of God's compassionate love in the history of every woman in the Bible. While not a full commentary on the Bible, Aguilar's work stands out for its comprehensive treatment of every female biblical character, including even the most obscure references.[13]

The first person to produce a full-blown feminist commentary on the Bible was Elizabeth Cady Stanton (1815–1902). A leading proponent in the United States for women's right to vote, she found that whenever women tried to make inroads into politics, education, or the work world, the Bible was quoted against them. Along with a team of like-minded women, she produced her own commentary on every text of the Bible that concerned women. Her pioneering two-volume project, *The Woman's Bible*, published in 1895 and 1898, urges women to recognize that texts that degrade women come from the men who wrote the texts, not from God, and to use their common sense to rethink what has been presented to them as sacred.

Nearly a century later, *The Women's Bible Commentary*, edited by Sharon Ringe and Carol Newsom (Westminster John Knox Press, 1992), appeared. This one-volume commentary features North American feminist scholarship on each book of the Protestant canon. Like Cady Stanton's commentary, it does not contain comments on every section of the biblical text but only on those passages deemed relevant to women. It was revised and expanded in 1998 to include the Apocrypha/Deuterocanonical books, and the contributors to this new volume reflect the global face of contemporary feminist scholarship. The revisions made in the third edition, which appeared in 2012, represent the profound advances in feminist biblical scholarship and include newer voices. In both the second and third editions, *The* has been dropped from the title.

---

12. The full title is *The Women of Israel or Characters and Sketches from the Holy Scriptures and Jewish History Illustrative of the Past History, Present Duty, and Future Destiny of the Hebrew Females, as Based on the Word of God.*

13. See further Eskenazi and Weiss, *The Torah: A Women's Commentary*, xxxviii; Taylor and Choi, *Handbook of Women Biblical Interpreters*, 31–37.

Also appearing at the centennial of Cady Stanton's *The Woman's Bible* were two volumes edited by Elisabeth Schüssler Fiorenza with the assistance of Shelly Matthews. The first, *Searching the Scriptures: A Feminist Introduction* (New York: Crossroad, 1993), charts a comprehensive approach to feminist interpretation from ecumenical, interreligious, and multicultural perspectives. The second volume, published in 1994, provides critical feminist commentary on each book of the New Testament as well as on three books of Jewish Pseudepigrapha and eleven other early Christian writings.

In Europe, similar endeavors have been undertaken, such as the one-volume *Kompendium Feministische Bibelauslegung*, edited by Luise Schottroff and Marie-Theres Wacker (Gütersloh, Gütersloher Verlagshaus, 2007), featuring German feminist biblical interpretation of each book of the Bible, along with apocryphal books, and several extrabiblical writings. This work, now in its third edition, has recently been translated into English.[14] A multivolume project, *The Bible and Women: An Encylopaedia of Exegesis and Cultural History*, edited by Irmtraud Fischer, Adriana Valerio, Mercedes Navarro Puerto, and Christiana de Groot, is currently in production. This project presents a history of the reception of the Bible as embedded in Western cultural history and focuses particularly on gender-relevant biblical themes, biblical female characters, and women recipients of the Bible. The volumes are published in English, Spanish, Italian, and German.[15]

Another groundbreaking work is the collection The Feminist Companion to the Bible Series, edited by Athalya Brenner (Sheffield: Sheffield Academic Press, 1993–2015), which comprises twenty volumes of commentaries on the Old Testament. The parallel series, Feminist Companion

---

14. *Feminist Biblical Interpretation: A Compendium of Critical Commentary on the Books of the Bible and Related Literature*, trans. Lisa E. Dahill, Everett R. Kalin, Nancy Lukens, Linda M. Maloney, Barbara Rumscheidt, Martin Rumscheidt, and Tina Steiner (Grand Rapids, MI: Eerdmans, 2012). Another notable collection is the three volumes edited by Susanne Scholz, *Feminist Interpretation of the Hebrew Bible in Retrospect*, Recent Research in Biblical Studies 7, 8, 9 (Sheffield: Sheffield Phoenix Press, 2013, 2014, 2016).

15. The first volume, on the Torah, appeared in Spanish in 2009, in German and Italian in 2010, and in English in 2011 (Atlanta, GA: SBL). Four more volumes are now available: *Feminist Biblical Studies in the Twentieth Century*, ed. Elisabeth Schüssler Fiorenza (2014); *The Writings and Later Wisdom Books*, ed. Christl M. Maier and Nuria Calduch-Benages (2014); *Gospels: Narrative and History*, ed. Mercedes Navarro Puerto and Marinella Perroni (2015); and *The High Middle Ages*, ed. Kari Elisabeth Børresen and Adriana Valerio (2015). For further information, see http://www.bibleandwomen.org.

to the New Testament and Early Christian Writings, edited by Amy-Jill Levine with Marianne Blickenstaff and Maria Mayo Robbins (Sheffield: Sheffield Academic Press, 2001–2009), contains thirteen volumes with one more planned. These two series are not full commentaries on the biblical books but comprise collected essays on discrete biblical texts.

Works by individual feminist biblical scholars in all parts of the world abound, and they are now too numerous to list in this introduction. Feminist biblical interpretation has reached a level of maturity that now makes possible a commentary series on every book of the Bible. In recent decades, women have had greater access to formal theological education, have been able to learn critical analytical tools, have put their own interpretations into writing, and have developed new methods of biblical interpretation. Until recent decades the work of feminist biblical interpreters was largely unknown, both to other women and to their brothers in the synagogue, church, and academy. Feminists now have taken their place in the professional world of biblical scholars, where they build on the work of their foremothers and connect with one another across the globe in ways not previously possible. In a few short decades, feminist biblical criticism has become an integral part of the academy.

Methodologies

Feminist biblical scholars use a variety of methods and often employ a number of them together.[16] In the Wisdom Commentary series, the authors will explain their understanding of feminism and the feminist reading strategies used in their commentary. Each volume treats the biblical text in blocks of material, not an analysis verse by verse. The entire text is considered, not only those passages that feature female characters or that speak specifically about women. When women are not apparent in the narrative, feminist lenses are used to analyze the dynamics in the text between male characters, the models of power, binary ways of thinking, and dynamics of imperialism. Attention is given to how the whole text functions and how it was and is heard, both in its original context and today. Issues of particular concern to women—e.g., poverty, food, health, the environment, water—come to the fore.

---

16. See the seventeen essays in Caroline Vander Stichele and Todd Penner, eds., *Her Master's Tools? Feminist and Postcolonial Engagements of Historical-Critical Discourse* (Atlanta, GA: Society of Biblical Literature, 2005), which show the complementarity of various approaches.

One of the approaches used by early feminists and still popular today is to lift up the overlooked and forgotten stories of women in the Bible. Studies of women in each of the Testaments have been done, and there are also studies on women in particular biblical books.[17] Feminists recognize that the examples of biblical characters can be both empowering and problematic. The point of the feminist enterprise is not to serve as an apologetic for women; it is rather, in part, to recover women's history and literary roles in all their complexity and to learn from that recovery.

Retrieving the submerged history of biblical women is a crucial step for constructing the story of the past so as to lead to liberative possibilities for the present and future. There are, however, some pitfalls to this approach. Sometimes depictions of biblical women have been naïve and romantic. Some commentators exalt the virtues of both biblical and contemporary women and paint women as superior to men. Such reverse discrimination inhibits movement toward equality for all. In addition, some feminists challenge the idea that one can "pluck positive images out of an admittedly androcentric text, separating literary characterizations from the androcentric interests they were created to serve."[18] Still other feminists find these images to have enormous value.

One other danger with seeking the submerged history of women is the tendency for Christian feminists to paint Jesus and even Paul as liberators of women in a way that demonizes Judaism.[19] Wisdom Commentary aims to enhance understanding of Jesus as well as Paul as Jews of their day and to forge solidarity among Jewish and Christian feminists.

---

17. See, e.g., Alice Bach, ed., *Women in the Hebrew Bible: A Reader* (New York: Routledge, 1998); Tikva Frymer-Kensky, *Reading the Women of the Bible* (New York: Schocken, 2002); Carol Meyers, Toni Craven, and Ross S. Kraemer, *Women in Scripture* (Grand Rapids, MI: Eerdmans, 2000); Irene Nowell, *Women in the Old Testament* (Collegeville, MN: Liturgical Press, 1997); Katharine Doob Sakenfeld, *Just Wives? Stories of Power and Survival in the Old Testament and Today* (Louisville, KY: Westminster John Knox, 2003); Mary Ann Getty-Sullivan, *Women in the New Testament* (Collegeville, MN: Liturgical Press, 2001); Bonnie Thurston, *Women in the New Testament* (New York: Crossroad, 1998).

18. J. Cheryl Exum, "Second Thoughts about Secondary Characters: Women in Exodus 1.8–2.10," in *A Feminist Companion to Exodus to Deuteronomy*, FCB 6 (Sheffield: Sheffield Academic Press, 1994), 75–97, at 76.

19. See Judith Plaskow, "Anti-Judaism in Feminist Christian Interpretation," in *Searching the Scriptures: A Feminist Introduction* (New York: Crossroad, 1993), 1:117–29; Amy-Jill Levine, "The New Testament and Anti-Judaism," in *The Misunderstood Jew: The Church and the Scandal of the Jewish Jesus* (San Francisco: HarperSanFrancisco, 2006), 87–117.

Feminist scholars who use historical-critical methods analyze the world behind the text; they seek to understand the historical context from which the text emerged and the circumstances of the communities to whom it was addressed. In bringing feminist lenses to this approach, the aim is not to impose modern expectations on ancient cultures but to unmask the ways that ideologically problematic mind-sets that produced the ancient texts are still promulgated through the text. Feminist biblical scholars aim not only to deconstruct but also to reclaim and reconstruct biblical history as women's history, in which women were central and active agents in creating religious heritage.[20] A further step is to construct meaning for contemporary women and men in a liberative movement toward transformation of social, political, economic, and religious structures.[21] In recent years, some feminists have embraced new historicism, which accents the creative role of the interpreter in any construction of history and exposes the power struggles to which the text witnesses.[22]

Literary critics analyze the world of the text: its form, language patterns, and rhetorical function.[23] They do not attempt to separate layers of tradition and redaction but focus on the text holistically, as it is in its

---

20. See, for example, Phyllis A. Bird, *Missing Persons and Mistaken Identities: Women and Gender in Ancient Israel* (Minneapolis: Fortress Press, 1997); Elisabeth Schüssler Fiorenza, *In Memory of Her: A Feminist Theological Reconstruction of Christian Origins* (New York: Crossroad, 1984); Ross Shepard Kraemer and Mary Rose D'Angelo, eds., *Women and Christian Origins* (New York: Oxford University Press, 1999).

21. See, e.g., Sandra M. Schneiders, *The Revelatory Text: Interpreting the New Testament as Sacred Scripture*, rev. ed. (Collegeville, MN: Liturgical Press, 1999), whose aim is to engage in biblical interpretation not only for intellectual enlightenment but, even more important, for personal and communal transformation. Elisabeth Schüssler Fiorenza (*Wisdom Ways: Introducing Feminist Biblical Interpretation* [Maryknoll, NY: Orbis Books, 2001]) envisions the work of feminist biblical interpretation as a dance of Wisdom that consists of seven steps that interweave in spiral movements toward liberation, the final one being transformative action for change.

22. See Gina Hens Piazza, *The New Historicism*, Guides to Biblical Scholarship, Old Testament Series (Minneapolis: Fortress Press, 2002).

23. Phyllis Trible was among the first to employ this method with texts from Genesis and Ruth in her groundbreaking book *God and the Rhetoric of Sexuality*, OBT (Philadelphia: Fortress Press, 1978). Another pioneer in feminist literary criticism is Mieke Bal (*Lethal Love: Feminist Literary Readings of Biblical Love Stories* [Bloomington: Indiana University Press, 1987]). For surveys of recent developments in literary methods, see Terry Eagleton, *Literary Theory: An Introduction*, 3rd ed. (Minneapolis: University of Minnesota Press, 2008); Janice Capel Anderson and Stephen D. Moore, eds., *Mark and Method: New Approaches in Biblical Studies*, 2nd ed. (Minneapolis: Fortress Press, 2008).

present form. They examine how meaning is created in the interaction between the text and its reader in multiple contexts. Within the arena of literary approaches are reader-oriented approaches, narrative, rhetorical, structuralist, post-structuralist, deconstructive, ideological, autobiographical, and performance criticism.[24] Narrative critics study the interrelation among author, text, and audience through investigation of settings, both spatial and temporal; characters; plot; and narrative techniques (e.g., irony, parody, intertextual allusions). Reader-response critics attend to the impact that the text has on the reader or hearer. They recognize that when a text is detrimental toward women there is the choice either to affirm the text or to read against the grain toward a liberative end. Rhetorical criticism analyzes the style of argumentation and attends to how the author is attempting to shape the thinking or actions of the hearer. Structuralist critics analyze the complex patterns of binary oppositions in the text to derive its meaning.[25] Post-structuralist approaches challenge the notion that there are fixed meanings to any biblical text or that there is one universal truth. They engage in close readings of the text and often engage in intertextual analysis.[26] Within this approach is deconstructionist criticism, which views the text as a site of conflict, with competing narratives. The interpreter aims to expose the fault lines and overturn and reconfigure binaries by elevating the underling of a pair and foregrounding it.[27] Feminists also use other postmodern approaches, such as ideological and autobiographical criticism. The former analyzes the system of ideas that underlies the power and values concealed in the

24. See, e.g., J. Cheryl Exum and David J. A. Clines, eds., *The New Literary Criticism and the Hebrew Bible* (Valley Forge, PA: Trinity Press International, 1993); Edgar V. McKnight and Elizabeth Struthers Malbon, eds., *The New Literary Criticism and the New Testament* (Valley Forge, PA: Trinity Press International, 1994).

25. See, e.g., David Jobling, *The Sense of Biblical Narrative: Three Structural Analyses in the Old Testament*, JSOTSup 7 (Sheffield: Sheffield University, 1978).

26. See, e.g., Stephen D. Moore, *Poststructuralism and the New Testament: Derrida and Foucault at the Foot of the Cross* (Minneapolis: Fortress Press, 1994); *The Bible in Theory: Critical and Postcritical Essays* (Atlanta, GA: Society of Biblical Literature, 2010); Yvonne Sherwood, *A Biblical Text and Its Afterlives: The Survival of Jonah in Western Culture* (Cambridge: Cambridge University Press, 2000).

27. David Penchansky, "Deconstruction," in *The Oxford Encyclopedia of Biblical Interpretation*, ed. Steven McKenzie (New York: Oxford University Press, 2013), 196–205. See, for example, Danna Nolan Fewell and David M. Gunn, *Gender, Power, and Promise: The Subject of the Bible's First Story* (Nashville, TN: Abingdon, 1993); David Rutledge, *Reading Marginally: Feminism, Deconstruction and the Bible*, BibInt 21 (Leiden: Brill, 1996).

text as well as that of the interpreter.[28] The latter involves deliberate self-disclosure while reading the text as a critical exegete.[29] Performance criticism attends to how the text was passed on orally, usually in communal settings, and to the verbal and nonverbal interactions between the performer and the audience.[30]

From the beginning, feminists have understood that interpreting the Bible is an act of power. In recent decades, feminist biblical scholars have developed hermeneutical theories of the ethics and politics of biblical interpretation to challenge the claims to value neutrality of most academic biblical scholarship. Feminist biblical scholars have also turned their attention to how some biblical writings were shaped by the power of empire and how this still shapes readers' self-understandings today. They have developed hermeneutical approaches that reveal, critique, and evaluate the interactions depicted in the text against the context of empire, and they consider implications for contemporary contexts.[31] Feminists also analyze the dynamics of colonization and the mentalities of colonized peoples in the exercise of biblical interpretation. As Kwok Pui-lan explains, "A postcolonial feminist interpretation of the Bible needs to investigate the deployment of gender in the narration of identity, the negotiation of power differentials between the colonizers and the colonized, and the reinforcement of patriarchal control over spheres where these elites could exercise control."[32] Methods and models from sociology and cultural anthropology are used by feminists to investigate

28. See Tina Pippin, ed., *Ideological Criticism of Biblical Texts: Semeia* 59 (1992); Terry Eagleton, *Ideology: An Introduction* (London: Verso, 2007).

29. See, e.g., Ingrid Rose Kitzberger, ed., *Autobiographical Biblical Interpretation: Between Text and Self* (Leiden: Deo, 2002); P. J. W. Schutte, "When *They, We,* and the Passive Become I—Introducing Autobiographical Biblical Criticism," *HTS Teologiese Studies / Theological Studies* 61 (2005): 401–16.

30. See, e.g., Holly Hearon and Philip Ruge-Jones, eds., *The Bible in Ancient and Modern Media: Story and Performance* (Eugene, OR: Cascade Books, 2009).

31. E.g., Gale Yee, ed., *Judges and Method: New Approaches in Biblical Studies* (Minneapolis: Fortress Press, 1995); Warren Carter, *The Gospel of Matthew in Its Roman Imperial Context* (London: T & T Clark, 2005); *The Roman Empire and the New Testament: An Essential Guide* (Nashville, TN: Abingdon, 2006); Elisabeth Schüssler Fiorenza, *The Power of the Word: Scripture and the Rhetoric of Empire* (Minneapolis: Fortress Press, 2007); Judith E. McKinlay, *Reframing Her: Biblical Women in Postcolonial Focus* (Sheffield: Sheffield Phoenix Press, 2004).

32. Kwok Pui-lan, *Postcolonial Imagination and Feminist Theology* (Louisville, KY: Westminster John Knox, 2005), 9. See also, Musa W. Dube, ed., *Postcolonial Feminist Interpretation of the Bible* (St. Louis, MO: Chalice Press, 2000); Cristl M. Maier and

women's everyday lives, their experiences of marriage, childrearing, labor, money, illness, etc.[33]

As feminists have examined the construction of gender from varying cultural perspectives, they have become ever more cognizant that the way gender roles are defined within differing cultures varies radically. As Mary Ann Tolbert observes, "Attempts to isolate some universal role that cross-culturally defines 'woman' have run into contradictory evidence at every turn."[34] Some women have coined new terms to highlight the particularities of their socio-cultural context. Many African American feminists, for example, call themselves *womanists* to draw attention to the double oppression of racism and sexism they experience.[35] Similarly, many US Hispanic feminists speak of themselves as *mujeristas* (*mujer* is Spanish for "woman").[36] Others prefer to be called "Latina feminists."[37] Both groups emphasize that the context for their theologizing is *mestizaje* and *mulatez* (racial and cultural mixture), done *en conjunto* (in community), with *lo cotidiano* (everyday lived experience) of Hispanic women as starting points for theological reflection and the encounter with the divine. Intercultural analysis has become an indispensable tool for working toward justice for women at the global level.[38]

Carolyn J. Sharp, *Prophecy and Power: Jeremiah in Feminist and Postcolonial Perspective* (London: Bloomsbury, 2013).

33. See, for example, Carol Meyers, *Discovering Eve: Ancient Israelite Women in Context* (New York: Oxford University Press, 1991); Luise Schottroff, *Lydia's Impatient Sisters: A Feminist Social History of Early Christianity*, trans. Barbara and Martin Rumscheidt (Louisville, KY: Westminster John Knox, 1995); Susan Niditch, *"My Brother Esau Is a Hairy Man": Hair and Identity in Ancient Israel* (Oxford: Oxford University Press, 2008).

34. Mary Ann Tolbert, "Social, Sociological, and Anthropological Methods," in *Searching the Scriptures*, 1:255–71, at 265.

35. Alice Walker coined the term (*In Search of Our Mothers' Gardens: Womanist Prose* [New York: Harcourt Brace Jovanovich, 1967, 1983]). See also Katie G. Cannon, "The Emergence of Black Feminist Consciousness," in *Feminist Interpretation of the Bible*, ed. Letty M. Russell (Philadelphia: Westminster, 1985), 30–40; Renita Weems, *Just a Sister Away: A Womanist Vision of Women's Relationships in the Bible* (San Diego: Lura Media, 1988); Nyasha Junior, *An Introduction to Womanist Biblical Interpretation* (Louisville, KY: Westminster John Knox, 2015).

36. Ada María Isasi-Díaz (*Mujerista Theology: A Theology for the Twenty-first Century* [Maryknoll, NY: Orbis Books, 1996]) is credited with coining the term.

37. E.g., María Pilar Aquino, Daisy L. Machado, and Jeanette Rodríguez, eds., *A Reader in Latina Feminist Theology* (Austin: University of Texas Press, 2002).

38. See, e.g., María Pilar Aquino and María José Rosado-Nunes, eds., *Feminist Intercultural Theology: Latina Explorations for a Just World*, Studies in Latino/a Catholicism (Maryknoll, NY: Orbis Books, 2007).

Some feminists are among those who have developed lesbian, gay, bisexual, and transgender (LGBT) interpretation. This approach focuses on issues of sexual identity and uses various reading strategies. Some point out the ways in which categories that emerged in recent centuries are applied anachronistically to biblical texts to make modern-day judgments. Others show how the Bible is silent on contemporary issues about sexual identity. Still others examine same-sex relationships in the Bible by figures such as Ruth and Naomi or David and Jonathan. In recent years, queer theory has emerged; it emphasizes the blurriness of boundaries not just of sexual identity but also of gender roles. Queer critics often focus on texts in which figures transgress what is traditionally considered proper gender behavior.[39]

Feminists also recognize that the struggle for women's equality and dignity is intimately connected with the struggle for respect for Earth and for the whole of the cosmos. Ecofeminists interpret Scripture in ways that highlight the link between human domination of nature and male subjugation of women. They show how anthropocentric ways of interpreting the Bible have overlooked or dismissed Earth and Earth community. They invite readers to identify not only with human characters in the biblical narrative but also with other Earth creatures and domains of nature, especially those that are the object of injustice. Some use creative imagination to retrieve the interests of Earth implicit in the narrative and enable Earth to speak.[40]

Biblical Authority

By the late nineteenth century, some feminists, such as Elizabeth Cady Stanton, began to question openly whether the Bible could continue to be regarded as authoritative for women. They viewed the Bible itself as

39. See, e.g., Bernadette J. Brooten, *Love between Women: Early Christian Responses to Female Homoeroticism* (Chicago and London: University of Chicago Press, 1996); Mary Rose D'Angelo, "Women Partners in the New Testament," *JFSR* 6 (1990): 65–86; Deirdre J. Good, "Reading Strategies for Biblical Passages on Same-Sex Relations," *Theology and Sexuality* 7 (1997): 70–82; Deryn Guest, *When Deborah Met Jael: Lesbian Feminist Hermeneutics* (London: SCM Press, 2011); Teresa Hornsby and Ken Stone, eds., *Bible Trouble: Queer Readings at the Boundaries of Biblical Scholarship* (Atlanta, GA: Society of Biblical Literature, 2011).

40. E.g., Norman C. Habel and Peter Trudinger, *Exploring Ecological Hermeneutics*, SymS 46 (Atlanta, GA: Society of Biblical Literature, 2008); Mary Judith Ress, *Ecofeminism in Latin America*, Women from the Margins (Maryknoll, NY: Orbis Books, 2006).

the source of women's oppression, and some rejected its sacred origin and saving claims. Some decided that the Bible and the religious traditions that enshrine it are too thoroughly saturated with androcentrism and patriarchy to be redeemable.[41]

In the Wisdom Commentary series, questions such as these may be raised, but the aim of this series is not to lead readers to reject the authority of the biblical text. Rather, the aim is to promote better understanding of the contexts from which the text arose and of the rhetorical effects it has on women and men in contemporary contexts. Such understanding can lead to a deepening of faith, with the Bible serving as an aid to bring flourishing of life.

Language for God

Because of the ways in which the term "God" has been used to symbolize the divine in predominantly male, patriarchal, and monarchical modes, feminists have designed new ways of speaking of the divine. Some have called attention to the inadequacy of the term *God* by trying to visually destabilize our ways of thinking and speaking of the divine. Rosemary Radford Ruether proposed *God/ess*, as an unpronounceable term pointing to the unnameable understanding of the divine that transcends patriarchal limitations.[42] Some have followed traditional Jewish practice, writing *G-d*. Elisabeth Schüssler Fiorenza has adopted *G*d*.[43] Others draw on the biblical tradition to mine female and non-gender-specific metaphors and symbols.[44] In Wisdom Commentary, there is not one standard way of expressing the divine; each author will use her or his preferred ways. The one exception is that when the tetragrammaton, YHWH, the name revealed to Moses in Exodus 3:14, is used, it will be without vowels, respecting the Jewish custom of avoiding pronouncing the divine name out of reverence.

---

41. E.g., Mary Daly, *Beyond God the Father: A Philosophy of Women's Liberation* (Boston: Beacon, 1973).

42. Rosemary Radford Ruether, *Sexism and God-Talk: Toward a Feminist Theology* (Boston: Beacon, 1983).

43. Elisabeth Schüssler Fiorenza, *Jesus: Miriam's Child, Sophia's Prophet; Critical Issues in Feminist Christology* (New York: Continuum, 1994), 191 n. 3.

44. E.g., Sallie McFague, *Models of God: Theology for an Ecological, Nuclear Age* (Philadelphia: Fortress Press, 1987); Catherine LaCugna, *God for Us: The Trinity and Christian Life* (San Francisco: Harper Collins, 1991); Elizabeth A. Johnson, *She Who Is: The Mystery of God in Feminist Theological Discourse* (New York: Crossroad, 1992). See further Elizabeth A. Johnson, "God," in *Dictionary of Feminist Theologies*, 128–30.

Nomenclature for the Two Testaments

In recent decades, some biblical scholars have begun to call the two Testaments of the Bible by names other than the traditional nomenclature: Old and New Testament. Some regard "Old" as derogatory, implying that it is no longer relevant or that it has been superseded. Consequently, terms like Hebrew Bible, First Testament, and Jewish Scriptures and, correspondingly, Christian Scriptures or Second Testament have come into use. There are a number of difficulties with these designations. The term "Hebrew Bible" does not take into account that parts of the Old Testament are written not in Hebrew but in Aramaic.[45] Moreover, for Roman Catholics, Anglicans, and Eastern Orthodox believers, the Old Testament includes books written in Greek—the Deuterocanonical books, considered Apocrypha by Protestants. The term "Jewish Scriptures" is inadequate because these books are also sacred to Christians. Conversely, "Christian Scriptures" is not an accurate designation for the New Testament, since the Old Testament is also part of the Christian Scriptures. Using "First and Second Testament" also has difficulties, in that it can imply a hierarchy and a value judgment.[46] Jews generally use the term Tanakh, an acronym for Torah (Pentateuch), Nevi'im (Prophets), and Ketuvim (Writings).

In Wisdom Commentary, if authors choose to use a designation other than Tanakh, Old Testament, and New Testament, they will explain how they mean the term.

Translation

Modern feminist scholars recognize the complexities connected with biblical translation, as they have delved into questions about philosophy of language, how meanings are produced, and how they are culturally situated. Today it is evident that simply translating into gender-neutral formulations cannot address all the challenges presented by androcentric texts. Efforts at feminist translation must also deal with issues around authority and canonicity.[47]

Because of these complexities, the editors of Wisdom Commentary series have chosen to use an existing translation, the New Revised

---

45. Gen 31:47; Jer 10:11; Ezra 4:7–6:18; 7:12-26; Dan 2:4–7:28.
46. See Levine, *The Misunderstood Jew*, 193–99.
47. Elizabeth Castelli, "*Les Belles Infidèles*/Fidelity or Feminism? The Meanings of Feminist Biblical Translation," in *Searching the Scriptures*, 1:189–204, at 190.

Standard Version (NRSV), which is provided for easy reference at the top of each page of commentary. The NRSV was produced by a team of ecumenical and interreligious scholars, is a fairly literal translation, and uses inclusive language for human beings. Brief discussions about problematic translations appear in the inserts labeled "Translation Matters." When more detailed discussions are available, these will be indicated in footnotes. In the commentary, wherever Hebrew or Greek words are used, English translation is provided. In cases where a wordplay is involved, transliteration is provided to enable understanding.

Art and Poetry

Artistic expression in poetry, music, sculpture, painting, and various other modes is very important to feminist interpretation. Where possible, art and poetry are included in the print volumes of the series. In a number of instances, these are original works created for this project. Regrettably, copyright and production costs prohibit the inclusion of color photographs and other artistic work. It is our hope that the web version will allow a greater collection of such resources.

Glossary

Because there are a number of excellent readily available resources that provide definitions and concise explanations of terms used in feminist theological and biblical studies, this series will not include a glossary. We refer you to works such as *Dictionary of Feminist Theologies*, edited by Letty M. Russell with J. Shannon Clarkson (Louisville, KY: Westminster John Knox, 1996), and volume 1 of *Searching the Scriptures*, edited by Elisabeth Schüssler Fiorenza with the assistance of Shelly Matthews (New York: Crossroad, 1992). Individual authors in the Wisdom Commentary series will define the way they are using terms that may be unfamiliar.

Bibliography

Because bibliographies are quickly outdated and because the space is limited, only a list of Works Cited is included in the print volumes. A comprehensive bibliography for each volume is posted on a dedicated website and is updated regularly. The link for this volume can be found at wisdomcommentary.org.

A Concluding Word

In just a few short decades, feminist biblical studies has grown exponentially, both in the methods that have been developed and in the number of scholars who have embraced it. We realize that this series is limited and will soon need to be revised and updated. It is our hope that Wisdom Commentary, by making the best of current feminist biblical scholarship available in an accessible format to ministers, preachers, teachers, scholars, and students, will aid all readers in their advancement toward God's vision of dignity, equality, and justice for all.

Acknowledgments

There are a great many people who have made this series possible: first, Peter Dwyer, director, and Hans Christoffersen, publisher of the academic market at Liturgical Press, who have believed in this project and have shepherded it since it was conceived in 2008. Editorial consultants Athalya Brenner-Idan and Elisabeth Schüssler Fiorenza have not only been an inspiration with their pioneering work but have encouraged us all along the way with their personal involvement. Volume editors Mary Ann Beavis, Carol J. Dempsey, Amy-Jill Levine, Linda M. Maloney, Ahida Pilarski, Sarah Tanzer, Lauress Wilkins Lawrence, and Seung Ai Yang have lent their extraordinary wisdom to the shaping of the series, have used their extensive networks of relationships to secure authors and contributors, and have worked tirelessly to guide their work to completion. Two others who contributed greatly to the shaping of the project at the outset were Linda M. Day and Mignon Jacobs, as well as Barbara E. Bowe of blessed memory (d. 2010). Editorial and research assistant Susan M. Hickman has provided invaluable support with administrative details and arrangements. I am grateful to Brian Eisenschenk and Christine Henderson, who have assisted Susan Hickman with the Wiki. There are countless others at Liturgical Press whose daily work makes the production possible. I am especially thankful to Lauren L. Murphy, Andrea Humphrey, Lauress Wilkins Lawrence, and Justin Howell for their work in copyediting.

Author's Introduction

Reading Books 2 and 3 of the Psalms (Pss 42–89)

Because seventy-three of the one hundred fifty psalms contain a superscription[1] linking them to King David (Hebrew: לדוד), many have concluded that the psalms speak in a masculine voice and therefore women cannot find a place in them. Certainly, royal psalms that concern the king (e.g., Ps 45) are overtly male focused, and the enthronement psalms (Pss 47, 93, 96–99) lift up God as King. The issue, however, is more nuanced. Marc Zvi Brettler suggests that women are excluded because the psalms were composed by male elites but that this does not exclude women from reciting them. Further, some psalms are "gender neutral" (e.g., 65 and 142), though one cannot say whether they are intentionally so.[2] Perhaps prayer, and especially women's prayer, was not part of the priestly cult, but rather the folk tradition of ancient Israel,[3] in which case the prayers of women outside of the Psalms may

---

1. The superscription is an introductory note, often printed in smaller type above the first verse of a psalm in most English Bibles. Superscriptions were added by ancient editors as the psalms were transmitted and collected.

2. See Marc Zvi Brettler, "Women and Psalms: Toward an Understanding of the Role of Women's Prayer in the Israelite Cult," in *Gender and Law in the Hebrew Bible and the Ancient Near East*, ed. Victor Matthews, Bernard Levinson, and Tikva Frymer-Kensky, JSOTSup 262 (Sheffield: Sheffield Academic Press, 1998), 25–56.

3. Israel Knohl, "Between Voice and Silence: The Relationship between Prayer and the Temple Cult," *JBL* 115 (1996): 17–30. Knohl argues that the priests performed cultic duties in silence.

be helpful. As Lisa Davison points out, eleven women in the Hebrew Bible (including Hagar, Rebekah, Miriam, Deborah, Naomi, and Hannah) and three in the Apocrypha (Esther, Susanna, and Judith) offer prayers that are recorded.[4] The prayers of these women can serve as "intertexts" (conversation partners) for interpretation of psalm prayer. This commentary will seek to use such intertexts and the stories of these praying women to suggest "plausible women's voices within and behind the text."[5] Teasing out these voices will require our imaginative interaction with Psalms 42–89.

Gender and feminist analysis will help tease out these plausible female voices in books 2 and 3 of the Psalms. Like feminist analysis, gender analysis "is not a method, but a lens."[6] Using these lenses can generate questions to ask of psalm texts but cannot dictate one method to answer questions about gender, ethnicity, power, and class. It does not suffice simply to search out female images for God or the speaker in the Psalms, since gender is socially constructed. Consequently, this study will use a variety of methods to interpret the psalms, including ideological and postcolonial criticism. Central to my approach is rhetorical-critical analysis of metaphor, "the most basic building block of poetry,"[7] since metaphor saturates the poetry of the book of Psalms. Derived from two Greek words, metaphor means literally to "carry across" or "transfer," that is, to understand a lesser-known thing in terms of a better-known thing by juxtaposing the two. Metaphors are meant to suggest "a network of associations"[8] that helps us see something new in the tension created by

---

4. Lisa W. Davison, "'My Soul Is Like the Weaned Child That Is with Me': The Psalms and the Feminine Voice," *HBT* 23 (2001): 155–67. See also the work by Amy Kalmanofsky on Daughter Zion (the personification of Jerusalem) in the book of Lamentations, whose prayers and tears connect her to the suffering of others: "Their Heart Cried Out to God: Gender and Prayer in the Book of Lamentations," in *A Question of Sex? Gender and Difference in the Hebrew Bible and Beyond*, ed. Deborah Rooke (Sheffield: Sheffield Phoenix Press, 2007), 53–65.

5. Athalya Brenner and Fokkelien Van Dijk-Hemmes, *On Gendering Texts: Female and Male Voices in the Hebrew Bible* (Leiden: Brill, 1993), 6.

6. Beatrice Lawrence, "Gender Analysis: Gender and Method in Biblical Studies," in *Method Matters: Essays on the Interpretation of the Hebrew Bible in Honor of David L. Petersen*, ed. Joel LeMon and Kent Harold Richards (Atlanta, GA: Society of Biblical Literature, 2009), 333–48, at 333.

7. William P. Brown, *Seeing the Psalms: A Theology of Metaphor* (Louisville, KY: Westminster John Knox, 2002), 3.

8. Janet Martin Soskice, *Metaphor and Religious Language* (Oxford: Clarendon Press; New York: Oxford University Press, 1985), 15.

bringing seemingly dissimilar or unconnected things together. Metaphor demands our imaginative engagement as readers in order to recognize this tension between the similar and dissimilar and sort through associations that such juxtaposition produces. The challenge is that different readers will not always agree on which associations are relevant, given both the choice of possibilities and the different life experiences readers bring to the text that shape those choices. The preoccupation of scholars with the setting from which the psalms emerged (cultic worship, family prayer, exile, Persian period) cannot be relied on to determine metaphorical associations. As Rolf Jacobson warns, there can be "no . . . rhetorical certitude" about the setting suggested by psalm metaphors because metaphors are multivalent.[9] We, as readers, are also multivalent.

We can, however, as Kirsten Nielsen argues, look for other biblical texts using the same metaphors ("intertexts") as keys to interpretation. The intertexts we choose can activate different nuances of the metaphor.[10] Again, the choice of intertext may differ, depending on the reader's gender, class, ethnicity, and other factors. Beth LaNeel Tanner has also looked at the Psalms through the lens of intertexuality, calling them a *bricolage* or mosaic patchwork "in which other texts are embedded implicitly or explicitly."[11] This patchwork produces "gaps" and "contradictions" in understanding that invite readers in. Tanner suggests that psalm superscriptions are a form of canonical intertextuality. These superscriptions give us permission to read other psalms and narratives alongside one another. Superscriptions point to the narrative performance of the psalms and make the general particular so that readers can connect with the psalmist's experience. This commentary will "imagine a superscription"[12] whenever possible, with an eye toward contemporary contexts and reader involvement.

An imagined superscription can tie the psalm to other figures in the biblical narratives, especially women, rather than exclusively to David.

9. Rolf Jacobson, " 'The Altar of Certitude': Reflections on 'Setting' and the Rhetorical Interpretation of the Psalms," in *My Words Are Lovely: Studies in the Rhetoric of the Psalms*, ed. Robert L. Foster and David M. Howard (New York: T & T Clark, 2008), 3–18, at 17.

10. Kirsten Nielsen, "Poetic Analysis: Psalm 121," in LeMon and Richards, *Method Matters*, 293–309, at 298–301.

11. Beth LaNeel Tanner, *The Book of Psalms through the Lens of Intertextuality*, StBibLit 26 (New York: Peter Lang, 2001), 6.

12. Dave Bland and David Fleer, eds., *Performing the Psalms* (St. Louis, MO: Chalice Press, 2005), 27.

Imagined superscriptions can also embody psalm metaphors so that the reader might more readily experience those metaphors rather than simply analyzing them. Jacqueline Lapsley urges reading strategies for biblical narratives that invite the reader to enter into the story and be shaped morally by it.[13] Reading strategies that help the reader empathize with female characters in narrative intertexts can also help the reader enter into psalm metaphors and recognize certain metaphorical associations overlooked in them. In Emanuel Levinas's terms, approaching the intertext as Other rather than as Object can lead to encounter with the psalm and its metaphors rather than simple, objective evaluation of them by those who stand outside.[14] This kind of involved reading of intertext and psalm can create the space for what Danna Nolan Fewell calls "interruption," a reading strategy of stopping and questioning the text and bearing responsibility for what goes on in it. She argues that "interruption is a strategy for both reading and living. To interrupt means to question the story being told, to imagine the story being told differently, and likewise, to question one's life and to imagine one's life being lived differently."[15]

Carol Meyers warns that we cannot use the Bible alone to study Israelite women and recover their voices because of the Bible's distorted focus on nation rather than family and because of the urban elite context of many of its authors. Instead, women's lives must be reconstructed in terms of their economic contributions to the family, social networking, and professional roles in the larger community. These women's structures have not been noticed, "but 'unnoticed' does not mean 'nonexistent.' "[16] Female guilds allowed for study, training, and the passing down of special knowledge in the areas of music traditions, prophetic roles, funerary services (professional keeners or reciters of dirges), psychological care and conflict resolution, and midwifery. Informal networks in peasant villages brought women together from several households to make bread and textiles and maintain the infrastructure of family and community

---

13. Jacqueline E. Lapsley, *Whispering the Word: Hearing Women's Stories in the Old Testament* (Louisville, KY: Westminster John Knox, 2005), 11.

14. Ibid., 12.

15. Danna Nolan Fewell, *The Children of Israel: Reading the Bible for the Sake of Our Children* (Nashville, TN: Abingdon Press, 2003), 34.

16. Carol Meyers, "Contesting the Notion of Patriarchy: Anthropology and the Theorizing of Gender in Ancient Israel," in Rooke, *A Question of Sex?*, 83–105, at 90.

life.[17] This study will draw on the context of women's lives in ancient Israel as a frame for psalm interpretation.

Other interpreters have also noted the presence of women in public celebration and mourning. Athalya Brenner and Fokkelien Van Dijk-Hemmes suggest that women participate in changing political situations with victory songs that both welcome warriors home and express public opinion, sometimes in a mocking or satirical way[18] (e.g., 1 Sam 18:6-7; Judg 5; 11:34a; Exod 15:20-21). In Lamentations 1, 2, and 4 the personified Lady Jerusalem mourns her destruction with numerous metaphors drawn from the world of women. God calls on the mourning women to come and raise a lament over Jerusalem in 9:10-11, 17-22 (see also Jer 22:18-19). David calls the "daughters of Judah" to weep over the death of Saul (2 Sam 1:24). These texts too can serve as intertexts for psalm interpretation. Ultimately, every psalm text is an intersection with other texts and offers "an indeterminate surplus of meaningful possibilities. Interpretation is always a production of meaning from that surplus."[19] This commentary invites readers to take part in such production.

17. Ibid., 95–99. Meyers suggests that we speak of heterarchy (fluid, lateral gender interdependence at the household level for certain economic and social functions) rather than patriarchy or hierarchy, which rank elements vertically in subordinate order.

18. Brenner and Van Dijk-Hemmes, *On Gendering Texts*, 32–34.

19. Timothy Beal, "Ideology and Intertextuality: Surplus of Meaning and Controlling the Means of Production," in *Reading Between Texts: Intertextuality and the Hebrew Bible*, ed. Danna Nolan Fewell (Louisville, KY: Westminster John Knox, 1992), 27–39, at 31.

Book 2 of the Psalter

(Pss 42–72)

The Psalter offers a "school of prayer"[1] that contains many different kinds of prayer articulating the entire range of human emotions. The book of Psalms as we have it emerged from a long process of transmission in ancient Israel. Editors divided the Psalter into five "books" to mirror the five-book division of the Torah (Pentateuch). Each of the five "books" ends with a doxology, that is, a speaking of praise to God (e.g., Ps 41:13). *Midrash Tehillim* explains this division: "As Moses gave five books of laws to Israel, so David gave five books of Psalms to Israel."[2] John Vassar suggests that the five Psalm books serve as "a marker moving the reader back to the Pentateuch"[3] as intertext (for "intertext," see above, p. xliii). This fivefold division was probably imposed on various independently circulating collections of psalms that were important to different groups in Israel in different locations at different times. The psalms seem to move from a preponderance of laments in the first

---

1. Roland Murphy, "The Faith of the Psalmist," *Int* 34 (1980): 229–39, at 237.

2. William G. Braude, *The Midrash on Psalms*, vol. 1 (New Haven, CT: Yale University Press, 1954), 5.

3. John Vassar, *Recalling a Story Once Told: An Intertextual Reading of the Psalter and the Pentateuch* (Macon, GA: Mercer University Press, 2007), 4.

three books to hymns of praise in books 4 and 5, ending with Psalm 150, the "Great Hallelujah": "Let everything that breathes praise the LORD."

Much of recent psalms scholarship has been devoted to the editing process that led to the final, canonical form of the Psalter. Interpreters suggest that this process narrates the history of Israel from the kingship of David and Solomon (books 1 and 2, Pss 1–72) to the divided monarchy and the destruction of Jerusalem (book 3, Pss 73–89, with its many laments), to the Babylonian Exile (book 4, Pss 90–106), and, finally, return to the land and God's rule (book 5, Pss 107–50).[4] Books 1–3 show the failure of the Davidic covenant (2 Sam 7), and books 4–5 respond to this crisis of the loss of land, temple, and king by proclaiming God's reign rather than the reign of an earthly Davidic king (especially Pss 93, 96–99). Many argue that this editing process also intentionally placed Psalms 1–2 at the beginning of the Psalter as an interpretive frame that moves the psalms out of worship into the realm of meditation and study of God's Torah, or "instruction" (Ps 1:2). The content of this theological instruction is presented in Psalm 2: God rules.[5] This understanding, if used exclusively, can undercut the performative power of the psalms and our imaginative participation in them.

---

4. Nancy deClaissé-Walford, "Psalms," in *Women's Bible Commentary*, ed. Carol A. Newsom, Sharon H. Ringe, and Jacqueline E. Lapsley, 3rd ed. (Louisville, KY: Westminster John Knox, 2012), 221–31, at 231.

5. J. Clinton McCann Jr., "The Book of Psalms," in *The New Interpreter's Bible*, vol. 4 (Nashville, TN: Abingdon Press, 1996), 639–1280, at 665. McCann suggests that God's reign is seen eschatologically, as awaiting fulfillment.

Psalm(s) 42–43

Tears of Connection

Psalm 42 begins book 2 of the Psalter. Multiple ancient manuscripts combine Psalms 42 and 43 as a unit. Most interpreters read them together as one psalm, especially since Psalm 43 lacks a superscription, though the Septuagint and Vulgate insert "a psalm of David" at the beginning of Psalm 43. Psalms 42 and 43 share vocabulary and a refrain, which divides the combined whole into three sections or strophes: 42:1-5; 42:6-11; 43:1-5. How those strophes are connected reveals much about the interpreter and his or her subject location.

The superscription of Psalm 42 connects it to the Korahites. Like all of the 117 superscriptions in the Psalter, this one is numbered as v. 1 in Hebrew texts but stands unnumbered (usually in smaller type) in Protestant and Catholic Bibles. Psalm 42–43 introduces a group of Korah psalms in book 2 that includes 42–49, 84–85, and 87–88. According to 1 Chronicles 6:31-48 the Korahites were a guild of Levitical temple singers commanded by King David to sing and play on musical instruments (1 Chr 15:16) in praise of God. They were perhaps responsible for collecting and transmitting particular psalms. Though Chronicles cites harps and lyres as the chief instruments in the religious music of ancient Israel, the archaeological record (iconography, figurines, and seals) shows that other instruments were widespread in the culture, including pipes, trumpets, drums, and rattles, and that music was not exclusively the

Psalm 42:1–43:5

To the leader. A Maskil of the Korahites.

¹As a deer longs for flowing
   streams,
      so my soul longs for you, O
      God.
²My soul thirsts for God,
   for the living God.
When shall I come and behold
   the face of God?
³My tears have been my food
   day and night,
while people say to me continually,
      "Where is your God?"

⁴These things I remember,
   as I pour out my soul:
how I went with the throng,
   and led them in procession to
   the house of God,
with glad shouts and songs of
   thanksgiving,
      a multitude keeping festival.

⁵Why are you cast down, O my
   soul,
   and why are you disquieted
      within me?
Hope in God; for I shall again
   praise him,
   my help ⁶and my God.

My soul is cast down within me;
   therefore I remember you
from the land of Jordan and of
   Hermon,
   from Mount Mizar.
⁷Deep calls to deep
   at the thunder of your cataracts;
all your waves and your billows
   have gone over me.
⁸By day the LORD commands his
   steadfast love,
   and at night his song is with
      me,
   a prayer to the God of my life.

⁹I say to God, my rock,

domain of men. The Bible records that drums and voices were used in religious celebrations and that women often played drums and danced, e.g., Judges 11:34-40 (Jephthah's daughter lamenting before her death); 1 Samuel 18:6 (groups of women celebrating battle victories of Saul and David); and Exodus 15:20 (Miriam and a group of women celebrating the crossing of the Reed Sea). The small hand or frame drum, תֹף, often translated as "tambourine," was even known as a "women's instrument."[1] Some contend that it was a sexual symbol in the Hebrew Bible; Jephthah's daughter bewails her virginity with a drum.[2]

1. Theodore Burgh, *Listening to the Artifacts: Music Culture in Ancient Palestine* (New York: T & T Clark, 2006), 34.
2. Joachim Braun, *Music in Ancient Israel/Palestine: Archaeological, Written, and Comparative Sources* (Grand Rapids, MI: Eerdmans, 2002), 30.

"Why have you forgotten me?
Why must I walk about mournfully
because the enemy oppresses
me?"
[10]As with a deadly wound in my
body,
my adversaries taunt me,
while they say to me continually,
"Where is your God?"

[11]Why are you cast down, O my
soul,
and why are you disquieted
within me?
Hope in God; for I shall again
praise him,
my help and my God.

[43:1] Vindicate me, O God, and defend my cause
against an ungodly people;
from those who are deceitful and
unjust
deliver me!

[2] For you are the God in whom I
take refuge;
why have you cast me off?
Why must I walk about mournfully
because of the oppression of
the enemy?

[3]O send out your light and your
truth;
let them lead me;
let them bring me to your holy hill
and to your dwelling.
[4]Then I will go to the altar of God,
to God my exceeding joy;
and I will praise you with the harp,
O God, my God.

[5]Why are you cast down, O my
soul,
and why are you disquieted
within me?
Hope in God; for I shall again
praise him,
my help and my God.

If we read Numbers 16–18 (the story of Korah's "rebellion") alongside Psalm 42–43, several intertextual allusions emerge. John Vassar suggests that Psalm 42:2, 4 and Psalm 43:3-4 address the community returning from exile and longing for the temple. Though in Numbers Korah is swallowed up by the ground as punishment for challenging Moses' authority, according to 1 Chronicles his sons eventually reestablish themselves in the temple. This sends a message of hope to the exiles. Korah may function as "the archetype of rebellion," but his descendants become "the archetypes of restitution and return."[3]

---

3. John Vassar, *Recalling a Story Once Told: An Intertextual Reading of the Psalter and the Pentateuch* (Macon, GA: Mercer University Press, 2007), 61. J. Clinton McCann Jr., "The Book of Psalms," in *The New Interpreter's Bible*, vol. 4 (Nashville, TN: Abingdon Press, 1996), 639–1280, at 852, also argues for an exilic audience by noting the many linguistic links between Ps 42–43 and Ps 44, a communal lament; these links suggest

Another allusion also emerges that is missed by many scholars, one that links Psalm 42–43, Numbers 16–18, and Numbers 12. Korah's revolt mirrors Miriam's challenge to Moses' autocratic authority in Numbers 12. Both Korah and Miriam are punished directly by God. Perhaps Miriam's voice can be heard in Psalm 42–43, lamenting her estrangement from God's presence. An imagined superscription to Psalm 42–43 might read: "A psalm of Miriam, when she was shut out of the camp for seven days after challenging Moses' leadership" (see Num 12:15).

Psalm 42–43 is an individual lament. Laments constitute one distinct literary psalm type identified by Hermann Gunkel in the 1920s in his pioneering work on form criticism. Others include hymns, thanksgivings, and royal psalms, each type having its own form and content growing out of a distinctive setting in life in which that psalm type functioned.[4] Nearly one-third of the 150 psalms are laments, yet the laments are seldom used in worship. As "a legitimate complaint in faith to God,"[5] a lament does more than complain. It seeks change from God with metaphorical, evocative, and provocative language, moving from complaint to praise in a process that can bring wholeness and healing to those experiencing brokenness and suffering. Basic trust in God's power and willingness to receive the lament and change the situation undergird the form. Thus it is not surprising to find that in Psalm 42–43 "God is omnipresent in a poem which complains of his [sic] absence."[6] God is mentioned twenty-two times.

The opening simile (a more explicit metaphor) immediately pulls us into the pathos of the psalmist who laments not being in God's presence in the sanctuary. Adele Berlin speaks of "a crossover effect" in the emotions of deer and human in vv. 1-2: "the deer longs (like a human) for water, and the human being thirsts (like a deer) for God."[7] Because the verb "long" is used twice in the first two lines and the verb "thirst" once

---

"that the 'I' of Psalms 42–43 speaks for the people." He points to a similar linkage at the beginning of book 3. The "I" of Ps 73 is followed by Ps 74, a communal lament; these are the first two psalms of the Asaph collection. These initial pairings provide a context for reading subsequent psalms.

4. Denise Dombkowski Hopkins, *Journey through the Psalms* (St. Louis, MO: Chalice Press, 2002), 29.

5. Ibid., 81. For what follows see pp. 82–121.

6. Konrad Schaefer, *Psalms*, Berit Olam (Collegeville, MN: Liturgical Press, 2001), 109.

7. Adele Berlin, "On Reading Biblical Poetry: The Role of Metaphor," in *Congress Volume* (Leiden: Brill, 1997), 25–36, at 31.

in the third line, "incrementation" suggests that "the psalmist's need for God is even greater than the deer's need for water."[8] Because these verbs are third-person feminine singular in form, we would expect a feminine singular noun for deer (doe), to correspond to the feminine singular noun נפש (42:1, 2, 4, 5, 6, 11; 43:5), translated incorrectly as "soul" in many English Bibles.[9] נפש is not to be conflated with the Greek idea of "soul" as separate from the body. The Hebrew literally means "throat," "animation," "vital self," "individual person."[10] The throat is the place where thirst is experienced (see Pss 63:1; 143:6).

Images of female deer with heads lowered to drink are frequently found on Judean seals and bullae from the eighth and seventh centuries BCE, representing the petitioner in prayer and worship. "The image of the doe is the projected 'soul,' the psalmist's personal self . . . the person's existential core, embodied in piety, fully dependent and vulnerable . . . like the doe whose head is stooped as it searches for water, her soul is 'downcast' "[11] (see 42:5, 6, 11; 43:5). The problem with this analysis from a feminist standpoint is that often the default position for women in society is "fully dependent and vulnerable." Perhaps this metaphor packs more transformative power for men of privilege. Renita Weems warns that "metaphors matter"[12]—they shape the way we view ourselves, one another, and the world. Consequently, readers must claim "our rights as readers to differ with authors" and, especially for the marginalized, must decide "whether the worlds that authors place us in are indeed worth inhabiting."[13]

---

8. Ibid.

9. איל ("stag") in the MT usually refers to a male deer or buck, but the verb is feminine. Perhaps haplography of the ת of the verb has occurred; read איילת, "doe."

10. Bernd Janowski, *Arguing with God: A Theological Anthropology of the Psalms*, trans. Armin Siedlecki (Louisville, KY: Westminster John Knox, 2013), 190.

11. William P. Brown, *Seeing the Psalms: A Theology of Metaphor* (Louisville, KY: Westminster John Knox, 2002), 150.

12. Renita J. Weems, *Battered Love: Marriage, Sex, and Violence in the Hebrew Prophets* (Minneapolis: Fortress Press, 1995), 106. On the damaging effects of metaphor, see also Jacqueline Grant, "The Sin of Servanthood and the Deliverance of Discipleship," in *A Troubling in My Soul: Womanist Perspectives on Evil and Suffering*, ed. Emilie M. Townes (Maryknoll, NY: Orbis Books, 1993), 199–218, at 200. She notes that "servanthood" as a metaphor for discipleship simply reinforces the social reality for black women in the United States that they have been "servants of servants"; "servanthood . . . has been servitude."

13. Weems, *Battered Love*, 10.

Godly Servitude

Society often attempts to conflate the will of God with the will of individuals and communities who operate out of privilege and attempt to propagate oppression. As a result, black women have unwittingly internalized paradigms of oppression in ways that foster our own subjugation. With that in mind, it is important to highlight that the doe in Ps 42:1 is longing for God. The "downcast" posture of dependency and service is aimed toward the deity and not human beings and social structures that attempt to do us harm. Jacqueline Grant cautions against the wholesale acceptance of models of servitude, arguing that this model of Christianity for black women has enabled our oppression. Rather than rejecting the model altogether, however, the womanist agenda cultivates a mind-set wherein we understand that our service to God need not be played out in ways that undercut our own interests. The imagery of the deer panting for water recalls the desperation brought on by the need to sustain and preserve one's own livelihood. Black women who have been disregarded by society must bow down to find life. In doing so we must acknowledge that the truest godly servitude we might undertake is our care for our own neglected humanity.

Yolanda Marie Norton

How ironic that the thirsting psalmist is virtually drowning in her own tears (v. 3a): "My tears have been my food day and night." Salty tears as solid food do not satisfy or sustain (see Pss 80:5; 102:9, where tears are a result of God's anger). "Through tears, the psalmist 'pours out' her soul. She is on the verge of dissolution."[14] One could say that the psalmist has become water because of the frequency and duration ("day and night") of her tears. Yet tears do not simply function negatively here. Tears seep through the numbness and isolation created by suffering; feeling nothing functions as an involuntary defense mechanism to keep trauma at bay.[15] From a pastoral care perspective, tears are part of "relationship behavior," that is, a way to express our need for connection, not simply an emotional release.[16] The psalmist needs to be connected

14. Brown, *Seeing the Psalms*, 133.

15. Kathleen O'Connor, *Jeremiah: Pain and Promise* (Minneapolis: Fortress Press, 2011), 59.

16. Judith Kay Nelson, *Seeing through Tears* (New York: Routledge, 2005), 6. Quoted in Denise Dombkowski Hopkins and Michael S. Koppel, *Grounded in the Living Word:*

to God, to "behold [ראה, 'see'] the face of God" (42:2b)[17] and be led to God's dwelling (the temple or sanctuary; see Ps 63:1-2, 5, 8-9) to praise God (43:3-4). "To turn one's face towards someone is the first condition for establishing communication."[18] "Face" (פנים) is the most common body part mentioned in the Psalms since it includes necessary organs for communication: eyes, mouth, ears. A repeated complaint in the laments is that God "hides" God's face, which means that God is experienced by the psalmist as absent (see Pss 13:2; 27:9; 44:25; 69:18; 88:15; 102:4; 143:7). Connection with God in the sanctuary means protection, deliverance, and worship joy for the psalmist, in contrast to the psalmist's current sense of abandonment and isolation.

The psalmist's tears may function positively as a prompt for God's hoped-for empathetic response.[19] Too often in many societies, however, tears are seen as a sign of weakness and are associated with women. Yet prominent men in the Hebrew Bible weep. Jacob and Esau weep when they meet in Genesis 33:4; Joseph weeps three times when reunited with his brothers in Egypt (Gen 42:24; 43:30; 45:2); David weeps over his dead son Absalom (2 Sam 18:33). Cultural bias against men who weep spills over into our God images. Consequently, when God weeps (Jer 9:1, 10) and grieves with and because of the people, desiring connection with them,[20] there is resistance. For example, the Hebrew MT of Jeremiah 9:10 uses a common first-person singular imperfect verb: "I will take up weeping"; the "I" refers to God. Yet the NRSV, following the Septuagint and Syriac, translates an imperative from God to the people: "Take up weeping." Some are reluctant to attribute grief to God because their core testimony affirms a God of strength. Tears signal "divine weakness and vulnerability."[21] Showing weakness and vulnerability are roles culture often assigns to women.

The Old Testament and Pastoral Care Practices (Grand Rapids, MI: Eerdmans, 2010), 145. Nelson works with attachment theory rooted in the parent-child bond.

17. Janowski, *Arguing with God*, 91–92.

18. Susanne Gillmayr-Bucher, "Body Images in the Psalms," *JSOT* 28 (2004): 301–26, at 306. In many Asian cultures, however, looking directly at someone is considered rude and disrespectful, suggesting that how the use of body parts is interpreted is culturally conditioned.

19. David Bosworth, "Weeping in the Psalms," *VT* 62 (2013): 36–46, at 37.

20. For a fuller discussion, see Hopkins and Koppel, *Grounded in the Living Word*, 145–48.

21. Ibid., 147, 179–86. For "core testimony," see Walter Brueggemann, *Theology of the Old Testament* (Minneapolis: Fortress Press, 1997).

The Tears of Black Women

As a black woman I find it difficult to hear that tears are a mechanism for connection because this highlights the isolation we experience in society. The very construction of and adherence to the "Strong Black Woman" paradigm necessitates black women "remaining emotionally strong."[22] There is no public space for our tears and thus there is no way for us to be connected to others. If our tears are the sustenance on which our souls must feed, this "Strong Black Woman" icon starves black women daily. In that vein, Beverly Wallace describes the ways in which expectations of acceptable emotional responses from black women as emotionally invincible reveal themselves through "African American women's anger, loneliness, and denial of pain."[23]

The lack of space in which to lament publicly, or even privately, is what renders black women speechless. Such space can help us to deal with the harshness and cruelty of life and grasp the totality of the trauma we experience through micro-aggression, emotional cruelty, physical violence, and being rendered invisible. Lack of such space fills us with platitudes when we try to answer the question: "Where is your God?" Ultimately this feeling of isolation facilitates the anger best described in an interaction between Shug and Celie in *The Color Purple*:

> She say, Miss Celie, You better hush. God might hear you.
> Let 'im hear me, I say. If he ever listened to poor colored women the world would be a different place, I can tell you.[24]

More than shining a spotlight on the ways in which black women's emotions have been stunted, Psalm 42–43 provides a challenge to examine the possibility of how black women might live. Emilie Townes explains that "womanist spirituality . . . is a social witness. It is born out of people's struggle and determination to continue to find ways to answer the question, 'Do you want to be healed' with the Yes! of our lives and the work we do for justice."[25] It is, indeed, too

---

22. Beverly Wallace, "A Womanist Legacy of Trauma, Grief, and Loss: Reframing the Notion of the Strong Black Woman Icon," in *Women Out of Order: Risking Change and Creating Care in a Multicultural World* (Minneapolis: Fortress Press, 2010), 43–56, at 43.

23. Ibid., 44.

24. Alice Walker, *The Color Purple* (New York: Harcourt Brace Jovanovich, 1982), 193.

25. Emilie Townes, *In a Blaze of Glory: Womanist Spirituality as Social Witness* (Nashville, TN: Abingdon Press, 1995), 10.

simplistic to suggest that the final message of Psalm 42–43 is one of absolute resolution and optimism. As most African American women will tell you, however, the experience of trauma does not preclude the experience and articulation of hope. The need to intertwine an acknowledgment of the persistence of trauma with an expectation that the triumph of the divine agenda facilitates a care and nurturing of the victim's soul—in this case in the healing of the souls of black women—can best be understood in the words of Alice Walker: "Black writers seem always involved in a moral and/or physical struggle, the result of which is expected to be some kind of larger freedom. Perhaps this is because our literary tradition is based on the slave narratives, where escape for the body and freedom for the soul went together, or perhaps this is because black people have never felt themselves guilty of global, cosmic sins."[26]

There is an eternal hope that one day God will listen to the cries and absorb the tears of black women, and the world will be a better place for it.

Yolanda Marie Norton

Too little water ("thirst") in v. 2 contrasts with too many tears in v. 3 ("day and night") and too much water in v. 7 ("deep [תהום] calls to deep"). The psalmist's tears release memories of worship, of the noisy communal procession with shouts and songs to the house of God (42:4). These memories persist in the land of the Jordan and Mount Hermon in the north (v. 6), where God's "house" (temple or sanctuary) is not and God's absence is felt. Most interpreters view the "deep" (תהום) as chaos waters (Tiamat) challenging God, borrowing from ancient Near Eastern myths such as the *Enuma Elish*. Yet God has controlled and confined the primeval waters by the divine word in Genesis 1. Here and in Jonah 2:6 and Ezekiel 26:19 the waters threaten the psalmist with drowning, and the image suggests Sheol, the abode of the dead (see Pss 18, 32, 69, 88, 124, 144).[27] This reading releases the reader from the mental gymnastics of trying to imagine "billows" and "waves," normally associated with seas, as characteristic of the less-than-mighty headwaters of the Jordan River (v. 6). Likewise, this

26. Alice Walker, *In Search of Our Mothers' Gardens: Womanist Prose* (San Diego, CA: Harvest Books, 1983), 5.

27. Rebecca Watson, *Chaos Uncreated: A Reassessment of the Theme of "Chaos" in the Hebrew Bible* (Berlin: de Gruyter, 2005), 98.

understanding underscores the paradox of juxtaposing God "my rock" (v. 9), "my help" (Pss 42:5, 11; 43:5) with the God whose absence threatens the psalmist with inundation by the waters of Sheol. Luis Alonso Schökel terms this contrast the heart of the psalm: "a dramatic tension in the soul between God and God,"[28] conveyed by the ambiguity of the image of water as both life-giving and life-threatening.

The psalmist grieves in Psalm 42–43 as a response to loss. Losses can be of several kinds.[29] The psalmist experiences material loss of the temple or sanctuary environs; relationship loss, that is, loss of connection with God; role loss as worshiper among other pilgrims; intrapsychic loss of an image of self as protected by God; and functional loss of vigor (being "cast down," 42:5, 11; 43:5). In short, the psalmist is traumatized. The psalmist asks "why?" frequently; the Hebrew words למה and מה are used ten times. Grief is heightened by the taunts of people demanding, "where is your God?" (42:3, 10; see also Pss 79:10; 115:2).

These taunts suggest the victory of the enemy over Israel and its God (see also Isa 10:9-10) and perhaps the experience of exile, though many other periods in Israel's history can also offer a context for them. Rolf Jacobson[30] argues that quoting this question from hostile others creates a role play in which the psalmist temporarily assumes the role of the other. In doing so, the psalmist dissociates from responsibility for the remark and expresses what is unacceptable, that is, his or her own doubt about God. Blasphemy becomes acceptable in the mouths of enemies. Consequently, "each time the enemies ask where the psalmist's God is, the psalmist makes a mental pilgrimage to Zion."[31] The psalmist also offers a self-quotation in anticipation of what she will say to God in 42:9: "Why must I walk about mournfully because the enemy oppresses me?"

---

28. Luis Alonso Schökel, "The Poetic Structure of Psalm 42–43," *JSOT* 1 (1976): 4–21, at 7. See Vassar, *Recalling a Story*, 60, who notes that God is "both succor and threat" in the Korah story of Num 16–18. Brown, *Seeing the Psalms*, 134, seems to minimize this paradox in his view of the interrelated controlling metaphors of God as water, self as water, and worship as water. The "roar of cascading waters" and the "din of restive worship" are bound together by hyperbole; "the voice of many waters and the voices of many at worship blend together."

29. For what follows, see Kenneth R. Mitchell and Herbert Anderson, *All Our Losses, All Our Griefs: Resources for Pastoral Care* (Louisville, KY: Westminster John Knox, 1983), 36–46.

30. Rolf A. Jacobson, *"Many Are Saying": The Function of Direct Discourse in the Hebrew Psalter*, JSOTSup 397 (Edinburgh: T & T Clark, 2004).

31. Ibid., 51.

This self-quotation juxtaposes the psalmist's faith with others' lack of faith. Together these two kinds of quotations both criticize enemies and, I would argue, lodge an implicit complaint against God, who allows the psalmist to suffer. They also self-characterize the psalmist in a way that negotiates community norms of what is acceptable speech about God. "Why are you cast down, O my 'soul'?" suggests that a faithful follower of God should not be so, given the community's theological portrait of a protective God of refuge. The question functions as rebuke.

Many interpreters contend that the refrain in 42:5, 11 and 43:5 charts the psalmist's progression from despair to pep talk to "shout of triumph,"[32] corresponding to a focus on the past, the present, and an envisioned future. J. Clinton McCann insists that the refrain expresses the possibility of hope, which is heard "more clearly" at the end of Psalm 42–43.[33] These assessments move the psalmist too quickly to resolution and undercut the complexity of the psalmist's internal conversation. Each occurrence of the refrain ends with a descriptive phrase for God: "my help and my God." The use of the possessive adjective "my" claims relationship, which simultaneously expresses hope and critique: this is how I remember it and how it should be now, but it is not. In this vein William Brown suggests that the "I" of Psalm 42–43 is cast dialogically by the psalmist as the speaking "I" and his "soul" (נפשׁ). These voices are interwoven but not fully melded, creating a "bifurcated" self not evident in 42:1-3. The refrain carries a "harsh, admonitory tone" that acts as prescriptive "critic" and "guide."[34] It is up to the speaker to resist or embrace this "I."

John Goldingay rightly sees no resolution in the psalm; God has not responded to the psalmist and little has changed. He appropriately suggests that the refrain functions as a motivation for God to act. God is meant to overhear the psalmist describing herself as being "cast down," since chances are that priest or prophet would rebuke her for saying so. Here an allusion to Hannah in 1 Samuel 1 emerges. Eli, the priest at the

---

32. Schaefer, *Psalms*, 110.

33. McCann, "The Book of Psalms," 853. McCann notes that this psalm was sung when Augustine was baptized on Easter Sunday, 387 CE. "To hope in God means we live eschatologically" (854).

34. William P. Brown, "The Psalms and 'I': The Dialogical Self and the Disappearing Psalmist," in *Diachronic and Synchronic: Reading the Psalms in Real Time*, Proceedings of the Baylor Symposium on the Book of Psalms, ed. Joel Burnett, W. H. Bellinger, and W. Dennis Tucker (Edinburgh: T & T Clark, 2007), 26–44, at 40–44.

Shiloh sanctuary, rebukes Hannah with an accusation of drunkenness when she prays silently for a son. Further, the barren Hannah is taunted by her enemy, Peninnah, in vv. 6-7a (Peninnah is the other wife of her husband, Elkanah), and she is described as weeping, literally, "pouring out my soul" (v. 15) and refusing food (v. 7b). Like the psalmist, Hannah does not express anger toward Peninnah or Eli; instead, "Hannah directs her emotion inwards."[35] We do not know the complete content of Hannah's prayer outside of the vow she makes in v. 11, but one can imagine a similar internal conversation as part of her silent prayer. Another superscription for Psalm 42–43 might read: "A prayer of Hannah, when she made pilgrimage to Shiloh to pray for a son."

Goldingay insists that in these refrains "the suppliant has to accept responsibility for his or her own encouraging."[36] Similarly, Nelle Morton speaks of "hearing to speech" in women's experience; women hear themselves or other women to expression.[37] If God is overhearing the refrain, then God becomes "the hearing one—hearing us [the psalmist] into our own responsible word."[38] Korean women struggle to hear themselves into speech and cut through passive obedience and the numbness of self-hate rooted in *han*, the feeling of oppression and anger stuck inside them with no outlet.[39] From a pastoral care perspective, this psalm can offer an outlet for their pain. As "an arena of contestation"[40] that draws God, the psalmist, the enemy, and the congregation into a "dialogic exchange," this psalm makes a True Self as it authorizes a sense of omnipotence by summoning God to action on the psalmist's behalf.

35. Ellen van Wolde, "Sentiments as Culturally Constructed Emotions: Anger and Love in the Hebrew Bible," *BibInt* 16 (2008): 1–24, at 12. Van Wolde notes that "none of the verbs [in the Hebrew Bible] designating anger are conceptualized with a female subject."

36. John Goldingay, *Psalms*, vol. 2 (Grand Rapids, MI: Baker Academic, 2007), 26. In Hannah's case, Elkanah does provide encouragement (1 Sam 1:8).

37. Nelle Morton, *The Journey Is Home* (Boston: Beacon Press, 1985), 127–28.

38. Ibid., 129.

39. Chung Hyun Kyung, *Struggle to Be the Sun Again* (Maryknoll, NY: Orbis Books, 1990), 36–52, discussed in Hopkins, *Journey through the Psalms*, 112.

40. Walter Brueggemann, "Psychological Criticism: Exploring the Self in the Text," in *Method Matters: Essays on the Interpretation of the Hebrew Bible in Honor of David L. Petersen*, ed. Joel LeMon and Kent Harold Richards (Atlanta, GA: Society of Biblical Literature, 2009), 213–32, at 226. Brueggemann says this in connection with Ps 35, but it applies to this psalm as well. He draws from Object Relations Theory as espoused by D. W. Winnicott and Heinz Kohut and the notion of "good enough mother," which expresses the notion of covenant.

As the psalmist is heard into speech she petitions God directly in 43:1 to "vindicate," "defend," and "deliver," as well as to send out "light and truth" to lead the psalmist to God (43:3). Just as God's "rod" and "staff" are personified in Psalm 23, so "light" and "truth" are personified here as guardians along the way to Zion.[41] This way can be taught, studied, and revealed. In both the Psalms and ancient Near Eastern literature, God's presence is expressed as light or solar theophany; "seeing God's face" is often associated with light or shining[42] and is rooted in temple theology. What the psalmist hopes for is light to pierce the darkness in which she finds herself wandering (42:9b, translated as "walk about mournfully" in NRSV). "Pathway . . . transforms the search for 'refuge' from aimless wandering into a pilgrimage."[43]

God is also repeatedly referenced as "refuge" in Ps 42–43. The network of associations spun by the idea of refuge includes such concrete images as "rock" (42:9), "help" (42:5, 11), and Zion, called "your holy hill" in Psalm 43:3. "Zion is the geographical embodiment of 'refuge' " (Ps 2:6).[44] In Psalm 43:2 the psalmist declares: "you are the God in whom I take refuge." These references express ambiguity. God as refuge is the psalmist's hope, but at the same time this metaphor functions as a critique of God's absence. This tension marks the life of faith.

41. Brown, *Seeing the Psalms*, 41.
42. Ibid., 84.
43. Ibid., 42.
44. Ibid., 19.

Psalm 44

Is Israel's Suffering Redemptive?

Several interpreters link Psalm 44 with the individual lament in Psalm 42–43 because of the shared themes of memory (42:4; 44:1-8), distance from God (42:1, 6, 9; 43:2; 44:9, 12, 24), and humiliation by others (42:3, 10; 43:1; 44:13-16),[1] and they claim that these themes are characteristic of the exilic period. Yet Psalm 44 has been dated anywhere from the eighth century BCE to the Maccabean period in the second century BCE and need not be tied to one particular time in Israel's history. Even though Adele Berlin classifies Psalm 44 as part of the literature of Exile (along with Psalms 69, 78, and 137 because of shared theological assumptions), she warns that dating psalms can entrap us in a hermeneutical circle and too easily follow general trends in dating other biblical texts.[2]

---

1. For example, J. Clinton McCann Jr., "The Book of Psalms," in *The New Interpreter's Bible*, vol. 4 (Nashville, TN: Abingdon Press, 1996), 639–1280, at 852. He argues that the "I" of Ps 42–43 speaks for the people and that book 3 begins in a way similar to book 2 (the Korah collection), with "I" Ps 73 followed by communal lament Ps 74 as the first two psalms in the Asaph collection. He claims that both books 2 and 3 address the exilic and postexilic eras.

2. Adele Berlin, "Psalms and the Literature of Exile: Psalms 137, 44, 69, and 78," in *The Book of Psalms: Composition and Reception*, ed. Peter W. Flint and Patrick D. Miller (Leiden: Brill, 2005), 65–86, at 66.

Psalm 44:1-26

To the leader. Of the Korahites. A Maskil.

¹We have heard with our ears, O God,
   our ancestors have told us,
what deeds you performed in their days,
   in the days of old:
²you with your own hand drove out the nations,
   but them you planted;
you afflicted the peoples,
   but them you set free;
³for not by their own sword did they win the land,
   nor did their own arm give them victory;
but your right hand, and your arm,
   and the light of your countenance,
for you delighted in them.

⁴You are my King and my God;
   you command victories for Jacob.
⁵Through you we push down our foes;
   through your name we tread down our assailants.
⁶For not in my bow do I trust,
   nor can my sword save me.
⁷But you have saved us from our foes,
   and have put to confusion those who hate us.
⁸In God we have boasted continually,
   and we will give thanks to your name forever.   *Selah*

⁹Yet you have rejected us and abased us,
   and have not gone out with our armies.
¹⁰You made us turn back from the foe,

Theological stakes are high in Psalm 44, the first communal lament in the Psalter. Is Israel's suffering redemptive? Are questions of theodicy (justification of God's justice in the face of evil and suffering) resolved? Those who argue for a progression toward hope in Psalm 42–43 tend to argue similarly for Psalm 44. Unlike individual laments, which often end with a confession of trust and a vow of praise in anticipation of future deliverance after the complaints and petitions have been offered,[3] "communal laments often end without any resolution,"[4] as in Psalms 44, 60, 74, 79, 80, 85, 94, 123, 137. As Peter Craigie puts it, Psalm 44 can

---

3. See Denise Dombkowski Hopkins, *Journey through the Psalms* (St. Louis, MO: Chalice Press, 2002), 81–82.

4. Frederico G. Villanueva, *The 'Uncertainty of a Hearing': A Study of the Sudden Change of Mood in the Psalms of Lament* (Leiden: Brill, 2008), 217.

and our enemies have gotten
spoil.
¹¹You have made us like sheep for
slaughter,
and have scattered us among
the nations.
¹²You have sold your people for a
trifle,
demanding no high price for
them.
¹³You have made us the taunt of
our neighbors,
the derision and scorn of those
around us.
¹⁴You have made us a byword
among the nations,
a laughingstock among the
peoples.
¹⁵All day long my disgrace is before me,
and shame has covered my
face

¹⁶at the words of the taunters and
revilers,
at the sight of the enemy and
the avenger.

¹⁷All this has come upon us,
yet we have not forgotten you,
or been false to your covenant.
¹⁸Our heart has not turned back,
nor have our steps departed
from your way,
¹⁹yet you have broken us in the
haunt of jackals,
and covered us with deep
darkness.

²⁰If we had forgotten the name of
our God,
or spread out our hands to a
strange god,
²¹would not God discover this?
For he knows the secrets of
the heart.

only end in desperate petition, leaving the lament questions unanswered; the psalm "points in the same direction as the book of Job."[5]

Those who see positive resolution in Psalm 44 focus on the opening vv. 1-8 and the inclusion (bracket or envelope) they form with the word חסד[6] in v. 26b: "Redeem us for the sake of your steadfast love [חסד]."[7] Nancy deClaissé-Walford, for example, notes the "two covenant-images of God" in vv. 1-3 and 26. Verses 1-3 rehearse the history of God's past action on Israel's behalf in the settlement of Canaan after the wilderness

5. Peter Craigie, *Psalms 1–50* (Waco, TX: Word Books, 1983), 335.
6. Katharine Doob Sakenfeld defines *ḥesed* as "something which is tested out in one's actions; it is action performed in accordance with and because of one's relationship to another." See *The Meaning of Ḥesed in the Hebrew Bible*, HSM 17 (Missoula, MT: Scholars Press, 1978), 217.
7. Nancy L. deClaissé-Walford, "Psalm 44: O God, Why Do You Hide Your Face?" *RevExp* 104 (Fall 2007): 745–59, at 752.

Psalm 44:1-26 (cont.)

22Because of you we are being
killed all day long,
and accounted as sheep for
the slaughter.

23Rouse yourself! Why do you
sleep, O Lord?
Awake, do not cast us off forever!

24Why do you hide your face?
Why do you forget our affliction
and oppression?
25For we sink down to the dust;
our bodies cling to the ground.
26Rise up, come to our help.
Redeem us for the sake of
your steadfast love.

wanderings, while vv. 4-8 testify to the present faithfulness of the community that continually thanks God. Verse 26 recalls this mutual covenant commitment with the word חסד. As a משכיל (from the root שכל, "to
have insight," "teach"), Psalm 44 therefore teaches us that we must
"remember and trust" and that sometimes the faithful "are not able to
understand the ways of God."[8]

An examination of the rhetorical function of the God descriptions in
44:1-8, however, suggests that they heighten the protest against God
voiced in vv. 9-22 and leave the question of theodicy open. Just as in
Psalm 42–43, God in 44:1-8 can be viewed as the object of either wistful
praise or irony-laced accusation. In a positive view of this rhetoric, God's
redemptive activity on Israel's behalf in the settlement of Canaan is celebrated. God's "hand" (vv. 2, 3) and "arm" (v. 3) "drove out the nations"
(v. 2; cp. Deut 7:17) and enabled the gift of land: "but them [Israel] you
planted" (v. 2a; cp. Deut 6:20-25). The divine body parts symbolize God's
power (cp. Exod 15:6, 13, 16; Ps 77:15). As divine warrior, God causes
Israel to "push down our foes" (v. 5; cp. Pss 60:12; 108:13; Isa 14:21; 63:6).
As "King" (v. 4), God commands victories.

In a negative view of this rhetoric, Israel's historical memory serves
to "'remind' God of how the Deity ought to act by citing past examples."[9]
God needs to act now in consonance with the divine character of old.
The present community argues in vv. 4-8 that it is faithful as the ancestors were, and thus God should act similarly now. Just as the ancestors
have told the story of God's salvific activity, this generation publicly and
liturgically thanks God (v. 8). Dalit Rom-Shiloni points to Psalm 44 as

---

8. Ibid., 757.
9. Loren Crow, "The Rhetoric of Psalm 44," *ZAW* 104 (1992): 394–401, at 395.

"nonorthodox protest"[10] against God that is found also in the book of Lamentations; it challenges the reigning orthodox theology that justifies God's actions.

Cultural Memory

Ronald Hendel suggests that "cultural memory (re)produces a past with present relevance, and since the relation between the past and the present shifts with every generation, this remembered past is continually revised to suit present circumstances. . . . In cultural memory, to paraphrase master Yoda, 'always in motion is the past.'"[11] In Psalm 44 the recollection of the past has an eye toward the future; however, that future need not bring resolution or hope. There are those members of minoritized communities who argue that hope is a tool of the oppressor to perpetuate subjugation.[12] The pairing of hope and God-speech can be incredibly dangerous; the marriage of the two has the potential to facilitate resignation and docility.

The psalmist's articulation that "with your own hand you drove out the nations . . . for not by their own sword did they win the land" does not absolve the oppressed from an obligation to fight. Instead, it releases them from the responsibility for victory. bell hooks argues that in African American intergenerational communal exchange "one had to understand beauty as a force to be made and imagined. Old folks shared their sense that we had come out of slavery into this free space and we had to create a world that would renew the spirit that would make it life-giving."[13] As such, the creation of a cultural memory that recalls deliverance forces a community to engage with the Deity for the sake of its own liberation. Consequently, the psalm has the potential to function as a call to arms for those who have been socially downcast.

Yolanda Marie Norton

---

10. Dalit Rom-Shiloni, "Psalm 44: The Powers of Protest," *CBQ* 70 (2008): 683–98, at 684.

11. Ronald Hendel, "Cultural Memory and the Hebrew Bible," *The Bible and Interpretation*, www.bibleinterp.com, July 2011.

12. Miguel De La Torre, Guest Lecture in Liberation Social Ethics (Vanderbilt University, Nashville, TN, November 19, 2013).

13. bell hooks, *Yearning: Race, Gender, and Cultural Politics* (Boston: South End Press, 1990), 104.

Verses 9-22 make it clear that God is not acting as warrior or king on Israel's behalf. The word אַף ("yet" in its adversative sense) at the beginning of v. 9, along with the notation סלה (some kind of liturgical instruction), signals a transition to protest. Rhetorical hints in vv. 1-8 set up this protest.[14] As John Goldingay notes, the very first word of v. 1, "O God," hints at criticism, since direct address to God "is more characteristic of protest than of praise," e.g., Psalms 38:1; 42:1 versus 46:1; 47:1; 48:1.[15] The vocabulary and motifs in vv. 1-8 are intentionally reversed in vv. 9-16[16] to underscore Israel's protest. For example, the glorious "days" of the ancestors in v. 1 contrast with the shame (v. 15) and slaughter (v. 22) experienced by Israel "all day long." The enemies were "put to confusion/shamed" (בוש) in v. 7 but shame now covers the psalmist's face in v. 15. God's salvific hand and arm (vv. 2-3) have been stilled, since God has "not gone out with our armies" (v. 9). The relentless repetition of "you" in second-person masculine singular verb forms in vv. 9-16 and vv. 1-8 emphasizes God's active role in Israel's life for both victory and defeat.

In the "loosely chiastic" structure[17] of Psalm 44 (vv. 1-3/4-8 // 9-16 // 17-23/23-26), God's violence in vv. 9-16 shocks Israel and raises the question of theodicy. God has made Israel "like sheep for slaughter" (vv. 11, 22; cp. Jer 12:3); the people experience constant shame and taunts (vv. 13-16). Herbert Levine notes the "bivalent" nature of the sheep metaphor; Israel needs to reconcile its suffering with its supposed protection as God's flock: "Because of you/for your sake we are being killed all day long" (v. 22). Jewish response to the Shoah (Holocaust) has often drawn on this verse and argued for the value of martyrdom. Levine argues that such uses of the metaphor "focus on Jewish powerlessness" but ignore the abuse of divine power against which Psalm 44 originally protested.[18] Martyrdom is not acceptable to the psalmist. David Blumenthal, who looks at psalms from the viewpoint of adult survivors of child abuse and the victims of the Shoah, also argues that there is no redemptive suffering

14. McCann argues that there is no preparation for this complaint in vv. 1-8. "The Book of Psalms," 857.

15. John Goldingay, *Psalms*, vol. 2 (Grand Rapids, MI: Baker Academic, 2007), 38.

16. Konrad Schaefer, *Psalms*, Berit Olam (Collegeville, MN: Liturgical Press, 2001), 112.

17. Crow, "Rhetoric," 394.

18. Herbert J. Levine, *Sing unto God a New Song: A Contemporary Reading of the Psalms* (Bloomington: Indiana University Press, 1995), 210.

in Ps 44; it is a "psalm of rage." Its righteous anger demands justice from God out of a "mutual covenantal debt" that will not let God "off the hook."[19] Laurel Dykstra similarly warns that prayer cannot be divorced from politics and justice. She dubs the viewing of movies like *Schindler's List*, *Blood Diamonds*, and *Twelve Years a Slave* "issue entertainment," in which we attempt to substitute "vicarious feeling" for "real-world action."[20]

God as King

The metaphor of God as King emerges out of the male-centered worldview of the Bible. God as King, Father, and Husband, reveals "the privilege granted to human kings, fathers, and husbands."[21] Many church hymnals take up these male images for God in what Brian Wren calls the KINGAFAP God metaphor, an acronym for "King-God-Almighty-Father-Protector."[22] Cultural contexts can also reinforce the male privilege of God images. "In Korean culture, for example, patriarchal God images combine with Confucian teachings about women submitting to male figures in their lives to shape negatively the identity and self-worth of Korean Christian women."[23]

Denise Dombkowski Hopkins

19. David Blumenthal, *Facing the Abusing God: A Theology of Protest* (Louisville, KY: Westminster John Knox, 1993), 107. Blumenthal draws parallels between 44:9-12 and the experience of Jews in the Shoah: shame included cutting men's beards, mass rape, defecating in clothes, putting Jews to flight in mass transports, tearing Jews to pieces by using their flesh for lampshades and soap, and handing Jews over like sheep to gas chambers, crematoria, and burn pits (p. 99).

20. Laurel A. Dykstra, *Set Them Free: The Other Side of Exodus* (Maryknoll, NY: Orbis Books, 2002), 124.

21. Julia M. O'Brien, *Challenging Prophetic Metaphor: Theology and Ideology in the Prophets* (Louisville, KY: Westminster John Knox, 2008), xvii.

22. Brian Wren, *What Language Shall I Borrow? God-Talk in Worship; A Male Response to Feminist Theology* (New York: Crossroad, 1989).

23. Denise Dombkowski Hopkins and Michael S. Koppel, *Grounded in the Living Word: The Old Testament and Pastoral Care Practices* (Grand Rapids, MI: Eerdmans, 2010), 61. See Simone Sunghae Kim, "A Korean Feminist Perspective on God Representation," *Pastoral Psychology* 55 (2006): 35–45.

These critiques challenge those like Hans-Joachim Kraus who claim that Psalm 44 suggests that "Israel is chosen for suffering."[24] McCann too quotes James Mays, who argues that "for your sake" "opens on the prospect of an understanding of suffering as a service to the kingdom of God. The prospect leads to the suffering servant of Isaiah 53, to Jewish martyrs, and to the cross of Calvary"[25] (cp. Rom 8:36). Such interpretation ignores the rage and irony that saturate Psalm 44. In this vein, Berlin questions those who interpret v. 17 as a denial of guilt before the exile and a rejection of the Deuteronomic idea that exile is the result of Israel's sin as the NRSV, AV, and NJPS translations suggest: "yet we have not forgotten you." Instead, NEB and REB apply this clause to the period of exile: "we do not forget despite being in exile." The people have not engaged in idolatry in exile, *"therefore the exile should end, because the reason for it no longer exists."*[26] Ironically, the psalmist uses the same Deuteronomic language to demand an end to exile as the prophets used to predict it.

The ending petition (vv. 23-26) shifts from the idea of an aggressor God to a God of inaction or indifference who seems to be comatose: "Why do you sleep, O Lord?" (v. 23b). Such juxtaposed images of God are characteristic of prophetic responses to the trauma of exile.[27] God is hiding God's face (v. 24a; cp. Pss 13:1; 27:9) and forgetting the oppressed Israelites (v. 24b; cp. Ps 42:9). Psalm 44 demands that God "rise up" (v. 26a), an action associated with God the warrior (cp. Num 10:35; Pss 10:12; 78:65), who was extolled in vv. 1-8. Core testimony about God asserts that God is not supposed to sleep (Ps 121:4), hide God's face (Ps 22:24), or forget (Isa 49:15; Ps 9:12). The ending petitions emerge out of the shame Israel experienced in displacement and the taunts of enemies. Though shame is often rooted in gender identity, W. Dennis Tucker[28] suggests that Israel's shame in Psalm 44 comes from a failure of reciprocity expected in the patron/client relationship that was common in ancient societies. God has failed to act as a good patron in a reciprocal way, and

---

24. Hans-Joachim Kraus, *Psalms 1–59: A Commentary*, trans. Hilton C. Oswald (Minneapolis: Fortress Press, 1989), 449.

25. McCann, "The Book of Psalms," 858.

26. Berlin, "Psalms and the Literature of Exile," 73.

27. See Kathleen O'Connor, *Jeremiah: Pain and Promise* (Minneapolis: Fortress Press, 2012).

28. W. Dennis Tucker, "Is Shame a Matter of Patronage in the Communal Laments?," *JSOT* 31 (2007): 465–80.

inaction produces shame for both God and God's client, Israel. The concluding appeal to God's חסד demands reciprocity.[29]

Scattered Among the Nations

The more than 45.2 million people who find themselves displaced by war today, including refugees, internally displaced people, and asylum seekers, must certainly resonate with v. 11: "you have scattered us among the nations."[30] Forced displacement is at an eighteen-year high in the world, and 55 percent of all refugees come from just five areas: Afghanistan, Somalia, Iraq, Syria, and Sudan. Reading v. 12—"you have sold your people for a trifle, demanding no high price for them"—within the context of human trafficking can jolt us into action. According to the 2009 United Nations Office on Drugs and Crime Global Report on Trafficking in Persons,[31] the most common form of human trafficking (79 percent) is sexual exploitation, and the victims are primarily women and girls. Forced labor makes up 18 percent of trafficking. Almost 20 percent of all trafficking victims are children. Most sobering is that such exploitation takes place close to home. Most sports enthusiasts don't know, for example, that the NFL Super Bowl is one of the largest sex-trafficking events in the United States each year.[32] How does the suffering of these women and children further the realm of God?

Denise Dombkowski Hopkins

29. Carleen Mandolfo, *God in the Dock: Dialogic Tension in the Psalms of Lament*, JSOTSup 357 (Sheffield: Sheffield Academic Press, 2002), 130, reminds us that "while the psalmists can admit that YHWH *acts* 'badly,' it does not follow for them that YHWH *is* bad." Ps 44 does not offer a blasphemous discourse.

30. From the Office of the United Nations High Commissioner for Refugees, Global Trends Report, June 2013. See www.unhcr.org/51c071816.html. Children under the age of eighteen make up 46 percent of all refugees.

31. See http://www.unodc.org/unodc/en/human-trafficking/index.html?ref =menuside.

32. See http://umc-gbcs.org/resources-websites/the-power-of-a-story. For a critique of this claim, see http://www.politifact.com/truth-o-meter/statements/2015 /jan/29/john-cornyn/does-sex-trafficking-increase-around-super-bowl/.

Psalm 45

When Being Lusted After Is Not Enough

Feminists have, for the most part, ignored Psalm 45, even though women figure prominently in vv. 9-15. Most interpreters consider the psalm to be a royal wedding song used at the marriage of an Israelite king to a foreign princess (see v. 12a), perhaps Jezebel, the wife of king Ahab (1 Kgs 16:31-33). Israelite kings often married foreigners to create alliances with other nations. Solomon, for example, "loved many foreign women" who "turned away his heart after other gods" (1 Kgs 11:1-8), a not-so-subtle stereotype of foreign women as dangerous temptresses and polluters of Israelite worship. The "strange" or "foreign" woman in many texts (see Deut 7:1-4; Ezra 10:1-17; Neh 13:23-27; Prov 2–7) represents a composite of all the women outside socially accepted categories.[1]

Interpreters note that the term "a love song" appears in the superscription for Psalm 45 and suggests a wedding context; this phrase is used only here in the Psalter. One wonders what love's got to do with it

---

1. Christine Roy Yoder, "Proverbs," in *Women's Bible Commentary*, ed. Carol A. Newsom, Sharon H. Ringe, and Jacqueline E. Lapsley, 3rd ed. (Louisville, KY: Westminster John Knox, 2012), 232–43, at 235.

Psalm 45:1-17

To the leader: according to Lilies.
Of the Korahites. A Maskil. A love song.

[1]My heart overflows with a goodly
  theme;
    I address my verses to the king;
    my tongue is like the pen of a
      ready scribe.

[2]You are the most handsome of
  men;
    grace is poured upon your lips;
    therefore God has blessed you
      forever.
[3]Gird your sword on your thigh, O
  mighty one,
    in your glory and majesty.
[4]In your majesty ride on victoriously
    for the cause of truth and to
      defend the right;
    let your right hand teach you
      dread deeds.

[5]Your arrows are sharp
    in the heart of the king's ene-
      mies;
    the peoples fall under you.
[6]Your throne, O God, endures for-
      ever and ever.
    Your royal scepter is a scepter
      of equity;
[7]you love righteousness and
      hate wickedness.
Therefore God, your God, has
      anointed you
    with the oil of gladness beyond
      your companions;
[8]your robes are all fragrant
      with myrrh and aloes
      and cassia.
From ivory palaces stringed in-
      struments make you glad;
[9]daughters of kings are among
      your ladies of honor;

when we consider the nature of marriage in ancient Israel. "In marriage the economic motivation was more important than the romantic. The chief goal of marriage was to have and raise children."[2] Marriage was patriarchal and contractual and subordinated the wife to her husband. The superscription also contains the phrase "according to Lilies," which many interpreters take to refer to some known melody to which the psalm was sung; see the superscriptions of Psalms 60, 69, 80. William Propp suggests that "lilies" sets the stage for Psalm 45 to be read as an erotic poem, since lilies are an erotic symbol for the mouth in the Song of Songs (see Song 2:16; 6:2-3; 5:13). Propp argues that Psalm 45 is full of "raunchy *double entendre*" that is "real and deliberate,"[3] such as the king's sword (v. 3a) and his arrows (v. 5a) as symbols of the genitals. He

---

2. Philip J. King and Lawrence E. Stager, *Life in Biblical Israel* (Louisville, KY: Westminster John Knox, 2001), 55.

3. William Henry Propp, "Is Psalm 45 an Erotic Poem?," *BRev* 20 (2004): 33–37, 42, at 34, 42.

at your right hand stands the queen in gold of Ophir.

[10]Hear, O daughter, consider and incline your ear;
forget your people and your father's house,
[11]and the king will desire your beauty.
Since he is your lord, bow to him;
[12]the people of Tyre will seek your favor with gifts,
the richest of the people [13]with all kinds of wealth.

The princess is decked in her chamber with gold-woven robes;

[14]in many-colored robes she is led to the king;
behind her the virgins, her companions, follow.
[15]With joy and gladness they are led along
as they enter the palace of the king.

[16]In the place of ancestors you, O king, shall have sons;
you will make them princes in all the earth.
[17]I will cause your name to be celebrated in all generations;
therefore the peoples will praise you forever and ever.

insists that this wedding song was meant to tease the royal couple. This argument becomes problematic for later Jewish and Christian interpretations of Psalm 45 as an allegory for the Messiah or a love song between the enthroned Christ the King and the church (Heb 1:8-9).

James Trotter, however, convincingly argues that Ps 45 belongs to a coronation ceremony for the king. "Love song" in the superscription offers one level of later interpretation, but not the only one. The closest parallels to Psalm 45 are the king's coronation psalms (2, 72, 110) and the enthronement-of-Yhwh hymns (Pss 47, 93, 95–99). The king is the primary focus throughout Psalm 45. The word המלך, "the king," is used five times (vv. 1, 5, 11, 14, 15), and twice the women around the king are described as "daughter(s) of the king" (vv. 9, 13). "The king steals every scene"; every word about the Queen Mother (v. 9b) and the princess and her retinue (vv. 10-15) "serves the ultimate function of enhancing the image of splendor and majesty surrounding the king."[4]

Both the princess (v. 11a) and the king (v. 2a) share the attribute of physical beauty; both are described by the word יפת—"to be handsome, beautiful." In short, the king's consort is the appropriate "arm candy"

---

4. James M. Trotter, "The Genre and Setting of Psalm 45," *ABR* 57 (2009): 34–46, at 38.

for God's anointed. Physical beauty "represents an ideal quality that should be possessed by kings"[5] (and their consorts). Parallels can be seen in references to the beauty of David (1 Sam 16:12) and his sons who sought to be king, Absalom (2 Sam 14:24) and Adonijah (1 Kgs 1:5).

John Goldingay notes that the description of the king's perfumed clothes (v. 8a) and stringed instruments (v. 8b) need not be interpreted as part of a wedding scene but could belong to any royal ceremonial occasion.[6] The poet opens and closes the song with a focus on the king, much like "a modern-day publicist."[7] The king is described as both warrior (vv. 3-5) and pretty boy (vv. 2, 8). His beauty and graceful speech have earned God's blessing (v. 2c); his fierce love of righteousness has resulted in God's anointing him (v. 7b; see Pss 2, 110). Each of God's actions is introduced by "therefore" (עַל־כֵּן), which structures the psalm and leads to the ultimate praise from "the peoples" forever (v. 17b, also introduced by "therefore").

The king's function in ancient Israel is clearly outlined: to defend the nation with his sword (v. 3), administer justice with his scepter (vv. 4, 6b), and beget heirs for his dynasty (v. 16). These are national and institutional concerns that leave little room for women and their roles except as heir incubators.[8] This is clear when the Queen Mother says to the bride in vv. 10b-11a: "forget your people and your father's house, and the king will desire your beauty." The word for "desire," from the root אוה in the Hithpael, often means "crave" in the more negative sense, as when Israel craved meat during the wilderness wanderings (Ps 106:14). This daughter is to content herself with being an object of male lust. These words of the bride's mother are countered by the words of another Queen Mother, to her son King Lemuel in Proverbs 31:1-9. This mother internalizes the fear and stereotypes of women by urging her son to practice self-restraint with both wine and women.[9]

Nancy Bowen argues that Psalm 45 is about a fairy-tale wedding, and "like most fairy tales, Psalm 45 presupposes asymmetry in its gender relationships,"[10] which can be damaging to women. Unfortunately, many

---

5. Ibid., 39.

6. John Goldingay, *Psalms*, vol. 2 (Grand Rapids, MI: Baker Academic, 2007), 58. Even in vv. 11-16 "the king remains the main character" (62).

7. Richard Clifford, *Psalms 1–72* (Nashville, TN: Abingdon Press, 2002), 226.

8. Carol Meyers, "Gender Imagery in the Song of Songs," in *A Feminist Companion to the Song of Songs*, ed. Athalya Brenner and Carole R. Fontaine (Sheffield: Sheffield Academic Press, 1993), 197–212, at 209.

9. Yoder, "Proverbs," 240.

10. Nancy R. Bowen, "A Fairy Tale Wedding? A Feminist Intertextual Reading of Psalm 45," in *A God So Near: Essays on Old Testament Theology in Honor of Patrick D.*

interpreters have embraced the fairy tale and romanticized the bride's situation in Psalm 45. Propp, for example, suggests that the ending verses of the psalm console the princess for the loss of her family;[11] people will seek her favor with gifts (v. 12) when she becomes the king's bride! Even Goldingay wonders if perhaps "love song" in the superscription refers to ordinary, rather than royal, marriage, "which might be more likely to involve love."[12] Whether Psalm 45 is a wedding song or part of a coronation ceremony, Bowen notes that the bride's voice is absent; intertexts featuring other biblical women might be able to fill in the gaps and surface assumptions about gender relations. She suggests that Abigail and Esther introduce tensions into the "idyllic wish" that the princess marry Prince Charming and live happily ever after.

The Pressure to Be Beautiful

Psalm 45 unfortunately adds to current global cultural pressure to be "beautiful." The International Society of Aesthetic Plastic Surgery (ISAPS) has released statistics for cosmetic surgical and nonsurgical procedures performed worldwide in 2013, noting that cosmetic surgery is on the rise on a global scale. More than 223 million procedures were performed, with those for women making up 87% of that total. The most popular surgeries included breast augmentation, liposuction, and blepharoplasty (creating or enlarging the eyelid crease many Asians lack). The United States led the pack (17%), followed by Brazil (9.1%), Mexico, Germany, and Spain.[13]

Furthermore, from 2005 to 2013 the American Society of Plastic Surgeons estimates that the number of cosmetic procedures performed on Asian Americans increased by 125%, Hispanics by 85%, and African Americans by 56%, while procedures on Caucasians increased just 35%. These figures are, in part, simply a mark of rising purchasing power; plastic surgery is nothing if not a sign that one has money to burn and status anxiety to spare.[14]

Denise Dombkowski Hopkins

Miller, ed. Brent Strawn and Nancy Bowen (Winona Lake, IN: Eisenbrauns, 2003), 53–71, at 56.

11. Propp, "Is Psalm 45 an Erotic Poem?," 41.

12. Goldingay, *Psalms*, 55.

13. http://www.isaps.org/Media/Default/Current%20News/ISAPS%202013%20Statistic%20Release%20FINAL%20(2).pdf.

14. See Maureen O'Connor, "Is Race Plastic? My Trip Into the 'Ethnic Plastic Surgery' Minefield," http://nymag.com/thecut/2014/07/ethnic-plastic-surgery.html.

Linked by shared vocabulary to Psalm 45, 1 Samuel 25 seems to show Abigail submitting to David, but she is no model wife. She gives orders; refers to her husband, Nabal, as a fool; and sides with his enemy: "there is almost a duplicitousness to her character."[15] Esther decenters the expectation of sexual, political, and theological loyalty to Persia's king, state, and gods. She will not forsake her family and people as Psalm 45 commands, but instead she risks her life to approach the king (Esth 4:16; 8:6). Vashti, the queen whom Esther replaces, had already called the idea of obedience into question (Esth 1:10-22) by refusing to appear before the drunken king when summoned. She is banished, and a decree is issued requiring women to honor their husbands. Katharine Doob Sakenfeld[16] notes that Vashti protests and is expelled while Esther makes changes from the inside. These two women offer two different models of resistance. One cannot claim that one model is always better than another, since context plays a role. Women face such choices every day.

Ruth 1:15-18 offers another intertext for Psalm 45. Ruth responds to her mother-in-law Naomi's urging that she return to her people in Moab and not follow Naomi to Bethlehem by saying: "Do not press me to leave you . . . your people shall be my people, and your God my God" (1:16). One can imagine that this is what the princess says to the Queen Mother in Psalm 45:10 after she commands her daughter to "forget your people and your father's house." Sakenfeld warns that "we must be cautious about generalizing Ruth's words to her mother-in-law as a desirable model for all women."[17] In other parts of the world this familial relationship can be abusive. Also, Ruth's words can become "a warrant for an assimilationist, melting-pot view of the proper role of immigrants to the United States."[18]

---

15. Bowen, "A Fairy Tale Wedding?," 58.

16. Katharine Doob Sakenfeld, *Just Wives? Stories of Power and Survival in the Old Testament and Today* (Louisville, KY: Westminster John Knox, 2003), 49–68.

17. Katharine Doob Sakenfeld, *Ruth* (Louisville, KY: Westminster John Knox, 1999), 34.

18. Ibid., 32.

Domestic Violence

Another intertext for Psalm 45 is Ezekiel 16, which combines sexual and theological fidelity in the metaphor of God's covenant relationship with Israel as marriage. Linda Day[19] notes that Ezekiel 16 shows God with an obsessive need to control his woman (Jerusalem) out of a distorted sense of gender relations; domestic violence results as God punishes unfaithful Jerusalem. Domestic violence "is a worldwide epidemic. A 2013 report of the World Health Organization (WHO) entitled 'Global and Regional Estimates of Violence Against Women: Prevalence and Health Effects of Intimate Partner Violence and Non-Partner Sexual Violence' found that intimate-partner violence affects 30% of women worldwide and is the most prevalent type of violence against women. The WHO estimates that 38% of all women murdered are killed by their intimate partners, although it recognizes that this is probably an underestimation. It also reports that 42% of women who had been sexually or physically abused by their partners were injured." Bowen questions whether Psalm 45 also participates in violence against women and concludes that the culture of Psalm 45 "is one of silent women, reproductively-focused sexuality, hierarchies, male rights, and vilified sexually-proactive women." In contrast, Song of Songs presents "an alternative fairy tale" in which women are strong with authority in the domestic sphere of rural life and can celebrate choice, passion, and sexual initiative.[20]

Denise Dombkowski Hopkins

---

19. Linda Day, "Rhetoric and Domestic Violence in Ezekiel 16," *BibInt* 8 (2000): 205–30.

20. See www.stopvaw.org/prevalence_of_domestic_violence; Bowen, "A Fairy Tale Wedding?," 68, 70.

Psalm 46

Imagining a World without War

In the midst of the cosmic and human chaos of Psalm 46, the voice of Israel's warrior God melts the earth and brings war to a halt. Rabbinic interpreters saw the battles preceding the Messianic Age in the poetry of Psalm 46. Martin Luther used the imagery of this psalm to sing of Jesus' battle against the Prince of Darkness in the hymn "A Mighty Fortress Is Our God." The very first verse of the psalm, however, describes God as "our refuge [מחסה] and strength." Though "refuge" can be a military term (e.g., Isa 25:12), here it communicates trust in God, who is affirmed as a reliable "helper" (עזרה, vv. 1, 5).[1] "Refuge" is almost "a one-word refrain" in books 1 and 2 of the Psalter.[2] The primary theme of protection and trust is picked up again in the refrain of vv. 7 and 11, in which משגב (protected high spot) is used for "refuge." The context of this refuge is not battle and war, as the rabbis and Luther's hymn would have it, but rather the end of war and the destruction of weapons, as Psalm 46:9 asserts. This is good news for women, children, and men everywhere.

---

1. See also Pss 10:14; 22:19; 28:7; 30:10; 33:20; 37:40. God sought such a "helper" for the man in the garden of Eden in Gen 2; she was to be for him an עזר כנגדו, "a companion corresponding to it" or "counterpart" in a relationship of mutuality and trust. Phyllis Trible, *God and the Rhetoric of Sexuality* (Philadelphia: Fortress Press, 1978), 88–90.

2. J. Clinton McCann Jr., "The Book of Psalms," in *The New Interpreter's Bible*, vol. 4 (Nashville, TN: Abingdon Press, 1996), 639–1280, at 864. This word appears twenty-four times in books 1 and 2, beginning in Ps 2:12.

*To the leader. Of the Korahites.
According to Alamoth. A Song.*

¹God is our refuge and strength,
    a very present help in trouble.
²Therefore we will not fear, though
    the earth should change,
    though the mountains shake in
    the heart of the sea;
³though its waters roar and foam,
    though the mountains tremble
    with its tumult.   *Selah*

⁴There is a river whose streams
    make glad the city of
    God,
    the holy habitation of the Most
    High.
⁵God is in the midst of the city; it
    shall not be moved;
    God will help it when the morn-
    ing dawns.
⁶The nations are in an uproar, the
    kingdoms totter;

Many classify Psalm 46 as a song of Zion, though no explicit mention is made of Jerusalem or Zion (a frequent poetic name for Jerusalem and for the temple mount area); other possible Zion psalms include 46, 48, 76, 84, 87, 122, and 132. Psalm 46 can be divided into three sections marked by סלה (a technical term indicating a pause) in vv. 3, 7, and 11 and by the refrain in vv. 7 and 11 (probably missing after v. 3). Repetition of the word "earth" (ארץ) ties the sections together (vv. 2, 6, 8, 9, 10) and suggests God's universal sovereignty. The psalm moves from chaos in nature (vv. 1-3) to chaos in history (vv. 4-7) to universal peace (vv. 8-11).

The first section claims that the agitated earth, mountains, and sea cannot cause fear because God is refuge. These verses show that confidence in God "is rooted in creation," both the creation of the world from the "deep" (Gen 1) and the creation of Israel, which passed through the waters of the Reed Sea (Exod 15).[3] Mountains "shake" (מוט) or "totter" in v. 2, recalling God's theophany on Sinai (Exod 19:18; Ps 68:7-8). Waters "roar" (המה) in v. 3, but "we will not fear." These verbs are repeated in the second section, tying the two sections together. In v. 6 the kingdoms "totter" (מוט) and the nations "are in an uproar" (המה). The NRSV translation obscures the repetition by using different translations of the same verb. We can imagine the worst in this "ancient version of a modern doomsday scenario," but since God is with us and reigns over all, it will not happen.[4] The word "strength" in v. 1 (עז, also "power," "fortress") is used often in psalms that proclaim God's reign and control (enthrone-

3. Peter Craigie, *Psalms 1–50* (Waco, TX: Word Books, 1983), 344–45.
4. McCann, "The Book of Psalms," 865.

he utters his voice, the earth melts. ⁷The LORD of hosts is with us; the God of Jacob is our refuge. *Selah* ⁸Come, behold the works of the LORD; see what desolations he has brought on the earth. ⁹He makes wars cease to the end of the earth;	he breaks the bow, and shatters the spear; he burns the shields with fire. ¹⁰"Be still, and know that I am God! I am exalted among the nations, I am exalted in the earth." ¹¹The LORD of hosts is with us; the God of Jacob is our refuge. *Selah*

ment psalms 29:1; 93:1; 96:7; 99:4); such a God brings joy and comfort to the entire created order.

Amid all this chaos and movement sits "the city of God" in v. 4; there God is present. This city, Zion, is the "still point"[5] of Psalm 46. As "the holy habitation of the Most High," it is the capital of God's realm and site of God's temple (see Pss 48:1, 2, 8; 87:3). The mountains and nations may "totter" or "shake," but this city "shall not be moved."[6] Verse 5 uses the same verb, מוט, as in vv. 2 and 6 to drive home the contrast, though the NRSV translation again obscures the repetition. Zion is stable because of God's presence and the presence of God's agent on earth, the king (see Pss 2:6-7; 89:19-37). The river whose streams gladden the city of God (v. 4) reinforces this sense of stability. Here the ambivalent value of water seen in Psalm 42–43 again appears. Water is an agent of joy and sustaining power for those inside the city but a symbol of chaos for those outside it. This is "no ordinary channel; it is uniquely a sanctuary stream, one that issues forth from God's holy residence."[7] This river in God's city

5. Konrad Schaefer, *Psalms*, Berit Olam (Collegeville, MN: Liturgical Press, 2001), 116.

6. Peter L. Trudinger, "Friend or Foe? Earth, Sea and *Chaoskampf* in the Psalms," in *The Earth Story in the Psalms and the Prophets*, ed. Norman C. Habel (Sheffield: Sheffield Academic Press, 2001), 29–41, argues that the *Chaoskampf* pattern (the battle between god[s] and forces of chaos represented by water-beings), which so many scholars see in poetic texts as a borrowing from the Enuma Elish creation story, is secondary in the Zion psalms. The Zion tradition "gives a central role to a *place*, not a battle" (p. 40). This frees the Earth and its components from their hostile stance against God's order and allows for free response to God.

7. William P. Brown, *Seeing the Psalms: A Theology of Metaphor* (Louisville, KY: Westminster John Knox, 2002), 117. See Ps 87:7.

evokes several associations: with the river that flowed out of Eden to water the garden in Genesis 2:10-14; the river flowing from the temple in Ezekiel 47:1-12; and the river flowing from the throne of God, which has replaced the temple in Revelation 22:1-12.

The underside of Zion as symbol of order and security for society is that it functions rhetorically to support the established political and cultic hierarchies there as immutable and divine. If Jerusalem is the symbol of security and refuge, then Jerusalem's rulers can argue that public life is in order; such "propaganda" allows no criticism.[8] As Coogan argues, "In the royal Judean ideology . . . deity, king, and city were linked."[9] Zion was thought to be inviolable because it was chosen as the dwelling place of both God and the Davidic king (Isa 37:35). One must ask how Jerusalem's leaders dealt with women, children, and the poor in service to this ideology, given repeated prophetic criticism of their economic policies.

The use of "Lord of hosts" as a title for God in the refrain of vv. 7 and 11 sets up expectations about God that are subverted in the third section of the psalm. The title "Lord of hosts" suggests that God is both divine king and warrior. "Hosts" refers to Israel's armies (1 Sam 17:45); God is enthroned invisibly in the ark of the covenant and accompanies Israel into battle (Num 10:35-36). "Hosts" also refers to the heavenly army of angelic beings who do God's bidding (Ps 89:6-8); the prophetic texts use this title often (e.g., Isa 6:3). Connected with the metaphor of the Warrior King is the destructive power of the divine voice; the Warrior King speaks and "the earth melts" (v. 6; cp. Pss 18:7-15; 29). Marc Brettler argues that God as warrior is prominent not only in Psalms 18, 24, and 68 but occurs in three-quarters of the psalms; it is a central metaphor for God complemented in Psalm 46 by the use of "refuge" as fortress protection. Verse 8 commands nature and nations to behold "desolations" this Warrior King God has brought. The word for "desolations" (שׁמּות) occurs only here in the form of a plural of intensity, showing that divine power is greater than human power to destroy. Instead of the expected list of God's destructive actions, however, this command is followed by the surprising declaration in v. 9 that God "makes wars cease" and destroys all the weapons of war. This warrior wages peace[10] and "is superlative in this

---

8. Robert D. Miller II, "The Origin of the Zion Hymns," in *The Composition of the Book of Psalms*, ed. Erich Zenger (Leuven: Peeters, 2010), 667–76.

9. Michael D. Coogan, *The Old Testament: A Historical and Literary Introduction to the Hebrew Scriptures* (Oxford: Oxford University Press, 2006), 278.

10. McCann, "The Book of Psalms," 866.

role."[11] We are surprised by this usage, perhaps because we can no longer imagine a world without war. The outrage expressed by some toward John Lennon's song "Imagine" comes to mind in this connection.

The security Psalm 46 imagines is based on God's stabilizing, nurturing presence rather than weaponry and war. Throughout human time, war has cruelly victimized women and children. Nowhere is this more clear than in Judges 4–5, the story of the judge Deborah, the Kenite woman Jael, and the mother of Sisera, the Canaanite general against whom Deborah urges Israel to battle. Jael must become a "seductive killer" (5:24) to survive, and the worried mother awaiting her general son's return assumes that he is gathering spoils of war: "a womb, two wombs" (5:30). She reduces the women of the enemy to their reproductive organs as she envisions their rape. These women "approve of or commit violent acts to help their men to become victorious. They serve a patriarchal agenda and do not seek its subversion."[12] Psalm 46 makes this kind of dehumanizing relationship among sisters unnecessary. Nations are to drop their weapons and stop warring, as God commands in 46:10: "Be still, and know that I am God!" The NRSV translation misses the point of God's action; "desist" might better express what is at stake (the word is the *hiphil* of רפה, "leave off, abandon, stop").

Women and War

Psalm 46 beckons us to reflect on the immeasurable and generational suffering experienced by women of color because of the brutal, inhumane "war" of slavery, servitude, patriarchy, and *machismo*.[13] This "war" is fought with the weaponry of marginalization and oppression and dehumanizes its victims. Psalm 46 proclaims that "God is our refuge." How is "refuge" experienced for African, Latina, African American, or Caribbean women who continue to be classified as ugly creatures and as property, solely because of their racial heritage? God's

---

11. Marc Brettler, "Images of YHWH the Warrior in Psalms," *Semeia* 61 (1993): 135–65, at 145. See also God's staff used to comfort rather than strike in Ps 23:4.

12. Susanne Scholz, "Judges," in *Women's Bible Commentary*, ed. Carol A. Newsom, Sharon H. Ringe, and Jacqueline E. Lapsley, 3rd ed. (Louisville, KY: Westminster John Knox, 2012), 113–27, at 118.

13. This cultural mind-set is found, *inter alia*, in Latino/a communities founded on patriarchy and male leadership in society and the household. Women are subjugated to the status of subservient and voiceless members of society who serve their men and maintain their households under the leadership of that patriarch.

refuge is not simply comfort for these women while they are ravaged by war. Rather, God's refuge is the end of war and the destruction of dehumanizing weapons.

Exploited, despised poor women of color, Shawn Copeland suggests, are the new anthropological subject.[14] When oppressors acknowledge this, they can then recognize and affirm the human dignity of God's precious creation, which also bears the imprint of God, the *imago Dei*. "The realization of humanity . . . of personhood . . . rooted in religious, intellectual, and moral conversion"[15] is refuge that facilitates the cessation of war. This realization challenges oppressors to destroy their weapons of war—racism, sexism, classism. Then and only then will women of color experience holistically God's healing refuge, so that the spiritual, emotional, and psychological wounds of battle may heal.

Audrey Coretta Price

For God to be "exalted" (v. 10), nations must stop their violence toward one another and toward their own people. Only then will the entire cosmos join in worship and exaltation of the One who is the only source of security. Will we recognize God's sovereignty or not? Yet one wonders whether Psalm 46 intends a universal peace. As Schaefer[16] argues, the refrain in vv. 7 and 11 is structured as a chiasm in an A/B//B*/A* pattern: A: Lord of hosts / B: (is) with us // B*: a refuge for us / A*: (is) the God of Jacob. The word "us," referring to Israel, is encompassed by God in God's role as Warrior King and God of a particular people. This particularism is echoed by Jesus, "God with us"/Immanuel (Matt 1:23), who becomes the new manifestation of God's presence as he preaches the reign or kingdom of God (Luke 4:14-15). We are confronted with the tension between the universal and the particular in both texts.

14. M. Shawn Copeland, *Enfleshing Freedom: Body, Race, and Being* (Minneapolis: Fortress Press, 2010), 93.

15. Ibid., 92.

16. Schaefer, *Psalms*, 116.

Psalm 47

Willing Worship?

The sounds of clapping, shouting, trumpets, and singing in Psalm 47 invite us to join in Israel's joyous celebration of God's coronation as king over the nations and the earth. Most interpreters continue to embrace James Muilenburg's long-standing argument that "there is no passage of more genuine universalism in the whole of the Old Testament."[1] To underscore God's universal sovereignty, God is referred to three times as "king" (vv. 6, 7, 8; see Pss 44:4; 48:2; 68:24; 74:12; 84:3) and once as "great king" (v. 2; see Ps 48:2; 2 Kgs 18:19, where the Assyrian king claims this title). Plural imperative verbs in vv. 1 and 6 also point to God's universal rule; for example, v. 1 commands "all you peoples" to shout with joy to God. Further, the phrase "all the earth" is used in vv. 2 and 7 to show the extent of God's rule. The phrase connects the two sections of the psalm and refers back to Psalm 46, which uses "earth" five times (vv. 2, 6, 8, 9, 11). In v. 9c, "the shields of the earth belong to God," recalls Psalm 46:9 with its assertion that God ends war (see Isa 2:4; 9:5; Zech 9:10); "shields" may also represent symbolically the kings of nations who now worship Israel's God. God "Most High" (יהוה עליון, v. 2; see Pss 46:4; 78:17, 35, 56; 82:6; 83:18; 91:9; 92:1) sits enthroned above every human king and every god.

---

1. James Muilenburg, "Psalm 47," *JBL* 63 (1944): 235–57, at 237.

Psalm 47:1-9

To the leader. Of the Korahites.
A Psalm.

¹Clap your hands, all you peoples;
    shout to God with loud songs
        of joy.
²For the LORD, the Most High, is
    awesome,
        a great king over all the earth.
³He subdued peoples under us,
    and nations under our feet.
⁴He chose our heritage for us,
    the pride of Jacob whom he
        loves.   *Selah*

⁵God has gone up with a shout,
    the LORD with the sound of a
        trumpet.

⁶Sing praises to God, sing
    praises;
        sing praises to our King, sing
            praises.
⁷For God is the king of all the
    earth;
        sing praises with a psalm.

⁸God is king over the nations;
    God sits on his holy throne.
⁹The princes of the peoples
    gather
        as the people of the God of
            Abraham.
For the shields of the earth belong
    to God;
        he is highly exalted.

The center point of the psalm rests in v. 5: "God has gone up with a shout." The notation סלה after v. 4 structures the focus on v. 5. This verse separates the two psalm sections introduced by imperatives of praise in vv. 1 and 6; praise surrounds God the king. As in a typical hymn structure, the imperatives are followed by reasons for the invitations, introduced by the particle כי ("for," "because"). Most interpreters argue that v. 5 indicates some kind of liturgical enthronement of God, and they point to a group of enthronement psalms—47, 93, 96, 97–99—all of which include the cry "YHWH has gone up." Few embrace Sigmund Mowinckel's once-dominant view of a specific New Year's festival of enthronement modeled on a Babylonian festival, since no direct references in Tanakh support it. Trumpets (v. 5b) accompany the coronation of earthly kings (1 Kgs 1:34, 39; 2 Sam 15:10; Ps 98:6). Clapping signals celebration (Nah 3:19; 2 Kgs 11:12; Ps 98:8). Shouts proclaim God's sovereignty in Psalms 66:1; 82:1; 95:1-2; 98:4, 6; 100:1 (see also Num 23:21; 1 Sam 10:21; 2 Sam 16:16). God's "going up" (עלה) suggests some kind of procession with the ark; 2 Samuel 6:15 reports that David "brought up" (עלה) the ark to Jerusalem with shouting and the sound of trumpets (cp. Pss 24:7-10; 132:8).

Aside from problems for women connected with the image of God as king (see Ps 44), Psalm 47 presents other challenges in the areas of ethnicity and the dynamics of power and imperialism. From Israel's perspective, God's universal sovereignty can be viewed only positively. God's universal kingship and role as judge of the world is celebrated liturgically during Rosh Hashanah ("new year") in Judaism, which has long incorporated the reading of Psalm 47 before the blowing of the shofar (ram's horn), signaling the festival's beginning. Christians use Psalm 47 on Ascension Day to celebrate Jesus' ascent into heaven after his last appearance to the disciples following his resurrection (Acts 1:2-11); he ascends to be enthroned at God's side (Eph 1:20-21; Rev 1:12-20) to rule the world. The universalism of both of these traditions bumps up against the particularity of a people, Israel, and a person, Jesus.

In Psalm 46, v. 2 calls the great king "awesome" (see also Pss 66:3, 5; 68:35), a word used in Exodus 15:11 in the Song of the Sea celebrating the Exodus, a constitutive event for Israel's identity. Further, v. 3 declares that God "has subdued peoples under us, and nations under our feet," an allusion to the conquest of Canaan (Josh 1:3). In v. 4, God "chose" Israel's "heritage" (נחלה, portion of the promised land that belongs to God; Lev 25:23). In v. 8 God as king "sits on his holy throne," probably a reference to the ark as God's portable throne that David brought to Jerusalem (2 Sam 6). Anne Moore argues[2] that Psalm 47, as a postexilic psalm, fits within the framework of Chronicles (515–300 BCE), which rewrites Israel's history in light of the absence of Davidic kingship and the presence of the Davidic dynastic promise (2 Sam 7). Chronicles claims that the promise is fulfilled in the theocracy rooted in the Jerusalem temple/Zion that was the Davidic dynasty's greatest achievement.

The connection Psalm 47 makes between God's universal kingship and the selection of Israel cannot escape the particularism of the conquest and of Jerusalem/Zion. Consequently, many commentators follow John Goldingay, who says that this psalm urges other nations "to come to recognize the truth expressed in that story and to see its implications for them."[3] One can label such an interpretation a "compliant" reading that trusts and accepts the text and adopts its values as God's values without question. Eric Seibert calls this "the default mode of readers who grow up in the church."[4] Denise Hopkins and Michael Koppel call this

---

2. Anne Moore, *Moving Beyond Symbol and Myth: Understanding the Kingship of God of the Hebrew Bible through Metaphor* (New York: Peter Lang, 2006), 188–92.

3. John Goldingay, *Psalms*, vol. 2 (Grand Rapids, MI: Baker Academic, 2007), 76.

4. Eric Seibert, *The Violence of Scripture: Overcoming the Old Testament's Troubling Legacy* (Minneapolis: Fortress Press, 2012), 55.

"consonant listening"[5] that hears only the commonalities it wants to hear. What is needed from a feminist viewpoint is a "conversant"[6] reading of the text or "dissonant listening"[7] that actively engages the text, critically evaluates it, and pays attention to the places of tension within it. What if the nations do not willingly worship Israel's God? What if they are not convinced by Israel's praise? How might a non-Israelite who worships a different god receive Israel's declarations?

Worship and Politics

The signifiers of ecstatic worship in Psalm 47 speak to the emotive worship embedded in African American Christian religious experiences. The raising and clapping of hands in v. 1 is considered a natural response for Israel, which acknowledges this God as "Most High" king. This attitude of praise resembles the African American ideology that worship is "acknowledgment of and response to the presence and power of God."[8]

As Hopkins and Koppel note, too often readers of the text uncritically conflate the theology of the text with the identity of God, failing to recognize the power of the intermediary ideologue, the scribe. Understanding this makes room for the rejection of political assertions embedded in the text that suggest that one mode of being is normative, in both a religious and a social context.

For an African American Christian reader what is important here is the idea that *"God* is king over the nations" (v. 8a). Most often, racist, imperial patriarchs have decided that they represent God and, as such, have the power and authority to exercise their will over nations and people in the name of God. Here it is important to remember Hopkins's intertextual connection to Rahab and to place that within the historical contexts in which the Joshua narrative was used to authorize imperial genocide.

However, for the African American reader it is easy to

---

5. Denise Dombkowski Hopkins and Michael S. Koppel, *Grounded in the Living Word: The Old Testament and Pastoral Care Practices* (Grand Rapids, MI: Eerdmans, 2010), 161.

6. Seibert, *The Violence of Scripture*, 56.

7. Hopkins and Koppel, *Grounded in the Living Word*, 161.

8. Melva Wilson Costa, *African American Christian Worship* (Nashville, TN: Abingdon Press, 2007), 79.

distinguish between the will and authority of people who would use God's name in vain to authorize destruction and the will of the God who has the capacity to operate in all spheres of the world. Thus the African American Christian experience of this psalm is one in which worshipers understand that God is operating on our behalf. While the text itself expresses this in a particular context, we understand that an experience of God is not limited to God's action in the canon. Thus we relive the praise of this psalm with the knowledge that God's enthronement gives life to our current situations.

Yolanda Marie Norton

A valuable intertext for dialogue with Psalm 47 on these points is the story of the foreign prostitute Rahab, read through the lens of postcolonial criticism, which seeks to analyze "unequal power relations of domination and subordination" from below and create "space for subalterns in which their voices and experiences are valued, not subjected or eradicated."[9] As Judith McKinlay argues, postcolonial interpretation resists imperialistic attitudes around land as divine promise because these attitudes lead to distortion of "complex histories and societies of indigenous peoples" like Rahab. "Rahab was created 'Other' in order to provide the 'Us' of Israel with an identity."[10] In this vein Robert Warrior offers a conversant/dissonant reading: God the Deliverer whom Israel praises in Psalm 47:3-4 has become God the Conqueror in the Joshua narratives, and Native Americans must identify with the Canaanites who already lived in the promised land but whose story has been silenced.[11]

If Rahab could speak "off the [i.e., Israel's] record," what would she say? As I have argued elsewhere, compliant/consonant readings of Joshua 2 "favor a co-opted Rahab who serves the purposes of the colonizing

9. Warren Carter, "Postcolonial Biblical Criticism," in *New Meanings for Ancient Texts*, ed. Steven L. McKenzie and John Kaltner (Louisville, KY: Westminster John Knox, 2013), 97–116, at 104.

10. Judith E. McKinlay, *Reframing Her: Biblical Women in Postcolonial Focus* (Sheffield: Sheffield Phoenix Press, 2004), 23, 47.

11. Robert Warrior, "A Native American Perspective: Canaanites, Cowboys, and Indians," in *Voices from the Margin: Interpreting the Bible in the Third World*, ed. R. S. Sugirtharajah (Maryknoll, NY: Orbis Books, 1995), 277–85.

Israelites claiming God on their side."[12] Christians put Rahab on a pedestal; she is listed as one of only five women in Matthew's genealogy of Jesus; compare the positive assessments of her in Hebrews 11:31 and James 2:25. Though some feminists would argue that Rahab subverts the patriarchal household when she negotiates for her family (Josh 2:13, 18; 6:23), Musa Dube warns that "imperialism in Rahab's story undercuts any use we can make of her for feminist ideals."[13] In Joshua 2:11, Rahab mimics the Israelites with her declaration: "The Lord your God is indeed God in heaven above and on earth below," akin to the claim Psalm 47 makes about God's universal sovereignty. This mimicry can be viewed as genuine confession or as subversion of patriarchy and imperialism by telling Israel what it wants to hear in order to save her family and herself from becoming spoils of war. The latter conversant/dissonant reading suggests that Rahab abandons her own people and becomes a traitor.[14] One can imagine that she does not do so willingly but that she acts with great resentment. In fact, Rahab is still called "the prostitute" in Joshua 6:25, even after she has saved the spies and begun living among the Israelites. What is the nature of her life among them? Does she remain as a reminder of the difference between "us" and "them"?

The ambiguity of Rahab's situation can shed light on the debate over the translation of Psalm 47:9ab. NRSV reads: "The princes of the peoples gather as the people of the God of Abraham."[15] Israelites and the nations are one in their recognition of God's sovereignty. This translation prompts

---

12. Hopkins and Koppel, *Grounded in the Living Word*, 154. An example of a compliant/consonant reading is that of Tikva Frymer-Kensky, who speaks of Rahab's "conversion" in Josh 2:9 ("I know") and the extensive parallels between the exodus stories and that of Rahab. Rahab is the "new Israel." See Tikva Frymer-Kensky, "Reading Rahab," in *Tehillah le-Moshe: Biblical and Judaic Studies in Honor of Moshe Greenberg*, ed. Mordechai Cogan, Barry L. Eichler, and Jeffrey H. Tigay (Winona Lake, IN: Eisenbrauns, 1997), 57–67, at 61–62 (quoted in Hopkins and Koppel, *Grounded in the Living Word*, 164–65).

13. Quoted in Hopkins and Koppel, *Grounded in the Living Word*, 167–68. See Musa Dube, *Postcolonial Feminist Interpretation of the Bible* (St. Louis, MO: Chalice Press, 2000), 70–75.

14. Hopkins and Koppel, *Grounded in the Living Word*, 170–71.

15. The Septuagint (LXX) reads "with the God of Abraham." The Greek has μετὰ ("with") where the Hebrew text has עַם ("people"). Keith Bodner, "The 'Embarrassing Syntax' of Ps. 47:10: A (Pro)Vocative Option," *JTS* (2003): 50–75, argues for a vocative reading of v. 9: "The princes of the people have been gathered together, O people of the God of Abraham." Bodner's is also a compliant/consonant reading and changes nothing about Rahab's situation.

questions: who gathers them? Do they come willingly? Most interpreters see an allusion to Genesis 12:3 and God's blessing of Abraham here: "in you all the families of the earth will be blessed." Moore argues that the idea of the nations coming to worship God is a trope present in the exilic and postexilic prophets (see Isa 52:7-10; Mic 4:2-5; Zeph 3:14-20).[16] Perhaps a postcolonial reading of Rahab can unmask exiled Israel's fantasies about power and Christian and Jewish desires for self-validation.

A Perspective from the Other

With imagery of a royal procession of God as "a great king over all the earth," Psalm 47 provides the reader with a liturgy and language of great "comprehensiveness" to celebrate the reign of a very "universal" God: "God is king of all the earth" (v. 7). At the same time, the reader catches a clear glimpse of the "exclusive" mindset of a people proclaiming the kingship of a very "particular" God: "He subdued peoples under us . . . sing praises to *our* King" (vv. 3, 6).

This inclusive *and* exclusive voice demands that "all you peoples" (v. 1) hear its authentic and undisputed word: "He chose our heritage for us, the pride of Jacob whom he loves" (v. 4). The voice fixing attention on us seeks power over *others*— "all you peoples." It claims unity in diversity (v. 9). The reader living in a world of fundamentally pluralistic relations may raise questions about this voice at the center that claims to "contain" other voices and mutes their expressions within the roar of the "seamless whole." The voice at the center does not take into consideration the reality of complex and ambiguous interrelationships with others, which often lead to the "mess" (i.e., separation, oppression, violence, prejudice, discrimination, brokenness, etc.) outside the system(s) behind the seamless whole.

This psalm perhaps reminds the reader of David's triumphal procession with the ark of God in 2 Samuel 6. When David celebrates Yʜwʜ's exaltation of his (David's) kingship above Saul (the "other"), he leaps and dances and presents himself as "degraded" in a nearly naked body. To Michal, David is only humiliating himself like "some vulgar fellow" (2 Sam 6:20). However, David declares that he will be held in כבד ("honor") by the "low" women his wife identifies—the slave women of

---

16. Moore, *Moving Beyond Symbol and Myth*, 237 n. 119.

his servants, the lowest of the low (2 Sam 6:22).

The reader of Psalm 47 hears that the people of the particular "God of Abraham" are elevated above the prestige of "the princes of the peoples"; the reader may also know that the reign of the universal God will be "coming down" to everyone, embracing the "lowest people" amid their fears, dangers, and life crises. If all peoples are invited to celebrate God's victory over all the earth, "we" may need to dislocate the "I" from the center of things and reread "our" achievements and resing "our" praises in relation to others.

. *Su Jung Shin*

Psalm 48

Inverting the Birth Metaphor

Though many classify it as one of the songs of Zion, along with Psalms 46, 76, 84, 87, and 122, Psalm 48 begins and ends with a focus on the God of Zion: "Great is the LORD" (v. 1) and "this is God, our God forever and ever" (v. 14). As Konrad Schaefer notes, "The political site becomes a theological premise."[1] Zion/Jerusalem witnesses to God, who within its citadels "has shown himself a sure defense" (v. 3; the same word, משגב, is translated as "refuge" in Ps 46:7, 11). God's presence ensures "physical protection and military security," which offers the possibility that God's city may become a symbol of peace.[2] As Psalm 46:4, 5, 9 declares, the God present in Zion ends all war. Psalm 48 shares with Psalms 46 and 47 a universal view of God's sovereignty: "Your name, O God, like your praise, reaches to the ends of the earth" (v. 10; cp. v. 2; Pss 46:8-11; 47:7-9). This phrase expresses "the spatial extension of God's reign," while "our God forever and ever" in v. 14 evokes its

---

1. Konrad Schaefer, *Psalms*, Berit Olam (Collegeville, MN: Liturgical Press, 2001), 121.
2. J. David Pleins, *The Psalms: Songs of Tragedy, Hope, and Justice* (Maryknoll, NY: Orbis Books, 1993), 117.

Psalm 48:1-14

A Song. A Psalm of the Korahites

¹Great is the LORD and greatly to
be praised
in the city of our God.
His holy mountain, ²beautiful in
elevation,
is the joy of all the earth,
Mount Zion, in the far north,
the city of the great King.
³Within its citadels God
has shown himself a sure
defense.

⁴Then the kings assembled,
they came on together.
⁵As soon as they saw it, they were
astounded;
they were in panic, they took to
flight;
⁶trembling took hold of them there,
pains as of a woman in labor,
⁷as when an east wind shatters
the ships of Tarshish.
⁸As we have heard, so have we
seen

"temporal extension."[3] God's "greatness" in v. 1 is an attribute often associated with God's universal sovereignty (see Pss 95:3; 96:4; 99:2).[4]

Despite the focus on God and the possibility for peace opened up by God's presence in Zion, Zion theology tethered to the king and the temple-state complex permeates Psalm 48 and raises possible roadblocks to peace. The seven epithets listed for Zion in vv. 2-3 hyperbolically praise the city itself. Their intentional arrangement forms a bracket with the word "city" and moves from the local aspect of "our God" to the universal aspect of "the great King," and from the localized epithet "his holy mountain" to the "joy of all the earth."[5] The word צָפוֹן, translated "in the far north" in v. 2, identifies Mount Zion with Mount Zaphon, associated with the god Baʾal in Canaanite myth (see Ps 89:12).[6] This conflation declares that " 'Zion is our Zaphon,' or, in classical Greek terms, that 'Zion is our Mount Olympus.' "[7] This language forms part of

3. J. Clinton McCann Jr., "The Book of Psalms," in *The New Interpreter's Bible*, vol. 4 (Nashville, TN: Abingdon Press, 1996), 639–1280, at 872. McCann quotes Robert Alter in this regard: "the towering ramparts of the fortress-city become a nexus for all imagined time and space." See Robert Alter, *The Art of Biblical Poetry* (New York: Basic Books, 1985), 124.

4. McCann, "The Book of Psalms," 871.

5. Michael Barré, "The Seven Epithets of Zion in Ps 48, 2-3," *Bib* 69 (1988): 558–60.

6. Robert D. Miller II, "The Origin of the Zion Hymns," in *The Composition of the Book of Psalms*, ed. Erich Zenger (Leuven: Peeters, 2010), 667, identifies this element as one of five that belong to the content of Zion hymns.

7. Robert P. Gordon, *Holy Land, Holy City: Sacred Geography and the Interpretation of the Bible* (Waynesboro, GA: Paternoster Press, 2004), 38.

in the city of the Lᴏʀᴅ of hosts,
in the city of our God,
which God establishes
    forever.   *Selah*

⁹We ponder your steadfast love, O
    God,
in the midst of your temple.
¹⁰Your name, O God, like your
    praise,
reaches to the ends of the
    earth.
Your right hand is filled with victory.

¹¹Let Mount Zion be glad,
let the towns of Judah rejoice
    because of your judgments.

¹²Walk about Zion, go all around it,
    count its towers,
¹³consider well its ramparts;
    go through its citadels,
that you may tell the next
    generation
¹⁴that this is God,
our God for ever and ever.
He will be our guide forever.

the "hyperbole" of sacred geography in Psalm 48 that undergirded the notion of Zion's inviolability and prompted the criticism of prophets like Jeremiah (see Jer 7). As Walter Brueggemann warns, the witness of the temple on Zion "becomes too often in fact the domestication of Y++++ in order to serve the interests of the established regime."[8] In this sense the psalm not only uses anthropomorphisms for God (God's "right hand" in v. 10) but also "sociomorphisms, in which the divine is interpreted according to patterns of social reality."[9] This social reality is rooted in the privileges of the male elite in ancient Israel, especially those associated with royal power, which was exercised at the expense of the people, and especially of women and children. Zion theology in Psalm 48 raises questions for feminist readers.

Verses 4-7 describe a great battle against the nations, which scholars note is one of the five features of content characteristic of Zion hymns; see Pss 46:4-7; 76:2-3, 5-6.[10] The chiasm in 48:10b-11 shows that Israel's gladness and rejoicing are encompassed by the "victory" in God's right hand (v. 10b) and God's "judgments" (v. 11c).[11] The enemy panics when

---

8. Walter Brueggemann, *Reverberations of Faith: A Theological Handbook of Old Testament Themes* (Louisville, KY: Westminster John Knox, 2002), 209.

9. Michael Hundley, *Gods in Dwellings: Temples and Divine Presence in the Ancient Near East* (Atlanta, GA: Society of Biblical Literature, 2013), 135.

10. Miller, "Origin of Zion Hymns," 667.

11. Schaefer, *Psalms*, 121–22. The Hebrew word translated "victory" is צדק, which means literally "what is right or just," "success." Many translate the word as "righteousness." The word translated "judgments" is משפתים, which means "legal decisions," "justice." These words take on a different nuance because of vv. 4-7. See Ps 97:3.

seeing Zion (vv. 4-7), but the people rejoice when considering its ramparts (v. 13). Just as in Psalm 47:3-4, in which Israel's praise of God's awesome greatness stems from God's choice of Israel and subduing of the nations, Israel's glad joy over God's "judgments" in Psalm 48:11 is connected with God's saving deeds on Israel's behalf (see Ps 97:8). Scholars disagree about whether an actual historical event is alluded to in vv. 4-7, perhaps the Assyrian withdrawal from Jerusalem in 701 BCE (2 Kgs 19:35-36), or whether these verses refer to a cultic reenactment of God's victory over Israel's enemies during a liturgical festival.

Much of the language of these verses echoes that of the Song of the Sea in Exodus 15, recalling the beginnings of God's actions on behalf of Israel. Psalm 48 connects the present sight of Zion with past salvation. As soon as the kings saw God's city on Zion they "were astounded; they were in panic" (v. 5ab; cp. the enemies who are "dismayed" in Exod 15:15); "trembling took hold of them" (v. 6a; cp. "trembling seized them" in Exod 15:15b); "pains" (v. 6b; cp. "pangs" in Exod 15:14); "east wind" (v. 7a and Exod 14:21). Verse 4 may recall the conquest of Canaan as well. "The kings assembled" (v. 4a) as they did at Hazor in Joshua 11:5; "they came on together" (v. 4b: עבר; cp. they "came on/passed through" in Josh 1:2; 3:16; 4:22; 10:29; 18:9; 24:11, 17). Yet God's salvation is not restricted to the past. The people declare in the temple that they have both heard about and seen God's salvation (v. 8). This declaration engages the issue of theodicy raised by another Korah psalm, 44, which questions the absence of signs of divine presence. The people have heard (Ps 44:1-3) but have not seen (44:23-25).[12]

Zion/Jerusalem is often referenced as female in Tanakh (cp. the "new Jerusalem, coming down out of heaven from God, prepared as a bride adorned for her husband" in Rev 21:2; see also Gal 4:26; Phil 3:20) and throughout the ancient Near East. The context for this personification in Tanakh is often that of military disaster; the conquered female city is portrayed as a victim of rape.[13] Zion is characterized as female in Psalm 48. Verse 11 declares: "let Mount Zion be glad, let the towns of Judah rejoice." The Hebrew word here translated "towns" is, in fact, "daughters" (בנות). In urban contexts, as Robert Alter notes, "daughters" refers to outlying hamlets, and the city is understood as "mother."[14] In addition,

12. Gordon, *Holy Land, Holy City*, 44.

13. Pamela Gordon and Harold C. Washington, "Rape as a Military Metaphor in the Hebrew Bible," in *A Feminist Companion to the Latter Prophets*, ed. Athalya Brenner (Sheffield: Sheffield Academic Press, 1995), 308–25, at 308.

14. Robert Alter, *The Book of Psalms* (New York: Norton, 2007), 170 n. 12.

though the NRSV translates pronouns and possessive adjectives for the city in vv. 12-13 as neuter "it" or "its," the Hebrew is in the third-person feminine singular form and literally reads "her": "go all around *her*," "consider well *her* ramparts."

Given this personification of Zion, Lamentations 2:15 can serve as helpful intertext for evaluating female Zion in Psalm 48:12-13. Zion/ Jerusalem is personified as "Daughter Zion" or "Daughter Jerusalem" (Lam 1–2) as she voices a funeral dirge over her military defeat, described as rape (see Jer 13:26; Isa 47:1-3). Lamentations 2:15 quotes Psalm 48:2 to contrast Zion's former beauty and joy with her current humiliated state. Passersby "hiss and wag their heads" at her now. Despite the exaltation of Zion in Psalm 48, subordination and abuse lurk behind her personification. "The intrinsic violence of the city-as-woman metaphor is grounded in men's violent control of women in ancient Near Eastern societies. . . . The city as an object of violence is always a *feminine* Other, reinforcing the status of the feminine as secondary, and facilitating a pornographic objectification of women by setting the female as the model victim."[15] Mark Boda expands this argument in his study of the summons to joy directed to the female Zion in the prophets, which he argues is always related to military victory, as in Psalm 48:11. In Lamentations 2, Daughter Zion must voice her lament uninvited and she expresses no joy. Boda charges that the male elite have "leveraged" the female image of the city in Lamentations 1–2 "to mourn the loss of their own privilege and hegemony over the vulnerable within the society." Daughter Zion is left "ever the victim in this new context."[16]

Another reference to females in Psalm 48:6 also raises questions. The hostile kings become undone when they view Zion: "trembling took hold of them there, pains as of a woman in labor." The Hebrew חיל means "labor pains." Carol Meyers argues that since contractions are not under one's control, the word is used figuratively to depict other situations of helplessness "in the face of an inevitable outcome."[17] In Psalm 48 this means the inevitable universality of God's sovereignty. Normally, however, the

15. Gordon and Washington, "Rape as a Military Metaphor," 318.

16. Mark Boda, "The Daughter's Joy," in *Daughter Zion: Her Portrait, Her Response*, ed. Mark Boda, Carol J. Dempsey, LeAnn Snow Flesher (Atlanta, GA: Society of Biblical Literature, 2012), 321–42, at 341.

17. Carol Meyers, "Ps 48:7, Woman in Labor," in *Women in Scripture: A Dictionary of Named and Unnamed Women in the Hebrew Bible, the Apocryphal/Deuterocanonical Books, and the New Testament*, ed. Carol Meyers and Toni Craven (Boston: Houghton Mifflin, 2000), 298–99.

expected outcome of labor pains is birth and new life, a positive experience. At the hands of the male elite and their Zion theology this metaphor has been turned upside down to signal defeat and death for the kings attacking Zion. Jeremiah uses the same metaphor in 4:31: daughter Zion is in labor, "fainting before killers" (the invading army) as a sign of Israel's punishment. In light of the Zion theology embedded particularly in Psalm 48:4-7 we are left, along with the worshipers in the temple, to "ponder" God's steadfast love (v. 9). The Hebrew verb translated "ponder" is דמה, which means "form an image in one's mind," "reflect." Psalm 48 reminds us, as feminist readers, to "ponder" how God's intentions may be distorted for our harm.

Birth Pangs and Black Liberation

As Walter Brueggemann suggests, too often the psalms are read within a context of affirming normative structures and power. White American males read a text about a God who defends them and use it as license to proliferate military and police power against all who oppose their agenda. However, it is crucial to remember that, despite its articulations otherwise throughout the canon, Israel was not an empire. Instead, we know that Israel most often lived in fear of and/or fell victim to empire.

When we read this psalm with the understanding that it is a statement against norms and power structures, it becomes a liberative tool for the marginalized. In this instance Israel is not on the attack but rather on the defensive; it is God who steps in and saves it from the aggressor. In this moment we should see the beginning work of the "God of the oppressed."[18] This psalm recalls a God who speaks in and through history. When it is read in a contemporary marginalized context, readers draw comfort from the notion that God protects those who are ill prepared for battle with their enemies.

In this instance the allusion to labor pains should not be seen as a reference to weakness. Instead, the writer paints a picture that highlights the intensity of the labor pains. Further, we can understand that these pains, while abortive for the oppressor, birth life and deliverance for the people of Israel in the text. When they read Psalm 48 in a contemporary context, black diasporatic Christians can understand themselves as those delivered through these birth pangs.

Yolanda Marie Norton

---

18. James H. Cone, *God of the Oppressed* (Maryknoll, NY: Orbis Books, 1997).

Psalm 49

You Can't Take It with You

Few psalms have given rise to more conflicting interpretations than Psalm 49. Most interpreters do agree, however, that it is a wisdom psalm concerned with wealth and death, favorite wisdom topics. Within the introduction (vv. 1-4), vv. 1-2 function as a teacher's summons to pay attention to instruction: "hear this" (Prov 4:1; 5:1, 7; 8:32). The psalmist in 49:4 suggests that if I incline my ear, then you who are being addressed must incline yours.[1] Verses 3-4 use words common in the wisdom lexicon: "wisdom" (חכמה), "understanding" (תבונות), "proverb" (משל), and "riddle" (חידה) (see Prov 1:1-7). Addressed in v. 1 are "all you peoples" and "all inhabitants of the world"; the "triumphal national perspective"[2] of Psalm 47:1 is absent. Rather, the summons indicates "that the wisdom about to be declared applies to all,"[3] in keeping with the international character of wisdom.

The psalmist/teacher need not be male. Proverbs 1:8–8:18 dispenses instruction in the household to a son about to enter the world of adults; the household is the setting "most associated with women in the ancient

---

1. John Goldingay, *Psalms*, vol. 2 (Grand Rapids, MI: Baker Academic, 2007), 99.
2. Robert Alter, *The Book of Psalms* (New York: Norton, 2007), 171.
3. Peter Craigie, *Psalms 1–50* (Waco, TX: Word Books, 1983), 358.

To the leader. Of the Korahites.
A Psalm.

¹Hear this, all you peoples;
    give ear, all inhabitants of the
        world,
²both low and high,
    rich and poor together.
³My mouth shall speak wisdom;
    the meditation of my heart
        shall be understanding.
⁴I will incline my ear to a proverb;
    I will solve my riddle to the
        music of the harp.

⁵Why should I fear in times of trouble,
    when the iniquity of my perse-
        cutors surrounds me,
⁶those who trust in their wealth
    and boast of the abundance of
        their riches?

⁷Truly, no ransom avails for one's
        life,
    there is no price one can give
        to God for it.
⁸For the ransom of life is costly,
    and can never suffice,
⁹that one should live on forever
    and never see the grave.

¹⁰When we look at the wise, they
        die;
    fool and dolt perish together
    and leave their wealth to oth-
        ers.
¹¹Their graves are their homes for
        ever,
    their dwelling-places to all gen-
        erations,
    though they named lands their
        own.

world."[4] Thus in Proverbs 1:8 and 6:20 the father of the household commends the mother's teaching to their son in addition to the father's own. Also, Wisdom is personified as female in Proverbs 1–8. She stands in the public square, normally the domain of men, to offer her instruction and warn against the "strange woman" who will lead foolish young men to ruin. These wisdom associations do not mean that Psalm 49 must be confined to the secular sphere. Though God is not addressed directly in this psalm, as Katharine Dell[5] writes, "the music of the harp" in v. 4 suggests a liturgical setting and argues against long-standing assumptions about the separation between wisdom and cult. Liturgical texts have a didactic function. Like wisdom, the cult was also concerned with keeping order.

The introduction is followed by two major sections, vv. 5-11 and 13-19, each concluded by a refrain (vv. 12, 20). Wealth emerges as a key motif

4. Christine Roy Yoder, "Proverbs," in *Women's Bible Commentary*, ed. Carol A. Newsom, Sharon H. Ringe, and Jacqueline E. Lapsley, 3rd ed. (Louisville, KY: Westminster John Knox, 2012), 232–42, at 234.

5. Katharine J. Dell, "'I Will Solve My Riddle to the Music of the Lyre' (Psalm XLIX 4 [5]): A Cultic Setting for Wisdom Psalms?," *VT* 54 (2004): 445–58.

¹²Mortals cannot abide in their
pomp;
they are like the animals that
perish.

¹³Such is the fate of the foolhardy,
the end of those who are
pleased with their
lot.   *Selah*
¹⁴Like sheep they are appointed
for Sheol;
Death shall be their shepherd;
straight to the grave they de-
scend,
and their form shall waste
away;
Sheol shall be their home.
¹⁵But God will ransom my soul
from the power of Sheol,
for he will receive me.   *Selah*

¹⁶Do not be afraid when some become rich,
when the wealth of their
houses increases.
¹⁷For when they die they will carry
nothing away;
their wealth will not go down
after them.
¹⁸Though in their lifetime they
count themselves happy
—for you are praised when you
do well for yourself—
¹⁹they will go to the company of
their ancestors,
who will never again see the
light.
²⁰Mortals cannot abide in their
pomp;
they are like the animals that
perish.

in Psalm 49, mentioned thirteen times in the psalm's twenty verses: 2, 6 (twice), 7, 8, 10, 11, 14, 15, 16 (twice), 17, and 18. A second motif, death, is expressed frequently in a variety of words, including "grave," "Sheol," "perish," "die," in vv. 9, 10, 11, 12, 14, 15, 17, 19, 20. The "riddle" the psalmist seeks to answer (v. 4) involves a comparison (מָשָׁל). If the refrains in vv. 12 and 20 answer the riddle, then it is this: "how are humans and animals alike?"[6] The answer is this: they die. Even the rich cannot buy themselves out of death, which is the great equalizer (v. 10). The psalmist addresses both the self-confidence of the rich (v. 18) and the fear of the poor (vv. 5, 16) that might prompt them to seek to acquire wealth as protection from death.

Both the psalmist's question in v. 5 ("why should I fear in times of trouble?") and admonition in v. 15 ("Do not be afraid when some become rich") suggest that a situation of distress is being addressed. The psalmist takes the role of counselor,[7] dealing with the fear on the part of the wise

6. J. Clinton McCann Jr., "The Book of Psalms," in *The New Interpreter's Bible*, vol. 4 (Nashville, TN: Abingdon Press, 1996), 639–1280, at 876.
7. Craigie, *Psalms 1–50*, 358.

and upright that the rich can buy themselves out of death. The psalmist addresses an experiential rather than a theoretical question of theodicy, a bit removed from the "first shock of disorientation."[8] The text uses the word כפר, "ransom" (vv. 7, 8, 15), perhaps a reference to the practice in some legal cases of paying "a ransom of life" to avoid the death penalty (see Exod 21:28-32; Prov 6:35). The psalmist is clear that no ransom is great enough to keep one from death (vv. 7-9)—you simply "can't take it with you" (vv. 10, 17). Employing many rhetorical techniques, including repetition, sound play (difficult to recognize in English translation), and semantic fields, the psalmist "expressed and overcame his [*sic*] feelings of fear."[9] The psalmist as counselor cannot erase the tension inherent in the riddle but can place it within a wisdom framework that allows one "to accept and live with the riddle."[10] J. David Pleins notes that Psalm 49, like Psalm 73, challenges "standard wisdom views about poverty and wealth" such as are found in Proverbs 10:15: "the wealth of the rich is their fortress; the poverty of the poor is their ruin" (see Prov 13:8; 18:11; 22:7, and the link between laziness and poverty in Prov 10:4; 19:15, 24; 21:5).[11] Ecclesiastes echoes Psalm 49 in its view of death as the great equalizer (Eccl 2:11, 18, 21; 6:6; 9:2, 10). Psalm 49:10 notes that the wise, fool, and dolt "perish together"; "fool" (כסיל) is a "distinctive term" in Ecclesiastes.[12] The response to the theodicy question in Psalm 49 nuances the notion of act/consequence (the theme of the Two Ways) that permeates wisdom thinking, namely, that the righteous are rewarded (often materially, e.g., Ps 112:1-3) and the wicked are punished.[13] The rewards of the righteous do not follow them to the grave (Ps 10:5-6; Luke 12:20).

The psalmist as counselor draws on personal testimony in a strong "confessional statement"[14] introduced by the disjunctive particle אך ("surely") in v. 16 (see the sage's personal testimony in Ps 37:25-26, 35-36). This verse has sparked intense controversy about whether or not the

---

8. Walter Brueggemann, *The Message of the Psalms* (Minneapolis: Augsburg, 1984), 106.

9. David J. Estes, "Poetic Artistry in the Expression of Fear in Psalm 49," *BSac* 161 (2004): 55–71, at 58.

10. Craigie, *Psalms 1–50*, 359.

11. J. David Pleins, *The Social Vision of the Hebrew Bible: A Theological Introduction* (Louisville, KY: Westminster John Knox, 2001), 430–33.

12. Alter, *Book of Psalms*, 172.

13. Denise Dombkowski Hopkins, *Journey through the Psalms* (St. Louis, MO: Chalice Press, 2002), 59–66.

14. Brueggemann, *The Message of the Psalms*, 109.

psalmist anticipates life after death. The psalmist declares that God will ransom her from Sheol, "for he will receive me." The Hebrew translated "receive" is לָקַח, which means "take." This verb appears in Genesis 5:24 and 2 Kings 2:3, 5, 9 in reference to Enoch and Elijah, respectively, who are "taken" by God. The verb also appears in Psalm 49:17, which insists that the rich "will carry/take nothing away" when they die, setting up a contrast filled with irony. Because "take" is also used in Psalm 18:16, in which God "takes" the king (rescues him from his enemies), the use of the verb in Psalm 49 suggests deliverance in this life, not the next; see Psalms 16:10-11; 30:3; 55:18; 86:13; 88:4-16; 116:1-6, 8-10, 15; Ezekiel 36:24; 37:21, all of which speak of God's redemption this side of the grave.

Psalm 49 uses the language of worship to describe and criticize the misplaced beliefs of the foolish rich. They "trust" in their wealth and "boast" about it (v. 6); their "wealth" (the Hebrew word כבוד literally means "glory" and is often used of God) will not "go down after them" (vv. 16-17); they "count themselves happy" (the Hebrew is "blessed," ברך) and are "praised" for doing well (v. 18). As Estes argues, "those who equate wealth with worth have in reality engaged in a form of idolatry, in which material possessions take the place that rightly belongs to God alone."[15] Wealth produces false confidence and fear.

Pseudo-Masculine Activity Versus "Beingness"

In an era in which common wisdom heralds material success over depth of understanding, progress over process, and financial security in the face of ever-diminishing fiscal assets, Psalm 49 comes to us as a prophetic voice. The psalmist reminds us that the majority's conscious pursuit of wealth and wisdom does not make one invulnerable to ultimate reality, that is, our own finitude. Psalm 49 asks us to take stock. What is it we are striving after? Do we waste our efforts on accumulating what distracts us rather than taking the time to look within and go down into our own depths?

The late British psychoanalyst Donald W. Winnicott describes pseudo-masculine activity as activity that is based on drive and instinct but entirely cut off from essential being*ness*, being that lays the foundation for primary creativity, authenticity. Acting out of the male element entirely cut off from the female,

---

15. Estes, "Poetic Artistry," 66.

though the two elements are essential for the growth and development of human personality and relationality, results in hyper-manic activity. This activity ever pushes one toward strenuous progress without a prior sense of knowing through being. In this mode, with a sense of unconscious devotion, one values *doing* over *being*, what Winnicott terms the male element of doing over the female element of being.[16]

Doing, disconnected from being, results in obsessional daily activity that disallows stillness, time to see what resides within, what may surprise, the place out of which true creativity springs. Hyperactivity cut off from a sense of being*ness* stems from a sense of fear, a fear of what one may find or experience if she is not compulsively compelled by her own drive and determination toward success. The psalmist here speaks to a concept similar to the one highlighted by Winnicott, urging us to reconsider this drive to

success and progress that is not first rooted in *being*. Hyperactivity deludes one about one's own invulnerability for, as the psalmist contends, in the end we humans are not different from the animals. This is not disdain for progress but rather a caution against activity that is not rooted first in a sense of being, being that births authenticity. From dust we came and to dust we return.

Psalm 49 forces us to ask these questions of ourselves: What is worth our time, here and now? What are we compulsively running after as a way of distracting us from going in and down, sitting still, *being* rather than finding satisfaction in compulsive *doing*, in one's progress and achievements? Rather than a constant striving toward progress or success, what might be different in our daily lives if we first allow ourselves simply to be? What might we find and experience?

Tiffany Houck-Loomis

---

16. "The study of the pure distilled uncontaminated female element leads us to BEING, and this forms the only basis for self-discovery and a sense of existing" (Donald W. Winnicott, *Playing and Reality* [London: Routledge Classics, 2005], 11).

TRANSLATION MATTERS:

Both rich and poor (v. 2) are taught by the psalmist that the proper object of fear is God. The development in the refrain drives this point home, even though the NRSV translates vv. 12 and 20 exactly the same. At issue are three words. The first (from יקר, "precious" or "costly") is translated "pomp" in both vv. 12 and 20 but is better rendered "riches," as in the NIV: "But man [*sic*] despite his riches, does not endure; he is like the beasts that perish." The notion of the foolish rich as animals is reinforced in v. 14, where they are compared to sheep shepherded by a personified Death into Sheol. The second word, in v. 12, is translated as "abide," from the root "spend the night" (ילין), suggesting that life is fleeting. Verse 20 does not use the same word but rather one that means "understanding"; this ties together the beginning and end of the psalm.[17] Without the understanding the psalmist is attempting to impart (v. 3), those with riches are like (משל, "compare"; see "proverb" in v. 4) the animals that perish. The rich who foolishly believe in the power of their wealth have no understanding. The sound play between the words underscores this point and implicitly pushes the readers/worshipers to choose what they will seek to possess—wealth or understanding. The psalmist does not offer comfort (cp. Eccl 12:1-8) but rather frames a choice about one's attitude in life.

Trust and Poverty

Walter Brueggemann argues that trust is the main issue in Psalm 49 and that it has to do "both with economic reality and religious commitment (cp. Matt 6:21),"[18] which cannot be spiritualized away. Brueggemann's warning is particularly important for women, "who bear a disproportionate burden of the world's poverty. Statistics indicate that women are more likely than men to be poor and at risk of hunger because of the systematic discrimination they face in education, health care, employment and control of assets."[19] According to the United Nations Development Programme, "six of ten of the world's poorest people are women."[20] Children are also

17. Ibid., 62.

18. Brueggemann, *The Message of the Psalms*, 110.

19. UN Women, http://www.unifem.org/gender_issues/women_poverty_economics/.

20. http://www.undp.org/content/undp/en/home/ourwork/povertyreduction/focus_areas/focus.

disproportionately poor. In the United States, for example, "children are the poorest age group in the nation." The United States "has one of the highest rates of child poverty among industrialized countries," and children of color are most at risk.[21] Psalm 49 can be misused to keep the poor "in their place," especially if it is dismissed because it does not support an afterlife. An eschatology that argues for God putting things right in the next life[22] can too easily let us off the hook in this life in terms of working to eradicate poverty and promoting social justice.

Denise Dombkowski Hopkins

21. http://www.childrensdefense.org/child-research-data.
22. Hopkins, *Journey through the Psalms*, 91.

Psalm 50

Protecting the Family

R ather than addressing God directly as most psalms do, Psalm 50 offers "first-person divine speech"[1] that criticizes Israel's sacrifices and behavior. Some argue that Psalm 50 belongs to the liturgy of a covenant renewal ceremony (Josh 24); others call it a didactic poem or a covenant lawsuit (ריב) brought by God against Israel (Isa 1:10-17; Mic 6:6-8).[2] Robert Alter calls it "a prophetic psalm, with God actually quoted in direct discourse for much of the poem, as in the literary prophets."[3] The "I" in Psalm 50 represents God speaking in oracles[4]

---

1. J. W. Hilber, *Cultic Prophecy in the Psalms*, BZAW 352 (Berlin: de Gruyter, 2005).

2. Konrad Schaefer, *Psalms*, Berit Olam (Collegeville, MN: Liturgical Press, 2001), 126, argues that "Psalms 50 and 51 belong together, as two parts of a lawsuit": the reprimand and the people's guilty plea, respectively.

3. Robert Alter, *The Book of Psalms* (New York: Norton, 2007), 176. See Raymond Tournay, *Seeing and Hearing God with the Psalms: The Prophetic Liturgy of the Second Temple in Jerusalem*, trans. J. Edward Crowley (Sheffield: JSOT Press, 1991), who argues that the Levitical singers of the Second Temple, inspired by God's spirit, acted as cultic prophets during the Second Temple period when prophetic activity had ended, and that Israel's psalms contain a clear "prophetic dimension" (230).

4. Susan Gillingham, "New Wine and Old Wineskins: Three Approaches to Prophecy and Psalmody," in *Prophecy and Prophets in Ancient Israel: Proceedings of the Oxford Old Testament Seminar*, ed. John Day (New York: T & T Clark, 2010), 370–90, at 372.

Psalm 50:1-23

A Psalm of Asaph.

¹The mighty one, God the LORD,
  speaks and summons the earth
  from the rising of the sun to its
  setting.
²Out of Zion, the perfection of
  beauty,
  God shines forth.

³Our God comes and does not
  keep silence,
  before him is a devouring fire,
  and a mighty tempest all
  around him.
⁴He calls to the heavens above
  and to the earth, that he may
  judge his people:
⁵"Gather to me my faithful ones,
  who made a covenant with me
  by sacrifice!"
⁶The heavens declare his righteousness,
  for God himself is judge. *Selah*

⁷"Hear, O my people, and I will
  speak,
  O Israel, I will testify against you.
  I am God, your God.
⁸Not for your sacrifices do I rebuke you;
  your burnt-offerings are continually before me.
⁹I will not accept a bull from your
  house,
  or goats from your folds.
¹⁰For every wild animal of the forest is mine,
  the cattle on a thousand hills.
¹¹I know all the birds of the air,
  and all that moves in the field
  is mine.

¹²"If I were hungry, I would not tell
  you,
  for the world and all that is in it
  is mine.
¹³Do I eat the flesh of bulls,

delivered by a prophet who need not necessarily be male. Tanakh identi-fies five women as prophets (הנביאה, feminine singular): Miriam (Exod 15:20), Deborah (Judg 4–5), Huldah (2 Kgs 22:8-14), the unnamed woman with whom Isaiah fathers a son (Isa 8:1), and Noadiah (Neh 6:14). Also, the daughters of Heman, along with their brothers ("all of these," 1 Chr 25:6), perform music in the temple under the direction of their father; their music is considered to be prophecy (1 Chr 25:1). As Psalm 68:24-25 suggests, women probably played the טף (small frame drum).[5]

The Talmud (b. Meg. 14a) lists seven female prophets: Sarah, Miriam, Deborah, Hannah, Abigail, Huldah, and Esther. Ezekiel 13:17 and Joel 2:28 speak generally of women and men prophesying. In many texts the mas-

---

5. Theodore W. Burgh, *Listening to the Artifacts: Music Culture in Ancient Palestine* (New York: T & T Clark, 2006), 103–4. See also Miriam in Exod 15:20; Jephthah's daughter in Judg 11:34; women celebrating David's victories in 1 Sam 18:6.

or drink the blood of goats?
[14]Offer to God a sacrifice of
thanksgiving,
and pay your vows to the Most
High.
[15]Call on me in the day of trouble;
I will deliver you, and you shall
glorify me."

[16]But to the wicked God says:
"What right have you to recite
my statutes,
or take my covenant on your
lips?
[17]For you hate discipline,
and you cast my words behind
you.
[18]You make friends with a thief
when you see one,
and you keep company with
adulterers.

[19]"You give your mouth free rein
for evil,

and your tongue frames de-
ceit.
[20]You sit and speak against your
kin;
you slander your own mother's
child.
[21]These things you have done and
I have been silent;
you thought that I was one just
like yourself.
But now I rebuke you, and lay the
charge before you.

[22]"Mark this, then, you who forget
God,
or I will tear you apart, and
there will be no one to
deliver.
[23]Those who bring thanksgiving as
their sacrifice honor me;
to those who go the right way
I will show the salvation of
God.

culine plural נביאים ("prophets") masks the presence of female prophets who "are lost to the binaries of grammar."[6] The NT names Anna (Luke 2:36), the virgin daughters of Philip (Acts 21:9), and females at Corinth (1 Cor 11:5) as prophets. Though only eleven psalms contain direct "God-quotations,"[7] H. G. M. Williamson argues that it "seems likely" that "the figure of the prophetess was not nearly so unfamiliar in monarchical Israel and Judah as our scant sources initially suggest." Prophecy as a "male preserve" has obscured the earlier social reality of female prophets.[8]

6. Wilda C. Gafney, *Daughters of Miriam: Women Prophets in Ancient Israel* (Minneapolis: Fortress Press, 2008), 15.

7. Rolf A. Jacobson, *"Many Are Saying": The Function of Direct Discourse in the Hebrew Psalter* (New York: T & T Clark, 2004). The eleven psalms are 2, 12, 50, 75, 81, 82, 89, 91, 95, 110, and 132.

8. H. G. M. Williamson, "Prophetesses in the Hebrew Bible," in Day, *Prophecy and Prophets in Ancient Israel*, 65–80, at 74, 76.

The tone of God's speech—does God come to criticize or praise Israel?—is not initially as clear as it is in a covenant lawsuit.[9] Verbs used with God as the subject in v. 1-7—"speak," "call," "judge," "testify"—are neutral and create ambiguity; they can be negative or positive depending on the context. The psalm moves from an opening theophany (vv. 1-7),[10] to a critique of misunderstandings about sacrifice and God (vv. 8-15) and of the life of the people (vv. 16-21), and finally to a closing summary (vv. 22-23). The storm imagery in v. 3 ("devouring fire" and "mighty tempest") communicates God's authority and sovereignty. This imagery evokes God's salvific coming on Sinai (Exod 19:16-19) and thus sets up positive expectations that are dashed by God's rebukes later in the psalm. God's self-identification in v. 7c, "I am God, your God," also communicates positive expectation. It suggests the covenant formula "I am the Lᴏʀᴅ your God" at the beginning of the Decalogue (in Jewish tradition this formula forms part of the first commandment; see Exod 20:25; Deut 5:6, 9; Ps 81:10). God ironically calls those summoned "my faithful ones" (v. 5), "my people" (v. 7). But these "covenant makers" (v. 5) become rebuked "covenant forgetters" later in the psalm (v. 22).[11] Rising suspense is expressed in v. 8: "not for your sacrifices do I rebuke you."[12] What, then, will God rebuke?

The images pile up in the theophany (vv. 1-7) in a "staccato manner" and create movement that fills the listener with expectation.[13] In v. 1, three names are used for God: אל, El or "mighty one"; אלהים, Elohim, translated "God"; and יהוה, Adonai or "Lord." These names chart a progression from the old general Semitic name for deity associated with pre-Davidic Jerusalem, Shechem, and Shiloh[14] to Israel's special name for God associated with Exodus and Sinai, again creating positive expectations. In v. 2, God comes "out of Zion," God's dwelling place, and "shines forth" to summon the earth (v. 1), the heavens (v. 4), and the people (v. 7). Deuteronomy 33:2 describes God's entrance into Canaan from Sinai as a salvific solar theophany using the same verb, again evoking positive expectations about God's coming. The eastern spatial orientation of the Jerusalem temple "in effect

---

9. Johanna W. H. Bos, "Oh When the Saints: A Consideration of the Meaning of Psalm 50," *JSOT* 24 (1982): 65–77, at 65, 67.

10. I agree with Bos, ibid., 66, who argues that v. 7 belongs to the announcement of speech and not the speech itself, as most argue.

11. Ibid., 70. Note that both terms are active participles in construct. Their grammatical form underscores their deliberate contrast.

12. John Goldingay, *Psalms*, vol. 2 (Grand Rapids, MI: Baker Academic, 2007), 113.

13. Bos, "Oh When the Saints."

14. Mark S. Smith, "El," *Eerdmans Dictionary of the Bible*, ed. David Noel Freedman (Grand Rapids, MI: Eerdmans, 2000), 384–86.

routinized and enshrined what was historiographically conveyed"[15] in Deuteronomy 33. The association of the sun with the divine presence "has its home in royal temple theology."[16] Psalm 50 makes it clear that Torah and covenantal expectations and promises are now relocated from Sinai to Zion, opening the door to the "internationalization" of both.[17]

The Earth Bears Witness

On June 24, 1988, Dr. James Hanson, a well-regarded NASA scientist, testified before a US Senate Committee and sounded as much like an Israelite prophet as he did a scientist. Hanson warned of a dangerous warming trend already underway, caused primarily by greenhouse gases released by the burning of fossil fuels. Hanson went on to say that unless we acted quickly to address "global warming," dangerous and unpredictable extremes in weather would only increase.[18]

In the intervening twenty-five-plus years we have offered up what makes God the angriest, according to the author of Ps 50: small, easy sacrifices, meant in large measure to give only lip service to the covenant God made with us and creation, while we continue our own unsustainable lives and lifestyles. As a result the planet continues to warm to dangerous levels, causing extreme weather patterns—storms, droughts, heat waves—that are already beginning to disrupt food and water supplies and have serious impacts on those who are most vulnerable and least responsible.[19]

From the beginning of Psalm 50, God calls on the earth to bear witness to the stark and violent ramifications of the disruption of the covenantal relationship: "Mark this, then, you who forget God, or I will tear you apart, and there will be no one to deliver" (v. 22).

---

15. William P. Brown, *Seeing the Psalms: A Theology of Metaphor* (Louisville, KY: Westminster John Knox, 2002), 88. Brown notes that the use of solar imagery was part of temple worship during the period of the monarchy and continued in popular circles much later.

16. Ibid., 86. For a critique or royal temple ideology, see Pss 46 and 48. See also Ps 84:10-11, which "solarizes" God with the epithet of "Sun" and evokes a sense of divine protection.

17. Walter Brueggemann, *Theology of the Old Testament: Testimony, Dispute, Advocacy* (Minneapolis: Fortress Press, 1997), 593.

18. Philip Shabecoff, "Global Warming Has Begun, Expert Tells Senate," *New York Times*, June 24, 1988.

19. Intergovernmental Panel on Climate Change, "Climate Change 2014: Impacts, Adaptation and Vulnerability" (2014); http://www.ipcc.ch/, accessed May 2, 2014.

And yet, there is hope. The psalmist tells us how to begin: with thanksgiving for the sufficiency of God's gifts. We declare in faith as another psalmist proclaimed: "The LORD is my shepherd, I shall not want" (Ps 23:1). We build on this foundation of thankfulness, renew our covenant with God and creation, and participate in what Joanna Macy and others call "The Great Turning."[20] We make real sacrifices and real change and "go the right way" so that we might enjoy "the salvation of God" (v. 23).

Beth Norcross

The command to "hear" that opens v. 7 does not constitute a wisdom invitation to instruction as in Psalm 49:1 but rather resonates with the first word of the *Shema* in Deuteromony 6:4 and evokes covenant obligations. This connection is strengthened by the superscription that indicates that Psalm 50 is one of the twelve psalms of Asaph; the others are Psalms 73–83. First Chronicles 16:7 traces Asaph back to David, who appointed Asaph to take charge of the ark liturgy as a permanent duty in Jerusalem. The ark contained the two tablets of the Decalogue, the essence of the covenant (Exod 25:21-22). Second Chronicles 29:30 refers to Asaph as "the seer," which would explain the prophetic tone of Psalm 50. Many of the Asaph psalms share references to the exodus (Pss 77:16-21; 78:12-14, 42-53; 80:9; 81:6-8) and covenant traditions (Pss 50, 74, 78).

Just as in prophetic texts, in Psalm 50:8-15 the criticism of sacrifice is not meant to abolish the sacrificial system (Amos 5:21-24; Hos 6:6; Isa 1:12-17). God refuses to accept a bull or goats for sacrifice (v. 9) because God already possesses these animals and many more (vv. 10-11). God's "extensive zoological wealth" shows that God does not need a sacrificial animal and, in fact, does not eat these animals when they are offered (see God's agitated rhetorical question in v. 13), contrary to popular belief. The progression in vv. 9-12 from bulls and goats to some animals to all animals to everything functions rhetorically to emphasize the gap between the sacrificial animal and the animals owned by God. The use of "you"/"your" and "my"/"mine" widens the gap. The result is that the

20. See Joanna Macy and Christopher Landry, "Joanna Macy and the Great Turning" (San Francisco: Video Project, 2014), "a short film about the societal shift now underway from an industrial growth society to a more sustainable civilization."

sacrificial animal is made to "look incredibly small and inconsequential."[21] Thus the people commit idolatry in their "distortion of God's nature."[22] Verse 15 (cp. v. 23) redefines proper worship as calling on God when in trouble; God will save and the people will glorify God with thanksgiving for deliverance (Deut 26:5-10).

The "sacrifice of thanksgiving" God recommends in v. 14 still requires animal sacrifice; תודה in Hebrew means both the attitude of thanksgiving and the thanksgiving sacrifice, often given in payment of vows (Pss 22:25; 61:8; 65:1; 116:14, 17-18). While the offerings of bulls and goats (v. 8) are wholly burned in fire for God, only a portion of the thanksgiving offering is burnt up; the rest is shared and eaten by the worshiper and the priests, all of whom serve as witnesses to God's deliverance. "Sacrifice . . . is conducted for the sake of God's *honor*, not appetite (v. 23)." This frees animals from their "instrumental status" for maintaining the God/human relationship.[23] Criticism shifts to the people's behavior with one another in vv. 16-21. "My faithful ones" (v. 5) become "the wicked" (v. 16). God accuses the people of hypocrisy; they recite the commandments (v. 16) but violate them. God takes it personally: you violate "my statutes," "my covenant" (v. 16), and "my words" (v. 17) through theft, adultery, and slander (corresponding to commandments 7, 8, and 9; see also Jer 7:9-10; Hos 4:1-3). In v. 21, God refuses to collude with them through divine silence; v. 3 had already given notice that "our God comes and does not keep silence." Clearly, "by being silent God would conform to the people's image of God: a god who opens its mouth only to receive the food which the faithful grant it."[24]

God's mention of theft and adultery as part of the people's hypocritical behavior underscores the precarious economic position of women and children in ancient Israel. Richard Horsley argues that the commandment about not committing adultery aimed to "protect the integrity and continuity of the family,"[25] which was the basic unit of production,

21. Richard Whitekettle, "Forensic Zoology: Animal Taxonomy and Rhetorical Persuasion in Psalm l," *VT* 58 (2008): 404–19, at 418. The psalm uses secondary taxa to make animals "more tangible and striking than primary level taxa" (416), which vividly engages the reader.

22. Bos, "Oh When the Saints," 73.

23. J. Clinton McCann Jr., "The Book of Psalms," in *The New Interpreter's Bible*, vol. 4 (Nashville, TN: Abingdon Press, 1996), 639–1280, at 154.

24. Bos, "Oh When the Saints," 72.

25. Richard A. Horsley, *Covenant Economics* (Louisville, KY: Westminster John Knox, 2009), 25.

reproduction, and socialization in Israel. Carol Meyers has shown the importance of women's roles in household maintenance activities such as food preparation and textile making for the survival of the household. The commandment against stealing is linked to other commandments prohibiting coveting (חמד) of house, fields, and wives that together make up the household (see Mic 2:2; Isa 5:8; Exod 22:1, 5). "Coveting" involves desiring and seizing. The commandment "you shall not steal" was meant to prohibit actions that could ruin a neighbor family economically.

The most ironic reversal in the psalm occurs in the summary, beginning with v. 22. Introduced by the same verb that ended Psalm 49, בין ("understand"; 49:20, but translated here as "mark this!"), God threatens: "I will tear you apart." The use of the lion as a simile for God, as suggested by the verb טרף ("tear to pieces"), is terrifying (Hos 5:14). Originating in folk sayings, this simile was applied to the king and then to God to illustrate the "antithetic activity" of God, who kills and gives life.[26] Verse 23 underscores this tension since it ends with God's promise to "show the salvation of God" to those who act rightly and bring thanksgiving.

26. Aaron Chalmers, " 'There Is No Deliverer (From My Hand)'—A Formula Analysis," *VT* 55 (2005): 287–92.

Psalm 51

Collateral Damage

Most interpreters consider Psalm 51 the quintessential model of repentance and humility. Not surprisingly, the Revised Common Lectionary assigns Psalm 51:1-17 to Ash Wednesday for Years A, B, and C to mark the beginning of the liturgical season of Lent. Traditionally, Jews pray v. 15 before the central prayer of the Jewish liturgy, the Amidah (or 18 Benedictions), a prayer of praise, petition, and thanks. Western Christian tradition has grouped Psalm 51 with six other so-called penitential laments: 6, 32, 38, 102, 130, and 143, though only Psalms 32 and 51 actually offer confession. The superscription of Psalm 51 ties confession to a narrative moment in the life of David in 2 Samuel 12. In this intertext the prophet Nathan rebukes David by means of a parable after he rapes Bathsheba and arranges for Uriah's murder. David then confesses to Nathan: "I have sinned against the Lord" (2 Sam 12:13), which scholars connect to Psalm 51:4, "against you, you alone, have I sinned." Robert Alter[1] notes the pun in the superscription revolving around the verb בא ("come, come into"): Nathan "comes" to David (enters his chambers), and David "comes into" Bathsheba (in intercourse). Pun and parable resonate with irony.

---

1. Robert Alter, *The Book of Psalms* (New York: Norton, 2007), 180 n. 2.

Psalm 51:1-19

*To the leader. A Psalm of David,
when the prophet Nathan came to him,
after he had gone in to Bathsheba.*

¹Have mercy on me, O God,
according to your steadfast
love;
according to your abundant mercy
blot out my transgressions.
²Wash me thoroughly from my
iniquity,
and cleanse me from my sin.

³For I know my transgressions,
and my sin is ever before me.
⁴Against you, you alone, have I
sinned,
and done what is evil in your
sight,
so that you are justified in your
sentence

and blameless when you pass
judgment.
⁵Indeed, I was born guilty,
a sinner when my mother conceived me.

⁶You desire truth in the inward
being;
therefore teach me wisdom in
my secret heart.
⁷Purge me with hyssop, and I
shall be clean;
wash me, and I shall be whiter
than snow.
⁸Let me hear joy and gladness;
let the bones that you have
crushed rejoice.
⁹Hide your face from my sins,
and blot out all my iniquities.

¹⁰Create in me a clean heart, O God,

In the first section of Psalm 51, vv. 1-9, the psalmist begs for cleansing. Verses 1-2 are saturated with imperatives from the vocabulary of forgiveness: חנני, "have mercy on me" (a better translation of חנני is "grace me"); מחה, "blot out"; כבסני, "wash"; טהרני, "cleanse." The issue is "not just cosmetic";[2] sin is so pervasive that a deep cleaning is required. Verses 2 and 7 form a chiasm with verbs in reverse order: כבס (to clean physically as in washing clothes) in vv. 2a and 7b, and טהר (ritual purification) in vv. 2b and 7a. Using the two words together "demonstrates the completeness of God's act of forgiveness,"[3] reaching both inside and out. The use of the verb מחה in vv. 1 and 9 forms an envelope for the psalm's first section. The word literally means "annihilation" (Gen 7:6), or "nuke" in modern terms; the NRSV translation downplays the verb's intensity.[4]

---

2. Claire Vonk Brooks, "Psalm 51," *Int* 49 (1995): 62–66, at 63.
3. Beth LaNeel Tanner, "Preaching the Penitential Psalms," *WW* 27 (Winter 2007): 88–98, at 89.
4. Ibid., 90.

and put a new and right spirit
within me.
[11]Do not cast me away from your
presence,
and do not take your holy spirit
from me.
[12]Restore to me the joy of your
salvation,
and sustain in me a willing
spirit.

[13]Then I will teach transgressors
your ways,
and sinners will return to you.
[14]Deliver me from bloodshed, O
God,
O God of my salvation,
and my tongue will sing aloud
of your deliverance.

[15]O LORD, open my lips,

and my mouth will declare your
praise.
[16]For you have no delight in sacrifice;
if I were to give a burnt offering,
you would not be pleased.
[17]The sacrifice acceptable to God
is a broken spirit;
a broken and contrite heart, O
God, you will not despise.

[18]Do good to Zion in your good
pleasure;
rebuild the walls of Jerusalem,
[19]then you will delight in right sacrifices,
in burnt offerings and whole
burnt offerings;
then bulls will be offered on
your altar.

The psalmist also piles up the vocabulary for sin, using synonyms for wrongdoing fourteen times: פשע, "transgressions"; עין, "iniquity"; הרע, "evil"; עון, "guilty"; חטאת, "sin." Konrad Schaefer notes that "sin, remarkably present in the beginning, gradually disappears and is replaced by God,"[5] who is named six times in the second major part of the psalm, which focuses on renewal (vv. 10-16). A striking rhetorical effect is produced by the repetition of the vocabulary of sin and forgiveness, expressed in twenty-one imperative petitions used throughout the psalm to underscore the psalmist's commitment to renewal. We are left with the image of a very humble David (if we take the superscription seriously as interpretive clue) who earns our sympathy. Interpreters have literally swooned over the emotional power of David's confession.

Unfortunately, the hyperbole of both text and interpreter serves to push the victims of David's transgressions—Bathsheba, Uriah, and the child born of rape who dies as punishment—into the background. This

5. Konrad Schaefer, *Psalms*, Berit Olam (Collegeville, MN: Liturgical Press, 2001), 129.

rhetorical effect is magnified by the appeals to God's character that support the psalmist's petitions. J. Clinton McCann, for example, thinks that Psalm 51 is "as much or more about God's character than it is about human sinfulness."[6] God is merciful, full of grace and steadfast love, cleansing, justified, creator, restorer, sustainer, and deliverer. Especially powerful from a feminist viewpoint is God's attribute of compassion, from the Hebrew רחם, which means "womb." The plural רחמיך ("your mercies") in v. 1b forms the abstract idea of compassion, mercy, and love. The NRSV translates "mercy," which obscures this feminine image of God; a better translation would be "womb-love"[7] (Gen 43:30; 1 Kgs 3:16-28; Exod 33:19; 34:6; Pss 25:6; 103:13; Jer 31:20; Isa 49:13).

The psalmist names God's womb-love as a warrant for forgiveness, which prompts associations with other God images that challenge the dominant, violent Warrior-Deliverer God metaphor. The "disjunctive metaphor" of womb-love joins those of God as Mother in Labor and Nurturing Mother in First and Second Isaiah (Isa 42:13-14; 45:9-10; 49:13-15; 66:10-13) to embody hope for the future of traumatized, exiled Israel.[8] "Womb-love" also gives hope to the sinful psalmist. How ironic that the king who abused his power calls on womb-love that challenges abusive power in order to save himself!

Interpreters have traditionally taken v. 5 to refer to original sin; contemporary interpreters have for the most part avoided this conclusion. They argue instead that "I was born guilty" does not support the biological or sexual transmission of sin but rather indicates the psalmist's own sense of personal, pervasive sinfulness. The psalmist makes this point, however, at the expense of women. The verb used with "my mother" in v. 5b, יחם, is connected with animals and means "to rut," "be in heat" (see Gen 20:14b; 30:10, 38-39). This verb prompts associations with Jeremiah's scathing, dehumanizing critique of personified Israel as "a wild ass . . . in her heat (אוה, literally 'desire') sniffing the wind" (Jer 2:24).[9]

---

6. J. Clinton McCann Jr., "The Book of Psalms," in *The New Interpreter's Bible*, vol. 4 (Nashville, TN: Abingdon Press, 1996), 639–1280, at 885.

7. Denise Dombkowski Hopkins and Michael S. Koppel, *Grounded in the Living Word: The Old Testament and Pastoral Care Practices* (Grand Rapids, MI: Eerdmans, 2010), 73–74.

8. L. Juliana M. Claassens, *Mourner, Mother, Midwife: Reimagining God's Delivering Presence in the Old Testament* (Louisville, KY: Westminster John Knox, 2012), 43–47.

9. *The Jewish Study Bible, Tanakh Translation*, ed. Adele Berlin and Marc Zvi Brettler (Oxford: Oxford University Press, 2004), 1339, notes that "the idea of the inherent sinfulness of humans is rarely expressed in the Bible, except for Gen 8:21. . . . Christianity developed the notion of original sin."

Schaefer rightly terms the psalmist's reference to sinful conception and birth "sheer exaggeration" and perhaps "a poetic attempt to abase oneself so as to win God's mercy."[10]

This observation opens the door to R. Christopher Heard's bold exploration of the interpretive effect of reading Psalm 51 against the background of its superscription. He notes that Nathan's parable in 2 Samuel 12:1-4 focuses on all the interpersonal sins David commits, drawing attention to all three offended parties—God, Bathsheba, and Uriah—but that David in both 2 Samuel 12:13 and Psalm 51:4 names only God. If we take the superscription seriously we must see that David "approaches confession as damage control and penitence as public relations," refusing to admit specific sins against Bathsheba and Uriah and misdirecting and obscuring the social/horizontal dimension of his crimes by stressing his vertical relationship with God.[11] The only recognition of his human victims can perhaps be seen in v. 14: "deliver me from bloodshed" (Hebrew דמים, literally "bloods"), which may refer to his fear of blood vengeance for the murder of Uriah or his own death by capital punishment.

The only punishment David accepts is purging with hyssop (v. 7), whose branches are used for sprinkling in purification rituals (see Num 19:6, 18; Lev 14:4). He does not even offer an animal sacrifice, something widows and orphans depend on for sustenance (Deut 14:22-29). Instead, David offers his speech (v. 14b, which links to Ps 50:14, 23). David here abuses his royal power and "proves himself once again to be 'that man,' loath to sacrifice an animal."[12]

The focus on God in Psalm 51 is underscored by the use of ברא ("create") in v. 10, linking Psalm 51 both to Genesis 1 and to Isaiah 40–55 and the "new thing" God is about to do in the exile (Isa 43:15-19); the verb is used only with God as subject. The request for a "clean heart" and "new spirit" parallels Ezekiel 36:25-27; Jeremiah 31:33; 32:39-40. God's רוח ("spirit" or "breath," v. 11) manifests God's creative activity, as in Genesis 2:7; 7:22. If this restoration (v. 13, *hiphil* of שוב, "restore") takes place, then the psalmist will teach others so that sinners will return (שוב) to God (v. 13a). The

---

10. Schaefer, *Psalms*, 131.

11. R. Christopher Heard, "Penitent to a Fault: The Characterization of David in Psalm 51," in *The Fate of King David: The Past and Present of a Biblical Icon*, ed. Tod Linafelt, Claudia Camp, and Timothy Beal (New York: T & T Clark, 2010), 163–74, at 173. See Barbara Ellison Rosenblit, "David, Bat Sheva, and the Fifty-First Psalm," *Cross Currents* (Fall 1995): 326–40, for what Heard (p. 168) terms an attempt at a "victim impact statement," something missing in Ps 51: an original drama that gives voice to Bathsheba as she overhears David praying Ps 51.

12. Heard, "Penitent to a Fault," 171.

promise of public praise (v. 14b) functions as a motivation for the granting of the psalmist's petitions. Because God's reputation is at stake, especially if David is the psalmist, the psalmist's praise has "PR value."[13] Kathryn L. Roberts argues that the psalmist's vows in vv. 14-15 are public, cultic acts, not simply inner feelings; the vows "put God on notice."[14]

Reading Psalm and Superscription in Reverse

The historical superscriptions to Psalms 51 and 59 (and others) tie those psalms to particular events in David's life. These are thought to be later additions, part of the compilation and editing of the Psalter rather than being original to the individual psalmic compositions.[15] The sum effect is to effectively "reshape the image of David, a complex and sometimes troublesome figure in the Samuel narrative, into a devout man, ever praying before his God."[16] The superscriptions "provide another way of reading the Samuel narrative" so that "both the story and David are given a marked religious character."[17]

When we read from story into psalm—so that the psalm expands or corrects the story—the psalm "fixes" the problem the story poses. David's terse exclamation of guilt (2 Sam 12:13) is amplified, via the superscription, into a full measure of repentance in Psalm 51. The speechless and curiously passive figure of David in 1 Samuel 19:11-17 is given voice in the ardent plea for help of Psalm 59.

Reading so that the psalm overwrites the story fits the linear way we tend to consume book-bound print, turning over leaves and recasting the information already consumed in light of the new information given. The story and its characters are restructured in

---

13. Denise Dombkowski Hopkins, *Journey through the Psalms* (St. Louis, MO: Chalice Press, 2002), 103–14.

14. Kathryn L. Roberts, "My Tongue Will Sing Aloud of Your Deliverance: Praise and Sacrifice in the Psalms," in *Psalms and Practice: Worship, Virtue, and Authority* (Collegeville, MN: Liturgical Press, 2001), 99–110, at 106.

15. See, e.g., ibid., 164; "Psalm 51," n. 11 in this commentary, and the discussion there of superscriptions as intertexts.

16. Vivian L. Johnson, *David in Distress: His Portrait through the Historical Psalms* (New York and London: T & T Clark, 2009), 1–2.

17. Ibid., 11, 140.

our minds through this new juxtaposition.[18] The effect of such sequential (re)reading, by "cleaning up" the problems of the story, also "cleans up" and out of the way the others involved and affected, as Denise D. Hopkins has noted. The deaths of Uriah and of the first infant Bathsheba bore to David are not referenced in Psalm 51, nor is the effect of David's sin on Bathsheba herself highlighted. Any memory of Michal, Saul's daughter and David's wife, is omitted from Psalm 59, even as the superscription implies events in which Michal was involved (1 Sam 19:11-17).

Yet the very fixedness of writing means that the order of reading can be inverted. The superscription need not be read as a dictate overwriting the story but can be seen as a hyperlink reopening the psalm by re-placing it into the messy narrative that is life. When psalm and superscription are read in reverse it is not David's image that is burnished but the human cost that is restored to view. The superscription implicates all the horizontal interpersonal relationships and actions that shape and are shaped by the vertical of human-divine that is the focus of the psalm-prayer. So read, the superscriptions rewrite the psalms, presenting the prayer not as the single action of an autonomous moral/religious actor but as grounded in the complex multiplicity of embodied life, what Pamela Cooper-White calls the "folding together (*com-plicatio*) not only of multiple roles and relationships, but also of multiple internal states of emotion and identity" that is a hallmark of women's lives.[19] The significance of the superscription is less its possible historicity than the way it invites the reader to reread the psalm in light of her own narrative so she can retell her life in light of the psalm.

Thus the superscription of Psalm 51 reconnects vertical

---

18. James W. Watts, *Psalm and Story: Inset Hymns in Hebrew Narrative* (Sheffield: Sheffield Academic Press, 1992), 191: "Psalms in narrative contexts invariably characterize their speaker(s), indirectly if not by direct description." These serve to "structure large blocks of material thematically, deepen the theocentric orientation of books and internal characterization of individuals, and actualize the narratives by eliciting reader participation in the songs" (197). The historical superscriptions do not operate in precisely the same fashion as do psalms directly woven within the narrative (e.g., 2 Sam 22), but the effect of recasting the narrative is similar.

19. Pamela Cooper-White, "Com/plicated Woman: Multiplicity and Relationality across Gender and Culture," in *Women Out of Order: Risking Change and Creating Care in a Multicultural World*, ed. Jeanne Stevenson-Moessner and Teresa Snorton (Minneapolis: Fortress Press, 2010), 7–21, at 9.

orientation of the prayer—"against you, you alone, have I sinned" (51:4)—to the horizontal cast of the narrative. The sin may be ultimately against the LORD alone, yet the LORD does not alone bear the hurt. The superscription recalls to the reader the effects of that sin on the man and woman and child otherwise unmentioned in the psalm and reminds her that relationship with God includes relationship with others. The messy narrative implicated by the superscription shines both judgment and hope on the messy reality of life, illumining the intersection of the planes, relationship with God and with neighbor, even as the psalm, connected by superscription to the narrative, serves as promise that relationship can be restored.

Similarly, the superscribed intersection of Psalm 59 with the narrative of 1 Samuel 19:11-17, where Michal takes initiative to plan and make good her husband's escape from her father's soldiers, reminds the reader that God's saving acts may be effected through human actors.

Katherine Brown

Cynthia Rigby speaks of "double agency" in Psalms 22 and 51; the psalmist is not passive but initiates deliverance with petitions and anticipates it with vows "that visibly manifest the reality of the divine/human reconciliation." Deliverance does not result in a quiet, happy withdrawal from the world, but rather in active partnership with God as in vv. 13-15.[20] Yet, one is forced to wonder about the nature of David's partnership with God following Nathan's parable in 2 Samuel 12, as his family and kingship are almost destroyed by his inability to do the right thing.

Many consider vv. 18-19 to be a later addition to Psalm 51 during the exile because of the petition to rebuild the walls of Jerusalem. Verse 19 repeats the anti-sacrificial vocabulary of v. 16—חפץ, "delight"; זבח, "sacrifice"; כליל, "burnt offering"—to show that sacrifices offered with a "broken [submissive] and contrite heart" (v. 17) are acceptable. Psalm 51 was one of ten psalms quoted in the Letter of Barnabas, written in the early second century CE, arguing that sacrifices had been abrogated. Interestingly, the Lectionary also leaves out vv. 18-19 in the Ash Wednesday reading.[21] If we view these verses as a later addition, David, as king,

20. Cynthia L. Rigby, "All God, and Us: Double Agency and Reconciliation in Psalms 22 and 51," in *Psalms and Practice*, 202–19, at 210, 208, 213.

21. Roberts, "My Tongue," 103.

becomes "the embodiment of the indicted, condemned, and sickened political nation, i.e., the disenfranchised and exiled ruling elite."[22] With its new ending Psalm 51 "neutralizes the critique" of sacrifice in Psalm 50[23] and brings it into line with Amos 5:21-24, which criticizes but does not advocate abolishing sacrifice. Nevertheless, David as mouthpiece for the elite means that we as readers must search even more diligently for traces of those on the margins.

22. Robert B. Coote, " 'Let This House Be Healed' (Psalm 51)," *Religion und Krankheit*, ed. Gregor Etzelmüller and Annette Weissenrieder (Darmstadt: Wissenschaftliche Buchgesellschaft, 2010), 217–30, at 218.
    23. Ibid., 228.

Psalm 52

Tree of Life

Psalm 52 expresses the primary wisdom theme of the Two Ways—the contrasting ways of the righteous and of the wicked and their consequences[1]—first introduced in the Psalter in Psalm 1. Since "antithesis seems to be the dominant textual strategy"[2] in Psalm 52, interpreters are right to classify it as a wisdom psalm, although some argue that it is a prophetic judgment speech containing accusation and announced punishment like Psalm 50. Wisdom influence can be seen throughout the Psalter, especially in book 5 (e.g., Ps 119). In the postexilic period wisdom is personified as Woman Wisdom (Prov 1–9; Wisdom; Sirach), and becomes embodied as Torah (Sir 24), "thereby inviting the reader to hear the voice of Woman Wisdom, the feminine iteration of YHWH" in wisdom psalms[3] like Psalm 52 (see also Pss 1, 32, 37, 49, 73, 78, 112, 119, 127, 128, 133, and 145).

1. Denise Dombkowski Hopkins, *Journey through the Psalms* (St. Louis, MO: Chalice Press, 2002), 59–66.

2. Johan Hendrik Potgieter, "The Profile of the Rich Antagonist and the Pious Protagonist in Psalm 52," *HTS* 69 (2013): 7 pp. (no pagination); http://hts.org.za /index.php/HTS/article/viewFile/1963/3645.

3. Nancy deClaissé-Walford, "Psalms," in *Women's Bible Commentary*, ed. Carol A. Newsom, Sharon H. Ringe, and Jacqueline E. Lapsley, 3rd ed. (Louisville, KY: Westminster John Knox, 2012), 221–31, at 226.

Psalm 52:1-9

To the leader. A Maskil of David,
when Doeg the Edomite came to Saul
and said to him, "David has come
to the house of Ahimelech."

¹Why do you boast, O mighty one,
  of mischief done against the
    godly?
All day long ²you are plotting
  destruction.
Your tongue is like a sharp razor,
  you worker of treachery.
³You love evil more than good,
  and lying more than speaking
    the truth.   *Selah*
⁴You love all words that devour,
  O deceitful tongue.
⁵But God will break you down for-
    ever;
  he will snatch and tear you
    from your tent;

he will uproot you from the
    land of the living.   *Selah*
⁶The righteous will see, and fear,
  and will laugh at the evildoer,
    saying,
⁷"See the one who would not
    take
  refuge in God,
but trusted in abundant riches,
  and sought refuge in wealth!"

⁸But I am like a green olive tree
  in the house of God.
I trust in the steadfast love of God
  forever and ever.
⁹I will thank you forever,
  because of what you have
    done.
In the presence of the faithful
  I will proclaim your name, for it
    is good.

Philippus J. Botha argues for a direct literary influence on Psalm 52
from Proverbs and Jeremiah 9 ("donor texts") and provides a long list
of deliberate allusions to support this view.[4] Chief among these is Psalm
52:6: "the righteous will see, and fear, and laugh at [יִשְׂחָקוּ] him" (the
wicked person in vv. 1-5 who will be punished by God). The verb "to
laugh" echoes Proverbs 1:26, in which Lady Wisdom warns the fools in
the streets who ignore her teaching that "I also will laugh [אֶשְׂחָק] at your
calamity; I will mock when panic strikes you" (see the contrasting use
of the same root, שׂחק, for delight in Prov 8:31). As much as Woman Wisdom in Proverbs 1–9 combines many positive aspects of divine and real
women, readers must appropriate her with a bit of caution. She, along
with the Woman of Substance with whom she coalesces in Proverbs
31:10-31, forms part of an envelope of "a book *intended for men* about

---

4. Philippus J. Botha, " 'I Am Like a Green Olive Tree': The Wisdom Context of
Psalm 52," *HTS* 69 (2013): 8 pp. (no pagination); http://hts.org.za/index.php/HTS
/article/viewFile/1962/3640.

living wisely in the everyday"; she is unrealistically idealized "to entice and promote the values of [heterosexual] men."[5]

In keeping with the wisdom focus on contrasting typical behaviors, Psalm 52 begins by addressing an anonymous "mighty one" (גבור, literally, "mighty man") who boasts of evil done to the godly (v. 1). The word גבור, which also means "hero" or "warrior," perhaps provides the connection to the curious superscription, which mentions Doeg the Edomite, one of the "mighty men" (גבורים) of Saul (1 Sam 14:52). Doeg endangers David by sharing his location with Saul and may be the model for the evil "mighty man" of the psalm, though "the house of God" in v. 8 does not exist in Saul's time, and Doeg is not a liar. In v. 1 the psalmist uses גבור ironically. It is a term often connected with God (e.g., Isa 10:24; Ps 50:1), but here it describes one who plots, lies, and uses his tongue "like a sharp razor" (v. 2b) to harm the righteous. Psalms 10:7; 12:3-4; 55:9, 21; and 57:4 describe the tongue as weapon, a favorite wisdom theme (Prov 10:18; 12:5-6; 21:6). The mighty one's tongue is so powerful with its "words that devour" that it is personified (Ps 73:9) and addressed directly in v. 4.

Contrasting pairs describe "the mighty one"(הגבור): "you love *evil* more than *good* and *lying* more than *speaking truth*" (v. 3). This is clearly the wicked person or fool of wisdom tradition. This fool's power, however, is momentary. In an ironic reversal, this "mighty man" (הגבור) becomes simply "the man" (הגבר) who is mocked by the righteous in v. 7 after the psalmist asserts God's future punishment of him. The English translation obscures this wordplay (גבר / גבור).

Though the wicked one dominates vv. 1-4, "he completely disappears from the text."[6] His future punishment is described in vv. 5-7 with powerful verbs of destruction: תצך, "break down" (a house); חתה, "snatch" (hot coals); נסח, "tear"; and שרש, "uproot" (v. 5). Though he plots evil "all day long" (v. 1), God will break him down "forever" (v. 5). The verb נסח ("tear away," "snatch") in v. 5 appears only here in Psalms and in Deuteronomy 28:63 and Proverbs 2:22 and 15:25, "proving a literary connection with Proverbs."[7] The "tent" from which he is snatched stands in antithesis to the security of "the house of God" (v. 8b). While the wicked one is "uprooted" like a tree, the righteous psalmist by contrast declares: "but I am like a green

---

5. Christine Roy Yoder, "Proverbs," in Newsom, Ringe, and Lapsley, *Women's Bible Commentary*, 232–42, at 241.

6. Konrad Schaefer, *Psalms*, Berit Olam (Collegeville, MN: Liturgical Press, 2001), 133.

7. Botha, " 'I Am Like a Green Olive Tree,' " 1.

olive tree in the house of God" (v. 8). The adversative ו ("but"), coupled with the independent personal pronoun "I" in v. 8, introduces a credo (Josh 24:15c) that begins the third section of the psalm (vv. 8-9), filled with the psalmist's gratitude in contrast to the greed of "the mighty man."

Though trees and gardens were common in temple areas throughout the ancient Near East, functioning as symbols of life and power, Psalm 52 uses tree imagery that "is found to be suspect elsewhere in biblical tradition."[8] The term רענן ("leafy," "fresh," "green") in v. 8 is often associated with pagan worship, e.g., Deuteronomy 12:1; 1 Kings 14:23; Jeremiah 2:20; 17:2; Isaiah 57:5; Ezekiel 6:13. The Canaanite fertility goddess Asherah, symbolized by the tree and pole/tree trunk (אשרה), is condemned frequently in Tanakh (see Deut 16:21; 2 Kgs 23). Why? Perhaps because Asherah functioned as God's consort or personified God's more feminine attributes in popular folk religion centered in the family where women played a major role; this folk religion clashed with the "official" religion of the Deuteronomists.[9] If Lady Wisdom is speaking in Psalm 52, and she is described as "a tree of life to those who lay hold of her" (Prov 3:18), then she is perhaps reclaiming this tree imagery in a positive way for the faithful, especially women.

The olive tree is chosen in Psalm 52 because "practically every aspect of daily life of both rich and poor was affected by the olive tree"[10] (see the parable in Judg 9:8-9). Olives were used for food, for medicine, for fuel for lamps, as a base for perfumes and oils, and in ritual contexts (anointing); olive wood was used for furniture. Like the long-lived, useful olive tree, the righteous psalmist is planted firmly within the temple (Ps 92:13-15), unlike the wicked, who are "chaff" blown away by the wind (Ps 1:4) or "uprooted" (Ps 52:5). The psalmist has found "refuge" (מעוז) in God's house that "the mighty man" had rejected (v. 7). As "a refuge and (botanical) conservatory, metaphorically a "hothouse" for growth in righteousness,"[11] "the house of God" (v. 8) provides security for the righteous to flourish like a well-rooted tree. This metaphor of refuge has moral force and contrasts with the lifestyle of greed of "the mighty man" who "sought refuge" (מעון) in wealth" (v. 7).

---

8. William Brown, *Seeing the Psalms: A Theology of Metaphor* (Louisville, KY: Westminster John Knox, 2002), 76.

9. William G. Dever, *Did God Have a Wife? Archaeology and Folk Religion in Ancient Israel* (Grand Rapids, MI: Eerdmans, 2005), 236–38.

10. Philip J. King and Lawrence E. Stager, *Life in Biblical Israel* (Louisville, KY: Westminster John Knox, 2001), 97.

11. Brown, *Seeing the Psalms*, 76.

The Courage to Walk Away

The first verses of Psalm 52 conjure for me one of the key scenes in Alice Walker's *The Color Purple*. Celie, the protagonist of the story, has endured a lifetime of abuse and neglect—first at the hands of her father and then from her husband, Mr._____. Finally reaching her emotional limits, she becomes audacious enough to leave. In her leaving, the reader bears witness to this exchange:

> I curse you, I say . . . I say,
> Until you do right by me,
> everything you touch will
> crumble.

> He laugh. Who do you
> think you is? . . . you
> black, you poor, you ugly,
> you a woman. Goddamn,
> he say, you nothing at all.

> Until you do right by me, I
> say, everything you even
> dream about will fail.[12]

Celie's words are the words of every oppressed person who takes her or his physical and emotional leave of subjugation. God will curse the powerful who exploit and mistreat God's people. This is the mantra of the womanist who stands on the shoulders of Alice Walker and her imagination, and these are the words of Israel, having endured the abuse of empire. Celie's words breathe life back into the lives of black women who have endured hardship at the hands of their white and black male counterparts. In the same manner Lady Wisdom's words breathe life and hope back into the hearts and minds of downtrodden Israel.

Yolanda Marie Norton

Rolf Jacobson notes that there are three kinds of speech in Psalm 52: the violent speech of "the mighty man" (vv. 1-4), the mocking speech of the psalmist (vv. 6-7), and the psalmist's first-person confession of trust (vv. 8-9). A quotation from the community, specifically from "the righteous" in v. 7, expresses what the psalmist desires or imagines people are saying or will say about "the mighty man" and the true source of "refuge" (see other communal quotations in Pss 58:11; 66:3; 70:4). They will "laugh at" ("mock," שׂחק) the conflict between the psalmist and his persecutors as a conflict "in which God is an active agent on the psalmist's side" who will bring about "a transformation of the present order."[13]

12. Alice Walker, *The Color Purple* (Orlando, FL: Harcourt Books, 1982), 204.
13. Rolf A. Jacobson, *"Many Are Saying": The Function of Direct Discourse in the Hebrew Psalter* (London and New York: T & T Clark, 2004), 138.

This quotation motivates God to act, aligns the psalmist with the community, and also "lends those future words a reality that functions to deny the apparent present victory of the wicked."[14]

The quotation also builds a foundation for the confession of trust in vv. 8-9, in which the psalmist witnesses to stability in God as refuge with the repetition of "forever" in contrast to the brevity of the fool's power. The community quotation creates a voice to which both male and female readers can relate. Whereas the mighty man trusts in riches, the psalmist trusts in God's חסד ("covenant loyalty," v. 8), which brackets the psalm. God's חסד is targeted by the mighty man in v. 1, though the NRSV reads with the Syriac and translates "the godly." The psalmist vows to thank God and wait for God's name "in the presence of the faithful" (חסידים, "covenant loyal ones," v. 9c), thus acting as witness within a community shaped by God's covenant loyalty.

---

14. Ibid., 139.

Psalm 53

The Fool and Sexual Violence

Psalm 53 begins by quoting an enemy attacking God. This quotation functions "to set up a theological problem that the psalmist answers in the rest of the psalm":[1] "Fools [the Hebrew is the singular נבל] say in their hearts, 'There is no God'" (Pss 2, 3, 11, 14, 115). Gerhard von Rad long ago called this "practical atheism" rather than theoretical atheism, meaning "the fool believes God is not active and present in the world in any effective way."[2] Walter Brueggemann notes that the real problem is not the refusal to speak about God (atheism) "but the temptation to engage in *wrong* speech" about God (idolatry).[3] Similar but not identical is Psalm 14. Psalms 14 and 53 were probably part of separate psalm collections, creating a doublet when the collections were brought together. Many interpreters call Psalm 53 a prophetic psalm (cp. Ps 50), while others note that the contrast between the "fool" and the righteous is typical of wisdom instruction (cp. Ps 49). Nevertheless, נבל ("fool")

---

1. Rolf A. Jacobson, *"Many Are Saying": The Function of Direct Discourse in the Hebrew Psalter* (London: T & T Clark, 2004), 49.

2. Ibid., 33.

3. Walter Brueggemann, *Theology of the Old Testament: Testimony, Dispute, Advocacy* (Minneapolis: Fortress Press, 1997), 136.

Psalm 53:1-6

To the leader: according to Mahalath.
A Maskil of David.

¹Fools say in their hearts, "There
is no God."
They are corrupt, they commit
abominable acts;
there is no one who does good.
²God looks down from heaven on
humankind
to see if there are any who are
wise,
who seek after God.
³They have all fallen away, they
are all alike perverse;
there is no one who does
good,
no, not one.

⁴Have they no knowledge, those
evildoers,
who eat up my people as they
eat bread,
and do not call upon God?
⁵There they shall be in great terror,
in terror such as has not been.
For God will scatter the bones of
the ungodly;
they will be put to shame, for
God has rejected them.
⁶O that deliverance for Israel
would come from Zion!
When God restores the fortunes of his people,
Jacob will rejoice; Israel will be
glad.

appears twice in Psalm 74 (vv. 18, 22), which is not a wisdom psalm, challenging this connection.

First Samuel 25 suggests itself as intertext for Psalm 53. Nabal ("fool"), the husband of Abigail in 1 Samuel 25, lives up to his name by dismissing a request for food from David's men, who have protected Nabal's fields and servants (v. 25). He hurls at them the contemptuous question: "Who is David?" (vv. 10-11). This taunt enrages David, who is persuaded by Abigail not to jeopardize his future kingship with bloodguilt by taking murderous revenge. Abigail's husband fits the description of a נבל "whose behavior is disruptive and disintegrative of family, community, and nation."[4] Fools make the wrong choices (see Josh 7:15; Judg 19:23; 1 Sam 13:13). The response in Psalm 53 to fools like Nabal who dismiss God and act abominably begins in v. 2: "God looks down from heaven on humankind," searching for any who are "wise," that is, "who seek after God." This verse constitutes "a confession of trust that God is active and present"[5] and stands sandwiched with tension between two sweeping declarations that "there is no one who does good" (vv. 1c, 3b). The

4. Marvin E. Tate, *Psalms 51–100* (Dallas, TX: Word Books, 1990), 42.
5. Jacobson, *"Many Are Saying,"* 33.

rhetorical question in v. 4 accuses the "evildoers" of having no knowledge; consequently they "do not call upon God" (v. 4c). The description of the evildoers in v. 4b as those "who eat [אכל] up my people as they eat [אכל] bread [לחם]" links Psalm 53 to Psalm 52, where "the mighty man" loves "all words that devour" (בלע, v. 4).

More Intertexts

Two verses in Psalm 53, 4 and 5, beg intertexts from opposing corners of the book of Judges. The reference to evildoers who "eat up my people as they eat bread" (53:4b) conjures the carnal, if comedic, story of Ehud and King Eglon (Judg 3:12-30). King Eglon is described as a portly Moabite lord over the Israelites, leading the reader to infer that he is literally eating up the Israelites through oppressive tribute demands. When Ehud penetrates Eglon's rotund belly (בטן [Judg 3:22], or "womb") with the thrust of his phallus (sword), he feminizes him and makes Eglon the butt of the macabre fat joke: Eglon will feast on anything!

"For God will scatter the bones of the ungodly" (53:5b) seems to be retributive answer to the ghastly story of the Levite's woman in Judges 19. After she is gang-raped and left for dead, the woman is dismembered by the Levite, who sends her limbs throughout the tribes of Israel to call them to action. These two bookended stories from Judges, one indicting a foreign ruler (outsider) and the other calling fellow Israelites (insiders) to justice, confirm the psalmist's declaration that "there is no one who does good, no, not one" (53:3).

In each story penetration is a violent assertion of masculinity at the expense of the feminine. Male power makes the feminine a laughingstock at one extreme and a tortured, raped, beaten, murdered, and dismembered shell of humanity at the other. For what kind of deliverance is there hope? Who will pay the price? It is little wonder that the only ones rejoicing at the conclusion of Psalm 53 are men.

Amy Beth Jones

Psalm 53:4 also invites an intertextual link to 2 Samuel 13, in which Amnon rapes his sister Tamar. If we enter into Tamar's story and allow ourselves to be shaped morally by it,[6] then as intertext it can help lead

6. Jacqueline E. Lapsley, *Whispering the Word: Hearing Women's Stories in the Old Testament* (Louisville, KY: Westminster John Knox, 2005), 11.

to an engaged encounter with Psalm 53 and its metaphors. Empathizing with Tamar might prompt readers to recognize certain metaphorical associations overlooked in Psalm 53. This kind of involved reading of intertext and psalm can create space for what Danna Fewell calls "interruption," a reading strategy of "stopping and questioning the text and bearing responsibility for what goes on in it."[7] This kind of reading helps to identify the plausible woman's voice behind Psalm 53—the voice of Tamar—amid the abundant shared vocabulary of the two texts.

In 2 Samuel 13, Amnon's friend, Jonadab, suggests a plan to Amnon, who is sickened by lust for Tamar. Amnon will trick her by feigning sickness, asking her to come to his room to prepare food (לחם, v. 5) for him, so that he "may eat [אכל] it from her hand" (v. 5). Tamar prepares cakes but Amnon refuses to eat; instead, he rapes her (v. 14). Further, in 2 Samuel 13:8 the narrative says Tamar makes "heart-shaped cakes," using the hapax הלבבות. The heart, as the seat of will, passion, and decision, links with the first line of Psalm 53: "a fool says in his heart [לב], there is no God." The heart-shaped cakes suggest Amnon's perspective. As Ilse Müllner argues, "Amnon's desire is not merely a superficial wish for food. Amnon's point of view dominates the narrative."[8] Amnon's sexual violence against his sister fits with the description of the fool in Psalm 53 who, according to v. 1b, "commits abominable acts." In v. 12 Tamar cries: "no, my brother, do not force me; for such a thing is not done in Israel; do not do anything so vile." The Hebrew for "anything so vile" is הנבלה הזות, literally "this foolish (thing)," connecting Amnon to the "fools" of Psalm 53:1 who commit abominable acts with disastrous consequences for family and nation. Amnon raped his sister as easily as he would have eaten up the bread she had prepared, and so he joins the ranks of the נבלים.

The damning irony is that Tamar is feeling the shame (חרפה, v. 13a) that Amnon should be feeling for having done "what is not done in Israel." Tamar's pointed comparison in verse 13 anticipating the consequences of Amnon's actions expresses this irony: ואני . . . ואתה—"as for me, where could I go with my disgrace [חרפתי]? And as for you, you would be one of the נבלים in Israel." Her shame is compounded when Amnon throws

---

7. Danna Nolan Fewell, *The Children of Israel: Reading the Bible for the Sake of Our Children* (Nashville, TN: Abingdon Press, 2003), 33.

8. Ilse Müllner, "Books of Samuel: Women at the Center of Israel's Story," trans. Linda M. Maloney, in *Feminist Biblical Interpretation: A Compendium of Critical Commentary*, ed. Luise Schottroff and Marie-Theres Wacker (Grand Rapids, MI: Eerdmans, 2012), 140–52, at 149.

her out (v. 17), referring to her as "this woman" (or better, "this thing," since the Hebrew says only את־זאת) rather than calling her by name. She goes to live with her brother Absalom, in perpetual disgrace (v. 20); the text uses a Qal feminine singular participle from שמם to describe her. Neither Absalom nor David punishes Amnon, although Absalom secretly plots to avenge Tamar's rape by killing him (vv. 22-39, esp. v. 32). His initial word, however, is "be quiet for now, my sister" (v. 20).

One can imagine that the now silenced Tamar voices her desire for justice with the words of Psalm 53:5 in prayer: "For God will scatter the bones of the ungodly; they will be put to shame [בוש], for God has rejected them." This is Tamar's confession of trust that God will oversee justice and that her disgrace (חרפה) will be countered by the shaming of Amnon. The words for "shame" are not identical, but they are synonyms. The terror Tamar probably felt while being raped will be visited upon Amnon; the word פחד ("terror") is used three times in Psalm 53:5a. Tamar envisions a role reversal that allows her to assume a position of dominance counter to her reality; unfortunately, social relationships based on honor/shame are not challenged.[9]

Tamar is abandoned by all the men in her life: Amnon, who rapes her and then throws her out; Absalom, who tells her to "be quiet for now"; and her father, who does nothing to punish Amnon because he loves him as his firstborn (v. 21). No wonder Tamar quotes the fool in v. 1 of Psalm 53: "there is no God." So it seems to her, as a "desolate" woman with no future; she will remain unmarried and childless. No wonder also that her voice haunts v. 3b: "there is not one who does good, no, not one." The psalmist pleads for deliverance to "come from Zion" (v. 6a), which echoes "there" at the beginning of v. 5. The use of the adverb "there" (שָׁם, *shēm*) may form part of a wordplay or pun with "name" (שֵׁם, *shām*), and the word "Jerusalem" (sometimes shortened to Salem), that "indirectly came to designate Jerusalem" and its deliverance;[10] see "there" in Psalms 46:9; 48:7. Tamar wants deliverance to come from the very place in which she was violated.

The narrative intertext has pulled us into Tamar's story and cultivated our empathy for her. Our encounter with 2 Samuel 13 as Other has

---

9. Amy C. Cottrill, *Language, Power, and Identity in the Lament Psalms of the Individual* (New York and London: T & T Clark, 2008), 92.

10. Raymond J. Tournay, *Seeing and Hearing God with the Psalms: The Prophetic Liturgy of the Second Temple in Jerusalem*, trans. J. Edward Crowley, JSOTSup 118 (Sheffield: Sheffield Academic Press, 1991), 103–5.

allowed for a connection that generates a set of associations for the metaphors of Psalm 53 different from those that have traditionally been put forward. As we "interrupt" the text we critique the links between sexual and political power. Based on these intertextual connections, one can imagine a superscription to Psalm 53 that reads: "A Psalm of Tamar, after her brother Amnon raped her."

Psalm 54

Dual Obligation

Its superscription anchors Psalm 54 firmly in the world of men and politics by referencing 1 Samuel 23:15-29 (esp. v. 19), in which David flees from Saul to the wilderness and is betrayed by the men of Ziph. Psalm 54 follows the structure of an individual lament: petition directed to God (vv. 1-2), complaint (v. 3), confession of trust (vv. 4-5), vow of praise and thanksgiving (vv. 6-7). The urgency of the psalmist's situation is emphasized by four imperatives in the petition: הושיעני, "save me"; תדינני, "vindicate me"; שמע, "hear my prayer"; האזינה, "give ear." The verb ישע ("save, deliver") in v. 1 often refers to military victory and supports the superscription, but the verb דין, translated as "vindicate," most often refers to judging in a legal context in terms of showing someone to be in the right. The speaker appeals to God's "name" and "might" in v. 1. God's name becomes very important in Deuteronomic theology as a quasi-manifestation of God's presence (see Solomon's prayer in 1 Kgs 8:22-53), but here it may simply indicate the essence of God's character: God is "mighty" (v. 1b) and "faithful" (v. 5b).

God's name may also represent God's honor; God must save the psalmist for the sake of God's own honor and reputation.[1] The complaint about the psalmist's enemies in v. 3c, "they do not set God before them," links Psalm 54 with Psalms 52:7 and 53:4 as a definitive statement both

---

1. Philippus J. Botha, "Psalm 54: The Power of Positive Patterning," *SK* 21 (2000): 504–16, at 512.

Psalm 54:1-7

To the leader: with stringed instruments.
A Maskil of David,
when the Ziphites went and told Saul,
"David is in hiding among us."

¹Save me, O God, by your name,
and vindicate me by your might.
²Hear my prayer, O God;
give ear to the words of my
mouth.

³For the insolent have risen
against me,
the ruthless seek my life;
they do not set God before
them.   *Selah*

⁴But surely, God is my helper;
the LORD is the upholder of my
life.
⁵He will repay my enemies for
their evil.
In your faithfulness, put an end
to them.

⁶With a freewill offering I will sacrifice to you;
I will give thanks to your name,
O LORD, for it is good.
⁷For he has delivered me from
every trouble,
and my eye has looked in triumph on my enemies.

of who the enemy is and who the psalmist is not. This verse offers an implicit motivation for God to intervene and save the psalmist by appealing to God's justice. Verse 3c is highlighted by the term *Selah* (indication of a pause) that follows it, as well as by its position as the third line in the only three-part line in the psalm. The NRSV translates "insolent" in v. 3a with several manuscripts, but the MT (= v. 5a) reads זרים ("foreigners," "strangers"), which prompts some interpreters to place Psalm 54 in the postexilic period.

The mood shifts abruptly to a confession of trust in v. 4 introduced by הנה ("but," "surely"), a particle that stresses the following noun, God. "Structurally . . . the affirmation comes in the midst of opposition"; vv. 3 and 5 refer to those opposed to the psalmist, while v. 4 states forcefully "the central theological assertion of the psalm: 'God is my helper' "[2] (Pss 10:14; 22:19). Whereas "the ruthless" were seeking the psalmist's life (v. 3b), God "upholds" it (v. 4b). There is some question in v. 5 as to whether God repays enemies for their evil, as the Qere᾽ reading (what is read) in the margin suggests, or whether the evil itself returns on the enemies (what goes around comes around) according to the Kethib (what is written in the text) in the MT. Either way, the enemies lose.

2. J. Clinton McCann Jr., "The Book of Psalms," in *The New Interpreter's Bible*, vol. 4 (Nashville, TN: Abingdon Press, 1996), 639–1280, at 894.

Verse 6 contains a vow to present a freewill offering and give thanks to God's name, creating a bracket with "your name" in v. 1a. Verse 7 prompts debate about whether the thanksgiving is offered after the deliverance or declared confidently in anticipation of the deliverance that has not yet occurred.

Affirmation in Opposition

Women of African descent live in constant tension between the evils of opposition and the graces of affirmation. Every milestone we reach and every success we achieve is born out of the dynamic and creative tension between opposition and affirmation. The sociological traumas of poverty, economic oppression, sexism, white supremacy, gender inequality, gender violence, and the devastating effects of centuries of colonization are overwhelming. Nevertheless, women of resilient faith know that the affirmation of *their* God is perpetually resurrected within, despite the oppositions they face. This is the affirmation of the psalmist.

Dr. Jeremiah A. Wright preaches prophetically about the presence of human company and holy company, which remind us that we are never alone.[3] This imagery is particularly powerful when seen through the eyes of black women throughout the African diaspora. Like the psalmist, we too lament and bring faithful complaint to God about our enemy's aggression; we rise from the despair of lament to cling resolutely to our human and holy company (v. 6). Our strength and tenacity uphold us and affirm our worth and relevance in the world. In between the oppositions (in vv. 3 and 5), affirmation blooms (v. 4). Nevertheless, we do not just receive the affirmation of human and holy company; we *become* the affirmation of the human and the holy. From Haiti to Harlem, the woman of African descent is the flower that pushes its way through the crack in the pavement to survive.

Lora F. Hargrove

Interpreters often explain the shift in Psalm 54 from petition and lament to confession of trust and vow of praise (see this shift in Pss 22, 56, 59, 61, 69, 71, 109) as response to a favorable oracle of salvation from the priest or cultic prophet; unfortunately, none of these oracles can be found

3. Jeremiah A. Wright, "In Seasons of Distress," a sermon preached at Elmwood Presbyterian Church, East Orange, NJ, September 2013.

in the Psalms. Tony Cartledge argues instead that it is the vow itself that creates the attitude of "trustful confidence" in v. 7. The vow is "based on *dual obligation*": if you deliver me, I will praise you; see Absalom's vow in 2 Samuel 15:8 and Hannah's vow in 1 Samuel 1:11.[4] We might call this "bargaining" but it crops up in human prayer across cultures repeatedly and in the structure of Western liturgies, e.g., when the pastoral prayer (often asking for things) follows the confession of trust. The psalmist believes that God "greatly desires" human praise; after all, "in death there is no remembrance of you; in Sheol who can praise you?" (Ps 6:5; Ps 88:10). Clearly, "without deliverance God will lose the psalmist's praise; the loss is God's."[5] The praise will come only if the psalmist's petition is granted; the psalmist's "certainty of an answer [v. 7] has obscured the underlying conditionality of the promise."[6]

The vow in Psalm 54:6 functions not only to motivate God to act favorably on the psalmist's behalf but also consequently to enhance God's reputation. Scoffers and enemies are watching to see if God saves (Pss 10:13; 79:9, 10), which suggests that the psalmist has "public relations value"[7] because of the praise she offers. Though this concept may prove disturbing to some, it takes seriously the covenantal relationship established at Sinai; there is "a kind of parity assumed in the relationship"[8] between God and the psalmist. The thanks the psalmist will give (ידה, v. 6b) becomes public testimony to deliverance in a worship setting accompanied by a sacrificial offering. The ending of v. 7: "and my eye has looked in triumph on my enemies" reads literally "and upon my enemies my eyes will look." The words "in triumph" in the NRSV are not found in the MT and are not necessary, since the Hebrew suggests a looking down on someone inferior. Not only God's reputation will be upheld, but the psalmist's as well. For the marginalized, the mutual obligations of covenant undergirding Psalm 54 can be empowering. Their praise matters to God. The hope is that it will matter as well to those who wield power.

4. Tony W. Cartledge, "Conditional Vows in the Psalms of Lament: A New Approach to an Old Problem," in *The Listening Heart: Essays in Wisdom and the Psalms in Honor of Roland E. Murphy*, ed. Kenneth G. Hoglund (Sheffield: JSOT Press, 1987), 77–94, at 81.

5. Denise Dombkowski Hopkins, *Journey through the Psalms* (St. Louis, MO: Chalice Press, 2002), 103.

6. Cartledge, "Conditional Vows," 91.

7. Hopkins, *Journey through the Psalms*, 103.

8. Walter Brueggemann, *The Message of the Psalms* (Minneapolis: Augsburg, 1984), 55.

Psalm 55

Prisoner of Disgrace

Several interpreters attempt to link Psalm 55 to 2 Samuel 15:31, in which Ahithophel betrays David during Absalom's revolt. The superscription, however, references David only obliquely: "a maskil [wisdom song put to music?] of [in honor of?] David." Others connect Psalm 55 with Jeremiah, especially 9:1-3 (a desire for escape and a tongue as weapon) and 9:4-8 (betrayal by neighbors and kin; see Jer 20:1-6 and Pashur's jailing of Jeremiah). As Ulrike Bail has shown, however, the metaphors in Psalm 55 can invite different connections. Bail links these metaphors to women's experience of violence, particularly the violence of rape. She argues that these metaphors "open up an imaginative space in which experiences can be located,"[1] allowing "the praying woman" in Psalm 55 to name the violence she has experienced and thus regain her identity. In other words, the spaces opened up by metaphor need not be filled by default with male experiences of war and kingship. We

---

1. Ulrike Bail, " 'O God, Hear My Prayer': Psalm 55 and Violence against Women," in *A Feminist Companion to Wisdom and Psalms*, FCB, 2nd ser., ed. Athalya Brenner and Carol Fontaine (Sheffield: Sheffield Academic Press, 1998), 242–63, at 248.

Psalm 55:1-23

To the leader: with stringed instruments.
A Maskil of David.

¹Give ear to my prayer, O God;
do not hide yourself from my
supplication.
²Attend to me, and answer me;
I am troubled in my complaint.
I am distraught ³by the noise of
the enemy,
because of the clamor of the
wicked.
For they bring trouble upon me,
and in anger they cherish en-
mity against me.
⁴My heart is in anguish within me,
the terrors of death have fallen
upon me.
⁵Fear and trembling come upon me,
and horror overwhelms me.
⁶And I say, "O that I had wings like
a dove!
I would fly away and be at rest;
⁷truly, I would flee far away;

I would lodge in the wilderness;   *Selah*
⁸I would hurry to find a shelter for
myself
from the raging wind and tempest."
⁹Confuse, O LORD, confound their
speech;
for I see violence and strife in
the city.
¹⁰Day and night they go around it
on its walls,
and iniquity and trouble are within it;
¹¹ruin is in its midst;
oppression and fraud
do not depart from its marketplace.

¹²It is not enemies who taunt me—
I could bear that;
it is not adversaries who deal in-
solently with me—
I could hide from them.

must "interrupt"[2] our reading on behalf of women to acknowledge different contexts for interpretation.

The Hebrew of the text is difficult, which has prompted many emen-
dations. The psalm is bracketed by the vocative "O God" in vv. 1 and
23; by two forms of the same verb, מוט ("move," "totter," "stagger"), in
vv. 3 and 22;[3] and by המה, "complain and moan," in vv. 2 and 17. The
enemy causes trouble to "totter" on the psalmist (v. 3), but God "will
never permit the righteous to be moved" (v. 22). The urgency of her
situation is expressed by the psalmist in four petitions in v. 1: האזינה, "give

2. Danna Nolan Fewell, *The Children of Israel: Reading the Bible for the Sake of Our
Children* (Nashville, TN: Abingdon Press, 2003), 32–36, at 33: "As a strategy of reading,
interruption is a way of stopping and questioning the text."

3. For inclusions that begin and end the two sections of the psalm with chiasm (vv.
1-3 / v. 17 and vv. 12-15 / vv. 20-23), see John S. Kselman and Michael L. Barré, "Psalm
55: Problems and Proposals," *CBQ* 60 (1998): 440–62.

¹³But it is you, my equal,
my companion, my familiar
friend,
¹⁴with whom I kept pleasant company;
we walked in the house of God
with the throng.
¹⁵Let death come upon them;
let them go down alive to
Sheol;
for evil is in their homes and in
their hearts.
¹⁶But I call upon God,
and the LORD will save me.
¹⁷Evening and morning and at
noon
I utter my complaint and moan,
and he will hear my voice.
¹⁸He will redeem me unharmed
from the battle that I wage,
for many are arrayed against me.
¹⁹God, who is enthroned from of
old,   *Selah*

will hear, and will humble
them—
because they do not change,
and do not fear God.
²⁰My companion laid hands on a
friend
and violated a covenant with
me
²¹with speech smoother than butter,
but with a heart set on war;
with words that were softer than oil,
but in fact were drawn swords.
²²Cast your burden on the LORD,
and he will sustain you;
he will never permit
the righteous to be moved.

²³But you, O God, will cast them
down
into the lowest pit;
the bloodthirsty and treacherous
shall not live out half their days.
But I will trust in you.

ear"; ואל־תתעלם, "do not hide;" הקשיבה לי, "attend to me"; עֵנני, "answer me." The plea "do not hide" suggests that she is feeling the absence of God in the midst of violence; God's "hiding" is the focus of frequent complaint in the laments (see Pss 13:1; 44:24; 69:17; 88:14; 89:46; 102:2).

Noteworthy is the role played by sound in Psalm 55. The psalmist hears "the noise of the enemy" and "the clamor of the wicked" in v. 3; see the enemy's wounding words in v. 22. The noise overwhelms her—a typical response to trauma—so that she becomes terrified (vv. 4-5). Amy Cottrill notes that the language of the body in the laments "is simultaneously a language of vulnerability, powerlessness, and distress, and also a claim to authority and power."[4] Such body language is found in v. 4; "the praying woman" cries: "my heart is in anguish within me." The

---

4. Amy C. Cottrill, *Language, Power, and Identity in the Lament Psalms of the Individual* (New York: T & T Clark, 2008), 30.

Hebrew translated "anguish" is from the root חיל, "dance, writhe, tremble, be born." Because this root is often associated with the pains of
childbirth (see Pss 51:5; 109:22), these psalm texts "overtly mingle the
language of making through birth and unmaking through pain and
suffering"[5] (see Isa 13:8; Job 15:20). One can add Esther 4:4 and Jeremiah
4:31 to this list. A key difference between the use of this verb in the psalms
and in the prophets, however, is that male prophets use the verb to
emasculate the elite male leadership by couching their punishment in
terms of the pain of childbirth; their writhing and convulsion will bring
not life but the undoing of life. When women use this verb in the Psalms
they acknowledge their vulnerability and suffering, claim their experience, and invite God to intervene and renew life. Thus this verb functions
very differently in different gender contexts.

The "topography of violence"[6] is demarcated in the contrast between
the city and the desert in Psalm 55. In vv. 9b-10 seven personifications
of negative behavior populate the city. The protective watchmen who
make their rounds on the city walls (v. 10a) are replaced by Violence and
Strife, who "surround," "go around," "encircle" (סבב) the city "day and
night," hemming the psalmist in. Bail suggests Genesis 19 and Judges
19 as intertexts since they share this verb in depictions of acts of violence:
the men of Sodom "surround" Lot's house to violate his visitors, and
the men of Gibeah "surround" the house of one who gave shelter to a
Levite and his concubine; the men gang-rape her and she dies. Other
personifications in Psalm 55 include Iniquity, Trouble, and Ruin within
the city (vv. 10b, 11a) and Oppression and Fraud, who persist in the
marketplace. The city is saturated with evil. No wonder "the praying
woman" feels surrounded: "horror overwhelms [Piel of כסה 'cover'] me"
(v. 5b). She is suffocated, much like the Egyptians who were "covered"
by the Reed Sea in Exodus 15:5. This Exodus text also shares other verbs
with Psalm 55: חיל ("tremble," "birth"); רעד ("shake"); and the phrase
"terror and dread fall upon them." The psalmist intentionally uses the
same words that describe the terrified oppressor Egyptians in Exodus
15 in order to contrast herself as different. In this way she both gains
God's sympathy in the midst of the undeserved violence she is experiencing and claims her place within the history of her people, Israel.

5. Ibid.
6. Bail, " 'O God, Hear My Prayer,' " 247.

The city is clearly a place of violence, which contradicts the true function of the city: protection behind its walls. The city no longer offers refuge; there is violence within. Note the repetition of "within" (קרב, "midst," plus the preposition ב, "with") in vv. 4, 11, 15. The desert (מדבר), usually seen as a threatening place of chaos, becomes "counter space" or refuge. "The praying woman" imagines it as a place of escape (vv. 6-8) in which she can find "rest" (v. 6b) and "shelter" (v. 8a), just as Hagar, Moses, David, and Elijah had done. Carleen Mandolfo suggests that this speech about "the relative safety of the 'wilderness', a region notorious in the Hebrew Bible for its dangers, only serves to emphasize the dire straits in which the supplicant finds herself" and should therefore be considered as part of the complaint.[7]

The verbs in vv. 6-8 express movement out of rather than the constriction of the city: אעופה, "I would fly away"; ארחיק, "I would flee"; אחישה, "I would hurry away." Bail notes that no keywords connect vv. 6-8 with the rest of the psalm, reinforcing the sense of contrast between the violent city and this "fictional place" in the desert. In v. 6 the psalmist is "trapped—within the construction of the sentence—by the subjunctive of desire: 'had I wings like a dove.'" The "I" of the psalm becomes a dove (יונה) who, as a substitute, does what the "I" cannot do: escape.[8] The dove, as "the prey of raptors," symbolizes innocence and vulnerability, and transports the psalmist to a place far from the "the house of God," i.e., from the temple in Jerusalem, where she was betrayed by her friend (vv. 13-14).[9] The dove constitutes what Bail calls a "survival strategy" that allows dissociation from the pain of rape and preserves the "I" from disintegration.[10] Mandolfo notes how the chaos of the supplicant's direct prayers to God, including three different approaches to describing the enemy (vv. 3, 9-11, and 12-14), stands in tension with the dialogic discourses in vv. 15, 19, and 22. Against this chaotic backdrop

7. Carleen Mandolfo, *God in the Dock: Dialogic Tension in the Psalms of Lament*, JSOTSup (Sheffield: Sheffield Academic Press, 2002), 78.

8. Ibid., 251. The dove in the flood story of Gen 8 also does something people in the ark cannot do. See also the book of Jonah (יונה, "dove") as a literary response to Ps 55 in Alastair G. Hunter, "Inside Outside Psalm 55: How Jonah Grew Out of a Psalmist's Conceit," *Psalms and Prayers*, OtSt 55 (Leiden: Brill Academic Publishers, 2006), 129–39.

9. William P. Brown, *Seeing the Psalms: A Theology of Metaphor* (Louisville, KY: Westminster John Knox, 2002), 145.

10. Bail, "'O God, Hear My Prayer,'" 262.

"the didactic interjections operate as a balm"[11] with their simplicity of assurances about God.

I suggest that the story of Tamar's rape by her brother Amnon in 2 Samuel 13 can, once again, serve as intertext for Psalm 55 and embody the metaphor of the dove explored by Bail so that the reader may enter into the metaphor experientially and empathetically. Tamar can only flee to her brother Absalom's house (2 Sam 13:20). She cannot escape the city of Jerusalem in which she experienced such violence. Tamar becomes a virtual prisoner of her disgrace, robbed of a future. The narrative describes her as "desolate," removed from society. Instead of a "lodging in the wilderness" that she longs for as refuge in Psalm 55:7, she must bear her disgrace (חרפה) in the midst of the violent city. As Ilse Müllner argues, Absalom takes away Tamar's words by ordering her to "be quiet for now" (2 Sam 13:20). "For Tamar, Absalom's house is not a place of security and restoration, but the place where she silently collapses."[12] The reader can imagine that Tamar recovers her voice in the words of Psalm 55.

Bail's interpretation of Psalm 55 challenges Rolf Jacobson's view that self-quotations in the present, as in vv. 6-8, serve to deemphasize the spontaneous emotions expressed; these emotions are opposed to "faith or the resolution of his [the psalmist's] will" that comes later in the psalm. The quotation inset distinguishes between these symbolic wishes and the literal requests of the rest of the psalm.[13] Herb Levine argues similarly that the psalmist "recants" the "unjustified flight of fancy" in vv. 6-8 because he no longer wishes to emulate what was spoken. His is a dialogue "with an earlier self" who had been wrong.[14] These male interpreters have unintentionally denied the psalmist her survival strategy, her living space. As Katie Cannon has argued, black women have had to "carve out a living space within the intricate web of racism, sexism, and poverty"[15] they experience daily; neither men nor the dominant culture can dictate what that living space should look like.

---

11. Mandolfo, *God in the Dock*, 81.

12. Ilse Müllner, "Books of Samuel: Women at the Center of Israel's Story," trans. Linda M. Maloney, in *Feminist Biblical Interpretation: A Compendium of Critical Commentary*, ed. Luise Schottroff and Marie-Theres Wacker (Grand Rapids, MI: Eerdmans, 2012), 140–52, at 150.

13. Rolf A. Jacobson, *"Many Are Saying": The Function of Direct Discourse in the Hebrew Psalter* (London: T & T Clark, 2004), 72–73.

14. Herbert J. Levine, *Sing unto God a New Song: A Contemporary Reading of the Psalms* (Bloomington: Indiana University Press, 1995), 123, 125.

15. Katie G. Cannon, *Black Womanist Ethics* (Atlanta, GA: Scholars Press, 1988), 7.

Young Black Men and the "Noise of the Enemy"

Nicole Paultre. Lucia McBath. Kadiatou Diallo. Sybrina Fulton. Lesley McSpadden. Esaw Garner. These women are not rape victims, but they have been victims of violence. These are mothers or spouses of black boys and men violently murdered. The stories of their sons/fiancées/husbands captured national attention, and as they lamented, mourned, cried for their loss, a community of people mourned with them. Yet while their hearts were still grieving, their distress was aggravated by the "noise of the enemy." The noise was defined by a nation of people willing to vilify their deceased loved ones. Trouble was heaped on them by the persistent effort of mainstream and social media to portray young black boys and black men as subhuman thugs. In this image of black males Kelly Brown Douglass's definition of "white culture" is sustained: it "promotes the sanctity of whiteness by devaluing that which is non-White."[16]

The metaphors in Psalm 55 give voice to these wailing, praying women to speak to God about the oppression they experience in their grief. This psalmist names the cruelty of an enemy who dehumanizes the innocent bystanders lost in the race war still raging in the United States. But the text also names the ridiculous inhumanity of having to suffer "respectability politics" spewed by certain members of the African American community. The bourgeoisie black media pundits and celebrities who suggest that if these boys had simply "put on a belt" or "turned down their music" they might have had a fighting chance, represent the "companion," the "familiar friend" (vv. 13-14) who heaps insult onto the injury of the perception of black men as an inherently imminent threat and thus justify their murder.

Yolanda Marie Norton

16. Kelly Brown Douglass, *Sexuality and the Black Church: A Womanist Perspective* (Maryknoll, NY: Orbis Books, 1999), 16.

Violence Against Women

Given the statistics gathered by the United Nations group UNITE to End Violence Against Women, language that facilitates the creation of living space for women who have been the victims of violence is needed more than ever. UNITE claims that "according to country data, up to 70 per cent of women experience violence in their lifetime"; the most common form of violence is physical, inflicted by an intimate partner. Other forms of violence include female genital mutilation, dowry murder, honor killing, trafficking in persons, female infanticide, and sexual harassment. Rates of sexual violence are difficult to establish because of the shame and stigma for women and their families that results in "significant underreporting." UNITE reports that "women aged 15–44 are more at risk from rape and domestic violence than from cancer, car accidents, war and malaria, according to World Bank data."[17] Rape continues to be employed as a tactic of war throughout the world in every war zone. This violence is not confined to a specific culture, country, or group in society.

Denise Dombkowski Hopkins

The pain of the psalmist's betrayal is underscored by multiple words describing the betrayer in v. 13: אנוש כערכי, "my equal"; אלופי, "my companion"; מידעי, "my familiar friend." "But you" (ואתה) at the beginning of v. 13 uses an adversative ו ("but") with the independent personal pronoun to contrast former intimacy with the betrayed present; it is countered by the same word, ואתה, "but you," referring to God, in v. 23. The contrast emphasizes the difference between an untrustworthy friend and the psalmist's dependable God. The use of the pronoun "you" supports Gerald Sheppard's[18] view that the psalmist complains in the hearing of both God and the worshiping community, within which the enemy is also present. This allows her to publicly expose the enemy with some protection, gain some relief, and perhaps generate a change in the enemy's behavior.

17. www.un.org/en/women/endviolence/pdf/pressmaterials/unite_the _situation_en.pdf; accessed May 1, 2014.

18. Gerald T. Sheppard, " 'Enemies' and the Politics of Prayer in the Book of Psalms," in *The Bible and the Politics of Exegesis*, ed. David Jobling, Peggy Day, and Gerald Sheppard (Cleveland, OH: Pilgrim Press, 1991), 61–82, at 75.

Psychic Contamination

The psalmist here laments a friendship gone wrong. Having trusted one with whom he walked in the house of God, he now finds himself deceived, estranged, and scorned, not from an enemy outside but from one within, a comrade and companion. We can hear this from an individual or from a collective perspective. Eric Neumann, a Jungian analyst, describes psychic contamination as the result of unconscious shadow projection at an individual and collective level.[19] Our own shadow, what we judge and condemn in ourselves yet of which we have little conscious understanding and which we have not yet owned, contaminates our understanding of self and other. The shadow becomes what we thrust on others and then feel obligated and vindicated to judge, condemn, and even kill off. Oh, how we would much rather "fly away and lodge ourselves into the wilderness" than face the turmoil around us and within us caused by those in our own communities and those whom our communities, whom we ourselves, have othered and called enemies! As the psalmist says, "it is not the enemy who taunts but one of my own kind."

I hear this through Carl Jung's articulation of the shadow and Neumann's understanding of psychic contamination. When we do not own our own shadow we project or throw it on others who are easier to hate, rather than see what we are ashamed of or hate within ourselves. When we become conscious of these aspects of our own shadow our heart may feel anguish within us, fear and trembling may come upon us, horror may overwhelm us. We can read this as the ways in which we feel betrayed by these other aspects of ourselves, our shadow aspects, when they start to make their way into consciousness. These other aspects feel intrusive and deceptive, challenging all that we have known and according to which we have lived. Suddenly we find ourselves unsure of what is certain, unfamiliar with how to move

---

19. "In the economy of the psyche, the outcast role of the alien is immensely important as an object for the projection of the shadow. The shadow—that part of our personality which is 'alien' to the ego, our own unconscious counter-position, which is subversive of our conscious attitude and security—can be exteriorized and subsequently destroyed. The fight against heretics, political opponents and national enemies is actually the fight against our own religious doubts, the insecurity of our own political position, and the one-sidedness of our own national viewpoint" (Erich Neumann, *Depth Psychology and a New Ethic*, trans. Eugene Rolfe [Boston and London: Shambhala, 1990], 52).

forward, how now to live. When we acknowledge, reconcile, and own these aspects of our shadow we can lessen the possibility of psychic contamination and projection upon individuals and entire groups of people. Taking back these projections will enable us to live with others who are different from us, who may even live contrary to our values, and help us to see them as others in their own right rather than as enemies to be annihilated.

Tiffany Houck-Loomis

The betrayer is one of "many who are arrayed against me" (v. 18b) who "do not change and do not fear God" (v. 19b); this definition links Psalm 55 to Psalms 52:7a; 53:4c; 54:3c. The words of the antagonists are "smooth" and "soft" but cut like "drawn swords" (v. 21). Given this military imagery, Cottrill argues that v. 21 shows that the enemy and the psalmist are "embattled warriors, fighting verbally for social dominance" within a framework of honor/shame that defines reputations and social worth. In fact, the psalmist even refers to "the battle that I wage" in v. 18. This means that the psalmist is not just a powerless victim; she engages the enemy who uses words like weapons on "a rhetorical battlefield."[20] Her "verbally aggressive language" reflects "a rhetorical position of empowerment."[21] This aggression emerges in the petition in v. 15 and the declaration in v. 23 that God will put an end to the enemies. They will "go down alive to Sheol" (v. 15b) and "not live out half their days" (v. 23b); that is, they will die in the prime of life. Problematic, however, is that a military mind-set of violence usually leads to conquered cities and raped women. With Audre Lorde one wonders if the master's house can be dismantled by using the master's tools.[22] Given this context of rhetorical swordplay, it makes sense that v. 22 is not an oracle of salvation as most interpreters claim, or a pep talk of self-encouragement; rather, it is the taunting speech of the enemy (Pss 22:8; 42:3, 10).[23]

20. Cottrill, *Language, Power, and Identity*, 80, 88.

21. Ibid., 89.

22. Audre Lorde, "The Master's Tools Will Never Dismantle the Master's House," in *Sister Outsider: Essays and Speeches* (Berkeley, CA: Crossing Press, 2007), 110–14.

23. Contra Mandolfo, *God in the Dock*, 78–82, and at 81, who notes how the chaos of the supplicant's direct prayers to God, including three different approaches to describing the enemy (vv. 3, 9-11, and 12-14), stands in tension with the dialogic discourses in vv. 15, 19, and 22. Against this chaotic backdrop, "the didactic interjections operate as a balm" with their simplicity of assurances about God.

Psalm 56

A Voice for Muted Women

The superscription for Psalm 56 connects us to Psalm 55 with the use of the word "dove": "according to The Dove on Far-off Terebinths." Most interpreters consider this to be the name of a melody accompanying the psalm. The Septuagint and Targums, however, translate the phrase "for the people removed far from the sanctuary." "Dove" (יונה, see Ps 55:6) becomes a symbol for Israel in exile, especially in conjunction with the psalmist's petition in v. 7 to "cast down the peoples." This leads some to suggest that the "I" represents the king speaking for the people in exile, adapting an individual lament for communal use. The superscription, however, links Psalm 56 directly to David: "when the Philistines seized him in Gath" (1 Sam 21:10-15). After the opening petition, Psalm 56 moves immediately to describe the enemies, using military language like "fight against" (v. 2), which could support the link to David if taken historically.

Taken metaphorically, however, Psalm 56 can be used in multiple contexts, including those of economic and social oppression. The enemies oppress (v. 1), trample (twice), fight against (v. 2), stir up strife, lurk, and watch (v. 7). They are relentless, as expressed by "all day long" in vv. 1, 2, and 5. In v. 6b they "hoped to have my life"; this phrase uses the verb קוה ("wait," "expect," "hope"); this verb is normally used for those who "wait for" or "hope in" God (Pss 25:3, 5, 21; 27:14; 37:34; 40:1; 52:9). The

Psalm 56:1-13

To the leader: according to The Dove
on Far-off Terebinths. Of David.
A Miktam, when the Philistines
seized him in Gath.

[1]Be gracious to me, O God, for
people trample on me;
all day long foes oppress me;
[2]my enemies trample on me all
day long,
for many fight against me.
O Most High, [3]when I am afraid,
I put my trust in you.

[4]In God, whose word I praise,
in God I trust; I am not afraid;
what can flesh do to me?

[5]All day long they seek to injure
my cause;
all their thoughts are against
me for evil.
[6]They stir up strife, they lurk,
they watch my steps.
As they hoped to have my life,
[7]so repay them for their
crime;

contrast serves to define the enemies over against the psalmist, who by implication is hoping in God. The primary purpose of the caricatured enemy "is to establish the worthy social identity of the psalmist."[1] God must deliver the worthy psalmist, not in the abstract, but through violent acts that dominate the hostile other. Consequently, the psalmist petitions God in v. 7 to put things right: "repay them . . . in wrath cast down the peoples." As Brian Doyle argues, the primary metaphor of God as absent/present unites the "small Psalter" comprised of Psalms 52–64: "The presence of God is revealed to the psalmist in the enemy's downfall."[2] This is problematic for women and children caught in the cycle of retributive violence.

As an individual lament, Psalm 56 exhibits "the fundamental basis of all the prayers for help: God is for me."[3] The psalmist's trust in God's desire and ability to deliver is highlighted by that very declaration in v. 9b and by the refrain in vv. 4 and 10-11 in which trust and fear are

1. Amy C. Cottrill, *Language, Power, and Identity in the Lament Psalms of the Individual* (New York: T & T Clark, 2008), 64.

2. Brian Doyle, "Where Is God When You Need Him Most? The Divine Metaphor of Absence and Presence as a Binding Element in the Composition of the Book of Psalms," in *The Composition of the Book of Psalms*, ed. Erich Zenger (Leuven: Peeters, 2010), 377–90, at 383.

3. Patrick D. Miller, *They Cried to the Lord: The Form and Theology of Biblical Prayer* (Minneapolis: Fortress Press, 1994), 128.

in wrath cast down the
peoples, O God!

⁸You have kept count of my tossings;
put my tears in your bottle.
Are they not in your record?
⁹Then my enemies will retreat
in the day when I call.
This I know, that God is for me.
¹⁰In God, whose word I praise,
in the LORD, whose word I
praise,

¹¹in God I trust; I am not afraid.
What can a mere mortal do to
me?

¹²My vows to you I must perform,
O God;
I will render thank offerings to
you.
¹³For you have delivered my soul
from death,
and my feet from falling,
so that I may walk before God
in the light of life.

juxtaposed: "in God I trust; I am not afraid." This refrain of trust anchors each of the two major parts of Psalm 56: vv. 1-7 and 8-13. Enemies
and petitions bracket the first section but recede into the background
in the second, which ends with a vow of thanksgiving (Pss 22:23-32;
32:6-11; 40:10-11; 51:15-17; 116:17-19) based on the certainty of
deliverance.

The contrast between the saving God and the merely mortal enemies
is highlighted in vv. 1, 4, and 11 by the use of three different terms for a
human being. The singular noun אנוש (v. 1), translated as the collective
"people" in NRSV, means "mortal"; the word בשר (v. 4) means literally
"flesh" or what is transitory, and the word אדם (v. 11) means a human
being (this word is repeatedly used to refer to Ezekiel in contrast to the
transcendent God). These three terms emphasize human dependence
and weakness compared to God's power (see 2 Chr 32:8). This language
can give hope to the marginalized that oppressors will be called to
account.

The psalmist opens Psalm 56 with a petition in v. 1: "be gracious to
me" (חנן, better translated "grace me"; cp. Pss 51:1; 57:1). For the psalmist,
"graced" is no abstract idea but rather means being able to "walk before
God in the light of life" (v. 13; cp. Ps 116:9). The psalmist wants to be in
God's presence on the right path in life, but her enemies "watch [her]
steps" (v. 6), waiting for the psalmist to stumble or fall so that she can
be pounced upon (cp. Pss 9:15; 25:15) and knocked off course. God's
"light" guides the psalmist on the path (Pss 43:3; 119:105) so that she

may flourish (Pss 13:3; 36:9; 38:10; 42:4). It is v. 8 that undergirds the psalmist's anticipation of walking before God: "you have kept count of my tossings" ("wanderings" is a better translation). In other words, God has noticed the psalmist. This assertion is emphasized by the wordplay between "my tossings/wanderings" (נֹדִי, *nōdî*) and "your bottle" (נֹאדֶךָ, *nōdekā*) in which the psalmist's tears are stored, as well as by the wordplay between "kept count" (סָפַרְתָּה, *sāpartāh*) and "record" (סִפְרָתֶךָ, "book," *siprātekā*). God's "book" or "record" is found also in Exodus 32:32; Malachi 3:16; Job 19:23; it is common in rabbinic tradition, especially in connection with Rosh Ha-Shanah (the New Year), when God sits in judgment and decides in which of three books each person will be inscribed for the coming year—of the righteous, the wicked, or balanced good and bad deeds. The "bottle" is actually a flask of animal skin that stores wine and milk, especially when traveling (Josh 9:4, 12-13; 1 Sam 16:20). In Psalm 56 it stores the psalmist's tears as part of God's record; her complaint has been filed and registered during her "wanderings" so that God can respond. William Brown points to the implication of these metaphors: "To record the psalmist's complaint, God must drink . . . the psalmist's tears!" Introducing the action by the emphatic imperative "put" (שִׂמָה), "the psalmist 'force-feeds' God with his tears."[4]

David Bosworth makes a case for weeping and tears as part of a range of behaviors that intensify interpersonal bonds. "Crying is part of a system of biologically based, inborn attachment behaviors that helps to establish and maintain the parent-child bond"[5] and other relationships past infancy. Crying functions in the laments to intensify the petitions and gain God's sympathy (Ps 39:12). Yet this motif is not common in the psalms; weeping appears in only nine of sixty-two petition psalms (14 percent). Sometimes the effect of tears can boomerang and provoke anger rather than pity (Ps 69:11), so perhaps the psalmists did not want to "overuse the motif lest it lose its power."[6] Ironically, this speculation about overuse may be shaped by societal norms of control and power that consider tears to be "feminine" signs of weakness.

---

4. William P. Brown, *Seeing the Psalms: A Theology of Metaphor* (Louisville, KY: Westminster John Knox, 2002), 119.

5. David A. Bosworth, "Weeping in the Psalms," *VT* 62 (2013): 36–46, at 37.

6. Ibid., 46.

"Tears Inscribed on God's Scroll": A Perspective from a Korean Woman

The psalmist's lament in Psalm 56 could be reread from the perspectives of Korean women—past and present—who, in the face of enduring social, gender, and/or economic oppression and discrimination sought alternatives of resistance through social movements, religious activities, and political actions rather than violence. The psalmist does not wallow in raw emotions of anger, sadness, and resentment but rather cries out for help from God, as an alternative truth who "is for me" (v. 9), and even praises God, regardless of whether the psalmist has experienced salvation (vv. 2 and 9). Note especially that the psalmist's laments in vv. 1-2 and 5-7 are each time followed by her praise of the *word* of God (and her assurance of deliverance) in vv. 3-4 and 10-11, even though enemies attempt to abuse her *words* (דבר, v. 5). The psalmist requests that her tears be inscribed on God's "scroll" (v. 8), so that God's *words* will testify to the psalmist's grief, hope, and praise.

When the psalmist cries out of the bitterness caused by the enemies' words and actions and requests that God "cast [them] down" (v. 7), she is fighting for her life and contending for freedom, independence, and equality, rather than asking for dominance over the enemy. The psalmist's demand that God collect her tears in a bottle (v. 8) forms part of her petition for deliverance—not for social, economic, or political power to overwhelm her enemies, but for life over death: "you have delivered my soul from *death* . . . so that I may walk before God in the light of *life*" (v. 13). For the women *and* men who suffer daily from the reality of inequality, opposition, and injustice, the psalmist displays the power that can overcome present situations of oppression and violence and change the future more actively and completely—the "power" of weeping with/in the word of God that is consistently accompanied by the praising of God's word, and thus will be lastingly inscribed on God's scroll.

Su Jung Shin

Interestingly, my search for women who cry/weep (בכה) in Tanakh surfaced only Hagar (Gen 21:16), Hannah (1 Sam 1:7, 8, 10), and Jephthah's daughter (Judg 11:37-38), though this last example may be a cult legend; Jerusalem personified weeps in Lamentations, and the crying Rachel serves as a metaphor for the exiles in Jeremiah 31:15. Men cry much more frequently: for example, Abraham (Gen 23:2), Jacob (Gen

29:11), Jacob and Esau (Gen 33:4), Hezekiah (2 Kgs 20:5), David (2 Sam 18:33; 19:1), David and his men (2 Sam 1:11-12), Jeremiah/God (Jer 9:1). True, some women functioned as professional mourners or keeners who led families and communities in funerary processions (2 Sam 1:24; Jer 9:17-20; Ezek 32:16) or in ritual acts of weeping in popular religion (Ezek 8:14 for Tammuz), but women who lament their own situations are few.

Perhaps this situation is connected to what Fokkelien Van Dijk-Hemmes terms the practice of "muting" women's songs and emotions. Jephthah's daughter, for example, comes out to meet her victorious father "with timbrels and dances" (Judg 11:34a), but we do not hear the words of her song; the narrator overrides them with a comment about her being Jephthah's only daughter (v. 34b) in order to emphasize the bitterness of her coming death for her father. In Exodus 15 "the song of Miriam and the women was shouted down by that of Moses and the Sons of Israel."[7] Psalm 56 gives muted women a voice, hearing them into speech,[8] accepting their tears and their praises (vv. 4, 10). Psalm 56 can help Korean women to dissolve the "lump" in their spirits and bodies called *han* that is formed by unexpressed anger and resentment of their social powerlessness.[9] These women have earned their tears and can resist having them wiped away too quickly (Rev 21:4). Instead, God carefully counts each tear and records them in God's book.

---

7. Athalya Brenner and Fokkelien Van Dijk-Hemmes, *On Gendering Texts: Female and Male Voices in the Hebrew Bible* (Leiden: Brill, 1993), 40.

8. Nelle Morton, *The Journey Is Home* (Boston: Beacon Press, 1985), 127–28.

9. Chung Hyun Kyung, *Struggle to Be the Sun Again* (Maryknoll, NY: Orbis Books, 1990), 36–52.

Psalm 57

God as Mother Bird

Psalms 56 and 57 share the same poignant opening line: "Be gracious [חנן] to me, O God," though the NRSV unfortunately translates the Hebrew with two different English words. The translation "grace me" better conveys the psalmist's heartfelt petition in both, since to be "graced" by God is not an abstract idea but rather the ability to give public testimony of praise and thanks to God "among the nations" (v. 9; cp. Ps 56:12, 13b). Also, because both psalms are individual laments that petition God to intervene by punishing the wicked (56:7) or shaming them (57:3) in order to relieve the psalmist's suffering, "graced" also means experiencing retributive deliverance from oppressive enemies.

The shaming (חרף) of the enemy in the Psalms does not seem to be tied to gender identity within an honor/shame framework as it is in the prophets and narrative texts. In those texts the marriage metaphor casts a woman as God's unfaithful spouse, Israel, who brings shame upon her aggrieved husband. In the Psalms, shaming is rooted instead in the patron-client relationship in which "the ideas of reciprocity and solidarity stand as foundational concepts."[1] Consequently, verse 3 (see also

---

1. W. Dennis Tucker Jr., "Is Shame a Matter of Patronage in the Communal Laments?," *JSOT* 31 (2007): 465–80, at 474. I argue that Tucker's argument about shame in the communal laments can be applied to individual laments as well.

Psalm 57:1-11

To the leader: Do Not Destroy.
Of David. A Miktam, when he fled
from Saul, in the cave.

[1]Be merciful to me, O God, be
merciful to me,
for in you my soul takes refuge;
in the shadow of your wings I will
take refuge,
until the destroying storms
pass by.
[2]I cry to God Most High,
to God who fulfills his purpose
for me.

[3]He will send from heaven and
save me,
he will put to shame those who
trample on me.   *Selah*
God will send forth his steadfast
love and his faithfulness.

[4]I lie down among lions
that greedily devour human prey;
their teeth are spears and arrows,
their tongues sharp swords.

[5]Be exalted, O God, above the
heavens.

v. 10) speaks of God sending forth "steadfast love" (חסד) and "faithful-ness" (אמת) as personified agents of God's deliverance of the psalmist; these two terms are often paired (Pss 25:10; 40:10-11; 61:7; 85:10; 89:14; 115:1; 138:2). As Katharine Doob Sakenfeld defines it, חסד "is action per-formed in accordance with and because of one's relationship to another."[2] Along with "trust" (בטח, see Pss 52:8; 55:23; 56:3, 11), these terms suggest reciprocity and solidarity in the relationship between God and the psalm-ist and/or community.

The psalmist's petition to God to "shame those who trample on me" (v. 3) suggests that both the psalmist and the God with whom she or he seeks refuge (v. 1) are being shamed by the enemy. God needs to restore honor for both the psalmist and God by upholding God's obli-gation to protect the psalmist. The structure of v. 3 reinforces this expectation. The enemies in 3b are enveloped by two lines that both begin with "God will send" in 3a and 3c. The self-encouragement in v. 8a also supports the reciprocity of God and psalmist: "Awake, my soul." In Hebrew, "my soul" is כבודי, literally "my glory," which plays on כבודך, "your glory," referring to God in vv. 5 and 11. Thus "the psalmist is a reflection of God's glory."[3] When the psalmist's glory is

---

2. Katharine Doob Sakenfeld, *The Meaning of Ḥesed in the Hebrew Bible*, HSM 17 (Missoula, MT: Scholars Press, 1978), 217.

3. Konrad Schaefer, *Psalms*, Berit Olam (Collegeville, MN: Liturgical Press, 2001), 142.

Let your glory be over all the
earth.
⁶They set a net for my steps;
my soul was bowed down.
They dug a pit in my path,
but they have fallen into it
themselves.   *Selah*
⁷My heart is steadfast, O God,
my heart is steadfast.
I will sing and make melody.
⁸Awake, my soul!
Awake, O harp and lyre!
I will awake the dawn.

⁹I will give thanks to you, O LORD,
among the peoples;
I will sing praises to you
among the nations.
¹⁰For your steadfast love is as
high as the heavens;
your faithfulness extends to
the clouds.

¹¹Be exalted, O God, above the
heavens.
Let your glory be over all the
earth.

tarnished or muted, so is God's because of their solidarity in the covenant relationship.

Unfortunately, the language about the cosmic God in Psalm 57 illustrates Brian Wren's KINGAFAP God of English hymnody: King-God-Almighty-Father-Protector who is transcendent, powerful, and in control,[4] and who reinforces male dominance of women in society. God is addressed as cosmic sovereign in v. 2: "Most High" (*El Elyon*). This epithet expresses the expectation that God, who first established order, will continue to maintain order, both cosmic and social. This proclamation about God's sovereignty invites the reader to consider what social order is being legitimated and for whose benefit. In v. 10 God's חסד is proclaimed to be "as high as the heavens" and God's אמת "extends to the clouds." The word "heavens" appears four times, in vv. 3, 5, 10, and 11. Also, the refrain in vv. 5 and 11 urges God to "be exalted" above the heavens and let the divine glory "be over all the earth" in a mighty theophany (Ps 50:1-3). Several interpreters have noted the intersections of this view with the Lord's Prayer: "Your will be done on earth as in heaven."

God as cosmic sovereign is not the only God image in Psalm 57. This psalm also shares with five others a mention of God's wings (v. 1c): Psalms 17, 36, 57, 61, 63, and 91. The wing metaphor introduces the possibility

4. Brian Wren, *What Language Shall I Borrow? God-Talk in Worship; A Male Response to Feminist Theology* (New York: Crossroad, 1989).

of experiencing God through the female imagery of a tender mother bird. Jesus uses just such an image in Matthew 23:37 in his lament over Jerusalem: "How often have I desired to gather your children together as a hen gathers her brood under her wings, and you were not willing!" Joel LeMon[5] notes the various ways in which God's wings have been interpreted in the Psalms: (1) as an image from nature of a mother bird, developed in Exodus 19:4 and Deuteronomy 32:10-12 in connection with the eagle; (2) as the winged sun disk; (3) as a general symbol for divine protection rooted in Egyptian symbolism; (4) as protecting mother goddesses found in eighth-century Samaritan ivories, highlighting the uniquely feminine aspects of God; and (5) as the winged cherubim of the temple and specifically of the ark throne in Jerusalem, rooted in traditions of theophany (e.g., Isa 6:1-3). LeMon argues that "God's supreme location—over the heaven and the earth—finds iconographic congruency . . . in the image of the winged sun disk in Syro-Palestinian art,"[6] an image that echoes representations of Mesopotamian and Egyptian solar deities. Often this art shows a personified pair of attendants (see Ps 57:3c) with the sun disk in a morning theophany (v. 8: "I will awake the dawn").

This winged deity fights for the psalmist against his or her foes, who are described as lions and hunters (57:4, 6). The winged deity fighting lions is common in ancient Near Eastern art and can be seen in Psalms 17 and 63. Images of a bird protecting its young do not appear in Syro-Palestinian art in the biblical period, but pervasive are images of the Horus falcon protecting the king. LeMon's "pictorial theology" warns against "the dangers of facile comparisons"[7] that are not supported by each psalm. Perhaps this means that the way in which the metaphor "mother bird" is understood must be modified to hold in tension aspects of "mother" as soft and as fiercely protective. As Silvia Schroer has argued, these wings can represent the protecting, regenerating wings of the goose vulture associated with goddesses in the ancient Near East. Israel's God has taken over this "motherliness."[8]

5. Joel M. LeMon, *Yahweh's Winged Form in the Psalms: Exploring Congruent Iconography and Texts* (Fribourg: Academic Press; Göttingen: Vandenhoeck & Ruprecht, 2010).

6. Ibid., 137.

7. Ibid., 193–94.

8. Silvia Schroer, " 'Under the Shadow of Your Wings': The Metaphor of God's Wings in the Psalms, Exodus 19.4, Deuteronomy 32.11 and Malachi 3.20, as Seen Through the Perspectives of Feminism and the History of Religion," in *Wisdom and Psalms*, FCB, 2nd ser., ed. Athalya Brenner and Carole Fontaine (Sheffield: Sheffield Academic Press, 1998), 264–82.

A Strong, Feminine God

Psalm 57 refers to God as both a nurturing mother hen (v. 1b) and a cosmic sovereign ruling over heaven and earth (vv. 2-3). Although the English pronoun "he" makes it seem as though the cosmic mighty God (vv. 2-3) is gendered male, Joel LeMon's observation about the "iconographic congruency" of the image of the winged sun disk permits a wider definition of femininity, to include cosmic reign. The psalm allows the reader to imagine a powerful feminine God with roles well beyond stereotypical childrearing or nurturing tasks.

In fact, women of the ancient world may have had more complex social roles than our preconceived, stereotyped images have allowed. Carol Meyers argues persuasively that ancient women were not slaves to a patriarchal machine but played significant roles in shaping their society. They performed important household maintenance tasks that served essential economic, social, and political functions and accorded them the prestige of skilled household managers. "This anthropological perspective of the gender dynamics implicit in women's maintenance activities," Meyers says, "suggests that Everywoman Eve was no less powerful than her partner, and perhaps more so in some ways."[9]

The psalm offers a feminine image of God who both reigns supreme and offers tender care, and both images find iconographic expression in the ancient world. Moreover, there is evidence that ancient women had a good deal of influence and power. If the image of a strong, feminine God seems incongruent, perhaps the problem is modern, not ancient.

Amy Beth Jones

The enemies from whom the psalmist seeks refuge in the shadow of God's wings are described with a combination of leonine and military imagery (vv. 4, 6). The refrain in v. 5 interrupts the description of enemies and functions not simply as a hymn of praise but as an urgent plea for God to intervene: "Be exalted!" God must show God's power as cosmic sovereign against enemies who are often likened to vicious wild animals, most frequently lions. This description of enemies means to gain sympathy from God for the vulnerable psalmist (see Pss 7:2; 10:9; 17:12; 22:13, 21; 35:17). Military similes in v. 4b describe the lions' teeth as weapons

9. Carol Meyers, *Rediscovering Eve: Ancient Israelite Women in Context* (New York: Oxford University Press, 2013), 187.

to convey the "discursive abuse,"[10] probably slander and false accusation, that the psalmist suffers. The enemies' teeth are "spears and arrows," and their tongues are "sharp swords." The metaphor shifts in v. 6 to the psalmist as prey being pursued by hunters who spread a net and dig a pit in the psalmist's path. In a stroke of retributive justice, the hunters fall into the pit themselves (see Prov 1:18-19; 26:27; 28:10; Eccl 10:8; Ps 141:10) and the mood of the psalm shifts. Immediately the psalmist declares that her heart is "steadfast" (v. 7a); after this declaration, praise and a vow of thanksgiving follow. The word pair in v. 3c is repeated in v. 10 as the reason for giving thanks. This suggests that the refrain in v. 11 expresses more confidence than in v. 5, showing movement within the psalm.

The psalmist declares that she will "awake the dawn" with harp and lyre (v. 8). Interpreters immediately link this phrase to David, who played the lyre for Saul (1 Sam 16:23); compare this to the superscription that ties Psalm 57 to "when David fled from Saul, in the cave" (1 Sam 24; 26). As Theodore Burgh points out, however, we cannot assume that men played most musical instruments and that women were only frame drummers and singers, since the sex and gender of musicians in writings and iconography are "often ambiguous."[11] Again, interpreters must not slip into default readings of texts without stopping to question what is actually known. The threefold repetition of "awake" in v. 8, in connection with the word "dawn," suggests a new future for the psalmist.

Some interpreters note that "dawn" may refer to one of a pair of beneficent Canaanite deities (Dawn and Dusk) connected with fertility of land and people. Building on this allusion, 1 Samuel 1, the story of Hannah's prayer for a son, emerges as intertext. In Psalm 57:2 the psalmist cries "to God who fulfills his purpose for me." The verb is גמר, which means "to complete or finish [something]." One thinks of Hannah in 1 Samuel 1 and all of the barren foremothers whose "completion" resided in bearing children according to the norms of the ancient world. Women petitioned God for children since it was God who provided them; 1 Samuel 1:5 and 6 note that the Lord had closed Hannah's womb (cp. Rachel and Leah in Gen 29:14–30:24). Hannah endured the taunts of Elkanah's other wife, Peninnah, who had several sons and daughters: "Her rival

---

10. William P. Brown, *Seeing the Psalms: A Theology of Metaphor* (Louisville, KY: Westminster John Knox, 2002), 138.

11. Theodore W. Burgh, *Listening to the Artifacts: Music Culture in Ancient Palestine* (New York: T & T Clark, 2006), 44.

used to provoke her severely, to irritate her" (1 Sam 1:6). This went on every year during the pilgrimage to Shiloh and resulted in Hannah's weeping and refusal to eat (1 Sam 1:7).

One can understand Peninnah's words and their effect on Hannah in terms of the language of Psalm 57:4, 6. Peninnah's weapon-words wounded Hannah; Peninnah set a trap for this wounding every year at Shiloh when Hannah went to the Lord's house to pray. Peninnah falls into her own pit when Hannah, the favorite wife of Elkanah (see Hannah's "double portion" in 1 Sam 1:5), gives birth to Samuel. Unfortunately, "the motif of female rivalry is intertwined with the motif of motherhood" in Hannah's story and functions "in the service of biblical sexual politics" that makes sisterhood difficult.[12] Another link is suggested by the psalmist's vow to give thanks and praise among the "peoples" and "nations" (57:9); this broad context resonates with Hannah's song in 1 Samuel 2, which is a national thanksgiving that refers to God as Creator and judge of "the ends of the earth." Thus we can imagine a superscription for Psalm 57 that links to Hannah's story: "A *maskil* when Hannah prayed for a son at the Shiloh sanctuary."

12. Esther Fuchs, "The Literary Characterization of Mothers and Sexual Politics in the Hebrew Bible," in *Women in the Hebrew Bible: A Reader*, ed. Alice Bach (New York: Routledge: 1999), 127–40, at 136.

Psalm 58

Broken Women's Bodies and the Health of Community

The intense, violent language of this imprecatory psalm reaches hyperbolic heights. It begins with a sarcastic and cynical pair of rhetorical questions (cp. Ps 52:1). These are directed not to God but rather to the אלם, a word that has generated much debate. NRSV translates "you gods," perhaps referencing the lesser gods assigned to different peoples and earthly tasks (Deut 32:8-9; Ps 82; Job 1:6; Exod 1:11); "mighty lords" is suggested in a footnote. NIV translates "you rulers," echoing the "mighty one" in Psalm 52:1. A third interpretation comes from the literal meaning of אלם—"muteness"— taken as an abstract collective noun, "mute ones." It is likely that the word functions in "a deliberately ambiguous way."[1] Whether those addressed are lesser gods or human leaders, they fail to decree what is right, judge fairly, or speak up at all on behalf of the oppressed, who by contrast are called בני אדם (v. 1b, literally "sons of adam"), merely "humans."

The expected negative answer to the initial rhetorical questions is introduced by the particle אף at the beginning of v. 2, which expresses

---

1. John Kselman and Michael Barré, "A Note on *'elem* in Psalm LVIII 2," *VT* 54 (2004): 400–402, at 400.

Psalm 58:1-11

To the leader: Do Not Destroy.
Of David. A Miktam.

¹Do you indeed decree what is
right, you gods?
Do you judge people fairly?
²No, in your hearts you devise
wrongs;
your hands deal out violence
on earth.

³The wicked go astray from the
womb;

they err from their birth, speaking lies.
⁴They have venom like the venom
of a serpent,
like the deaf adder that stops
its ear,
⁵so that it does not hear the voice
of charmers
or of the cunning enchanter.

⁶O God, break the teeth in their
mouths;

emphasis or contrast—"surely." Unfortunately, most translations ignore it. These abusively powerful ones "devise wrongs" in their hearts (cp. Mic 2:1) and carry them out with their hands; they are "all in" when it comes to violence. In fact, their wickedness is congenital (v. 3): "from the womb." As is common in the laments, the antagonists in Ps 58 are personified as vicious animals: snakes (vv. 4-5) and lions (v. 6). These verses focus on the mouths of the animals—their teeth and fangs—which are deadly (cp. Pss 52:2-4; 55:21; 57:4), and connect with the speaking (דבר) of lies in v. 3b and unjust decrees in v. 1a. These snakes cannot be charmed because they are deaf to the charmer's voice; they cannot be curbed by human means. Only God can stop them.

The violent curses in vv. 6-9 take the form of imperatives directed to God to "break" and "tear out" the teeth and fangs of the wicked (v. 6), as well as jussives—"let them be . . ." (vv. 7-9). The psalmist wants God to make the wicked disappear like snails dissolving into slime (when sprinkled with salt, a gardener's trick), or a miscarriage, or water that vanishes. Many believers are shocked by the violence of this language and point to Jesus' instruction to "love your enemies" (Luke 6:27-31; Matt 5:43-46; Mark 12:28-34; see also Deut 6:4-5; Lev 19:17-18). Since this is a communal lament, it is not about personal vengeance but about systemic justice and putting things right. These enemies are more than human. They represent all that is opposed to *shalōm* and order in God's world. "The violence of the enemy language in laments also emerges out of the this-worldly focus of the Hebrew Bible. . . . Injustices had to be put right here and now in this life" since there was no thought of life

tear out the fangs of the young lions, O LORD!
⁷Let them vanish like water that runs away;
like grass let them be trodden down and wither.
⁸Let them be like the snail that dissolves into slime;
like the untimely birth that never sees the sun.
⁹Sooner than your pots can feel the heat of thorns,

whether green or ablaze, may he sweep them away!

¹⁰The righteous will rejoice when they see vengeance done;
they will bathe their feet in the blood of the wicked.
¹¹People will say, "Surely there is a reward for the righteous;
surely there is a God who judges on earth."

after death in any meaningful sense until the second century BCE onward.[2] This urgency regarding injustice can correct what Roland Murphy called "an exaggerated eschatologism which fails to meet squarely the realities of this life."[3] Repeated words forming brackets support this view. The wicked "deal out violence on *earth*" (v. 2b), and the psalmist declares that God "judges on *earth*" (v. 11b). "Justice, in the spiritual economy of the psalmist, is a profoundly this-worldly category."[4] Consequently, the "gods" who do not *judge* fairly (v. 1b) are *judged* by God on earth (v. 11b).

Verses 10-11 correspond to the usual confession of trust and vow of praise at the end of many laments, in anticipation of deliverance that has not yet occurred. The psalmist asserts that the righteous "will rejoice" at the downfall of the wicked and "bathe their feet in [their] blood" (v. 10b). This gory image is used elsewhere to describe the defeat of enemies in battle, for example in Psalm 68:23; Deuteronomy 32:42; 1 Kings 22:38; Isaiah 63:1-6, and in the Anath cycle in Ugaritic poetry. Marti Steussy notes that if righteousness is "the ordering of relationships to support the flourishing of all," then the psalmist's desire "is itself no

2. Denise Dombkowski Hopkins, *Journey through the Psalms* (St. Louis, MO: Chalice Press, 2002), 89–90.

3. Roland Murphy, "The Faith of the Psalmist," *Int* 34 (1980): 229–39, at 238, quoted in ibid., 90.

4. Gary A. Anderson, "King David and the Psalms of Imprecation," *ProEccl* 15 (2006): 267–80, at 269.

vision of mutual flourishing" but rather "full of wounding and brokenness."[5] Yet the psalmist does not act on this desire; it is left to God.

The psalm ends in v. 11 with a quotation from אדם, first mentioned in v. 1b and translated in both verses as the collective "people." This quotation is introduced in each line of v. 11 by the particle of emphasis and contrast, אך, suggesting that what the people are saying is contrary to their present experience: "*surely* there is a reward [literally, "fruit"] for the righteous; *surely* there is a God who judges on earth." This is a hypothetical quotation like those found in Psalms 35, 40, 52, and 70 and functions "to motivate God to answer the psalmist's prayer" by speaking the praise God will receive if God intervenes on behalf of the righteous[6] (Gen 18:25). Justice demands that God act, and the psalmist feels free to remind God of that, given their patron/client relationship with its mutual obligations.

Psalms 57, 58, and 59 share the words "do not destroy" in their superscriptions. The rabbis argued that this phrase links the psalms to the two times (1 Sam 24 and 26) when David had the opportunity to kill Saul in a cave and assume the throne. "Do not destroy" are the words David speaks to Abishai, who is ready to kill Saul the second time (1 Sam 26:8); David insists instead that vengeance must come only from God. According to the rabbis, David does not act on his words in Psalm 58 but rejects his desire for vengeance and becomes for us a moral model to emulate.[7] The narrative takes pains to keep David from bloodguilt (see also 1 Sam 25:32). But if justice and righteous behavior are at stake in both these narratives about David as they are in Psalm 58, could or should women who are the victims of violence in Tanakh mimic David and overcome their desire for vengeance, which is a desire for justice? For them no throne hangs in the balance. Should self-control become their model?

Alice Keefe's intertextual study of the rape of Dinah (Gen 34), the gang rape of the Levite's concubine (Judg 19), and the rape of Tamar by Amnon (2 Sam 13)[8] can help to answer this question. In Genesis 34, Dinah's body becomes a metonym (a part signifying the whole) for cultural encounter between the Hivites and the Israelites, and her rape becomes the catalyst for more male violence. In Judges 19 the concubine is raped and hacked

---

5. Marti J. Steussy, *Psalms* (St. Louis, MO: Chalice Press, 2004), 138–39.

6. Rolf A. Jacobson, *"Many Are Saying": The Function of Direct Discourse in the Hebrew Psalter* (New York: T & T Clark, 2004), 141.

7. Anderson, "King David," 271.

8. Alice A. Keefe, "Rapes of Women/Wars of Men," *Semeia* 61 (1993): 79–93.

into twelve pieces as a symbol of social chaos among the twelve tribes of Israel: "in those days there was no king in Israel" (Judg 19:1; see also the violation of expected behaviors in 19:30). This kind of chaos, a type of disgraceful folly expressed by the word נבלה that all three stories share, is suggested by vv. 4-5 in Psalm 58: the snake that is deaf and cannot hear its charmer, and thus cannot be controlled.

Second Samuel 13 suggests itself as intertext for Psalm 58. In this story we can enter into the psychological trauma of Tamar's rape; she speaks, as the other two raped women do not. We can concretize the venomous words of the serpent in 58:3-5 with the literal words of Amnon to Tamar after he rapes her: "put this out of my presence" (2 Sam 13:19); she is no more than a piece of trash, as conveyed by the demonstrative pronoun "this" with no other qualifying word. His violence against Tamar "is multidimensional—physical, emotional and social."[9] She laments with ashes and torn robe and weeps; her future is declared bleak: "So Tamar dwelt, a desolate woman, in her brother Absalom's house" (v. 20). Like Jacob, who does nothing in response to his daughter Dinah's rape, or the Levite and his host, who do not protect the concubine but actually hand her over to the mob, David does nothing about Amnon except to become "very angry" (13:21), which creates a vacuum that Absalom fills with more bloodshed.

The men in these rape stories are the "mute ones" of Psalm 58:1 who do not "decree what is right," whose hearts and hands cause violence (58:2). As Keefe argues, "Woman's body as a sign for community, connectedness, and covenant in these Hebrew narratives offers, through images of victimization and violation, powerful rhetorical figures of witness against the realities of brokenness within the human community," and, I would argue, concretizes the violence decried in Psalm 58. Further, the mention in a negative context of "womb" in 58:3a and "untimely birth" in 58:8b also connect Psalm 58 to these rape stories by perverting the reverence for life generated from woman's womb as a symbol of community and people.

---

9. Ibid., 91.

Multiplying Trauma

How do we multiply Tamar's trauma across a generation? Can we estimate the physical and psychological trauma of six hundred abducted, abused women? At the conclusion of Judges 21 more than six hundred women are abducted and raped in order to preserve the Benjaminites from complete annihilation. This is cloaked as an act of "compassion" for the Benjaminites, which minimizes the brutality and enhances the male plot by acknowledging only the male benefit from the violence. Even more disconcerting, framing this as "compassion" alienates the reader from the horror, putting readers in the position of literary bystanders, passively perpetuating the pain of these women. There is violence inherent in the narrative retelling of these atrocities. These women are physically raped *and narratively raped.*[10] Reading Psalm 58 alongside stories like that of Tamar or Judges 21 resensitizes the reader to the pain and trauma of the text and, for a moment, allows the welfare of women to speak louder than male ambitions. If we can permit ourselves to feel the sting of the words of Psalm 58, maybe we can begin to actively confront the violence.

Amy Beth Jones

---

10. J. Cheryl Exum, *Fragmented Women: Feminist (Sub)versions of Biblical Narratives* (Valley Forge, PA: Trinity Press International, 1993), 170–201.

Psalm 59

Protestation of Innocence

The superscription of Psalm 59 places it firmly within a man's world, specifically the world of kings in 1 Samuel 19:11-17, which tells the story of David's escape from the murderous Saul. Michal, Saul's daughter and David's wife, makes David's escape possible, but she is not mentioned in the superscription.[1] Interpreters generally agree that Psalm 59 is a communal lament in which the king speaks for the nation. They draw on several features to support this view: the enemies are "all the nations" (vv. 5, 8); military imagery is used in addresses to God as "the LORD God of hosts" (v. 5), "my strength" (v. 9), "my fortress" (vv. 9, 16, 17), and "our shield" (v. 11); the psalmist prays that God's punishment of the enemies "will be known to the ends of the earth" (v. 13); God "laughs" at the nations and holds them "in derision" (v. 8), just as God does in royal Psalm 2:4.

Double refrains structure the psalm: (1) almost identical complaints in vv. 6-7 and 14-15 compare the enemies to howling dogs, a term of derision associated with death and uncleanness (cp. 1 Sam 17:43; 1 Kgs 14:11; 21:19; Ps 22:16, 20; Isa 56:11), and (2) similar confessions of trust in vv. 9-10 and 17 call God a "fortress" (see "protect" in v. 1b, which comes from the same root as "fortress," שגב); this protecting God shows חסד (covenant

---

1. See Katherine Brown's comments on Ps 51 above, 76–78.

Psalm 59:1-17

To the leader: Do Not Destroy.
Of David. A Miktam,
when Saul ordered his house
to be watched in order to kill him.

¹Deliver me from my enemies, O
my God;
protect me from those who rise
up against me.
²Deliver me from those who work
evil;
from the bloodthirsty save me.
³Even now they lie in wait for my
life;
the mighty stir up strife against
me.
For no transgression or sin of
mine, O LORD,
⁴for no fault of mine, they run
and make ready.

Rouse yourself, come to my help
and see!

⁵You, LORD God of hosts, are
God of Israel.
Awake to punish all the nations;
spare none of those who
treacherously plot
evil.   *Selah*
⁶Each evening they come back,
howling like dogs
and prowling about the city.
⁷There they are, bellowing with
their mouths,
with sharp words on their
lips—
for "Who," they think, "will hear
us?"

⁸But you laugh at them, O LORD;
you hold all the nations in derision.
⁹O my strength, I will watch for
you;
for you, O God, are my fortress.

loyalty). Repetitions of words from the same root, עזז, unfavorably contrast the arrogance of the enemy with God's power: the enemies are
called עזים, "the mighty," in v. 3, but the confessions of trust in vv. 9 and
17 call God עזי, "my strength" (cp. עזן, "might" in v. 16a). Enemy arrogance is also expressed by the contemptuous question in v. 7, "who will
hear us?" (cp. Isa 29:15), which is immediately countered by "but you
laugh at them" in v. 8 (Pss 2:4; 37:13; 59:9; 104:26). God's laughter suggests that God does hear and will respond.

The enemy's question voices the psalmist's own doubts expressed in
the petitions to a sleeping, hidden God in vv. 4b and 5b: "rouse yourself
. . . awake to punish" (see also Pss 7:6; 44:23; 78:65; 121:4; Isa 51:9). This
doubt continues in v. 9; the psalmist declares, "I will watch for you,"
perhaps reminding God what God is supposed to do: watch out for the
psalmist (Pss 12:7; 146:9). These doubts are overcome in v. 16 when the
psalmist bursts forth with a confession of trust: "but I will sing." The
adversative ו with the independent first-person pronoun builds on "but

¹⁰My God in his steadfast love will
meet me;
my God will let me look in triumph on my enemies.

¹¹Do not kill them, or my people
may forget;
make them totter by your
power, and bring them
down,
O Lᴏʀᴅ, our shield.
¹²For the sin of their mouths, the
words of their lips,
let them be trapped in their
pride.
For the cursing and lies that they
utter,
¹³consume them in wrath;
consume them until they are
no more.
Then it will be known to the ends
of the earth
that God rules over
Jacob.   *Selah*

¹⁴Each evening they come back,
howling like dogs
and prowling about the city.
¹⁵They roam about for food,
and growl if they do not get
their fill.

¹⁶But I will sing of your might;
I will sing aloud of your steadfast love in the morning.
For you have been a fortress for
me
and a refuge in the day of my
distress.
¹⁷O my strength, I will sing praises
to you,
for you, O God, are my fortress,
the God who shows me steadfast love.

you" in v. 8 (adversative ו with the second-person masculine singular personal pronoun) that speaks of God's laughter at the nations. The psalmist is moved from watching for God to an anticipation of praising God after God has intervened to save.

The metaphor of the enemies "howling like dogs" in vv. 6 and 14 proves central to the meaning of Psalm 59 for several reasons.[2] The parallelism between the mouth and lips of the dogs in v. 7ab and the mouth and lips of the enemy in v. 12ab ties the psalm together. Also, the verb ארב, meaning "to lie in wait" (v. 3), is used for setting an ambush against cities in warfare (see Judg 9:34; Josh 8:2) as well as for animals lurking after prey (see Ps 10:9; Lam 3:10-11). Similarly, the verb סבב, which means "go in a circle, surround," can connote hostile action (vv. 6, 14; Ps 55:9-10). The enemies are described as a pack of wild dogs

---

2. Brian Doyle, "Howling Like Dogs: Metaphorical Language in Psalm LIX," *VT* 54 (2004): 61–82.

searching for food (אכל, *'okel*—note the wordplay with כלב, *keleb*, "dog") in v. 15.

As many interpreters have noted, the psalmist expresses a seeming contradiction: in v. 11 God is petitioned not to kill the enemies so that they may exist as an object lesson, but in v. 13 the psalmist demands that God "consume them in wrath . . . until they are no more." Brian Doyle does not see a contradiction here but rather a deliberate word choice meant to relate "the devouring dogs (אכל/כלב) to the consuming deity"[3] (כלה in the Piel, which means to finish or destroy). The metaphor of howling dogs allows the psalmist to invite God to act like the enemy in order to punish; animal metaphors are often used this way in the imprecatory psalms. Similarly, Goeran Eidevall argues that the ambivalence about the enemies in vv. 11 and 13 is deliberate *"because someone has to play their part* in the process of shaping individual and collective religious identity"; such ambiguity can "avoid a demonization of YHWH."[4] Without human enemies, God becomes the enemy in a world of suffering and conflict.

If feminist readers take the superscription as simply one possible interpretative frame among many rather than as historical, and if they search for traces of women's voices embedded in the psalm, different connections can emerge. For example, in the book of Lamentations, Daughter Zion (the personified city of Jerusalem destroyed by the Babylonians in 587 BCE) uses some of the same vocabulary and metaphors as Psalm 59. In 59:3 the enemies "lie in wait" (ארב), which suggests lurking and watching, waiting for the right moment to pounce. Anxiety is associated with being the object of constant scrutiny, making the psalmist feel vulnerable, shamed, and the "object of unsympathetic gaze"; "looking . . . connotes power, control, and dominance."[5] Consequently, deliverance will involve a reversal: the psalmist will turn an unsympathetic gaze upon the enemy once God intervenes: "my God will let me *look* in triumph [not in the Hebrew] on my enemies" (59:10b; Ps 54:7). Daughter Zion prays for the same reversal in Lamentations 1:21-22 (3:64-66).

---

3. Ibid., 78.

4. Goeran Eidevall, "Images of God, Self, and the Enemy in the Psalms: On the Role of Metaphor in Identity Construction," in *Metaphor in the Hebrew Bible*, ed. Pierre van Hecke (Leuven: University Press, 2005), 55–65, at 65.

5. Amy C. Cottrill, *Language, Power, and Identity in the Lament Psalms of the Individual* (New York and London: T & T Clark, 2008), 87.

Black Women and Community

Cheryl Townsend Gilkes argues that, "in spite of the discrimination they face, the commitment of African American women to the organizational integrity of black churches and communities means that their definitions of feminist or womanist are first and foremost communalist."[6] Black women have a long history of willingness and ability to speak to the heart of both oppression and hope. They have been fierce agents of change, shining a light on systemic subjugation. There is a legacy of audacity enmeshed in the African American female experience, from Sojourner Truth's articulation: "Religion without humanity is very poor human stuff" and the commentary it provided on the perverseness of religious justifications of chattel slavery, to Fannie Lou Hamer's cry: "I'm sick and tired of being sick and tired," and the position she assumed as face and voice of the Jim Crow South. Black women have buttressed the call for human and civil rights throughout history. These women have been the "everyman" reflecting grief and projecting hope while the tyrannical, domineering "dogs" and "bears" circle, waiting to attack.

Yolanda Marie Norton

The key to the psalmist's seeing retributive reversal of her situation is God's seeing: "Rouse yourself, come to my help and *see*!" (v. 4b). Similarly, the narrator in Lamentations 1:7 describes Jerusalem/Daughter Zion's suffering: "the foe *looked on*, mocking over her downfall" (cp. Lam 2:16; 3:61-63). Jerusalem is shamed by the unsympathetic, continuous gaze and mocking of the foe. She has "no one to comfort her" (Lam 1:2, 9, 17, 21), so she begs both passersby and God to see: "All you who pass by . . . *Look* and *see*, if there is any sorrow like my sorrow?" (Lam 1:12); "O Lord, *look* at my affliction" (Lam 1:9c; cp. 1:11c, 20; 2:20; and 5:1 spoken by the voice of the community). The repeated petitions to "look" suggest that God is not looking or even present. As in Psalm 59:10b, deliverance in Lamentations means Daughter Zion will switch places with the enemy:

---

6. Cheryl Townsend Gilkes, "Go and Tell Mary and Martha: The Spirituals, Biblical Options for Women, and Cultural Tensions in the African American Religious Experience," in *Womanist Theological Ethics: A Reader*, ed. Katie Geneva Cannon, Emilie M. Townes, and Angela D. Sims (Louisville, KY: Westminster John Knox, 2011), 217–36, at 233.

"Bring on the day you have announced, and let them be as I am. . . . Deal with them as you have dealt with me" (Lam 1:21c, 22b).

In addition, the same verb, "lie in wait" (ארב), used for the enemies in Psalm 59:3, is used of God, who takes the form of a bear and a lion (Lam 3:66) rather than a howling dog. This complaint is spoken by a lamenting woman of Jerusalem who "gives voice to the grief and hopes of an entire community in the persona of an 'everyman.' "[7] She also expresses doubt that God is paying attention by declaring that she will weep "until the Lord from heaven looks down and sees" (Lam 3:50). In Psalm 59:6, 14, the howling dogs prowl at night but the psalmist anticipates singing of God's חסד "in the morning" (v. 16a; cp. Ps 30:5). Lamentations 3:22-23 echoes this hope: "The חסד of the Lord never ceases. . . . They [God's mercies] are new every morning." God's response in the morning is anticipated also in Lamentations 2:19, in which the narrator instructs the people to "cry out in the night." Also, in Psalm 59:13 the psalmist petitions God to consume (כלה, "finish" in the Piel) the enemy. Daughter Zion says in Lamentations 2:22 that her children have been "destroyed" (כלה in the Piel) by the enemy, and the narrator notes that the consuming God has given "full vent [כלה in the Piel] to his wrath" and kindled a fire that "consumed" (אכל) Zion in Lamentations 4:11.

Thus a new superscription suggests itself for Psalm 59: "a lament of Daughter Zion after the Babylonian destruction." She has accepted her guilt (Lam 1:8, 18; 2:17), but she wants God to see that her punishment now is more than she can bear. The protestation of innocence in Psalm 59:3-4 makes sense as a check on God's excessive punishment experienced in starvation, shame, and grief. Like Psalm 59, "Zion's prayer in Lamentations 1–2 is that God see her as she sees herself"[8] and be moved out of passivity to action.

---

7. John H. Hobbins, "Zion's Plea That God See Her as She Sees Herself: Unanswered Prayer in Lamentations 1–2," in *Daughter Zion: Her Portrait, Her Response*, ed. Mark Boda, Carol Dempsey, and LeAnn Snow Flesher (Atlanta, GA: Society of Biblical Literature, 2012), 149–76, at 169.

8. Ibid., 150. Hobbins rejects the usual interpretation that a male survivor of Jerusalem's destruction speaks in Lam 3. He notes that a woman as speaker of grief is supported by cross-cultural studies and that we must distinguish between the poet-performer and the scribe.

Psalm 60

Co-opting the "Other" Woman

Psalm 60 is one of thirteen psalms attached by its superscription to events in David's life. Second Samuel 8, 10 and 1 Chronicles 19 report David's decisive and swift military victories over the lands mentioned in Psalm 60; women do not appear in these narratives. The psalm itself takes the form of a national lament, perhaps spoken by the king on behalf of the people, asking God for help in overcoming these enemies. Placing the psalm in this narrative context serves to "tone down the image of David as military hero" and to "recast David into a model of repentance and piety."[1] David enjoys success only because God made it possible in response to David's prayer when he was in trouble.

Psalm 60 falls into three parts: complaint and petition in vv. 1-5, God's address in vv. 6-9, and renewed complaint and petition with confession of trust in vv. 10-12. The people's defeat is connected with God's rejection (vv. 1, 10) and anger (v. 1), as is often the case in communal laments (see Pss 44:9, 23; 74:1; 77:7; 89:38). The psalmist addresses God directly and describes God's actions in military terms: "you have broken [from the root פרץ, literally 'make a breach,' 'tear down,' 'break through'] our defenses" (v. 1; cp. 2 Kgs 14:13; Isa 5:5), presumably to allow the enemy to

---

1. Vivian L. Johnson, *David in Distress: His Portrait through the Historical Psalms* (New York and London: T & T Clark, 2009), 131, 140.

Psalm 60:1-12

To the leader: according to the Lily of the Covenant. A Miktam of David; for instruction; when he struggled with Aram-naharaim and with Aram-zobah, and when Joab on his return killed twelve thousand Edomites in the Valley of Salt.

¹O God, you have rejected us,
   broken our defenses;
   you have been angry; now re-
      store us!
²You have caused the land to quake;
   you have torn it open;
repair the cracks in it, for it is
      tottering.
³You have made your people suf-
      fer hard things;
   you have given us wine to
      drink that made us
      reel.
⁴You have set up a banner for
   those who fear you,
   to rally to it out of
      bowshot.   *Selah*
⁵Give victory with your right hand,
   and answer us,

attack. The land also suffers the consequences of Israel's behavior and God's anger. Verse 2 describes an earthquake, a phenomenon associated with God's life-giving theophany (e.g., Exod 19:16-19) but used metaphorically in Psalm 60 to suggest the destruction that war brings (cp. Jer 4:23-26; Isa 13:13; 24:18-20).

God makes Israel and its enemies alike drink from God's cup of wrath (v. 3; cp. Ps 11:6; Isa 51:17, 21; Jer 25:15-29; Ps 75:8). The "hard things" the people suffer (v. 3a), along with the plea to "give victory with your right hand" (v. 5a), recall both enslavement in Egypt (Exod 1:14; 6:9; Deut 26:6) and the liberation of exodus (Exod 15:6, 12). In Psalm 60, Israel cries out for a new exodus, but the irony is that God is the new taskmaster.[2] To reinforce the petition, the ones lamenting are described as "those who fear you," that is, worshipers (v. 4a), and "those whom you love" (v. 5b). The God whom Israel experiences as absent is reminded about the covenant relationship with Israel. This reminder is meant to motivate divine intervention; perhaps these phrases suggest a protestation of innocence (cp. Ps 44:17-22).

The response to the petition in v. 5a, "answer us," comes from recalling a previous oracle from God in vv. 6-9. Psalm 60:5-12 occurs also in Psalm 108:6-13, suggesting that oracles were reused in different situations because they contain patterned, stereotypical speech. Language marked by "you" (God) and "us" (the "innocent" community) in vv. 1-5 shifts to the divine "I," "mine," "my," and "me" in vv. 6-9, returning to "you" and "us" in vv.

2. J. Clinton McCann Jr., "The Book of Psalms," in *The New Interpreter's Bible*, vol. 4 (Nashville, TN: Abingdon Press, 1996), 639–1280, at 916.

so that those whom you love
may be rescued.

⁶God has promised in his sanctuary:
"With exultation I will divide up
Shechem,
and portion out the Vale of
Succoth.
⁷Gilead is mine, and Manasseh is
mine;
Ephraim is my helmet;
Judah is my scepter.
⁸Moab is my washbasin;
on Edom I hurl my shoe;

over Philistia I shout in triumph."
⁹Who will bring me to the fortified
city?
Who will lead me to Edom?
¹⁰Have you not rejected us, O
God?
You do not go out, O God, with
our armies.
¹¹O grant us help against the foe,
for human help is worthless.
¹²With God we shall do valiantly;
it is he who will tread down our
foes.

10-12. In this structure Israel and the king encircle God as the center of life and salvation. In vv. 6-9 God declares divine ownership of the land and speaks as a warrior dividing up the spoils of war. The mention of Shechem (v. 6), where Joshua (Josh 24) called the people to renew the covenant, in connection with the verb "divide up" (חלק, "divide, allot, give shares to") recalls Israel's entry into the Promised Land and the distribution of land to the tribes in Joshua 13–22.

God calls Ephraim (often a name for the northern kingdom) "my helmet" and Judah "my scepter" (v. 7; cp. Gen 49:10), which suggests both protection and aggression[3] and indirectly reaffirms God's promise of land made to Abraham in Genesis 12:7. Consequently, God terms Moab "my washbasin," Edom a place to throw dirty shoes,[4] and Philistia the object of triumphant shouts of victory; these nations are all mentioned in Exodus 15:14-15. Verse 9 is also spoken by God, contrary to those who group it with vv. 10-12; God asks a rhetorical question to remind Israel of its part in the covenant. God's speech in vv. 6-9 stands between the petitions of the people (in vv. 1b, 5, and 11) and "will serve both to *remind God* that God should keep those promises, and also . . . to *remind the community* that God has made such a promise"[5] and will keep it.

3. John Goldingay, *Psalms*, vol. 2 (Grand Rapids, MI: Baker Academic, 2007), 231.

4. Ibid. I agree with Goldingay that hurling a shoe at Edom does not suggest taking possession, as some argue in connection with Deut 25:9-10 and Ruth 4:7-8.

5. Rolf A. Jacobson, *"Many Are Saying": The Function of Direct Discourse in the Hebrew Psalter* (New York: T & T Clark, 2004), 118.

A God for Those Who "Suffer Hard"

The observation that "women do not appear" in the texts referenced in the superscription, paired with the psalmist's declaration that God has rejected "us" (v. 1) and "made your people suffer hard" (v. 3), helps us to glimpse what is unsaid in Psalm 60. After all, when kings—men of political, social, and economic power—act, it is the everyday people who "suffer hard" and whose depths of suffering often go unseen. We must imagine that the unnamed, unacknowledged women of the text are the ones who silently pay the price for David's actions and reactions, yet these women are among the worshipers who have heard God's promises in the sanctuary (v. 6).

It is not difficult to imagine this reality. In the 1940s, when men went to war in the United States, it was women who were left behind to maintain economic stability and work in places where they had not before. When wars declared by men of power break out, women are often the victims of physical and sexual violence. Yet those who have the least, who have been disregarded or mistreated in the midst of larger political battles, cling most fervently to God, as Deborah Little argues. In her chapter "Theologies of the Poor" she describes a woman who is plagued by pain, homeless, and alone except that she "has God."[6] Those at the bottom of the socio-economic ladder who suffer most from political decisions often cling to God for hope when humanity has failed them. They worship a God they perceive as bigger than their situation and the community that has failed or ignored them. This hope for deliverance from God persists despite pushback within marginalized communities from voices insisting that God is the taskmaster who perpetuates their struggle.

Yolanda Marie Norton

The community renews its complaint in v. 10a with a rhetorical question addressed to God: "have you not rejected us, O God?" The use of the second-person independent personal pronoun "you" in v. 10 challenges the oracle in vv. 6-9: you may have promised us land, but our experience is that "you do not go out with our armies" (v. 10b). This counter-testimony rooted in the lived experience of God's absence chal-

---

6. Deborah Little, "Theology of the Poor," in *Handbook of U.S. Theologies of Liberation*, ed. Miguel De La Torre (St. Louis, MO: Chalice Press, 2004), 274–80, at 275.

lenges the core testimony[7] of the oracle (the affirmation of God's presence). Couched in military language, this complaint articulates the tension of life lived between the promise of land and its fulfillment. God is challenged to act like the Lord of Hosts who takes Israel's side in battle, a role that undergirds Holy War and is associated with the ark of the covenant on which God is invisibly enthroned (see Num 10:35-36; 14:42-45; Josh 6:1-16; Judg 4:12-16). This tension leads to a renewed petition for God's help in v. 11, coupled with an acknowledgment that "human help is worthless" (Ps 146:3-4). Isaiah 63:1-6 may be a response to this petition, since it uses some of the same vocabulary and metaphors as Psalm 60 ("tread down," Edom staggering like a drunkard);[8] Israel switches places with its foe as just retribution. The psalm concludes with a confession of trust in God's future action to "tread down" Israel's foes.

A Perspective from the Other

The psalmist(s) desperately recounts and laments God's violent actions (vv. 1-3) toward "us," the people whom God loves (v. 5). At the same time, the psalmist petitions God to trample "them" down (v. 12). Problematically, this psalm treats violence not as something contrary to God's purposes but as a means of exercising God's will toward both the people of God and their enemies. God's potential reign over the peoples and the lands (vv. 6-8) rests on God's violent actions toward all. What is questionable, according to the psalmist, is that God acts violently toward "us" rather than toward "our" enemies.

The psalmist complains that this God no longer goes out with "our" armies (v. 10). The psalmist's community desires to combat violence with violence, just as God is depicted as resorting to violence (vv. 2-3, 12). The reader observes how the use of arms and aggression could be justified by an image of a warring God who is involved in securing and maintaining political and military interests. The psalm opens up the polemical "truth" (קשט) of a combative God raising the militaristic "banner for rallying" (v. 4) that has violently affected

---

7. Walter Brueggemann, *Theology of the Old Testament* (Minneapolis: Fortress Press, 1997), 400.

8. Graham S. Ogden, "Psalm 60: Its Rhetoric, Form, and Function," *JSOT* 31 (1985): 83–94.

the regions of Palestine and Israel and ruined (in)visible innocent lives of women, men, and children, and does so even today. Violence multiplies violence. Hatred multiplies hatred. A God of "all" may be present in the psalmist's community, but the only experience of God that "all" share is the experience of God's anger. Perhaps this God awaits the vibrant coexistence that can be achieved—in any sociocultural, theological/ideological, or political sphere—by facing differences actively, fearlessly, and nonviolently.

Su Jung Shin

God as warrior and the divine promise of land to Israel center Psalm 60. This psalm continues the conflict between the nations and God that begins in Psalm 2 and ends in Psalm 149 with the subjugation of the nations. This conflict "reveals that there is no such thing as world peace in the Psalms," but instead a *Pax Judaica* characterized by particularism.[9] Consequently, it is imperative to read with "interruption,"[10] that is, stopping and questioning the text to create an ethical moment of decision on behalf of women and children who are victimized by war and whose voices are often absent from the psalms. Israel sees itself as gifted by God with the land; the land shapes Israel's self-identity. The "Other" does not share in this gift unless she or he surrenders her or his identity, as both Ruth and Rahab did. Israel developed boundary markers to distinguish Us from Other, including "a stock figure, a female embodiment of evil 'Otherness' that could be used again and again," fleshed out in the figures of the "outsider" woman in Proverbs 2; 5; 7, Jezebel, Ruth, Rahab, and the Syrophoenician woman.[11] In the Rahab story, land plays a central role; Rahab is co-opted by Israel to affirm its claim on the land. She even uses Holy War language in her speech to the spies (Josh 2:9-11), who repeat her words when they report back to Joshua (2:24).

---

9. Harm van Grol, "War and Peace in the Psalms: Some Compositional Explorations," in *Deuterocanonical and Cognate Literature Yearbook 2010: Visions of Peace and Tales of War*, ed. Jan Liesen and Pancratius Beentjes (Berlin and New York: de Gruyter, 2010), 173–206, at 178–79.

10. Danna Nolan Fewell, *The Children of Israel: Reading the Bible for the Sake of Our Children* (Nashville, TN: Abingdon, 2003), 33–34.

11. Judith E. McKinlay, *Reframing Her: Biblical Women in Postcolonial Focus* (Sheffield: Sheffield Phoenix Press, 2004), 30–31.

Like Rahab, Ruth is an "Other" from Moab; Moab is mentioned in Psalm 60:8 as God's washbasin. The story of Ruth unfolds "in the days when the judges ruled" (Ruth 1:1). The judges were military deliverers who overcame resistance from the inhabitants of Canaan; "this is a tale told in the context of land wars."[12] In this context Ruth gives up her homeland, language, and religion to birth a male heir who serves Israelite dominance of the "Other." We are left asking with Judith McKinlay, "what happens to women who refuse to do that?"[13]

Reading with Interruption from Rahab

"As a critic from Asia, where sex tourism is a flourishing business and some countries can be considered 'the brothel of the world,' I read Rahab's story from the perspective of women compelled to provide sexual labor as an integral part of global markets and military buildup. In southeast Asia, institutionalized prostitution began with the establishment of American military bases during the Vietnam War. American soldiers were sent to cities in southeast Asia for 'rest and recreation.' After the war, promoting tourism to sustain the entertainment businesses led to the formation of an institutionalized sex industry. . . . The sex industry remains intimately connected with militarism; the sexual use of women, along with alcohol and drugs, is regarded as a necessary channel for letting off steam from military life."[14]

Kwok Pui-Lan

---

12. Ibid., 52.

13. Ibid., 56.

14. Kwok Pui-lan, "Sexual Morality and National Politics: Reading Biblical 'Loose Women,'" in *Engaging the Bible: Critical Readings from Contemporary Women*, ed. Choi Hee An and Kathryn Pfisterer Darr (Minneapolis: Fortress Press, 2006), 21–46, 134–37, at 38.

Psalm 61

God's Nurturing Protection

At first glance Psalm 61 appears to be yet another psalm rooted in the world of men and war. The superscription labels it "of David." The psalm begins with petitions typically found in individual laments—"hear my cry," "listen to my prayer"—and then moves to complaint (v. 2a), renewed petition (vv. 2b-4), confession of trust (v. 5), a prayer for the king (vv. 6-7), and a concluding vow of praise (v. 8). In v. 2 the psalmist locates herself at "the end of the earth," מקצה הארץ, which can also be translated as "the border of the land" in the sense of "outpost." This could suggest a military context, especially when viewed with "refuge" and "strong tower" in v. 3, making vv. 6-7 a prayer before battle offered by the soldiers of the king on his behalf. Other interpreters suggest that "the end of the earth" refers to the exile or that it is not a geographical term at all but rather a metaphor for someone who feels separated from God spiritually in a situation of suffering.

A closer look at the metaphors of Psalm 61 reveals other possibilities for understanding. First of all, the psalmist describes herself in v. 2 as calling to God "when my heart is faint." Her diminished body is a "somatic idiom of distress"[1] that suggests powerlessness and vulnerability

---

1. Amy C. Cottrill, *Language, Power, and Identity in the Lament Psalms of the Individual* (New York and London: T & T Clark, 2008), 30.

Psalm 61:1-8

To the leader: with stringed instruments.
Of David.

¹Hear my cry, O God;
    listen to my prayer.
²From the end of the earth I call to
        you,
    when my heart is faint.

Lead me to the rock
    that is higher than I;
³for you are my refuge,
    a strong tower against the
        enemy.

⁴Let me abide in your tent for-
        ever,
    find refuge under the shelter of
        your wings.   *Selah*

⁵For you, O God, have heard my
        vows;
    you have given me the heri-
        tage of those who fear
        your name.

⁶Prolong the life of the king;
    may his years endure to all
        generations!
⁷May he be enthroned forever be-
        fore God;
    appoint steadfast love and
        faithfulness to watch
        over him!

⁸So I will always sing praises to
        your name,
    as I pay my vows day after day.

within the God/psalmist patronage relationship; the psalmist's language has relational power that roots itself in the loyalty of mutual interdependence. The pairing of "steadfast love" (חסד) and "faithfulness" (אמת) in v. 7 reinforces this sense of loyal interdependence, emphasizing that God is dependable in a time of crisis. Further, the petition in v. 2b, "lead me to the rock," lifts up God's protective nature as experienced in the wilderness (Exod 13:17, 21; Pss 77:20; 78:14, 52-53) and suggests pastoral-shepherd imagery. Such imagery "bespeaks tenderness, gentleness, and attentiveness"; this God "has *maternal* qualities, and in these verbs does what a mother does,"[2] leading her child along a pathway of safety and nurture.

The psalmist's petition to "find refuge under the shelter of your wings" in v. 4b (Pss 17:8; 36:7-8; 57:1; 63:7; 91:1-4) also links to God's protective, maternal nature. Silvia Schroer rejects the association of "wings" here with the winged sun disk, since the sun is not suited to offer protection, especially shade. Rather, she argues that God is implicitly referred to in

---

2. Walter Brueggemann, *Theology of the Old Testament* (Minneapolis: Fortress Press, 1997), 204. This maternal aspect is strengthened when combined with the use of verbs of feeding, e.g., in Ps 23.

this passage as a bird, through the image of protecting wings; the wild bird most frequently referred to in Tanakh is the goose vulture (see Exod 19:4; Deut 32:11); the word "eagle" in these texts has come to us from the Septuagint. The goose vulture feeds on carrion and has a bald head (Job 39:27-30; Prov 30:17; Mic 1:16). The ancient Near East held the goose vulture in great esteem; it was often associated with goddesses who give birth to life and devour it at the end. The goose vulture becomes a symbol of regeneration and healing in Psalm 103:5 and Isaiah 40:30-31. God in Psalm 61 integrates "the dimension of motherliness from the powers and qualities associated clearly with goddesses," so that God's wings "no longer protect only kings and the deceased [as with the winged sun disk], but also the living women and men who pray the Psalms."[3]

A Perspective from the Other after the Exile

How might postexilic peoples—those "from the end of the earth" (v. 2) and those within the war-devastated "promised land" who daily suffered insufficient food, clothing, and shelter—have interpreted the psalmist's prayer? In a context of such uncertainty the psalmist's request for "rock," "tent," "refuge," "strong tower," and "shelter" could surely have inspired them with hope for a secure community, as well as for protection from "others" among whom they struggled to survive. Having lived without a king, however, some might have taken a sideways glance at the psalmist's petition, which perhaps seeks to reestablish the preexilic form of the institution with its temple and military complex. The psalmist's vision of the king's everlasting reign (vv. 6-7) is followed by the conditional offer to sing praises and renew vows (v. 8). From the psalmist's perspective the audience would not praise God amid the realities of postexilic life without the polemical vision of masculine, militant kingship, which makes the language and content of the psalm contestable.

Would these people, like the psalmist, praise God daily if they knew the monarchy

---

3. Silvia Schroer, "'Under the Shadow of Your Wings': The Metaphor of God's Wings in the Psalms, Exodus 19.4, Deuteronomy 32.11 and Malachi 3.20, as Seen through the Perspectives of Feminism and the History of Religion," in *Wisdom and Psalms*, FCB, 2nd ser., ed. Athalya Brenner and Carole Fontaine (Sheffield: Sheffield Academic Press, 1998), 264–82, at 280–81.

"enthroned forever before God" would never revive after Jehoiachin? Or would they lament the absence of kingship and its expected order, security, and certainty? What if they argued that the fixed, secure imagery of "rock" and "strong tower" no longer resembled the design of an exodus community that moved freely and humbly with God? Some might hope that the prestige of kingship would soon return to save their community. Others might argue against the desire to reestablish the imperial structure *and* still sing praises.

Su Jung Shin

Given the references to God's nurturing protection in Psalm 61, one can imagine that this psalm was prayed by the young slave girl in 2 Kings 5, who had been taken captive from the land of Israel during an Aramean raid (2 Kgs 5:2). The slave girl served the wife of Naaman, commander of the Aramean army. This little slave girl functions simply as an "agent" in this story; she moves the plot along. After she mentions to Naaman's wife that the prophet Elisha could cure her husband's skin disease, the little girl disappears from the narrative. She is simply "an everyday reality of the violence that helps realize the imperial dream."[4] Connecting her with Psalm 61 serves to "interrupt," that is, stop and question the text in order to view history not from the perspective of kings and military leaders but from the underside, where women and children suffer; this creates an "ethical moment" in which we can imagine and live differently.[5] Separated from her family and homeland, she calls to God "from the end of the earth" in Aram with a faint heart (Ps 61:2), like so many women and children who suffered as the spoils of war in the ancient world (and today). Living among the enemy, she desires to be led by God to "the rock higher than I" (v. 2b), that is, to a place where she is no longer vulnerable, above the tumult of war and captivity. By using Psalm 61 the slave girl prays to be led away from danger rather than for divine violence against the enemy. She seeks the "shelter" of God's

4. Cameron B. R. Howard, "1 and 2 Kings," in *Women's Bible Commentary*, ed. Carol A. Newsom, Sharon H. Ringe, and Jacqueline E. Lapsley, 3rd ed. (Louisville, KY: Westminster John Knox, 2012), 175.

5. Danna Nolan Fewell, *The Children of Israel: Reading the Bible for the Sake of Our Children* (Nashville, TN: Abingdon, 2003), 33–34.

wings; the word is סתר, which means "hiding or secret place." This phrase suggests that the stance of Psalm 61 can be characterized as "defensive rather than aggressive."[6] One suspects that as a captive she has witnessed and experienced enough of violence. The heaping up of terms of safety underscores this point: rock, refuge, strong tower, tent, shelter (vv. 2b-4).

Many commentators romanticize the nameless little girl and insist that she does God's work quietly on the margins or provides the locus of healing in the midst of war and domination, or chooses to love rather than hate, or expresses a childlike hope that things can be better for everyone. The hidden transcript in the story suggests that her co-opted voice makes a theological point about God's sovereignty over all political power. Women and children as spoils of war understand the brutality of war that drowns out hope; compare this with Jael in Judges 5 and modern examples from Mali, the Sudan, Liberia, Nigeria, Syria, and the former Yugoslavia in which children are recruited into the army and young girls are sexually abused by soldiers.[7] Where the little girl wants to be is in God's tent (v. 4a). In her isolating captivity in this foreign land, abiding in God's tent "forever" suggests the intimacy and security she presently lacks. We can imagine a new superscription for Psalm 61: "To the leader: with stringed instruments. When Naaman's slave girl prayed in Aram."

She reminds God in Psalm 61:5 that "you have given me the heritage of those who fear your name." "Heritage" comes from the root ירש, "possess," and refers to land. It does not make sense to emend the text from ירשת (*yerushat*, "inheritance") to ארשת (*ʿareshet*, "plea"), as several scholars suggest. The MT reading constitutes the girl's declaration that she is still an Israelite who worships Israel's God (Pss 25:12; 34:8-10; 112:1) and as such is entitled to both God's protection, even in this faraway place, and a return to her land. Similarly, W. H. Bellinger notes that "to dwell (worship) in the temple carried with it the privilege of dwelling on the land."[8] This was true as well for residents of the northern kingdom who looked not to the Jerusalem Temple for worship but to the main sanctuaries at

---

6. Joel M. LeMon, *Yahweh's Winged Form in the Psalms: Exploring Congruent Iconography and Texts* (Fribourg: Academic Press; Göttingen: Vandenhoeck & Ruprecht, 2010), 148.

7. For the complete discussion of the little slave girl in 2 Kgs 5, see Denise Dombkowski Hopkins, "2 Kings 5:1-4," at www.goodpreacher.com, Proper 9, July 7, 2013.

8. W. H. Bellinger, *A Hermeneutic of Curiosity and Readings of Psalm 61*, Studies in Old Testament Interpretation (Macon, GA: Mercer University Press, 1995), 52–53.

Bethel and Dan. Confident of her loyal connection with God, she assumes God has heard her vows (v. 5a). Her prayer for the king in vv. 6-7 suggests Psalm 72, which describes the king as defender of the poor and instrument of divine justice and abundance for the people and individual worshipers. She wants the king to enable her to return to worship at the northern kingdom sanctuaries, where she will "sing praises" and "pay vows" (v. 8) with others who fear God's name. As Marvin Tate maintains, Psalm 61 "serves to diminish distance and enhance nearness and presence."[9] The little slave girl understands her relationship with God as nearness to the sanctuary in communal worship and knows that only God can make this happen through the agency of the king. The irony is that it is the king who contributed to her enslavement through his reckless policies; her prayer thus functions as both plea and rebuke.

---

9. Marvin E. Tate, *Psalms 51–100* (Dallas, TX: Word Books, 1990), 116.

Psalm 62

The Positive Value of Silence

Psalm 62 is bracketed by two other psalms of trust that offer an assurance of God's loyalty, dependability, and power in response to the preceding string of laments. Several repeated words link Psalms 61, 62, and 63:[1]

חסד ("covenant loyalty"; "steadfast love" in NRSV) in 61:7; 62:12; 63:3

נפש ("soul" in NRSV; a better translation is "being" or "self") in 62:1, 5 and 63:1, 5, 8

"rock" in 61:2b; 62:2, 6, 7

"refuge" in 61:3, 4; 62:7, 8

"shelter/shadow of your wings" in 61:4 and 63:7

עז ("power"/ "strength") in 61:3; 62:11b; 63:2

שלם ("pay"/"repay") in 61:8; 62:12

God showed covenant loyalty to Israel from the beginning of God's relationship to Israel (Exod 15:13) and the psalmist counts on it now.

---

1. J. Clinton McCann Jr., "The Book of Psalms," in *The New Interpreters Bible*, vol. 4 (Nashville, TN: Abingdon Press, 1996), 639–1280, at 922. McCann suggests that these psalms "form a sort of trilogy of trust."

Psalm 62:1-12

To the leader: according to Jeduthun.
A Psalm of David.

¹For God alone my soul waits in
silence;
from him comes my salvation.
²He alone is my rock and my salvation,
my fortress; I shall never be
shaken.

³How long will you assail a person,
will you batter your victim, all
of you,
as you would a leaning wall, a
tottering fence?

⁴Their only plan is to bring down a
person of prominence.
They take pleasure in falsehood;
they bless with their mouths,
but inwardly they curse. *Selah*

⁵For God alone my soul waits in
silence,
for my hope is from him.
⁶He alone is my rock and my salvation,
my fortress; I shall not be
shaken.
⁷On God rests my deliverance and
my honor;

The superscription ties Psalm 62 to Jeduthun (see also Pss 39; 72),
which probably refers to one of David's chief musicians and singers
(along with Asaph and Heman; see 1 Chr 9:16; 16:38, 42; 25:6). Like Psalm
42–43, Psalm 62 expresses the struggle between the speaking "I" and her
נפש as enemies plot against her (vv. 3-4). The psalm moves from an inner
dialogue between the "I" and the נפש (vv. 1-7) to outward-directed public
instruction (vv. 8-11), and finally to direct address to God (v. 12). At the
end of the psalm the "I" and the נפש have become one voice, uniting the
psalmist and the speaker of the psalmist's words and putting "the frac-
tured self back together."[2]

The sixfold use of אך at the beginning of vv. 1, 2, 4, 5, 6, and 9 testifies
to this struggle between the "I" and the נפש and their eventual union.
The NRSV, NJPS, and NIV mute the power of this particle by sometimes
translating it as "alone" and other times ignoring it altogether. אך can
have an emphatic/asseverative ("surely," "indeed," "truly") or restrictive
meaning to indicate something exceptional ("only," "however," "but");[3]
both senses seem to be at work in Psalm 61. Given the frequent changes
in address in the psalm, revealing the agitation of the speaker—self in

2. William P. Brown, "The Psalms and 'I': The Dialogical Self and the Disappearing
Psalmist," in *Diachronic and Synchronic: Reading the Psalms in Real Time* (London and
New York: T & T Clark International, 2007), 26–44, at 44.

3. Ronald J. Williams, *Williams' Hebrew Syntax*, 3rd ed., rev. and exp. by John Beckman
(Toronto: University of Toronto Press, 2010), 140–41.

my mighty rock, my refuge is in
God.

⁸Trust in him at all times, O people;
pour out your heart before him;
God is a refuge for us.   *Selah*

⁹Those of low estate are but a
breath,
those of high estate are a delu-
sion;
in the balances they go up;
they are together lighter than a
breath.

¹⁰Put no confidence in extortion,
and set no vain hopes on
robbery;
if riches increase, do not set
your heart on them.

¹¹Once God has spoken;
twice have I heard this:
that power belongs to God,
¹²and steadfast love belongs to
you, O LORD.
For you repay to all
according to their work.

vv. 1-2, enemies in v. 3, talk about the enemies in v. 4, self-address again
in vv. 5-7, instruction to the congregation in vv. 8-11, and finally address
to God in v. 12—the repeated particle each time introduces an affirmation
the psalmist struggles to embrace, an affirmation about God, the reality
of enemies, and the nature of life.

"God alone" (vv. 5, 7) protects and saves the psalmist in the midst of
the pain and injustice of the world. This repetition underscores the
psalmist's ongoing struggle. Yet v. 5 ups the ante with urgency by using
an imperative the NRSV fails to translate: "find rest, O my soul, in God
alone" (NIV). The staccato use of אַךְ pushes the psalmist to embrace what
she was uncertain about: God is the only source of trust because God is
rock, salvation, fortress, and refuge; the enemies are hypocrites who plot
destruction; life is ephemeral for all; riches are not to be trusted. Only
when the psalmist claims God as "*my* refuge" (v. 7) can she turn to the
congregation and proclaim, "God is a refuge for *us*" (v. 8). She must
practice affirmation by calling God "my salvation" four times (vv. 1, 2,
6, 7) and "my rock" three times (vv. 2, 6, 7) before this can happen. In v.
7, her "I" and נפשׁ come together in a verse beginning with "on God" and
ending with "in God"; "structurally and theologically, the reality of God
encompasses the psalmist,"[4] who realizes that everything, including
deliverance and honor, depends on God.

With the psalmist's instruction to the people in v. 8 to "pour out" (שׁפך)
their hearts before God who is their refuge (Ps 42:4; the superscriptions

---

4. McCann, "The Book of Psalms," 923.

of Pss 102; 142:2), the story of Hannah and the birth of Samuel suggests itself as intertext. In 1 Samuel 1:15, Hannah responds to Eli's accusation that she is drunk at the Shiloh sanctuary by insisting, "No, my lord . . . but I have been pouring out [שָׁפַךְ] my soul [נֶפֶשׁ] before the Lord." One can imagine that she was praying Psalm 62 as a prelude to her vow (1 Sam 1:11); she, like the psalmist, is searching for the unity of her "I" and her נֶפֶשׁ. Eli thought she was drunk because he saw her lips moving but heard no sound. The narrator tells us that "Hannah was praying silently" (literally, "in her heart," v. 13), which provides another link to Psalm 62. The psalmist gives positive instruction about the heart in v. 8 ("pour out your heart") and also negative instruction in v. 10 ("do not set your heart on them [riches]").

The psalm and Hannah's story are also linked by the idea of silence, especially if we translate 62:1a with Robert Alter: "Only in God is my being quiet."[5] Literally, the phrase is a nominal clause: "only to/toward God my נֶפֶשׁ (is) silence." Commentators have injected the sense of waiting (the Hebrew root קָוָה) into their translation of this feminine singular noun. As in both Psalm 19 (creation's silent speech) and 1 Kings 19:12 (Elijah's experience of God in silence) "silence gains a positive significance. . . . Silence need no longer represent His [God's] anger or rejection but can express His [God's] Presence as well as or better than the word."[6] Silence becomes a medium for approaching God in both Psalms 62 and 65:1a and in 1 Samuel 1.

Hannah describes herself to Eli as "deeply troubled" and speaking out of "great anxiety and vexation" (1 Sam 1:15). Why? Peninnah, the "other" (literally, "second") wife of Hannah's husband, Elkanah, had children, but Hannah was barren because "the LORD had closed her womb" (1:5). Peninnah "used to provoke her severely, to irritate her" (1:6); she rubbed her own fertility in Hannah's face when the wives would accompany Elkanah to Shiloh on his yearly pilgrimage: "so it went on year by year; as often as she went up to the house of the LORD, she used to provoke her" (1:7). Hannah's response was to weep and refuse to eat (v. 7); her silence stands in sharp contrast to Peninnah's constant verbal assaults. Did Hannah imagine challenging Peninnah

---

5. Robert Alter, *The Book of Psalms* (New York: W. W. Norton, 2007), 213.

6. Andre Neher, *The Exile of the Word: From the Silence of the Bible to the Silence of Auschwitz*, trans. David Maisel (Philadelphia: Jewish Publication Society of America, 1981), 85, quoted in Herbert J. Levine, *Sing unto God a New Song: A Contemporary Reading of the Psalms* (Bloomington: Indiana University Press, 1995), 222.

with the words of Psalm 62:3: "How long will you assail [literally: 'shout at'] a person, will you batter [the Hebrew root is from רצח, 'kill'] your victim?"[7] "How long?" is not a question for information but rather a cry of pain.[8] Hannah cannot take it anymore; this verbal abuse has been going on for far too long and is literally killing her.

The victim in Psalm 62:3b is like "a leaning wall, a tottering fence," which suggests Hannah's imminent collapse. To keep herself from falling apart, one imagines that Hannah counters v. 3b with the desperately hopeful declaration in v. 6b (also v. 2): "I shall never be shaken" (Pss 13:4; 15:5; 16:8; 21:7; 30:6; 112:6). The fact that Peninnah was engaged in such vicious verbal assault on Hannah during visits to worship at the Shiloh sanctuary is expressed by v. 4b of the psalm: "they [the enemies] bless with their mouths, but inwardly they curse." The hypocrisy is shocking. Threatening speech is often cited in the laments to underscore the vulnerability of the psalmist and convince God to act; this will be important when Hannah petitions God for a son and makes her vow (1 Sam 1:11). The fact that Elkanah's second wife, Peninnah, is threatening to topple Hannah, his first wife, links to Psalm 61:4a (though the Hebrew is difficult): "their only plan is to bring down a person of prominence." Hannah's "prominence" comes from Elkanah's devotion to her (v. 8); she was his "favorite" (v. 5) and Peninnah knew it. Entering into Hannah's narrative fleshes out the metaphors of Psalm 62 in an experiential way.

Psalm 62:10 and Psalm 120 "problematize the use of violence and evidence caution and restraint."[9] The psalmist instructs: "put no confidence in extortion (or "oppression"), and set no vain hopes on robbery." The phrase "vain hopes" comes from the Hebrew word הבל (what is worthless, empty breath, used often in Qoheleth). Hannah's instruction rebukes Peninnah; Hannah trusts in God to remedy the abusive situation (vv. 8, 12).

---

7. In only two other psalms does the psalmist address enemies directly: 4:2-3 and 52:1-5. One would expect more examples if Gerald Sheppard is correct in arguing that the enemies, community, and God were all addressed in local worship settings. See Gerald T. Sheppard, " 'Enemies' and the Politics of Prayer in the Book of Psalms," in *The Bible and the Politics of Exegesis*, ed. David Jobling, Peggy Day, and Gerald Sheppard (Cleveland, OH: Pilgrim Press, 1991), 61–82, at 78.

8. Denise Dombkowski Hopkins, *Journey through the Psalms* (St. Louis, MO: Chalice Press, 2002), 83.

9. Amy C. Cottrill, *Language, Power, and Identity in the Lament Psalms of the Individual* (New York and London: T & T Clark, 2008), 97 n. 116.

A Childless Woman

Even though Hannah's husband, Elkanah, insists that her childlessness does not matter to him ("Am I not more to you than ten sons?" [1 Sam 1:8]), it matters to her. Elkanah was wealthy enough to afford a second, fertile wife, Peninnah. As a childless woman probably much younger than her husband, Hannah risked sinking into poverty once Elkanah died. Without a male in her kinship group—husband, son, son-in-law—she would remain on the fringes of society. "Hannah . . . needed children: for her future support . . . but also for her position in the society she lived in."[9] Hannah would acknowledge this in praying Psalm 62:7: "on God rests my deliverance and my honor."

Hannah's כבוד ("honor" / "respect") in society was based in part on her fertility. Peninnah's constant provocations damaged Hannah's honor and shamed her. To restore her honor, Hannah goes to God and makes a vow (1 Sam 1:11), acknowledging that God has closed her womb and is the only One to open it. Also, based on the offering of firstfruits of animals and harvest to God to ensure future yields, Hannah probably makes her vow to give her son to God "in hopes of receiving more children in return."[10] First Samuel 2:21 relates that this does happen: "and the Lord took note of Hannah; she conceived and bore three sons and two daughters."

Denise Dombkowski Hopkins

What puts everything in perspective for the psalmist and for Hannah is v. 9. All humans, rich and poor alike (see Ps 49:2; Isa 40:15, 17), are but a transitory breath so insubstantial that on a scale, breath would weigh more. Peninnah's striving to usurp Hannah's position as first wife is futile in this bigger picture. The psalm ends with an implicit reference to the idea of act-consequence, or reward-punishment for one's deeds: God will "repay to all according to their work." Despite the bigger picture, perhaps Hannah wishes that Peninnah will get hers after all. Often women turn against one another within the larger social location of patriarchy (see Sarah and Hagar in Gen 16).[12]

10. Jo Ann Hackett, "1 and 2 Samuel," in *Women's Bible Commentary*, ed. Carol A. Newsom, Sharon H. Ringe, and Jacqueline E. Lapsley, 3rd ed. (Louisville, KY: Westminster John Knox, 2012), 150–63, at 154.

11. Ibid.

12. Renita J. Weems, "A Mistress, a Maid, and No Mercy," in *Just a Sister Away* (Philadelphia: Innisfree Press, 1988), 1–23.

God Defines Us

In the movie *The Color Purple*, Celie endures years of emotional, physical, verbal, and sexual abuse from her husband, with whom she was forced into marriage and whom she calls Mister, an indication of her subjugated role. Walker describes Mister as brutish, sexually aggressive, unloving, and lazy. He is not in love with Celie and does not value her as a person. Rather, Mister receives her as his property.

One day, Celie realizes that the source of her strength and liberation is transcendent and she confronts Mister. Celie says, "I curse you. Until you do right by me everything you think about is gonna crumble!" Mister responds, "Who you think you is? You can't curse nobody. Look at you. You're black, you're poor, you're ugly, you're a woman, you're nothing at all!"[13]

For centuries, women of color were viewed through such a hateful and disempowering lens and suffered horrifying abuse. Women were sacrificed to satisfy the appetite of dominance and power. Like Hannah, these women were deeply troubled and suffered in silence. Celie, suffering silently, musters enough strength to trust God and seek liberation because she realizes that Mister is mere breath and possesses no power over her (Ps 62:9). In response to Mister's hateful declaration, Celie proclaims: "I'm poor, black, I might even be ugly, but dear God, I'm here. I'm here." Celie, like the psalmist in v. 7, now understands that God defines who she is, and in God her human dignity, liberation, and hope are found and secured.

God has no intention for Celie's body, life, or even soul to be sacrificed in the manner Mister had perpetrated. God is the only source of trust because God is rock, salvation, fortress, and refuge (v. 7); God offers hope and salvation. Now knowing there is no shame in being black, poor, and a woman, Celie escapes her bondage, walks away from her captivity, and claims her salvation.

Audrey Coretta Price

13. *The Color Purple*, book by Alice Walker, screenplay by Menno Meyjes, film production by Steven Spielberg, Kathleen Kennedy, Frank Marshall, Quincy Jones, and Jon Peters (Amblin Entertainment, Guber-Peters Company, Warner Brothers, 1985). Quotations are from the film.

Psalm 63

Body-Based Prayer

The emotional intensity of Psalm 63 is conveyed through body parts: thirsty throat (נפש, v. 1), fainting flesh (בשר, v. 1), beholding eyes (v. 2), praising lips (v. 3b), uplifted hands (v. 4b), sated body (נפש, v. 5a), praising mouth (v. 5), joyful lips (v. 5b), clinging person (נפש, v. 8a), upholding right hand (of God, v. 8), preyed-upon life (נפש, v. 9a), mouths of liars (v. 11c). The NRSV translation of נפש as "soul" in vv. 1, 5, and 8 and "life" in v. 9 does not take into account the nuances of the term in each verse and its function of characterizing the changing feelings and emotions of the psalmist.[1] In somatic parallelism with "flesh" in v. 1, the psalmist metaphorically locates her search for God in her "throat"; her longing for God is a thirst. Just as a parched land needs water, the psalmist needs God. Her body also needs divine nourishment; her flesh "faints" for God. Once again the thirsty and hungry body communicates the psalmist's vulnerability (Pss 42:1-2; 143:6) and reminds us that life depends on God. Perhaps this explains why later editors linked Psalm 63 to David with the superscription "when he was in the wilderness of Judah." The dry land "where there is no water" in v. 1b suggests the wilderness to which the vulnerable David flees when Saul seeks to kill him (1 Sam 23:14-25; 24:1-2).

---

1. Susanne Gillmayr-Bucher, "Body Images in the Psalms," *JSOT* 28 (2004): 301–26, at 304–5.

Psalm 63:1-11

A Psalm of David, when he was in the Wilderness of Judah.

¹O God, you are my God, I seek you,
  my soul thirsts for you;
my flesh faints for you,
    as in a dry and weary land
      where there is no water.
²So I have looked upon you in the sanctuary,
  beholding your power and glory.

³Because your steadfast love is better than life,
  my lips will praise you.
⁴So I will bless you as long as I live;
  I will lift up my hands and call on your name.

⁵My soul is satisfied as with a rich feast,
  and my mouth praises you with joyful lips

The Psalmist's נפש in the Wilderness

This psalm may surprise the audience with its dissonance and contradictions about the condition and location of the psalmist's נפש ("living being"). The psalmist complains that the נפש thirsts for God and stands desperately in need of water (v. 1); however, the psalmist soon confesses that the נפש is fully satisfied as with "a rich feast" (v. 5). Situated in the "wilderness," the psalmist laments the desolate and solitary state of "flesh" (v. 1); in the next verse, however, this same psalmist, located in the "sanctuary," experiences the strength and abundance of God (v. 2). The psalmist's נפש fully attaches to God, whose hand protects it (v. 8), and yet this נפש is threatened by those who attempt to destroy its life (v. 9). In this multilayered view of the נפש the psalmist escapes the control of the audience's judgment on its condition and location and invites us as readers to contemplate the condition and location of our own נפש.

What is even more striking to the audience is that the speaker in this psalm is, in fact, identified with a "king" in the last verse (v. 11). The audience may be reminded of David's experiences of life and death in the wilderness when he tries to escape from Saul's attacks (1 Sam 24 and 26). Saul is unsuccessful in his attempts to kill David, and David ultimately succeeds in making Saul acknowledge "who David is" and in removing him as king with the sword of the Philistines (1 Sam 26:10; Ps 63:10). Just as Saul acknowledges David as the king of Israel while in the desert of En-gedi (1 Sam 24:20), the psalmist reveals his identity as the king to the audience in the

⁶when I think of you on my bed,
and meditate on you in the
watches of the night;
⁷for you have been my help,
and in the shadow of your
wings I sing for joy.
⁸My soul clings to you;
your right hand upholds me.

⁹But those who seek to destroy
my life

shall go down into the depths
of the earth;
¹⁰they shall be given over to the
power of the sword,
they shall be prey for jackals.
¹¹But the king shall rejoice in God;
all who swear by him shall
exult,
for the mouths of liars will be
stopped.

most unexpected place—the wilderness. Surprisingly, the psalmist praises God with "lips," "hands," "mouth," "body," and "soul" (vv. 3, 4, 5, 7, 11), not in a royal palace of cedar but in the dislocated place of desert—an unlikely location in which a king would exult and rejoice in God (v. 11) and a humbling reminder to those in power about where power ultimately lies: in God.

Su Jung Shin

If we read the verb חזיתיך in 63:2 in the perfect as NRSV does—"so I have looked upon you"—the memory of worship in the sanctuary fuels the psalmist's desire. If we read this verb as a perfect of certitude[2]—"so I will look upon you"—it is the anticipation of worship that fuels her desire (Pss 65:4; 84:2-4, 10). This latter reading works better with the imperfects used in vv. 3-5. Either reading shows that "the direction of desire leads ineluctably to God," the only worthy goal of desire in the Psalms.[3] God is the end stage of the process of reaching happiness, a

2. Ronald J. Williams, *Williams' Hebrew Syntax*, 3rd ed., rev. and exp. by John Beckman (Toronto: University of Toronto Press, 2010), 68, section 165. The perfect of certitude describes a future event as if it has already happened.

3. William P. Brown, "Happiness and Its Discontents in the Psalms," in *The Bible and the Pursuit of Happiness: What the Old and New Testaments Teach Us about the Good Life*, ed. Brent A. Strawn (Oxford: Oxford University Press, 2012), 95–116, at 109.

process begun in Psalm 1:1—"how happy [אשרי]"—which orients the whole Psalter toward human flourishing through obedience to God.[4] Because of God's faithfulness or covenant loyalty (v. 3a, חסד, "steadfast love" in NRSV), the psalmist anticipates that her parched lips will offer God praises and blessing (vv. 3b, 4a), accompanied by uplifted hands (v. 4b), a typical ancient Near Eastern prayer posture.

In v. 5, the use of נפש signals a shift to the psalmist's confident hope that her needs and desires will be met: "my soul [better: 'being'] is satisfied as with a rich feast," literally "with choicest fat/marrow and fat of the olive," or rich food and drink. This phrase suggests a sacrificial meal at the sanctuary. The mouth and lips that eat and drink their fill will respond with praises in public worship (v. 5b). The use of the verb "satisfied" (שבע, "sate," "eat one's fill") in v. 5a calls to mind Psalms 104:13, 28 and 107:9, in which God the creator "fills with good things" (food and drink) the earth and all creatures. God's "glory [כבוד, 'radiance,' 'majesty']" in 63:2b links the psalm to the covenant meal on Sinai (Exod 24:16; see also Exod 40:34; 1 Kgs 8:11). Israel's remembered past is also often linked with food.

The psalmist's focus shifts from public worship to private meditation in the present in v. 6, introduced by the conjunction אם. I translate v. 6 with Marvin Tate, not as a subordinate clause to v. 5 but as beginning a new sentence and a new section of Psalm 63: "As I remember you upon my bed."[5] The psalmist "meditates" in the night watches, just as the psalmist "meditates" on God's Torah day and night in Psalm 1:2. Some interpreters suggest that this phrase refers to a night vigil in the sanctuary, especially when coupled with "in the shadow of your wings" (v. 7b), which may refer to the cherubim atop the ark of the covenant. As Silvia Schroer has argued, however, these wings are the protecting, regenerating wings of the goose vulture associated with goddesses in the ancient Near East. Israel's God has taken over this "motherliness."[6]

---

4. Ibid., 97.

5. Marvin E. Tate, *Psalms 51–100* (Dallas, TX: Word Books, 1990), 123.

6. Silvia Schroer, " 'Under the Shadow of Your Wings': The Metaphor of God's Wings in the Psalms, Exodus 19.4, Deuteronomy 32.11 and Malachi 3.20, as Seen through the Perspectives of Feminism and the History of Religion," in *Wisdom and Psalms*, FCB, 2nd ser., ed. Athalya Brenner and Carole Fontaine (Sheffield: Sheffield Academic Press, 1998), 264–82.

Carol Meyers on Festivals as Food Events Involving Women

The "rich feast" the psalmist anticipates in v. 5a can be viewed in a larger anthropological context. Carol Meyers cites archaeological evidence that supports the practice of feasting at neighborhood, village, regional, and national shrines and temples, and ethnographic materials that indicate gender inclusivity in these community feasts (Deut 16:14). Coupling this evidence with her study of women's roles in food preparation, she concludes that "women in social reality (as opposed to biblical texts) were likely to have been frequent participants in festivals, which were food events." Whether these festivals are regular or *ad hoc* affairs, they are more than a form of ritual activity; they have psychological, political, and economic functions as well.

Feasts, whether local or national, share characteristics: they are all commensal, i.e., food and drink are shared and consumed; the food and drink are more abundant and/or of better quality than an ordinary meal; the meal lasts much longer; the number of participants is greater than in an individual household. All these features contribute to the emotional intensity of the feast by heightening anticipation, providing entertainment in "something of a carnival atmosphere," providing a break from "agrarian anxiety," and providing visual, olfactory, and auditory stimuli from the slaughtering process itself.

In addition, feasts functioned religiously to affirm one's loyalty to God, politically to affirm and legitimate the unequal power relations of political and priestly elites, and economically to redistribute foodstuffs brought to the festival and sold/traded to those attending. The festival foods become "material mnemonics connecting people to their remembered past and to one another"; food created social cohesion and solidified group identity and values.[7]

Denise Dombkowski Hopkins

---

7. Carol Meyers, "The Function of Feasts: An Anthropological Perspective on Israelite Religious Festivals," in *Social Theory and the Study of Israelite Religion: Essays in Retrospect and Prospect*, ed. Saul M. Olyan (Atlanta, GA: Society of Biblical Literature, 2012), 141–68.

This view fits well with the intimacy of the God/psalmist relationship experienced by the psalmist in the present in v. 8, based on memory and anticipation of the future: "my נפש clings to you." The declaration that God's right hand upholds the psalmist adds to this sense of intimacy. "Cling" (דבק) is the same verb that speaks in Genesis 2:24 of a man clinging to his woman in sexual union, and in 2 Kings 5:27 for disease that clings to a person; compare this to the military usage of the verb in 2 Samuel 23:10 and 1 Samuel 14:22 in terms of battle and pursuit of the enemy. It is a verb of fierce connection. Ruth expresses her strong desire for connection to Naomi by "clinging" to her (Ruth 1:14) and refusing to turn back to Moab as Orpah had done.

A God Who Suckles

The psalmist wants a maternal God who can nurture, satisfy, and satiate; a God who holds her child close, protects her young with the strength of her outstretched wing, and provides the richest food possible. The intimacy of the language is evocative of a breastfeeding mother who quenches her baby's hunger with the cream of her milk, produced from the richness of her own body. A suckling infant clings close to its nursing mother, cradled in the crook of her arm, shielded from the distractions and dangers of the world. The lips of the nursing infant utter the deepest praise possible, first with the loud, hungry swallows of mother's milk and then with the sated, gaping, drowsy mouth asleep on the mother's breast. The intensity of the embodied language of the psalm points to a female God, uniquely able to meet the needs of her young.

The breastfeeding relationship is reciprocal, however. A mother will produce only as much milk as her nursing child needs, not more and not less. The physical comfort of the mother depends on the child draining the breast of milk; otherwise she risks engorgement and possible infection. An ineffective nursing infant yields an infirm mother. The mother needs the child as much as the child needs her mother. The milk-laced lips of the sated sleeping child are a mother's affirmation of her existence. Beneath the intensity of the embodied language of the psalm, rife with the human desire for physical intimacy, is a subliminal sense that the deity needs this relationship too. The mouthfuls of praise, the awe-struck gaze, and the fainting flesh are not simply involuntary reflexes of gratitude but part of what the relationship requires, just as the lactating mother needs her child to suckle to complete satiation.

Amy Beth Jones

The final use of נפש in Psalm 63:9 again shifts the tone, this time to a vengeful triumphalism against those who seek to destroy the psalmist's life (נפשי). Here the sated psalmist exults that the enemies will become "prey for jackals" (v. 10b). The psalmist receives life from God's presence, but the enemy descends into the earth's depths (v. 9b), probably Sheol, the realm of the dead. The juxtaposition of a "rich feast" for the psalmist with enemies who become "prey for jackals" points again to the importance of food in this psalm. Food often functions in Tanakh in the literary motif of "judgment at the table"; "it is through food events that YHWH exhibits his justice."[8] This motif also supports the patronage system that characterizes the God/psalmist relationship. God as patron is expected to protect the psalmist, who deserves such protection. After all, the psalmist has declared that God's חסד is "better than life" (v. 3).

Other contrasts pepper Psalm 63.[9] For example, while the mouth and lips of the psalmist offer up praise to God, the "mouths of liars will be stopped" (v. 11c); the thirsting, hungry psalmist will be sated; God's power will overcome human hostility; God's power contrasts with human fainting. All oppositions dissolve in God. Just as in Psalm 61:6, a prayer for the king is included, but this does not mean that the king is the speaker in the psalm; he simply represents God's justice on earth.

Food and reversals also play a large part in three stories about women: Hannah, Ruth, and Abigail, each of whom could have prayed Psalm 63. The Song of Hannah (1 Sam 2:5-6, 7-8) takes place at the annual feast at Shiloh and anticipates God's judgment: the full "have hired themselves out for bread" while the formerly hungry "are fat with spoil"; God "brings to life . . . and down to Sheol." The house of Eli falls because Eli and his sons fattened themselves on the choicest parts of offerings (1 Sam 2:29, 36), while Hannah is raised up because she refused to eat (1 Sam 1:7). The opening chapter of Ruth is framed by food. It begins with famine in Bethlehem (the "house of bread"), which forces Naomi and her husband and sons to leave, and it concludes with the beginning of the barley harvest, prompting Naomi's return to Bethlehem with Ruth. Death is overcome by life and birth (chap. 4). Boaz gives Ruth extra portions when she gleans; she eats in the field "until she [is] satisfied" (שבע, 2:14, 18; cp. Ps 63:5). Psalm 63:7 and Ruth 2:12 (see 3:9) also share the seeking

---

8. Nathan MacDonald, *Not Bread Alone: The Uses of Food in the Old Testament* (Oxford: Oxford University Press, 2008), 167, 172.

9. Konrad Schaefer, *Psalms*, Berit Olam (Collegeville, MN: Liturgical Press, 2001), 153.

of refuge under "God's wings." The rabbinic midrash on Ruth likewise centers on food and punishment. Elimelech was wealthy but fled rather than help the starving, so he and his sons died as punishment.[10] Abigail's story unfolds during a sheep-shearing feast (1 Sam 25). Her husband, Nabal, refuses to feed David and his men as protection insurance. Abigail foils David's retaliatory attack by bringing food and drink to him and his men (25:18). Nabal dies after the feast when he learns what she has done, and David considers it God's justice (25:39).

10. Kirsten Nielsen, *Ruth*, OTL (Louisville, KY: Westminster John Knox, 1997), 18, referring to *Ruth Rabbah*.

Psalm 64

Sharp Tongues

As a tightly constructed individual lament, Psalm 64 uses repetition, reversals, irony, and metaphor to convince God to carry out retributive justice against the wicked. That the threat is unbearable for the psalmist is conveyed by the petitions in vv. 1-2. Her very life is at stake, and God must preserve it (v. 1b). The urgency of her situation is amplified by the description of the enemies that follows in vv. 3-6. Drawing on military metaphors of swords and arrows in "a language of wounds and weapons" frequently found in the Psalter, the psalmist makes her pain visible to God and the public, forcing it to be addressed while at the same time gaining sympathy from both. With "tongues like swords" and "bitter words like arrows" (v. 3), the speech of the evildoers functions as "a tool of violence, a weapon of attack"[1] against the psalmist (Pss 52:2-3; 55:21; 57:4; 58:3-5; 59:7; 63:9, 11; 140:3). In this way the psalmist defines herself as vulnerable and the other as evil aggressor, which allows for some rhetorical control over the situation.

When the psalm shifts in v. 7 from direct address to God to third-person talk about God and what God will do, irony becomes apparent. God and the enemies act in the same way, so that "their images mirror

---

1. Amy C. Cottrill, *Language, Power, and Identity in the Lament Psalms of the Individual* (New York and London: T & T Clark, 2008), 39, 80.

Psalm 64:1-10

To the leader. A Psalm of David.

¹Hear my voice, O God, in my
complaint;
preserve my life from the
dread enemy.
²Hide me from the secret plots of
the wicked,
from the scheming of evildoers,
³who whet their tongues like
swords,

who aim bitter words like
arrows,
⁴shooting from ambush at the
blameless;
they shoot suddenly and
without fear.
⁵They hold fast to their evil
purpose;
they talk of laying snares
secretly,
thinking, "Who can see us?

each other"² and accentuate the notion of retributive justice. The enemies may shoot their arrows (חץ, vv. 3-4), but God will retaliate in kind,
shooting divine arrows (חץ; Ps 7:12-13) at the evildoers (v. 7a). Just as the
enemies shoot "suddenly" (v. 4b), so will God: "they [the evildoers] will
be wounded suddenly" (v. 7b). Yet God and the wicked do not share the
same motives for their actions; the relational function of the archer metaphor is different for each vis-à-vis the psalmist. God is vindicator/helper,
while the wicked are aggressors. God and the psalmist share these mutual enemies and create common cause against them; the enemies are
necessary to avoid a demonization of God.³ The end result is that the
psalm's initial focus on the enemies shifts to the "righteous" and "upright" in v. 10; "plots" and "snares" give way to rejoicing and glory in
an "antithetic inclusion."⁴

Retribution anchors Psalm 64, as it does many laments. God is expected to do to the wicked what the wicked have been doing to the
psalmist (see Pss 7:15-16; 9:15; 18:25-26; 35:7-8; 37:14-15). Psalm 1:6 states
the principle of retribution in general terms: God rewards the righteous
and punishes the wicked (Gal 6:7-8). This view undergirds the wisdom
tradition, the prophets, Deuteronomy, the parables of Jesus, and the book
of Revelation. It is expressed in *lex talionis*, "proportionate punishment,"

---

2. Goeran Eidevall, "Images of God, Self, and the Enemy in the Psalms: On the
Role of Metaphor in Identity Construction," in *Metaphor in the Hebrew Bible*, ed. P. Van
Hecke (Leuven: University Press, 2005), 55–65, at 62.

3. Ibid., 63.

4. Philippus J. Botha, "The Textual Strategy and Social Background of Psalm 64 as
Keys to Its Interpretation," *JSem* 11 (2002): 64–82, at 72.

[6]Who can search out our crimes? We have thought out a cunningly conceived plot." For the human heart and mind are deep.	all who see them will shake with horror. [9]Then everyone will fear; they will tell what God has brought about, and ponder what he has done.
[7]But God will shoot his arrow at them; they will be wounded suddenly. [8]Because of their tongue he will bring them to ruin;	[10]Let the righteous rejoice in the LORD and take refuge in him. Let all the upright in heart glory.

in Exodus 21:23-25; Leviticus 24:17-21; Deuteronomy 19:19-21, and can be traced back to the Code of Hammurabi (ca. 1750 BCE).[5] Several interpreters argue that the psalmist's desire for retribution stems not from "a *realization of fantasies of vengeance*, but a *restoration of justice* through God's saving righteousness,"[6] especially since the psalmist transfers her own vengeance to God, who is petitioned to carry it out.

Frequent reversals and wordplays in Psalm 64, in addition to the use of military imagery discussed above, support the central idea of retribution. The wicked who believed they were invisible in v. 5b—"who can see us?"—will be exposed in v. 8b: "all who see them will shake with horror" after God retaliates. The verb ראה, "see," in both verses serves to heighten the reversal. Once again (Ps 59:7), the quotation of the enemy marks the transition from the complaint in vv. 3-6 to the confession of trust and exhortation to the congregation in vv. 7-10. The vocabulary of the quotation ties the two sections together and provides the central arguments addressed in the psalm, namely, that God is absent and/or powerless to stop the wicked. The enemy quotation provides a way of "circumventing *theologically determined* limits that delineated how far the psalmist could go in her complaint against God." Quoting the enemy "dissociates the psalmist from the responsibility for the assertions."[7]

---

5. Gordon J. Wenham, *Psalms as Torah: Reading Biblical Song Ethically* (Grand Rapids, MI: Baker Academic, 2012), 112.

6. Bernd Janowski, *Arguing with God: A Theological Anthropology of the Psalms*, trans. Armin Siedlecki (Louisville, KY: Westminster John Knox, 2013), 125.

7. Rolf A. Jacobson, *"Many Are Saying": The Function of Direct Discourse in the Hebrew Psalter*, JSOTSup 397 (Edinburgh: T & T Clark, 2004), 54, 55.

Michal and Words as Weapons

Cheryl Exum's study of Michal, Saul's daughter and David's wife, can help readers flesh out the metaphors of swords and arrows in Psalm 64. Exum notes that Michal acts as an agent in her own right in 1 Samuel 19 when she helps David to escape from the murderous Saul. She also shows agency in 2 Samuel 6 when she censures David for exposing himself to the help while dancing before the ark of the covenant "as any vulgar fellow might shamelessly uncover himself" (2 Sam 6:20). Yet Michal is "killed off as a narrative presence" (p. 45),[8] because she loses the "battle of words" with David, who "holds the power" (p. 55) in their relationship. In his stinging rebuke of her criticism David reminds her that God chose him over her father (2 Sam 6:21-22). The narrator denies her a reply; that David's words have fatally wounded her can be seen in v. 23: the narrator immediately announces that "Michal the daughter of Saul had no child to the day of her death." Michal is denied a child and thus her identity, since "patriarchal texts identify women in terms of reproductive function" (p. 57). By leaving the safety of her house and power sphere and publicly criticizing the king's behavior, Michal essentially commits "verbal suicide" (p. 55). Saul's house is now out of the way, securing the future of David's house. Even worse, Michal's own words isolate her from other women at the mercy of men in their lives by implying that David has uncovered himself in front of women of inferior status— servants of the male servants (v. 20). Her words create a class divide "to obscure the gender issue," which is "one of the strategies of patriarchal ideology" (p. 61).

Denise Dombkowski Hopkins

Another reversal tinged with irony emerges in vv. 3a and 8a. The wicked with "their tongues [לשונם] like swords" will find that their tongues (לשונם) will be their undoing, illustrating "the boomerang effect of evil (see Ps 7:16)."[9] While the wicked shoot "from ambush" (v. 4a, from the root סתר, "hide"), the psalmist petitions to be hidden (v. 2a, from the root סתר) by God from their plotting. At the end of the psalm, however, the

8. J. Cheryl Exum, "Murder They Wrote: Ideology and the Manipulation of Female Presence in Biblical Narrative," in *The Pleasure of Her Text: Feminist Readings of Biblical and Historical Texts*, ed. Alice Bach (Philadelphia: Trinity Press International, 1990), 45–68.

9. Konrad Schaefer, *Psalms*, Berit Olam (Collegeville, MN: Liturgical Press, 2001), 155.

righteous are encouraged to "take refuge" in God (v. 10), not in hiding, but in rejoicing and exultation. The downfall of the fearless wicked who plot secretly with impunity will cause "everyone" to "fear" (v. 9a).

Another aspect of retribution present in Psalm 64 is rooted in the Decalogue. Gordon Wenham[10] argues that though lawgiving at Sinai is "mostly absent" in the Psalter, Psalm 64 and other psalms focus on violations of the ninth commandment: "you shall not bear false witness against your neighbor" (Exod 20:16). Proverbs deals with the immediate consequences of the vices and virtues of the tongue (e.g., Prov 15:2; 18:21), but the psalms relate speech to God; the tongue should be used to praise God rather than wound one's neighbor (Jas 3:9-10; Ps 62:4). Proper speech should "tell what God has brought about" (v. 9b) and "rejoice in the Lord" (v. 10a).

Sharp-Tongued Biblical Women

Two women of 2 Samuel, the wise woman of Tekoa (2 Sam 14) and the wise woman of Abel (2 Sam 20), have some of the sharpest tongues in the Bible. The wise woman of Tekoa lures David to indict himself with her prophetic story about feuding sons. The wise woman of Abel saves her village from a rampaging Joab by invoking the city's reputation as a peaceful place of counsel and rhetorically asking him if he would destroy the "city that is a mother in Israel." The confrontational speech of both women rises to what Claudia Camp calls "psychological warfare," which she defines as "psychological manipulation that is applied by the prophets and wise women, who use the parables to create the two conditions—of distancing and re-involvement—necessary for a person blinded by proximity to a problem to achieve a new perspective on it."[11] The pointed words of these women interrupt the male plot of their stories, temporarily pausing and redirecting male ambitions with female intellect. The weapon-like words cut deeper and pose a greater challenge than any physical armament in the story. The psalmist acknowledges impotence to combat the verbal cunning unaided. It is *God* who will battle the word-slinger. The text avoids lingering with women for too long, but the effect of their words and actions reverberates. The impact of provocative words is arguably greater than the impact of penetrating swords.

Amy Beth Jones

10. Wenham, *Psalms as Torah*, 98, 107–9.

11. Claudia Camp, "The Wise Women of 2 Samuel: A Role Model for Women in Early Israel?," *CBQ* 43 (1981): 14–29, at 21.

The focus on violent retribution in Psalm 64 calls to mind 1 Samuel 25 as intertext. The story intersects with and counters Psalm 64 as foil in several places. Nabal, the rich husband of Abigail, uses his words as weapons in response to the request of David's outlaw men for the equivalent of protection money (food from the sheep-shearing festival): "Who is David? . . . There are many servants today who are breaking away from their masters. Shall I take my bread and my water and the meat that I have butchered for my shearers, and give it to men who come from I do not know where?" (1 Sam 25:10-11). True to his name, which means "fool," Nabal insults David. His "bitter words" aimed "like arrows" (Ps 64:3) prompt David to prepare for retaliation; he and his men strap on their swords (1 Sam 25:13), physical instruments of wounding that rival the power of Nabal's wounding words.

Abigail is introduced as the opposite of Nabal in 1 Samuel 25:3: "the woman was clever and beautiful, but the man was surly and mean." She uses her words and acts very differently from both men. Hurrying with abundant supplies to meet David, she launches into an extended speech before David has a chance to say a word. She uses the phrase "my Lord" twelve times in reference to David, showing her subordination to him. As Katharine Doob Sakenfeld[12] notes, Abigail uses "a rhetorically effective strategy" by speaking as if David's plans for retaliation have already been canceled; she shows him another way that will keep him from bloodguilt. Sakenfeld quotes Judette Gallares, who calls Abigail "a faithful pacifist, an advocate of active non-violence and peace, [who] offers us an alternative value system . . . that relies more on the power of peace and reconciliation than on the power of hate and vengeance."[13]

Alice Bach[14] speaks of Abigail's "providential persuasion"; with her "verbal power" of prophecy Abigail recognizes David as the future king. She sets limits to David's anger. Unfortunately, she is labeled by some as "the good-sense wife" in comparison with Bathsheba and Michal, an expansion perhaps of the good wife in Proverbs 31, who "opens her mouth with wisdom, and the teaching of kindness is on her tongue" (Prov 31:36). This is not the tongue of David or Nabal. Yet Bach criticizes this view because Abigail loses her agency and becomes simply what is

12. Katharine Doob Sakenfeld, *Just Wives? Stories of Power and Survival in the Old Testament and Today* (Louisville, KY: Westminster John Knox, 2003), 85.

13. Ibid., 87, quoting Judette A. Gallares, *Images of Faith: Spirituality of Women in the Old Testament* (Maryknoll, NY: Orbis Books, 1992), 124.

14. Alice Bach, "The Pleasure of Her Text," *USQR* 43 (1989): 41–58, at 44, 43, 46–49.

"advantageous to men in the story." As Abigail is absorbed into David's household, she loses her voice. Sadly, retribution does take place in the story, as it is hoped for in Psalm 64. "When David heard that Nabal was dead, he said, 'Blessed be the LORD who has judged the case of Nabal's insult to me; . . . the LORD has returned the evildoing of Nabal upon his own head" (1 Sam 25:39).

Psalm 65

The Earth's Praise

Psalm 65 begins in silence and ends with shouts and singing. As a thanksgiving psalm it contrasts with the string of laments that precedes it. Its multiple metaphors evoke our joyful imagination as the psalmist praises God the redeemer, creator, and sustainer. Building to a crescendo of praise, Psalm 65 unfolds in three sections, each focusing on God's activity in the temple, cosmos, and earth, and the response to that activity. The first section, vv. 1-4, opens in Hebrew with the word "to you" in v. 1a, which occurs again in 2a and 2b. Along with the independent personal pronoun ("you") in v. 3b, these words focus our attention on God in the temple, perhaps as a counter to those who would attribute the earth's bounty (vv. 9-13) to Ba'al, the Canaanite god of storm and fertility. Though the NRSV translates v. 1a as "praise is due to you," following the LXX and Syriac, the Hebrew reads literally "to you silence is praise." Rather than connoting passive resignation, as in Psalm 39:2, this silence perhaps conveys the sense of "confident expectation"[1] as in Psalm 22:2. Robert Alter argues more convincingly that "the subject of

---

1. Howard N. Wallace, "*Jubilate Deo omnis terra*: God and Earth in Psalm 65," in *The Earth Story in the Psalms and the Prophets*, ed. Norman C. Habel (Cleveland, OH: Pilgrim Press; Sheffield: Sheffield Academic Press, 2001), 51–64, at 54.

Psalm 65:1-13

To the leader. A Psalm of David.
A Song.

¹Praise is due to you,
O God, in Zion;
and to you shall vows be performed,
²O you who answer prayer!
To you all flesh shall come.
³When deeds of iniquity overwhelm us,
you forgive our transgressions.
⁴Happy are those whom you
choose and bring near
to live in your courts.

We shall be satisfied with the
goodness of your house,
your holy temple.

⁵By awesome deeds you answer
us with deliverance,
O God of our salvation;
you are the hope of all the ends of
the earth
and of the farthest seas.
⁶By your strength you established
the mountains;
you are girded with might.
⁷You silence the roaring of the seas,
the roaring of their waves,

the poem, God's greatness, is beyond what language can express."[2] The God who can appear in silence, as before Elijah in 1 Kings 19:11-12, can receive silence as praise (Ps 19:1-4).

Such silent praise comes from all parts of the created order, fulfilling their God-given mandate to work in harmony with one another for the good of all (Ps 104). Not all praise of God is silent, however. Pastures, hills, meadows, and valleys "shout and sing for joy" (vv. 12-13). The earth's bounty is itself testimony to God's care as sustainer of the created order. Terence Fretheim suggests that "the natural order is certainly not understood to be passive; to the contrary, it is a *coparticipant* in God's creative activity,"[3] with intrinsic rather than simply instrumental value. Earth itself has a voice. While Psalms 89, 96, 98 and Isaiah 35:1-10 express the joy of nature, they do not do so in the context of fertility and harvest as Psalm 65 does. Those psalms that deal with fertility—67, 85, 126—do not include the motif of the joy of nature; Psalm 65 is "unique."[4] One wonders whether earth's voice is still singing for joy today, or singing at all.

2. Robert Alter, *The Book of Psalms* (New York: Norton, 2007), 221.
3. Terence E. Fretheim, "God, Creation, and the Pursuit of Happiness," in *The Bible and the Pursuit of Happiness: What the Old and New Testaments Teach Us about the Good Life*, ed. Brent A. Strawn (Oxford: Oxford University Press, 2012), 33–56, at 50.
4. Wallace, "*Jubilate Deo*," 61.

the tumult of the peoples.
⁸Those who live at earth's farthest
bounds are awed by your
signs;
you make the gateways of the
morning and the evening
shout for joy.

⁹You visit the earth and water it,
you greatly enrich it;
the river of God is full of water;
you provide the people with
grain,
for so you have prepared it.
¹⁰You water its furrows abundantly,
settling its ridges,

softening it with showers,
and blessing its growth.
¹¹You crown the year with your
bounty;
your wagon tracks overflow
with richness.
¹²The pastures of the wilderness
overflow,
the hills gird themselves with joy,
¹³the meadows clothe themselves
with flocks,
the valleys deck themselves
with grain,
they shout and sing together
for joy.

In v. 1a, God is addressed in Zion, the spatial "center"[5] of the psalm; from Zion come all good things, including Torah (Isa 2:3), blessing (Ps 134:3), and water (Ps 46:4). Ellen Davis calls Zion an "icon: a holy, healing image whose function is to invite worshipers into a different experience of the world and their own humanity."[6] "Zion" in v. 1 and "your courts," "your house," and "your holy temple" in v. 4 frame the first section. Between vv. 1 and 4 God "answers prayer" (v. 2a) and "forgive[s] . . . transgressions" (v. 3b). This structure anchors the section in worship in the Jerusalem temple. Vows are performed to God in the temple (Ps 65:1b), probably as thanksgiving sacrifices (see Ps 116:17-18), which involved a common meal. Carol Meyers notes that because of women's important role in food preparation in ancient Israel, "women in social reality (as opposed to biblical texts) were likely to have been frequent participants in festivals, which were food events."[7] The use of "satisfied"

5. Konrad Schaefer, *Psalms*, Berit Olam (Collegeville, MN: Liturgical Press, 2001), 156.

6. Ellen Davis, *Scripture, Culture, and Agriculture: An Agrarian Reading of the Bible* (Cambridge: Cambridge University Press, 2009), 163.

7. Carol Meyers, "The Function of Feasts: An Anthropological Perspective on Israelite Religious Festivals," in *Social Theory and the Study of Israelite Religion: Essays in Retrospect and Prospect*, ed. Saul M. Olyan (Atlanta, GA: Society of Biblical Literature, 2012), 151.

(שבע, "sated") in v. 4b may also refer to a communal meal in the temple (Ps 64:5); the word anticipates the fertility described in vv. 9-13.

Unusual is the use of the Hebrew word כפר (literally, "cover") for "forgive" in v. 3b. This word is used in the Psalms in connection with God's atoning for human sin only three times: here and in Psalms 78:38 and 79:9. Normally the verb is used for human atoning in Exodus and Leviticus. Those forgiven and chosen to be "brought near" to God in the temple courts (v. 4) respond to God's graciousness with the recognition of being "happy" (v. 4a). The temple offers safe haven for worshipers because God resides there as king (see Ps 48:1-3). God's kingship in Zion, however, "functions as a guarantor for the political claims of the Davidic dynasty."[8] This may be good news for the elites, but not necessarily for the peasantry and for the women whose household maintenance activities were crucial for the survival of the peasant household. Taxes levied to support the royal court, standing army, temple, and international alliances often pushed peasant families into poverty and land forfeiture.

The second section of the psalm, vv. 5-8, expands the idea found in v. 2b that to God in Zion "all flesh shall come" (Isa 2:2). God, who redeems the sinful in the first section, is addressed as God the creator of Israel and the cosmos in the second section. The psalm moves out beyond Zion to "the ends of the earth" (v. 5b) and the "earth's farthest bounds" (v. 8a); these bookends suggest that "the whole world is Zion's intended hinterland."[9] Zion becomes the universal center of the cosmos. The God who hears prayer in Zion (v. 2) "answers" with "awesome deeds" (v. 5a) and "signs" (v. 8a). These words refer to God's work in Israel's history in the exodus experience (see Pss 78:43; 105:27; 106:22; 135:9) as well as God's work in creation (see Pss 74:12-17; 95:4-5). The world's peoples respond in "awe" to God's "awesome deeds"; both words come from the root ירא, "fear."

God does not speak creation into being as in Genesis 1 but rather bullies it into submission with "strength"; God is "girded [from גבר, 'be strong'] with might" (v. 6); compare this to sin that "overwhelms" (from גבר in v. 3). God's strength as creator "established the mountains" (see Ps 93:1). God silences seas, waves, and peoples in v. 7 (see Pss 46:3, 6, 10; 89:9-10; 107:29), which echoes "to you silence is due" in v. 1, providing another link between the two sections. The second section

8. Walter Brueggemann, *Theology of the Old Testament* (Minneapolis: Fortress Press, 1997), 657.

9. Ibid., 165.

presents a very masculine God, the KINGAFAP God found in Christian hymnals, as described by Brian Wren: "King-God-Almighty-Father-Protector," who is aloof, transcendent, powerful, and in control.[10] This God can reinforce social domination of one group or gender over another. Just as the political realm is ordered by the God of Zion in the first section, the cosmos is ordered by the Creator in this second section.

The image of the KINGAFAP God gives way to a delightful metaphor of God as farmer or gardener. The word ארץ in v. 5 shifts from its cosmic meaning to the sense of cultivated land, which God "visits" (פקד, v. 9) with a divine watering can. The verb "visit" often connotes God's punishing activity (e.g., Ps 59:5), but here it is used in the sense of caring divine action (cp. Pss 8:4; 80:14; 106:4), which results in a bountiful harvest. God's caring is expressed by making God the subject of multiple verbs: God visits, waters, enriches, provides, prepares, settles ridges, softens, blesses, crowns. The "river of God" (v. 9) is often associated with the temple (see Pss 36:7-9; 46:4; Isa 33:21; Ezek 47:1, 8, 12) or with the garden of Eden (Gen 2:10-14) from which it waters the whole earth. It was conceived of also as a channel to bring rain to the earth (Job 38:25-26). The roaring seas of v. 7 have been domesticated to become God's nurturing river and rain. Earth's delightful metaphorical response is to dress up: "the hills gird themselves with joy" (v. 12b; see also God "girded with might" in v. 6b), "the meadows clothe themselves with flocks" (v. 13a), and "the valleys deck themselves with grain" (v. 13b).

All "shout and sing together" (v. 13). Human and earthly praise join voices. Psalm 65 "assumes an intricate connection between the activity in the sanctuary, the orderliness of the cosmos and the nations, and the fertility of Earth"[11] (see Deut 11:13-17, in which divine forgiveness for sin is prerequisite for winter rains and good harvests). Perhaps Psalm 65 was sung during the feast of Sukkot/Tabernacles in the fall at the end of the summer harvest and beginning of the rainy season.

---

10. Brian Wren, *What Language Shall I Borrow? God-Talk in Worship; A Male Response to Feminist Theology* (New York: Crossroad, 1989).

11. Wallace, *"Jubilate Deo,"* 62.

Joining Creation in Praise

Environmental activists are a busy bunch. And who can blame them? The ongoing unraveling of earth's natural systems is quite possibly irreversible. It is time for action.

Even though it is harvest time and there is work to be done, the community in Psalm 65 stops to praise and give thanks—exuberantly, passionately—for much-needed rain, for the land and the provision from it. Earth even gets into the act. Pastures, herds, and meadows are decking themselves out and singing in praise. But is the earth's voice still heard? Some thirty years ago, Annie Dillard wrote: "Did the wind used to cry, and the hills shout forth praise? Now speech has perished from among the lifeless things of earth, and living things say very little to very few."[12]

At a time when humanity is silencing the earth, can we, should we, take the time to praise and to thank? After all, there are laws to be passed, solar panels to be installed, native gardens to be planted. Psalm 65 answers by reminding us that praise is never simple, let alone simplistic. As early as v. 3, the psalmist frames thanksgiving in the context of communal repentance. As we in the First World praise, we also ask forgiveness for forgetting that the earth is a gift from God to be honored, respected, and shared. Verse 4 tells us too that the basis for praise and gratitude is satisfaction, satiation, enoughness. Everyone is to gather as much as required and no more, so that everyone might have what she or he needs (Exod 16:16-18).

Thanks/praise done the psalmist's way is perhaps the most radical act in which we could engage. Gratitude can, if thoughtfully considered, stop us in our tracks. Wangari Maathai, the irrepressible Nobel-winning creator of the Kenyan women's Green Belt Movement, said: "Gratitude is the simple acknowledgment of the bounty with which you have been blessed, and a sense of responsibility for using it wisely."[13] We might consider the psalmist's approach: join creation in praise and thanks, admit our complicity in the Earth's destruction, satisfy ourselves with the Creator's abundant provision, and then join the community in the work ahead of us.

Beth Norcross

---

12. Annie Dillard, *Teaching a Stone to Talk* (New York: HarperCollins, 1982), 70.

13. Wangari Maathai, *Replenishing the Earth: Spiritual Values for Healing Ourselves and the World* (New York: Doubleday, 2010), 105.

The Ethics of Agriculture

Psalm 65 suggests that we look more closely at agricultural practices around the world. Ellen Davis argues that "agriculture has an ineluctably ethical dimension. . . . Food production entails at every stage judgments and practices that bear directly on the health of the earth and living creatures, on the emotional, economic, and physical well-being of families and communities, and ultimately on their survival. Therefore, sound agricultural practice depends upon knowledge that is at one and the same time chemical and biological, economic, cultural, philosophical, and (following the understanding of most farmers in most places and times) religious. Agriculture involves questions of value and therefore of moral choice, whether or not we care to admit it."[14] The Food and Agricultural Organization of the United Nations published a report in 2011[15] estimating that 925 million people are currently undernourished. Closing the gender gap in agricultural yields could decrease that number by as much as 100–150 million people. Women make up about 43 percent of the agricultural labor force in developing countries, but they have less access than men to productive resources and opportunities.

Denise Dombkowski Hopkins

14. Davis, *Scripture, Culture, and Agriculture*, 22.

15. Food and Agricultural Organization of the United Nations, *The State of Food and Agriculture* (Rome 2011), http://www.fao.org/docrep/013/i2050e/i2050e.pdf.

Psalm 66

Women's Daily Victories of Survival

Thanksgiving Psalm 66 centers on fulfillment of the vow (נדר) made when the psalmist was "in trouble" (v. 13b). This brief and very general reference to the psalmist's distress enables almost anyone to pray the psalm by particularizing "trouble" with his or her own personal experience. Thanks is expressed in part by telling others of deliverance: "I will tell what [God] has done for me" (v. 16a). This telling demands an audience, so the psalmist invites all who "fear God" to "come and hear" (v. 16a) her testimony. As an act of worship, the vow is fulfilled at the temple: "I will come into your house with burnt offerings" (v. 13a; cp. "your house" in Psalm 65:4). Because of the public dimension of the vow, Psalm 66 ties together both the communal memory of God's deeds on Israel's behalf in vv. 1-12 and the individual testimony about God's rescue in vv. 13-20, moving from the plural "we" to the singular "I."

Unlike Phoenician and Punic stelae inscriptions, with which Psalms 66 and 116 share vocabulary and structure, Psalm 66 is "community-directed" rather than individually focused, offering "new evidence" of God's faithfulness from the psalmist's personal experience, evidence the congregation is invited to affirm.[1] The vow is fulfilled because God "has

---

1. Julia O'Brien, "Because God Heard My Voice: The Individual Thanksgiving Psalm and Vow-Fulfillment," in *The Listening Heart: Essays in Wisdom and the Psalms*

Psalm 66:1-20

To the leader. A Song. A Psalm.

¹Make a joyful noise to God, all
the earth;
²sing the glory of his name;
give to him glorious praise.
³Say to God, "How awesome are
your deeds!
Because of your great power,
your enemies cringe be-
fore you.
⁴All the earth worships you;
they sing praises to you,
sing praises to your
name."   *Selah*

⁵Come and see what God has
done:
he is awesome in his deeds
among mortals.

⁶He turned the sea into dry land;
they passed through the river
on foot.
There we rejoiced in him,
⁷who rules by his might forever,
whose eyes keep watch on the
nations—
let the rebellious not exalt
themselves.   *Selah*

⁸Bless our God, O peoples,
let the sound of his praise be
heard,
⁹who has kept us among the living,
and has not let our feet slip.
¹⁰For you, O God, have tested us;
you have tried us as silver is
tried.

listened; [God] has given heed to the words [literally, 'voice'] of my prayer" (v. 19; cp. Ps 65:2). Just as the community instructs "all the earth" (v. 1) to "come and see what God has done" (v. 5), the psalmist instructs "all you who fear God" to "come and hear" what God has done for her (v. 16). Konrad Schaefer speaks of the "symmetry" in this juxtaposition: "what Israel is to the nations . . . the individual is for the devout community."[2] Consequently, "our God" (v. 8) becomes "my Lord" (v. 18), a narrowing that illustrates the "necessary reciprocity" of individual and communal praise.[3] Such reciprocity enables the individual story to become part of the larger story of God's faithfulness in the life of the community. The Song of Hannah in 1 Samuel 2 does the same thing. God's

---

in Honor of Roland E Murphy, OCarm, JSOTSup 58 (Sheffield: Sheffield Academic Press, 1987), 281–98, at 291, 293.

2. Konrad Schaefer, *Psalms*, Berit Olam (Collegeville, MN: Liturgical Press, 2001), 161.

3. Frederick Gaiser, " 'I Will Tell You What God Has Done for Me' (Psalm 66:16): A Place for 'Testimony' in Lutheran Worship?," *WW* 26 (Spring 2006): 138–48, at 141.

¹¹You brought us into the net;
  you laid burdens on our backs;
¹²you let people ride over our heads;
  we went through fire and
    through water;
yet you have brought us out to a
  spacious place.

¹³I will come into your house with
  burnt offerings;
  I will pay you my vows,
¹⁴those that my lips uttered
  and my mouth promised when
    I was in trouble.
¹⁵I will offer to you burnt offerings
  of fatlings,
  with the smoke of the sacrifice
    of rams;
I will make an offering of bulls and
  goats.   *Selah*

¹⁶Come and hear, all you who fear
  God,
  and I will tell what he has done
    for me.
¹⁷I cried aloud to him,
  and he was extolled with my
    tongue.
¹⁸If I had cherished iniquity in my
  heart,
  the LORD would not have lis-
    tened.
¹⁹But truly God has listened;
  he has given heed to the
    words of my prayer.
²⁰Blessed be God,
  because he has not rejected
    my prayer
  or removed his steadfast love
    from me.

gift of a son to Hannah is coupled with the gift of a king to Israel (vv. 5 and 10).

In Tanakh both men and women make vows, or conditional promises to God: Jacob (Gen 28:20-22; 31:13); Jephthah, with lethal consequences for his daughter (Judg 11:30-39); Hannah (1 Sam 1:11); Absalom (2 Sam 15:7-8); the queen mother of Lemuel (Prov 31:2); the "strange" woman (Prov 7:14-15); the sailors on the ship carrying Jonah to Tarshish, and Jonah himself (Jonah 1:16; 2:9); Judeans (wives included) in Egypt who make vows to the queen of heaven (Jer 44:25). Vows were taken very seriously; once made, they had to be "paid," from the verb root שלם, which means "complete, pay, fulfill" in the Piel (as in Ps 66:13b; Num 30; Deut 23:21-23; Pss 22:25; 50:14; 56:12-13; 65:1; 76:11; 116:14). Payment could be in the form of either an unblemished animal eaten in a communion sacrifice (Lev 7:16-17; 22:17-25; 27:16-28) or money, with specific values for each animal (Lev 27).

Vows

Vows have a subtle underlying economic component. For example, the Nazirite vow (Num 6) stipulates no restrictions on who is eligible, and clearly allows both men and women to voluntarily take the vow. Still, the implicit assumption is that those who do so will have the economic means to make the final offering or any additional offerings if the vow goes awry. The vow is not as democratizing as it may first seem. It is unattainable for any except the richest, alienating the poor.[4]

The switch from first-person plural to first-person singular in this psalm may have a similar alienating effect. The first-person plural of vv. 10-12 describes the difficulties of deliverance experienced by everyone. God "tested us" and "laid burdens on our back." The very next verses switch to singular, "I will come to your house with burnt offerings; I will pay you my vows" (v. 13). Everyone pays the price for deliverance in the form of terror and trauma, but only some can afford to fulfill the vows uttered in the midst of the hardest times. Is this a psalm the whole community can pray together? Or are the most vulnerable, with the fewest resources, subtly uninvited to the party?

Amy Beth Jones

What is offered in payment becomes a thank offering, though Psalm 50:13-14 insists on praise rather than bulls and goats for the sacrifice of thanksgiving. Payment of vows came to be centralized in Jerusalem (Deut 12:6, 11, 17, 26). Verses 15 and 16 of Psalm 66 promise an over-abundance of offerings—fatlings, rams, bulls, and goats—that Erhard Gerstenberger suggests "transcends normal private capacities." He describes this as exaggeration or else joint offerings of the congregation who share in the communal feasting, family by family (1 Sam 1:1-4; 2:12-17, and Hannah's payment of her vow).[5]

---

4. Susan Niditch, "Defining and Controlling Others Within: Hair, Identity, and the Nazirite Vow in a Second Temple Context," in *The "Other" in Second Temple Judaism: Essays in Honor of John J. Collins*, ed. Daniel C. Harlow, Karina Martin Hogan, Matthew Goff, and Joel S. Kaminsky (Grand Rapids, MI: Eerdmans, 2011), 67–85, at 80.

5. See the commentary on Ps 63 and Carol Meyers's writing on festivals as food events involving women.

**Katharine Doob Sakenfeld
on the Vow**

According to Numbers 30, a man's vow could not be cancelled but a woman's vow could be overturned by her father or husband, that is, by a male with authority over her (Num 30:3-15). If she were a widow or divorced, her vow could not be overturned (v. 9). There is "very little evidence" in Tanakh about the subjects of women's vows, though they seem to be concerned with fertility, as in Hannah's case (1 Sam 1) and the queen mother of Lemuel (Prov 31:2). Sakenfeld suggests that what women vowed might have included fasting, sexual abstinence, or an economic payment promised in some kind of women's ritual that existed "alongside the more official male world of religious practice attested in the Bible." Overturning the woman's vow may have functioned to keep male economic control within the household. If women vowed what Hannah did, that child would be "lost to the economic future of the family or perhaps be redeemed for a payment according to the categories laid out in Leviticus 27:1-8. A vow involving animal sacrifice might likewise affect the economic status of a family rather substantially." The ancient purpose of the law in Numbers 30 about women and vows "seems to be the promotion of family stability within a culture of male-dominated households."[6]

Denise Dombkowski Hopkins

While the details of the psalmist's personal situation of distress are absent, Psalm 66 offers several brief allusions to Israel's salvation history. The psalmist instructs "all the earth" (vv. 1, 4) to acknowledge in v. 3 that God's "deeds" are "awesome" (נורא, v. 3, repeated in v. 5b); God's great power makes the enemies "cringe." This little "inset hymn" in v. 3 with its direct address to God was perhaps sung by the congregation.[7] The adjective "awesome" is a Niphal masculine singular participle from ירא, "fear," and occurs in the singular in Exodus 15:11 to describe God and in the plural in 2 Samuel 7:23, where God's "awesome things"

6. Katharine Doob Sakenfeld, "Numbers," in *Women's Bible Commentary*, ed. Carol A. Newsom, Sharon H. Ringe, and Jacqueline E. Lapsley, 3rd ed. (Louisville, KY: Westminster John Knox, 2012), 79–87, at 86.

7. Erhard Gerstenberger, *Psalms, Part 2, and Lamentations* (Grand Rapids, MI: Eerdmans, 2001), 25.

include driving out the nations and their gods before the Israelites (Deut 28:58; Pss 47:2; 45:4 [in reference to the king]).

Perhaps the exodus and entry into the promised land have been telescoped by the psalmist, as they are in v. 6: God "turned the sea into dry land; they passed through the river on foot" (v. 6). Verse 6 suggests both the crossing of the Reed Sea (Exod 14:16, 21-22) and the crossing of the Jordan River into Canaan (Josh 3:14-17). The adverb "there" in v. 6c may refer to Miriam and the women rejoicing at the Reed Sea (Exod 15:20-22). Perhaps the general references to "testing" (v. 10a) and "fire and water" (v. 12a) suggest the exile. The mention of metal refining—"you have tried us as silver is tried" (v. 10b)—parallels prophetic language about exile (Isa 48:10; Jer 6:29; 9:7; Zech 13:9) and supports this view. On the other hand, these terms may simply synthesize a number of communal crises in Israel's experience involving "enemies" (v. 3), "rebellious" nations (v. 7), and people whom God "let ride over our heads" (v. 12). Whatever the cause of national distress, it is bracketed by God's deliverance in vv. 9 and 12c; the power of the universal sovereign cannot be thwarted (Ps 2).

The LXX and the Vulgate add the title "psalm of the resurrection" to Psalm 66, which has prompted Christian use of this psalm during the Easter season. This makes sense in light of v. 9, which speaks of "our God" "who has kept us among the living." In the end, the focus of Psalm 66 is not so much on the big events of Israel's history in which men played such a prominent role but on the little deliverances of daily life in which women played a crucial part and that illustrate God's continuing faithfulness. Women in ancient Israel were involved in the daily struggle for life in their childbearing and food preparation. "With grain-based foods supplying the bulk of the caloric intake in most households, protective procedures associated with preparing dough, for example, took on a life-death quality no less than did reproductive rituals."[8] Proper offerings could ensure the fertility of the lands and animals necessary for household survival. The psalmist declares God "blessed" (v. 20) because God did not remove חסד from her; God heard her voice in the household rituals over which she presided. Her blessing of God elevates the psalm as a vehicle "to celebrate small, daily victories of survival, and to strengthen one another in the community and in relation with a dependable Deity."[9]

---

8. Carol Meyers, "Women's Religious Life in Ancient Israel," in Newsom, Ringe, and Lapsley, *Women's Bible Commentary*, 354–60, at 360.

9. Gerstenberger, *Psalms*, 31.

Psalm 67

Universal Gratitude for God's Bounty

At first glance, Psalm 67 seems to express universal joy unsullied by "specific references to divine victories or demonstrations of power"[1] over other nations, as found in many other psalms (e.g., Pss 2, 18, 47, 48, 58, 60, 68, 110). Contrasting bumper stickers in the United States make the same point: "God Bless America" and "God Bless All Nations: No Exceptions"; unfortunately, the former have been much more visible. Psalm 67 begins and ends with divine blessing; the congregation ("us") invites it (v. 1a), affirms it (v. 6b), and prays for its continuation (v. 7a). The refrain in vv. 3 and 5 divides the psalm into three parts: vv. 1-2, 4, and 6-7. Verse 4, the only three-line verse in the psalm, stands at the center; it is bracketed by the hoped-for praise of God from "the peoples" (עמים) and highlighted by the term *Selah* (perhaps a pause) immediately following it. The repetition of "all" in vv. 2, 3, 5, and 7 and "earth" in vv. 2, 6, and 7; the movement from "us" to "all the earth" in vv. 1 and 7; and the use of "nations" and "peoples" eight times in vv. 2-5, all serve to convey the universalism and inclusive sweep of Psalm 67.

---

1. Erhard Gerstenberger, *Psalms, Part 2, and Lamentations* (Grand Rapids, MI: Eerdmans, 2001), 32.

Psalm 67:1-7

To the leader: with stringed instruments.
A Psalm. A Song.

¹May God be gracious to us and
bless us
and make his face to shine
upon us,   *Selah*
²that your way may be known
upon earth,
your saving power among all
nations.
³Let the peoples praise you, O God;
let all the peoples praise you.

⁴Let the nations be glad and sing
for joy,

for you judge the peoples with
equity
and guide the nations upon
earth.   *Selah*

⁵Let the peoples praise you, O
God;
let all the peoples praise you.
⁶The earth has yielded its increase;
God, our God, has blessed
us.
⁷May God continue to bless us;
let all the ends of the earth
revere him.

The Monarch Butterfly and Universalism

The nearly five-thousand-mile migration of the monarch butterfly is one of nature's most spectacular and mysterious phenomena. From their wintering grounds in Mexico and southern California, thousands of monarchs make their way to the eastern United States and Canada in a few generations, stopping along the way to rest, feed, and reproduce. In autumn, prompted by changes in light and temperature, the monarchs produce a "super-generation" that makes it all the way back to its wintering grounds in a single generation.

In recent years the monarchs have not been faring very well. Timber harvesting in the Mexican mountains has eliminated hibernating habitat. Droughts in Texas have dried up important water sources. Increasing use of herbicides on Midwest farmland has eliminated much of the milkweed on which the species relies.

The manifestation of God's blessing in Genesis 1:22 to the monarch—and other creatures—"be fruitful and multiply" is directly connected with the ecological health of each and every state and nation through which it passes. Moreover, it is more often than not the human creature that acts to interrupt God's blessing on the monarch as well as on other humans and non-humans alike.

Migratory ecology affirms the universalistic message of Psalm 67. God's blessings are not only expansive and universal but also intermingled and entangled. They cannot be separated out or distinguished. Accordingly, the fates of all the creatures, even the one created to image the divine, rise and fall together within this big, beautiful web of creation we share.

Beth Norcross

Because of the universalism of Psalm 67 (cp. Ps 66), some interpreters argue for its postexilic date. Walter Beyerlin, for example, sees links to the Priestly source and late prophecy, especially Second Isaiah.[2] Jon Berquist notes that sharing language and singing praise and thanks united people beyond national boundaries into the Persian Empire and beyond; "the radical inclusion perhaps has no direct social referent, but the rhetoric allows for feelings of connectedness and solidarity."[3] These arguments are not convincing, since blessing is understood in part as bountiful harvests (v. 6; cp. Ps 65:9-13), hope for which is not confined to the postexilic period in the moderate- to high-risk agricultural environment of ancient Israel. Ironically perhaps, in traditional Jewish practice Psalm 67 is recited at the end of every Sabbath,[4] a day of rest and "visible cessation of production" in service of empire; Sabbath resists consumerism and puts God at the center of life.[5]

Verse 1 clearly echoes the Aaronic benediction in Numbers 6:24-26 by using the same verbs, but they are spoken directly by the congregation rather than by a priest. The people pray that God's "face" may "shine" upon them. William P. Brown notes that "face" serves to "heighten the personal dimension" of God's relationship with the community and represents the fullness of God's presence (synecdoche); God's face "both saves and instructs" and with the solar nuance of

2. Walter Beyerlin, *Im Licht der Traditionen: Psalm LXVII and CXV: ein Entwicklungszusammenhang*, VTSup 45 (Leiden: Brill, 1992).

3. Jon L. Berquist, *Judaism in Persia's Shadow: A Social and Historical Approach* (Minneapolis: Fortress Press, 1995), 194.

4. J. Clinton McCann Jr., "The Book of Psalms," in *The New Interpreter's Bible*, vol. 4 (Nashville, TN: Abingdon Press, 1996), 639–1280, at 939.

5. Walter Brueggemann, *Reverberations of Faith: A Theological Handbook of Old Testament Themes* (Louisville, KY: Westminster John Knox, 2002), 180–81.

"shining" is "life-giving."[6] The blessing is invoked for a purpose, as v. 2 shows: "so that your way may be known upon earth" (note the ל of purpose with ידע). In light of this purpose, several interpreters speak of the missional function of Psalm 67 and connect it to Abraham's commission in Genesis 12:1-3—"and in you all the families of the earth shall be blessed." Joel Kaminsky, however, criticizes "the Christian tendency to reduce Israel's election to her service to the larger world" and suggests instead an acknowledgment of God's "mysterious act of divine love" in Israel's election (Deut 7:7-8).[7]

Erhard Gerstenberger suggests that perhaps an element of "divine competition" exists in v. 4; the prophets constantly contended against the Canaanite fertility god Baʾal (Hos 2; 1 Kgs 18) or the queen of heaven (Jer 44, the fertility goddess Ishtar or Astarte?). He also argues that the reference to God judging the peoples with equity in verse 4b (Pss 9:8; 72:1-7; 96:13; 97:2; 98:9; 99:4) may hide a prediction of punishment or destruction of foreign nations (Pss 58:10-11; 75:2-10; 82). He cautions us not to view the psalm, however, through "nationalistic glasses" and "aggressive monotheism" that becomes "a projection and usurpation, taking hostages spiritually, so to speak." Instead, he urges us to recognize the "gratitude for yearly sustenance shared naturally by all other ethnic groups."[8] If we were to do so, what would the world's food distribution systems and farming practices look like today in light of Psalm 67? How might a universal reading of Psalm 67 contribute to the flourishing of undernourished children everywhere?

---

6. William P. Brown, *Seeing the Psalms: A Theology of Metaphor* (Louisville, KY: Westminster John Knox, 2002), 172–73.

7. Joel Kaminsky, *Yet I Loved Jacob: Reclaiming the Biblical Concept of Election* (Nashville, TN: Abingdon Press, 2007), 84.

8. Gerstenberger, *Psalms*, 32–33.

Psalm 68

Conflicting Images of Women

At first glance Psalm 68 appears to be a disjointed collage of biblical references with no clear structure. Too many of its Hebrew words appear here and nowhere else, making translation a challenge. Interpreters offer widely different classifications for the psalm: victory hymn, communal thanksgiving, enthronement psalm. Moreover, a liturgical celebration follows quite abruptly a very gory section in vv. 21-23 that focuses on brutal military practices that ultimately victimize women. Yet a closer look from the context of those on the margins suggests that the heart of this psalm resides in vv. 5-6, which transform the psalm's problematic aspects into hope and praise for God's sovereignty. These verses also bring women and children into a more caring focus: "Father of orphans and protector of widows is God in his holy habitation" (v. 5).

Unfortunately, "the manner in which Psalm 68 makes the case for God's sovereignty or power is . . . difficult . . . to accept"[1] when interpreters focus on the violence and relegate vv. 5-6 to the periphery of the psalm. These interpreters consider the summons to worship in v. 32—"sing to

---

1. J. Clinton McCann, "Preaching the Psalms, Ps 68:1-10, 32-35, Ascension Sunday," *Journal for Preachers* 31 (Easter 2008): 17–20, at 17.

Psalm 68:1-35

To the leader. Of David. A Psalm.
A Song.

¹Let God rise up, let his enemies
    be scattered;
  let those who hate him flee be-
    fore him.
²As smoke is driven away, so
    drive them away;
  as wax melts before the fire,
  let the wicked perish before
    God.
³But let the righteous be joyful;
  let them exult before God;
  let them be jubilant with joy.

⁴Sing to God, sing praises to his
    name;
  lift up a song to him who rides
    upon the clouds—
  his name is the LORD—
  be exultant before him.

⁵Father of orphans and protector
    of widows
  is God in his holy habitation.
⁶God gives the desolate a home
    to live in;
  he leads out the prisoners to
    prosperity,
  but the rebellious live in a
    parched land.

⁷O God, when you went out be-
    fore your people,
  when you marched
    through the
    wilderness,   *Selah*
⁸the earth quaked, the heavens
    poured down rain
  at the presence of God, the
    God of Sinai,
  at the presence of God, the
    God of Israel.

God, O kingdoms of the earth"—to be "an order to surrender"² rather than an invitation to worship Israel's God. If these brutal images remain the focus of the psalm we run the risk of engaging in "reckless irresponsibility" by taking the psalm's "angry rhetoric literally" as an "excuse" for genocide.³ To read the whole psalm is "to stand in solidarity with the lowly, protesting the evil of those who oppose God"; this is why Psalm 68 is used on Ascension Sunday at the end of the Easter season: Jesus Christ, the resurrected one, is still the crucified one. The "power and strength" God gives to the people (v. 35b) "are not to be construed triumphalistically" as privilege, reward, or power over others but as a charge to confront opposition to God⁴ and perhaps to invite other nations to join in worship of such a God (v. 32).

2. Erhard Gerstenberger, *Psalms, Part 2, and Lamentations* (Grand Rapids, MI: Eerdmans, 2001), 42.

3. Daniel Smith-Christopher, *Jonah, Jesus, and Other Good Coyotes: Speaking Peace to Power in the Bible* (Nashville, TN: Abingdon Press, 2007), 172.

4. McCann, "Preaching the Psalms," 19.

⁹Rain in abundance, O God, you
showered abroad;
you restored your heritage
when it languished;
¹⁰your flock found a dwelling in it;
in your goodness, O God,
you provided for the
needy.

¹¹The Lord gives the command;
great is the company of those
who bore the tidings:
¹²"The kings of the armies,
they flee, they flee!"
The women at home divide the
spoil,
¹³though they stay among the
sheepfolds—
the wings of a dove covered with
silver,
its pinions with green gold.

¹⁴When the Almighty scattered
kings there,
snow fell on Zalmon.

¹⁵O mighty mountain, mountain of
Bashan;
O many-peaked mountain,
mountain of Bashan!
¹⁶Why do you look with envy, O
many-peaked mountain,
at the mount that God desired
for his abode,
where the Lord will reside forever?
¹⁷With mighty chariotry, twice ten
thousand,
thousands upon thousands,
the Lord came from Sinai into
the holy place.
¹⁸You ascended the high mount,
leading captives in your train

Cheryl Townsend Gilkes on Psalm 68:5

Cheryl Townsend Gilkes notes that a fragment of Psalm 68:5 in the KJV—"father to the fatherless"—has become entrenched in the African American Christian worship tradition of songs, sermons, and prayers, where it was linked to "mother of the motherless," "brother to the brotherless," and "sister when you're sisterless." This linkage "extends the image of God to include the feminine and maternal in worship language" (p. 57)[5] and offers a resource for liberation from racism. It also illustrates a technique of Afrocentric reading of the Bible, that is, "the extension of or an enlargement

5. Cheryl Townsend Gilkes, " 'Mother to the Motherless, Father to the Fatherless': Power, Gender, and Community in an Afrocentric Biblical Tradition," *Semeia* 47 (1989): 57–85.

Psalm 68:1-35 (cont.)

and receiving gifts from
people,
even from those who rebel
against the LORD God's
abiding there.
¹⁹Blessed be the LORD,
who daily bears us up;
God is our salvation.   *Selah*
²⁰Our God is a God of salvation,
and to God, the LORD, belongs
escape from death.

²¹But God will shatter the heads of
his enemies,
the hairy crown of those who
walk in their guilty ways.
²²The LORD said,
"I will bring them back from
Bashan,
I will bring them back from the
depths of the sea,

²³so that you may bathe your feet
in blood,
so that the tongues of your
dogs may have their
share from the foe."
²⁴Your solemn processions are
seen, O God,
the processions of my God, my
King, into the sanctuary—
²⁵the singers in front, the musicians last,
between them girls playing
tambourines:
²⁶"Bless God in the great congregation,
the LORD, O you who are of Israel's fountain!"
²⁷There is Benjamin, the least of
them, in the lead,
the princes of Judah in a body,

upon a passage to tailor the imagery of the text to concrete circumstances" (p. 58).

The extension of the fragment in Psalm 68:5 presents God as father and mother, and that understanding was fixed in popular consciousness by the gospel song "Surely Our God Is Able," written by the Reverend Herbert Brewster. The song connected the God of Moses, Daniel, and Ezekiel with slavery and black suffering and involved listeners in call and response. "In time, the song and its traditional foundations came to be part of what 'everybody knows' in the black church, that 'God is a mother to the motherless and a father to the fatherless'" (p. 63). Gilkes suggests that the "slaves' view of themselves as motherless addressed the powerlessness of their family and community systems" (p. 65) as well as the cultural humiliation of violence against and sexual abuse of women in the slave system.

Psalm 68:5-6 names God as parent, liberator, judge, and bringer of justice to the least in society, but by and large the historical-critical interpreters did

the princes of Zebulun, the
princes of Naphtali.

28Summon your might, O God;
show your strength, O God, as
you have done for us
before.
29Because of your temple at Jerusalem
kings bear gifts to you.
30Rebuke the wild animals that live
among the reeds,
the herd of bulls with the
calves of the peoples.
Trample under foot those who lust
after tribute;
scatter the peoples who delight
in war.
31Let bronze be brought from
Egypt;

let Ethiopia hasten to stretch
out its hands to God.

32Sing to God, O kingdoms of the
earth;
sing praises to the LORD, *Selah*
33O rider in the heavens, the ancient heavens;
listen, he sends out his voice,
his mighty voice.
34Ascribe power to God,
whose majesty is over Israel;
and whose power is in the
skies.
35Awesome is God in his sanctuary,
the God of Israel;
he gives power and strength to
his people.

Blessed be God!

not "commend" the psalm to the church. The black community, however, "commended" it by its frequent use. African Americans saw themselves referenced in v. 31 by the word Ethiopia/ Cush. Instead of a declaration of submission of one of Israel's enemies, black worshipers "perceived a universal invitation to share a particular story" (p. 68). The reference to Ethiopia "became a promise that affirmed their humanity, ethnic identity, and community" (p. 69).

Denise Dombkowski Hopkins

Samuel L. Adams
on Widows and Orphans
in Second Temple Judea

Psalm 68:5 calls God "father of orphans and protector of widows." If Psalm 68 is an exilic or postexilic psalm, what was their status during that time? Samuel L. Adams argues that the "ancient sources pay close attention to the situation of widows and for good reason: these women lacked the security of the 'house of the father' structure. . . . [If the dead husband's family] rejected her, the widow could become unmoored from her social standing, losing the essential benefits of the marital union." Pentateuchal laws recognize this situation and protect widows by allocating them food (see the Covenant Code, Exod 22:22-24 and Deut 24:17-21, 27-29). Later sources also show concern for widows (Mal 3:5; Sir 35:17-19; Tob 1:8). "Unless they could rely on property holdings or some other measure of security, widows faced the prospect of poor social standing, destitution, and possibly death." Often a widow lost her husband's land after he died, "especially if they had no living sons"; she also lost support from her dead husband's relatives. Adams suggests that "the fact that the Hebrew Bible often groups widows with orphans and resident aliens (e.g., Deut 14:29) demonstrates the power of the patrilineal system and the need to be part of a functioning household with property holdings" (pp. 51–52).[6]

As far as children in the Second Temple period are concerned, Adams warns that "'childhood' is a modern phenomenon." Subsistence farming left little time for childhood. "Parents needed the contributions of their children to make the household function and had considerable expectations for productiveness after the period of infancy and before adulthood." Work began at an early age (as early as six) and many progeny were needed because of the demanding agrarian lifestyle of most of the population and a high infant mortality rate (pp. 58–59). "An elaborate system of tenant farming left older sons and daughters vulnerable to debt slavery, especially if their father lost his land and owed sizeable amounts to lenders and/or the ruling power" (cp. Neh 5:2-5). "Not just orphans but also those belonging to a struggling household often reached a point where inheritance subsided as a possibility and survival became the sole concern" (pp. 78, 80).

Denise Dombkowski Hopkins

---

6. Samuel L. Adams, *Social and Economic Life in Second Temple Judea* (Louisville, KY: Westminster John Knox, 2014).

Verses 1-3 serve as a kind of summary introduction to the way of this God whose sovereignty is universally acknowledged. These verses outline the Two Ways prominent in wisdom tradition (cp. Ps 1): The "wicked" are punished (vv. 1-2); they are scattered and flee and perish quickly like smoke and wax. The righteous are rewarded by a just God; they are joyful (v. 3). Verse 1 taps a historical memory of the wilderness wanderings by quoting Numbers 10:35: "Arise, O LORD, let your enemies be scattered, and your foes flee before you." God invisibly enthroned on the ark guides the Israelites and leads them in battle against enemies as the Divine Warrior. Other allusions to Israel's story abound in vv. 4-18: Exodus (vv. 4-6), Sinai (v. 8), conquest (v. 9, נחלה or "heritage," frequent in the book of Joshua; "spoil" in Judg 5:30), making Jerusalem God's dwelling place (vv. 15-18).

The first verse sets the stage for both the battle referenced in vv. 17-18, 21-23 and the liturgical procession to Jerusalem's sanctuary in vv. 24-27 (e.g., the use of the ark in liturgical processions in Pss 24:7-10; 132:7-8; Josh 3). God's oracle in vv. 22-23 declares that the people will bathe their feet in enemy blood and that dogs' tongues will lick it up. These are "stereotyped expressions of victory"[7] used throughout Tanakh (Isa 63:3; 1 Kgs 14:11; 16:4; 21:19; 22:38; 2 Kgs 9:10, 36). Mention of God as a cloud rider in vv. 4 and 33 evokes mythological themes, since Baʾal rides the clouds in Ugaritic myth, defeating Sea and Death. One can recognize a "polemical thrust"[8] in the declaration "his name is the LORD" in v. 4c (cp. Exod 15:3; Deut 33:26; Ps 18:9-13; Isa 19:1). Israel's God, and not Baʾal, controls the rain and fertility (see vv. 9a and 34c; 1 Kgs 17–19). Likewise, Bashan competes in a mythological war with Zion as the holy center of the earth (vv. 15-16), where God is especially present as "king" (v. 24). The violently "archaic description of enemies"[9] in v. 21a—"hairy skull" and "shattered heads"—alludes to the ancient myth of Marduk, the Babylonian storm god who defeated the goddess Tiamat by crushing her skull with his mace in the Enuma Elish.

The structure of Psalm 68 underscores its liturgical use and relegates the military violence to a mythological and historical memory that strengthens the present community, perhaps in exile. The exilic audience was "not actually capable" of engaging in this level of violence against

---

7. Gerstenberger, *Psalms*, 41.

8. J. Clinton McCann Jr., "The Book of Psalms," in *The New Interpreter's Bible*, vol. 4 (Nashville, TN: Abingdon Press, 1996), 639–1280, at 945.

9. Gerstenberger, *Psalms*, 40.

enemies or collecting the tribute mentioned in v. 29; the brutal language represents a colonized people's dream of rising up to destroy the colonizer and expresses their "anger and frustration."[10] In this regard Egypt is described as "the wild animal that [lives] among the reeds" (v. 30).

Liturgical clues suggest that the violence is contained. Praise brackets the psalm: "sing to God" (vv. 4a and 32a), as does the epithet for God, the "rider of the clouds/heavens" (vv. 4b, 33a; cp. Pss 18:9-11; 104:3). "Blessed be the Lord" in vv. 19 and 35 divides the psalm into two major sections. This phrase also interrupts the battle language in vv. 17-18 and 21-23 and redirects it to liturgy that memorializes God's power and perhaps envisions a peaceful coexistence with all who come to praise God. This vision is eschatological, anticipated by the address to an international audience in v. 32: "kingdoms of the earth." God present in the temple claims center stage (vv. 5, 16-18, 24, 19, 35); the temple is the locus of God's sovereignty and the center from which flows God's care for the dispossessed. Constant toggling between second-person direct address and third-person description also reinforces the argument for a liturgical setting.

Psalm 68 mentions women three times: once in v. 25 (female drummers), once in v. 5 (widows), and also indirectly in v. 12. There the Hebrew reads literally "the dweller of the house" (from the verb נוה, "dwell, abide"), in a feminine singular construct phrase used collectively. The phrase may suggest women waiting at home for warriors to return from battle. Carol Meyers notes the double irony of this verse. While the kings of the armies flee (v. 12a), the women indulge in a "false sense of security" by "already dividing up the expected booty that will never come" (v. 12b). These women will themselves become booty to be divided up as spoils of war.[11] This verse echoes v. 30 in the ancient poem, the Song of Deborah (Judg 5), which also links violence and sexuality and offers several different portraits of women. Deborah leads troops for battle (vv. 7, 12, 15); Jael seduces and kills the enemy general, Sisera (v. 24); Sisera's mother worries about his return from battle (v. 28); wise women give her counsel (v. 29); and women reduce other women to their reproductive organs by calling them "wombs" that are being gathered as booty: "Are they not finding and dividing the spoil?—A womb or two for every man" (v. 30). Sisera's mother expects women to be raped in war. As

---

10. Smith-Christopher, *Jonah, Jesus*, 171.

11. Carol Meyers, "Women Dividing the Spoil, Ps 68:12," in *Women in Scripture*, ed. Carol Meyers (Boston: Houghton Mifflin, 2000), 299–300.

Susanne Scholz notes, "None of the women speak with each other, support each other, or even meet the other women. . . . [They] approve of or commit violent acts to help their men to become victorious. They serve a patriarchal agenda and do not seek its subversion."[12]

In Psalm 68:25 a somewhat different picture of women emerges. Referred to as עלמות, or women of marriageable age (fem. pl.), these young girls take part in the joyous procession of God, the King, into the Jerusalem sanctuary, playing the תוף, or small hand drum (inaccurately translated "tambourine"). Many biblical texts show women participating in acts of public celebration and mourning. Athalya Brenner and Fokkelien Van Dijk-Hemmes suggest that women participate in changing political situations with victory songs that both welcome warriors home and express public opinion, sometimes in a mocking or satirical way[13] (e.g., 1 Sam 18:6-7; Judg 5; 11:34a; Exod 15:50-21). Meyers argues that "women were almost certainly part of many ensembles, even when the gender of the musicians is unspecified"[14] (cp. Ps 149:2-3).

Harmonized with a Male Voice? Victimized by Masculine Violence?

Given the psalm's depiction of women and war, some in the audience could easily find the tone and focus of the authorial voice(s) curious or even troubling. The audience hears the actions of women described with language that both mimics the voices speaking about a warring God, the nation, and the people (i.e., men), and highlights masculine military activities. At the lord's command there is a great "company of those [women] who bore the tidings" (v. 11). While enemies of their men flee, the women, accordingly, participate in sharing in the spoils (v. 12), despite their supposedly passive role in the battle. The celebration of the women casts a shadow over their passivity and detachment from the "real" male-dominated world. In

---

12. Susanne Scholz, "Judges," in *Women's Bible Commentary*, ed. Carol A. Newsom, Sharon H. Ringe, and Jacqueline E. Lapsley, 3rd ed. (Louisville, KY: Westminster John Knox, 2012), 113–27, at 118.

13. Athalya Brenner and Fokkelien Van Dijk-Hemmes, *On Gendering Texts: Female and Male Voices in the Hebrew Bible* (Leiden: Brill, 1993), 32–34.

14. Carol Meyers, "Women's Religious Life in Ancient Israel," in Newsom, Ringe, and Lapsley, *Women's Bible Commentary*, 359.

addition, some women are described as following the group of male singers and musicians in rejoicing and celebrating the victorious procession of God (v. 25). Unlike the violent military scenes that eliminate women from playing a central role, here young women may have been placed in the middle to hold a performance for the warrior(s) returning from battle. What a precarious position to occupy!

Are these women adapting to the male model for attaining security, comfort, and success? Are they benefiting after all by following the disciplines of a masculine "militaristic" world? Or are they used and victimized by the authoritative and androcentric perspectives of the text? Amid these tensions the audience hears about an alternate image of God—resembling more a nurturing and forbearing mother than a ruthless militaristic warrior—who protects "the fatherless" (v. 5), "widows" (v. 5), "the desolate" (v. 6), "the prisoners" (v. 6), and "the needy" (v. 10), that is, the people who may not have male patrons to guide and support them and who thus must make decisions for themselves in order to survive. If, in fact, God hates the people "who delight in war" (v. 30) and dwells not in a war zone but in a separate place ("holy habitation," v. 5) with the poor, the lowly, and the exiled (v. 18), then perhaps this discovery releases us—both women and men—from the shackles of hierarchy and violence. We are freed from a world that reinforces our blindness to the other, including orphans, widows, the poor, refugees from war or economic disaster, political prisoners, and the stateless exiled all over the world.

Su Jung Shin

Psalm 69

Women's Tears

Like Psalm 42:1-3, Psalm 69 plunges us immediately into water and tears. Up to her neck (נפש, v. 1b) in water, the psalmist appears to be drowning. Three words for water in vv. 1-2—מים, "waters"; מעמקי־מים, "deep waters"; and שבלת, "flood"—reinforce this image (cp. Jonah 2:5-6). The use of ביון, "mire" in v. 2a, found only here and in Psalm 40:2, also contributes to the sense of sinking (v. 14a with its synonym for "mire"). The psalmist's tears extend the water imagery (v. 3a; cp. Ps 22:14-15). These tears function positively and negatively. Positively, they anticipate God's hoped-for empathetic response.[1] Too often in many societies, however, tears are seen as a sign of weakness and are associated with women. Yet prominent men in the Hebrew Bible weep. Jacob and Esau weep when they meet in Genesis 33:4; Joseph weeps three times when reunited with his brothers in Egypt (Gen 42:24; 43:30; 45:2); David weeps over his dead son Absalom (2 Sam 18:33).

---

1. David Bosworth, "Weeping in the Psalms," *VT* 62 (2013): 36–46, at 37.

Psalm 69:1-36

To the leader: according to Lilies.
Of David.

¹Save me, O God,
  for the waters have come up to
    my neck.
²I sink in deep mire,
  where there is no foothold;
I have come into deep waters,
  and the flood sweeps over me.
³I am weary with my crying;
  my throat is parched.
My eyes grow dim
  with waiting for my God.

⁴More in number than the hairs of
    my head
  are those who hate me without
    cause;
many are those who would de-
    stroy me,

my enemies who accuse me
    falsely.
What I did not steal
  must I now restore?
⁵O God, you know my folly;
  the wrongs I have done are not
    hidden from you.

⁶Do not let those who hope in you be
    put to shame because of me,
  O LORD God of hosts;
do not let those who seek you be
    dishonored because of me,
  O God of Israel.
⁷It is for your sake that I have
    borne reproach,
  that shame has covered my
    face.
⁸I have become a stranger to my
    kindred,

Rizpah

Rizpah knows the power of saturating grief without communal or familial support. In 2 Samuel 21, David, in order to end a three-year famine, permits the brutal execution of seven innocent sons of Saul at the hands of the Gibeonites as expiation for the alleged bloodguilt of Saul. The "word of the Lord" is manipulated to serve political ends, and, ironically, the unjust death of blameless men is intended to restore order in the natural world even as it adds chaos to the moral fabric of the social world. Two of the victims are Rizpah's own sons. She keeps vigil for months on the rock where the unburied bodies of the impaled men lie, from the beginning of the harvest "until rain from the sky fell on the bodies" (2 Sam 21:10).

It is only when the very earth weeps with Rizpah that David notices the travesty and injustice of the brutalized, desecrated bodies. As for the psalmist, Rizpah's tears alone are not enough to gain the attention of those in power (divine or human), but when her tears intersect with the cosmic waters,

an alien to my mother's children.

[9]It is zeal for your house that has
consumed me;
the insults of those who insult
you have fallen on me.
[10]When I humbled my soul with
fasting,
they insulted me for doing so.
[11]When I made sackcloth my
clothing,
I became a byword to them.
[12]I am the subject of gossip for
those who sit in the gate,
and the drunkards make songs
about me.

[13]But as for me, my prayer is to
you, O LORD.
At an acceptable time, O God,

in the abundance of your steadfast love, answer me.
With your faithful help [14]rescue me
from sinking in the mire;
let me be delivered from my enemies
and from the deep waters.
[15]Do not let the flood sweep over
me,
or the deep swallow me up,
or the Pit close its mouth over
me.

[16]Answer me, O LORD, for your
steadfast love is good;
according to your abundant
mercy, turn to me.
[17]Do not hide your face from your
servant,
for I am in distress—make
haste to answer me.

Rizpah's vigil becomes a powerful act of protest that prods David, and then God, to action. Dulcie Abraham suggests that tears have rhetorical and political power that allow the voiceless to be heard.[2] Rizpah's vigil is active, creative participation in God's concern for humanity. Abraham also draws a connection between women from across the globe who have enacted Rizpah's protest in their own context through human rights protests, testimony against injustice, and imprisonment.

Amy Beth Jones

2. Dulcie Abraham, "Rizpah's Story: II Samuel 21:1-14," in *Women of Courage: Asian Women Reading the Bible*, ed. Lee Oo Chung, et al. (SaDang Publishing House, 1992), 29–31.

Psalm 69:1-36 (cont.)

¹⁸Draw near to me, redeem me,
    set me free because of my
        enemies.

¹⁹You know the insults I receive,
    and my shame and dishonor;
    my foes are all known to you.
²⁰Insults have broken my heart,
    so that I am in despair.
I looked for pity, but there was
        none;
    and for comforters, but I found
        none.
²¹They gave me poison for food,
    and for my thirst they gave me
        vinegar to drink.

²²Let their table be a trap for them,
    a snare for their allies.
²³Let their eyes be darkened so
    that they cannot see,

and make their loins tremble
    continually.
²⁴Pour out your indignation upon
        them,
    and let your burning anger
        overtake them.
²⁵May their camp be a desolation;
    let no one live in their tents.
²⁶For they persecute those whom
        you have struck down,
    and those whom you have
        wounded, they attack
        still more.
²⁷Add guilt to their guilt;
    may they have no acquittal
        from you.
²⁸Let them be blotted out of the
        book of the living;
    let them not be enrolled among
        the righteous.

Negatively, tears signify a diminished body that has been worn out by weeping (v. 3a); the psalmist's tears mingle with the flood waters to threaten her life. The body "rhetorically marks the site of the lamenter's public and private powerlessness, suffering, and incapacitation."[3] Tears wear her out; her eyes "grow dim" (v. 3c) waiting for God. Ironically, in the midst of all of these waters the psalmist's throat is "parched" (v. 3b), perhaps from calling out repeatedly to God. The psalmist's tears "do not quench thirst; they are, rather, testimony to deprivation,"[4] that is, the absence of God's presence, communal and family support, and nutritional sustenance.

Rather than represent the cosmic threat of primordial chaos, the waters of Psalm 69 combine with enemy language in vv. 14-15 to form a meta-

3. Amy C. Cottrill, *Language, Power, and Identity in the Lament Psalms of the Individual* (New York and London: T & T Clark, 2008), 29.

4. William P. Brown, *Seeing the Psalms: A Theology of Metaphor* (Louisville, KY: Westminster John Knox, 2002), 120.

²⁹But I am lowly and in pain;
let your salvation, O God, protect me.

³⁰I will praise the name of God
with a song;
I will magnify him with thanksgiving.
³¹This will please the LORD more
than an ox
or a bull with horns and hoofs.
³²Let the oppressed see it and be
glad;
you who seek God, let your
hearts revive.

³³For the LORD hears the needy,
and does not despise his own
that are in bonds.

³⁴Let heaven and earth praise him,
the seas and everything that
moves in them.
³⁵For God will save Zion
and rebuild the cities of Judah;
and his servants shall live there
and possess it;
³⁶the children of his servants
shall inherit it,
and those who love his name
shall live in it.

phor for Sheol, the place in the bowels of the earth where all the dead go to exist as shades of their former selves (Jonah 2:4). The three elements of chaos imagery—chaos, creation, and combat—are missing from Psalm 69.[5] There is no conflict with the sea; in fact, the seas are called upon in v. 34 to join with the whole cosmos in praise of God. In v. 15 the psalmist petitions that God not let "the deep swallow me up, or the Pit close its mouth over me." As John Goldingay argues, "being drowned by the flood means being swallowed by the earth, by the grave, by Sheol (106:17; Exod 15:12; Num 16:30, 32, 34). . . . Death is personified as a monster that threatens to swallow us."[6] The shame imposed by hostile others makes the psalmist feel as if Sheol is closing in, sucking her down to her death (Ps 124:3-4).

Shame words appear multiple times in two parallel panels of petition and complaint (vv. 1-13b and 13c-20). Their frequency serves to intensify the sense of the psalmist's suffering: "reproach" (חרפה, vv. 7a, 9b, 10b, 19a, 20a where the NRSV translates "insult"); "shame" (NRSV translation of a word from the root כלם in v. 7b, better translated "insult," and v. 19, where the NRSV translates "dishonor"); and "shame" (בוש, v. 19). The

5. Rebecca S. Watson, *Chaos Uncreated: A Reassessment of the Theme of "Chaos" in the Hebrew Bible* (Berlin: deGruyter, 2005), 369.
6. John Goldingay, *Psalms*, vol. 2 (Grand Rapids, MI: Baker Academic, 2007), 346.

psalmist feels keenly the public and social aspects of shame in the gossip of "those who sit in the gate" (the elders) and the "drunkards'" songs (v. 12) about her. The petitions "save" and "protect" (vv. 1 and 29) bracket this shame.

As William P. Brown notes, "The psalmist is drowning in shame"; she is "sunk" by slander and insults that are swallowing her up.[7] To reinforce the petitions, the psalmist uses "self-abasement language" such as "needy" (v. 33), "lowly" (v. 29), "oppressed," and "servant" (v. 17). The psalmist's acceptance of her dependence on God by using these terms "reinforces God's power, but also God's obligation"[8] in the patron/client relationship.

In addition, relational "loyalty language" reinforces "mutual interdependence"[9] between God and the psalmist. She calls on God's חסד ("covenant loyalty," vv. 13, 16) as grounds for granting her petition and for reminding God of their binding connection. Other loyalty language includes רחמים, "mercy" (v. 16), and אהב, "love" (v. 36). Especially powerful from a feminist viewpoint is God's attribute of mercy, from the Hebrew רחם, which means "womb." The plural רחמים in v. 16 forms the abstract idea of compassion. The NRSV translates "mercy," which obscures this feminine image of God; a better translation would be "womb-love"[10] (cp. Gen 43:30; 1 Kgs 3:16-28; Exod 33:19; 34:6; Pss 25:6; 103:13; Jer 31:20; Isa 49:13). The psalmist names God's womb-love as a warrant for forgiveness, which prompts the surfacing of other God images that challenge the dominant violent Warrior-Deliverer God metaphor found in vv. 22-28.

The psalmist demands that God "pour out your indignation" (v. 24) on the enemies in retribution; God's anger must "drown" the enemies, reversing the psalmist's drowning in shame. The enemies will be "blotted out of the book of the living" (v. 28a, a later rabbinical reference to the ledger opened on Rosh Hashanah). While the psalmist was given "poison for food" and "vinegar to drink" (v. 21; cp. Matt 27:34, 38; Mark 15:23; Jer 8:14; 9:15; 23:15) by the enemies, God must now "let their table be a trap for them" (v. 22a). The violent tit-for-tat rhetoric of reversal

7. Brown, *Seeing the Psalms*, 114.

8. Cottrill, *Language, Power, and Identity*, 118.

9. Ibid., 122.

10. Denise Dombkowski Hopkins and Michael S. Koppel, *Grounded in the Living Word: The Old Testament and Pastoral Care Practices* (Grand Rapids, MI: Eerdmans, 2010), 73–74.

provides a psychological release for anger and frustration for the psalmist and Israel; it comes from a time when Israel "was not actually capable" of carrying out these actions (exile).[11] The "disjunctive metaphor" of womb-love joins those of God as Mother in Labor and Nurturing Mother (Isa 42:13-14; 45:9-10; 49:13-15; 66:10-13) and embodies hope for the future of traumatized, exiled Israel in Isaiah[12] and for the less-than-perfect psalmist and her community in exile (v. 5).

The two parallel panels of petition and complaint in Ps 69 also share the phrase "you know" (see Jer 12:3; 15:15; 17:16; 18:23). God knows that the psalmist is not perfect (v. 5) and knows the insults she has received (v. 19) because of her zeal for God's house (v. 9a; cp. John 2:17) and her loyalty to God: "the insults of those who insult you have fallen on me" (v. 9b). Such are the consequences of the reciprocal relationship between God and the psalmist. The psalmist insists that "it is for your sake that I have borne reproach" (v. 7). Suffering for God's sake appears in Jeremiah's laments (11:18-20; 15:15-18; 17:14-18; 18:23); Lamentations; Psalm 44:22, 24; Isaiah 53; and Job. These texts are all shaped by the experience of exile, as is Psalm 69, which asserts that God "will save Zion and rebuild the cities of Judah" (vv. 35-36, probably a later addition).

The psalmist also presents herself as a paradigm for others with zeal for God, described as "those who hope in you" (v. 6a) and "those who seek you" (v. 6b); they are addressed directly by the psalmist in v. 32b. The psalmist pleads that these faithful ones not "be put to shame because of me" (v. 6a) or "be dishonored because of me" (v. 6b). Others (both the enemies and the faithful) are watching how God treats the psalmist. The psalmist has "public relations (PR) value"; without deliverance, God will lose the psalmist's praise, damage God's own reputation and prestige, and discourage believers.[13]

Most interpreters point to male figures in the Bible who suffer for God's sake as embodiments of the rhetoric of Psalm 69. Do any female biblical characters qualify? Given the links already noted between Psalm 69 and the book of Job, Job's unnamed wife comes to mind. Perhaps Psalm 69 provided the outlet for Job's wife that is denied her in the MT. Carol

11. Daniel Smith-Christopher, *Jonah, Jesus, and Other Good Coyotes: Speaking Peace to Power in the Bible* (Nashville, TN: Abingdon Press, 2007), 171.

12. L. Juliana M. Claassens, *Mourner, Mother, Midwife: Reimagining God's Delivering Presence in the Old Testament* (Louisville, KY: Westminster John Knox, 2012), 43–47.

13. Denise Dombkowski Hopkins, *Journey through the Psalms* (St. Louis, MO: Chalice Press, 2002), 103–4.

Newsom describes Job's wife as "the prototypical woman on the margin whose iconoclastic words provoke defensive condemnation but whose insight serves as an irritant that undermines old complacencies."[14] No lesser figures than Augustine and Calvin condemn her as an aide to Satan. Though she speaks only one abrasive line in the MT, she is given a more extended speech in the LXX that draws our sympathy. That sympathy makes it easier, however, to patronize her and dismiss what she says.

In 2:9 (LXX) she laments that Job's "memorial" is "abolished," a reference to their dead children, whom she describes as the "pangs and pains" of her womb. She calls herself "a wanderer and a servant from place to place and house to house, waiting for the setting of the sun, that I may rest from my labors and my pangs which have now beset me." Her self-designation as *latris*, or "hired servant" (cp. the use of "servant" in Ps 69:17a), expresses her own sense of alienation from the community. Her words echo Job's about his communal and familial alienation in 19:13-19. Her need for rest from the "pangs" involved in hiring herself out to sustain them both suggests the reproaches, insults, and shame she must have encountered daily.

As Job's wife, this woman is tainted by association. Unlike Job, whose three friends initially sit in silence with him for seven days and seven nights, "for they saw that his suffering was very great" (2:13), she "looked for pity, but there was none; and for comforters, but found none" (Ps 69:21). She finds only poisoned food and vinegar to drink (v. 21), "images of personal estrangement."[15] In Psalm 69 "family solidarity, essential for survival, has given way to distrust and hostility."[16] Job's wife craves human support; finding none, she turns to God in Psalm 69 and petitions "draw near to me" (v. 18a, only here and in Psalm 119:69 in the Psalter). God will be her *goʾel*, her redeemer (v. 18b; see Lev 25:25), a position normally filled by the next of kin. Job cannot act in that capacity since he has removed himself from society to the trash heap outside of the city to scrape his sores.

---

14. Carol A. Newsom, "Job," in *Women's Bible Commentary*, ed. Carol A. Newsom, Sharon H. Ringe, and Jacqueline E. Lapsley, 3rd ed. (Louisville, KY: Westminster John Knox, 2012), 208–15, at 212.

15. Konrad Schaefer, *Psalms*, Berit Olam (Collegeville, MN: Liturgical Press, 2001), 166.

16. Erhard Gerstenberger, *Psalms, Part 2, and Lamentations* (Grand Rapids, MI: Eerdmans, 2001), 49.

Perhaps Psalm 69 expresses for Job's wife the equivalent of his initial refusal in chapters 1 and 2 to abandon the client-patron relationship. In the end she moves beyond Psalm 69 with her radical challenge in Job 2:9: "Do you still persist in your integrity? Curse God and die." She recognizes what is at stake in the conflict between Job's integrity and an affirmation of God's goodness. Unfortunately, all she gets for her deep theological analysis is harsh condemnation in both the MT and the LXX; Job calls her one of the "foolish women" (2:10). One can imagine a new superscription for Psalm 69: "A prayer of Job's wife, while he was sitting on the dung heap."

Psalm 70

Shame and Retribution

The story of Susanna in the Apocrypha (Dan 13:1-63 LXX) particularizes the urgency, shame, and contrasts between the righteous and the wicked that infuse Psalm 70 and thus suggests itself as an intertext for our interpretation. Susanna's story does not tell us what she cries out "with a loud voice" in the garden in v. 24 after she realizes that she is "completely trapped" (v. 22) by the two lying, lusting elders. One can imagine that she is hurling Psalm 70 at God in a panic, as her "groaning" suggests. Psalm 70 begins and ends with petitions to "make haste" (from the Hebrew root חוש, vv. 1b, 5a) to save the psalmist. Both petitions use the masculine singular imperative of the verb with an emphatic *ah* ending that lends urgency to the psalmist's pleas. The urgency of Susanna's situation is clear. The elders tell their lies immediately after she cries out, and the next day she is formally accused. She directs an audible, recorded prayer to God later, after the assembly has condemned her to death for adultery: "and now I am to die, though I have done none of the wicked things that they have charged against me" (v. 43). God hears her cry "just as she was being led off to execution" (v. 45). The use of "now" (ἰδοὺ in Greek, often translated "behold!," "lo!") extends the sense of urgency she had felt in the garden. Susanna has no time to lose; God must intervene immediately.

Psalm 70 clearly contrasts the way of the righteous and the way of the wicked. The righteous are described as "all who seek you" and "those

Psalm 70:1-5

To the leader.
Of David, for the memorial offering.

¹Be pleased, O God, to deliver me.
O LORD, make haste to help
me!
²Let those be put to shame and
confusion
who seek my life.
Let those be turned back and
brought to dishonor
who desire to hurt me.

³Let those who say, "Aha, Aha!"
turn back because of their
shame.

⁴Let all who seek you
rejoice and be glad in you.
Let those who love your salvation
say evermore, "God is great!"
⁵But I am poor and needy;
hasten to me, O God!
You are my help and my deliverer;
O LORD, do not delay!

who love your salvation" (vv. 4a and 4b). The word "love" (אהב) belongs to the language of covenant loyalty and mutual commitment. The psalmist includes herself among the righteous by describing herself as "poor and needy" (v. 5a; cp. Pss 69:29, 33; 70:5). The wicked, by contrast, are those "who seek my life" (v. 2b), those "who desire to hurt me" (v. 2d), and "those who say 'Aha, Aha'" (v. 3a). The book of Susanna also sets forth these oppositions. The narrator describes Susanna as "one who feared the Lord" (v. 2) and her parents as "righteous" (v. 3). We are told that her parents "had trained their daughter according to the law of Moses" (v. 3). By contrast, the two elders who ambush Susanna never mention the name of God. They lie in wait to trap her out of their desire to possess and hurt her and they lie about her adultery. By accusing Susanna of adultery with a young man not her husband, the elders literally "seek her life," since adultery was punishable by death (Lev 2:10; Deut 22:21-24; John 8:4-5). Susanna indeed fears she will die (v. 43) without God's intervention. Susanna and her accusers illustrate Psalm 70's point, that "the righteous submit to God's rule and recognize God's provisions as the only source of security. . . . The wicked think themselves autonomous, independent of God's reign; that sense of self-sufficiency leads to the oppression of others."[1]

In a series of five jussives (an expression of desire or wish in the third person, often translated with "may" or "let"), the psalmist reinforces the contrast between righteous and wicked. She desires that the wicked be

---

1. Jerome F. D. Creach, "Psalm 70," *Int* 60 (2006): 64–66, at 65.

"put to shame" (v. 2a) and "turned back and brought to dishonor" (v. 2b) and that they "turn back because of their shame" (v. 3b). "The expression 'be put to shame' and its synonyms signify social and possibly physical annihilation to be effected by divine powers or sanctions."[2] By contrast, the psalmist wishes that the righteous will "rejoice" (v. 4b) and proclaim "God is great" (v. 4d; cp. Ps 69:30). As Erhard Gerstenberger notes, "imprecation and praise are mutually dependent . . . [as] a structural phenomenon in complaint songs and ceremonies."[3] Shame (from the root בוש) defines both the psalmist and the hostile others with whom the psalmist deals.

Shame also permeates the story of Susanna. The elders who falsely accuse her each lusted after her but did not tell the other, "for they were ashamed to disclose their lustful desire to seduce her" (v. 11). Adulterous lust did not befit their status as elders. Susanna's servants "felt very much ashamed" when the elders told their fabricated story, because "nothing like this had ever been said about Susanna" (v. 27); they assumed her guilt. The accusation brought dishonor to the household and thereby to them as well. Both these verbs are from the Greek verb καταισχύνω, "be ashamed." Though the verb for shame is not used to describe Susanna, she does experience public humiliation. Being "a woman of great refinement and beautiful in appearance" (v. 31), Susanna is ordered by the elders to be unveiled "so that they might feast their eyes on her beauty" (v. 32). The weeping of those with her and all who saw her testifies to their sense of her humiliation and their own (v. 33).

Psalm 70 shows that "the psalmist directly connects deliverance as dominance with the other's shame"; the psalmist can "escape shame by imposing shame on others" rhetorically.[4] The narrator accomplishes this in Susanna's story through the agency of Daniel, who heaps insults upon the two elders while cross-examining them separately (vv. 52-53, 56-57). Truly, the "confusion" of "those who seek my life" prayed for in Psalm 70:2a emerges in Daniel's cross-examination, as the elders contradict one another's stories. The retributive principle governing Psalm 70 is succinctly stated by the narrator in Susanna: "they did to them as they had wickedly planned to do to their neighbor" (v. 61). Just as Psalm 70

---

2. Erhard Gerstenberger, *Psalms, Part 2, and Lamentations* (Grand Rapids, MI: Eerdmans, 2001), 56.

3. Ibid., 57.

4. Amy C. Cottrill, *Language, Power, and Identity in the Lament Psalms of the Individual* (New York and London: T & T Clark, 2008), 97, 90.

prays for the public shaming of the hostile other, the elders who falsely accuse Susanna are put to death (v. 62). The elders who "desire[d] to hurt" Susanna are "brought to dishonor" (Ps 70:2cd).

In Psalm 70:3 the wicked are quoted as saying "Aha!" (cp. Pss 35:21, 25; 40:15; Mark 15:29, used during Holy Week). This speech of the enemy is contrasted with the speech of the righteous who shout "God is great" in v. 4d. "Aha" is "an exclamation of joy at another's downfall" that helps to create "an 'unbalanced' comparison": "her enemies simply scorn her but her supporters praise God."[5] This comparison helps to align the community with the psalmist and God in praise. Susanna's silence serves to highlight the lies of the two elders and creates a similar imbalance that leads (after God stirs up the holy spirit of Daniel to intervene) to an alignment between God, Susanna, and her family that prompts their praise (v. 63): "Hilkiah and his wife praised God for their daughter Susanna, and so did her husband Joakim and all her relatives." Ultimately, however, Susanna is at the mercy of the male elites among a people who do not raise questions on her behalf and are "easily swayed." "The readers are left to consider how best to make their own voices heard in the face of adversity without marginalizing others who lack the power to speak out on their own behalf."[6]

---

5. Rolf A. Jacobson, *"Many Are Saying": The Function of Direct Discourse in the Hebrew Psalter*, JSOTSup 397 (Edinburgh: T & T Clark, 2004), 51, 136.

6. Nicole Tilford, "The Greek Book of Daniel," in *Women's Bible Commentary*, ed. Carol A. Newsom, Sharon H. Ringe, and Jacqueline E. Lapsley, 3rd ed. (Louisville, KY: Westminster John Knox, 2012), 426–31, at 430.

Politics of Prayer

If we imagine the words of Psalm 70 on Susanna's lips we must consider the unspoken politics of prayer. Only when Susanna begs for divine intervention in Daniel's presence is her voice heard. What other women might have prayed this psalm? Hagar? God answers Hagar only after her son cries out. Hannah? Eli overhears her prayer before she gains divine attention. Did Jephthah's daughter pray this prayer? The Levite's concubine? These women are not so fortunate. Must a woman plead to God in the presence of a man in order to receive divine attention? Contrast Susanna's experience with Daniel's. It is difficult to imagine Psalm 70 on Daniel's lips, since God allows Daniel to receive favor and compassion from the palace master before Daniel has to beg (Dan 1:9). Is it possible that the gender of the supplicant makes a greater impact on the divine ear than the urgency of the language of a prayer? Does God hasten only for men?

Amy Beth Jones

Psalm 71

Persistence in the Midst of Doubt

Because Psalm 71 is one of eight psalms that lack a super-scription, many interpreters assume that it must be coupled with Psalm 70, which precedes it (see also Pss 9–10; 42–43). Similar phrases tie the two psalms together, as does the repetition of words from the root בוש, "shame," "disappointment"[1] (reading with JPS) in 70:2; 71:13, 24. The story of Susanna in the Apocrypha was suggested as intertext for Psalm 70 and can function similarly for Psalm 71. Psalm 71 moves from petition and complaint to trust and praise three times: from vv. 1-4 to vv. 5-8; from vv. 9-13 to vv. 15-17; and from v. 18 to vv. 19-24, showing the persistence of the psalmist's faith.[2] This same persistence takes center stage in the Susanna story. Even after Susanna is condemned to death in v. 41 because of the false testimony of the two dishonest judges, she prays "with a loud voice" to God so that all the people can

---

1. Yael Avrahami, "בוש in the Psalms—Shame or Disappointment?," *JSOT* 34 (2010): 259–313.
2. J. Clinton McCann Jr., "The Book of Psalms," in *The New Interpreter's Bible*, vol. 4 (Nashville, TN: Abingdon Press, 1996), 639–1280, at 958.

Psalm 71:1-24

¹In you, O Lᴏʀᴅ, I take refuge;
let me never be put to shame.
²In your righteousness deliver me
and rescue me;
incline your ear to me and
save me.
³Be to me a rock of refuge,
a strong fortress, to save me,
for you are my rock and my
fortress.

⁴Rescue me, O my God, from the
hand of the wicked,
from the grasp of the unjust
and cruel.
⁵For you, O Lᴏʀᴅ, are my hope,
my trust, O Lᴏʀᴅ, from my youth.
⁶Upon you I have leaned from my
birth;
it was you who took me from
my mother's womb.
My praise is continually of you.

⁷I have been like a portent to many,
but you are my strong refuge.

⁸My mouth is filled with your
praise,
and with your glory all day long.
⁹Do not cast me off in the time of
old age;
do not forsake me when my
strength is spent.
¹⁰For my enemies speak concerning me,
and those who watch for my
life consult together.
¹¹They say, "Pursue and seize that
person
whom God has forsaken,
for there is no one to deliver."

¹²O God, do not be far from me;
O my God, make haste to help
me!
¹³Let my accusers be put to
shame and consumed;
let those who seek to hurt me
be covered with scorn and disgrace.
¹⁴But I will hope continually,

hear (vv. 42-43). God responds to her prayer by stirring up the holy spirit of young Daniel to defend her.

Two sections in Psalm 71, vv. 6-16 and 17a-24, focus on memory and form a kind of literary two-panel hinged painting.[3] In vv. 5-6a the psalm-ist speaks of leaning on God "from my birth," and in v. 17a she remem-bers that God has taught her "from my youth." The narrator notes that Susanna had been trained by her righteous parents in the "law of Moses" while growing up (v. 3); this training helps her to refuse to submit to the two lecherous judges. Susanna's memory of parental instruction in Torah (made explicit by the narrator for the reader) saves her from their

3. Konrad Schaefer, *Psalms*, Berit Olam (Collegeville, MN: Liturgical Press, 2001), 170.

and will praise you yet more
and more.
15My mouth will tell of your righteous acts,
of your deeds of salvation all
day long,
though their number is past my
knowledge.
16I will come praising the mighty
deeds of the LORD God,
I will praise your righteousness, yours alone.
17O God, from my youth you have
taught me,
and I still proclaim your wondrous deeds.
18So even to old age and gray hairs,
O God, do not forsake me,
until I proclaim your might
to all the generations to come.
Your power 19and your righteousness, O God,
reach the high heavens.

You who have done great things,

O God, who is like you?
20You who have made me see many
troubles and calamities
will revive me again;
from the depths of the earth
you will bring me up again.
21You will increase my honor,
and comfort me once again.

22I will also praise you with the
harp
for your faithfulness, O my
God;
I will sing praises to you with the
lyre,
O Holy One of Israel.
23My lips will shout for joy
when I sing praises to you;
my soul also, which you have
rescued.
24All day long my tongue will talk
of your righteous help,
for those who tried to do me harm
have been put to shame, and
disgraced.

clutches. L. Juliana M. Claassens argues that Psalm 71 "creates space for remembrance" that is necessary for rebuilding life in the midst of trauma.[4] Susanna, who is wise and a God-fearer (v. 2), is devastated by the charges of adultery from the two dishonest judges, so much so that she "groans" before she refuses to submit to them. Psalm 71 may have helped give Susanna the space to function in her trauma. She admits that she is "trapped," knowing that the only one she can depend on is God. Psalm 71 reinforces this idea of life dependent on God by referring to God fourteen times, often with the possessive, showing an intimate relationship: "my rock," "my fortress," "my God." This God is righteous, as the

4. L. Juliana M. Claassens, *Mourner, Mother, Midwife: Reimagining God's Delivering Presence in the Old Testament* (Louisville, KY: Westminster John Knox, 2012), 74.

bracketing of Psalm 71 by God's "righteousness" in vv. 2 and 24 asserts. God can be counted on to do the right thing in every situation and bring about justice.

Despite Susanna's training and righteous reputation, and despite the contrast the psalmist draws between herself and the wicked, both figures express doubts about God. The psalmist expresses her doubt in two places. In v. 11 she quotes the enemies as saying "seize that person whom God has forsaken, for there is no one to deliver." As Rolf Jacobson argues, the enemies name the theological problem of God's loyalty[5] in the covenant relationship, and the psalmist can hide behind their words to express her own doubts.

The second instance occurs in v. 20: "you who have made me see many troubles and calamities will revive me again." Here, the psalmist "vacillates between praying to God for deliverance and holding God responsible for the calamities that have befallen him."[6] The same ambiguity can be seen in Susanna v. 43, in which Susanna shouts to God: "you know that these men have given false evidence against me. And now I am to die." She acknowledges that God is there and knows what is going on; because she believes in God as deliverer she accuses God of not doing anything about it. "The implication is that if God does not act, he is as guilty as the people who condemn her."[7]

Where Susanna and Psalm 71 part ways is at the end of Susanna's story; she lapses into silence. It is left to "the whole assembly" (v. 60) and her relatives to praise God (v. 63). Susanna's trauma has taken away her speech. Unlike the psalmist, who vows to praise God (vv. 14-16, 22-24), she has no desire to praise God in the midst of a people who are "easily swayed by the voice of the few," despite the contradiction of her long-standing righteous character (v. 27).[8]

In vv. 9 and 18, the psalmist pleads twice, using the same word as the enemies quoted in v. 11: "do not *abandon* [עזב] me" in old age (vv. 9, 18). Many interpreters suggest that this plea means the psalmist is old and sick and is reflecting back on his life as the enemies circle around him to

---

5. Rolf A. Jacobson, *"Many Are Saying": The Function of Direct Discourse in the Hebrew Psalter*, JSOTSup 397 (Edinburgh: T & T Clark, 2004), 39.

6. Claassens, *Mother, Mourner, Midwife*, 74.

7. Nicole Tilford, "The Greek Book of Daniel," in *Women's Bible Commentary*, ed. Carol A. Newsom, Sharon H. Ringe, and Jacqueline E. Lapsley, 3rd ed. (Louisville, KY: Westminster John Knox, 2012), 430.

8. Ibid.

bring him down in his weakened condition. Because his experience tells him that God will deliver once again, the psalmist asserts that those who try to shame (בוש) the psalmist (v. 1) will themselves be put to shame (בוש, v. 24) in an act of retributive justice. Other interpreters argue that the psalmist is not old but rather looking toward the future: "he is actually praying *towards* old age and not *lamenting over* its presence."[9] The psalmist wants the same favors experienced before to be continued into old age. In the same way, Susanna is looking toward her future in her silence. She has been blessed with a rich husband, children, servants, and dedicated parents, but none of them has spoken up for her. She is silent at the end of her story, but vv. 9 and 18 of Psalm 71 may be on her mind; one imagines that she prays them silently.

Juliana Claassens on God as Midwife

Claassens focuses on the metaphor of God as Midwife in Psalm 71:6b—"it was you who took me from my mother's womb." She notes that this metaphor of birth and new life seems out of place in the "military-oriented context" of the psalm, with its references to enemies and impenetrable places like fortresses and sheltering rocks. "However, this language contributes to the transformation of the memory of God as Deliverer into a redeeming memory." The verb in verse 6b is a *hapax* masculine singular participle from גזה, which means "sever" or "cut off." It suggests that God is the one who severs the baby from its mother's womb when baby and/or mother are in danger. This action captures the vulnerability of the speaker, who is in a life-threatening situation, and holds together the "tension of life in the midst of death." The metaphor offers an image of power "to give life or to rescue life from death." The midwives Shiphrah and Puah illustrate this power (Exod 1) as they save Hebrew babies from Pharaoh's decree of death.

God's deliverance of the baby "does not eliminate the agency of the mother." People serve as God's partners to promote life. A newborn needs care. Claassens reads v. 21 as reflecting that care, with the verb סבב taken as "surrounding" or "embracing" rather than as "once again" (NRSV). The usually threatening image emerging from סבב is

---

9. Ignatius M. C. Obinwa, *Yahweh My Refuge: A Critical Analysis of Psalm 71* (Frankfurt: Peter Lang, 2006), 208.

overturned here (enemies and animals "surround"), and instead "represents comforting" that a newborn requires. "It thus seems that liberation does not end with the act of redemption, but that survival depends on the cultivation of meaningful relationships based on comfort and support. . . . The community is obliged to take responsibility for caring for one another; the image of God as Deliverer thus finds extension in the life of community."[10]

Unfortunately for her, the community failed Susanna; only Daniel argued for her.

Denise Dombkowski Hopkins

10. Claassens, *Mourner, Mother, Midwife*, 74–79.

Psalm 72

Irony as Criticism

Several audiences are addressed by the words of royal Psalm 72. The imperative petition in v. 1 frames the psalm as an address to God: "give the king your justice, O God." The verbs that follow are mostly imperfects that can either be translated as statements ("he will . . .") or as wishes ("may he . . ."). These verbs outline shared expectations for kings throughout the ancient Near East. Walter Houston argues that Psalm 72 offers a "discourse of persuasion"; as discourse it becomes a "transaction between speaker and audience"[1] that multiple audiences can overhear. Since the king overhears this prayer offered to God about the king he is also addressed and pressured rhetorically to fulfill what is expected of him. The psalm becomes a warning for the king in its function as a "mirror"[2] that allows him to evaluate his reign. The doxology in vv. 18-19 not only closes book 2 of the Psalter but functions perhaps to remind the king that his rule is only possible through God: "Blessed be the LORD, the God of Israel, who *alone* does wondrous things."

Also overhearing the psalm are the king's subjects, both peasants and the elite. If we take note of the superscription, which labels Psalm 72 as

---

1. Walter Houston, "The King's Preferential Option for the Poor: Rhetoric, Ideology and Ethics in Psalm 72," *BibInt* 7 (1999): 341–67, at 342.

2. Ibid., 361.

Psalm 72:1-20

Of Solomon.

¹Give the king your justice, O God,
and your righteousness to a
king's son.
²May he judge your people with
righteousness,
and your poor with justice.
³May the mountains yield prosperity for the people,
and the hills, in righteousness.
⁴May he defend the cause of the
poor of the people,
give deliverance to the needy,
and crush the oppressor.

⁵May he live while the sun endures,
and as long as the moon,
throughout all genera-
tions.
⁶May he be like rain that falls on
the mown grass,
like showers that water the
earth.
⁷In his days may righteousness
flourish
and peace abound, until the
moon is no more.

⁸May he have dominion from sea
to sea,
and from the River to the ends
of the earth.
⁹May his foes bow down before him,
and his enemies lick the dust.
¹⁰May the kings of Tarshish and of
the isles
render him tribute,
may the kings of Sheba and Seba
bring gifts.
¹¹May all kings fall down before him,
all nations give him service.
¹²For he delivers the needy when
they call,

"of Solomon," as well as the description of gift-bearing rulers in vv. 10-11, 15 (cp. 1 Kgs 10), we can imagine that a special member of the elite audience, the Queen Mother Bathsheba, also overhears this prayer. Interpreters ignore her in this connection. It seems certain that the woman who "plays an active, vocal role in Solomon's accession to the throne"[3] in 1 Kings 1–2 would be present at her son's coronation. Paying attention to how Bathsheba might receive the words of Psalm 72 in light of her experience with King David in 2 Samuel 11 and 1 Kings 1, as well as in the aftermath of Solomon's bloody ascent to his father's throne, can help readers to surface and enter into the contradictions inherent in the royal ideology of the psalm.

Psalm 72 roots itself in God's promise made in 2 Samuel 7:13, 16 of a perpetual dynasty for David and his descendants; a Davidic king will

---

3. Cameron B. R. Howard, "1 and 2 Kings," in *Women's Bible Commentary*, ed. Carol A. Newsom, Sharon H. Ringe, and Jacqueline E. Lapsley, 3rd ed. (Louisville, KY: Westminster John Knox, 2012), 164–79, at 167.

the poor and those who have
no helper.
¹³He has pity on the weak and the
needy,
and saves the lives of the
needy.
¹⁴From oppression and violence
he redeems their life;
and precious is their blood in
his sight.

¹⁵Long may he live!
May gold of Sheba be given to
him.
May prayer be made for him continually,
and blessings invoked for him
all day long.
¹⁶May there be abundance of
grain in the land;
may it wave on the tops of the
mountains;

may its fruit be like Lebanon;
and may people blossom in the
cities
like the grass of the field.
¹⁷May his name endure forever,
his fame continue as long as
the sun.
May all nations be blessed in him;
may they pronounce him
happy.

¹⁸Blessed be the Lord, the God of
Israel,
who alone does wondrous
things.
¹⁹Blessed be his glorious name
forever;
may his glory fill the whole
earth.
Amen and Amen.

²⁰The prayers of David son of
Jesse are ended.

reign "forever." Psalm 72:8-11 expresses this idea with hyperbolic language of time and space to describe the king's reign: "until the moon is no more" (vv. 5, 7) and "dominion from sea to sea" (vv. 8-11; cp. Ps 2). Hyperbole continues in v. 9 (the king's enemies will "lick the dust") and in v. 11 (foreign kings will "fall down before him"). Such actions are usually directed toward God and were rarely experienced by Israel's monarchy. This ideal portrait (see also royal Ps 2) may suggest that Psalm 72 functioned as a piece of royal propaganda outlining the way in which the monarchy saw itself or wished to be seen by its subjects and other nations, akin to the function of an inaugural address today. The rhetoric of this ideal, however, "is at odds with itself."[4] Babylonian exile and the end of monarchy (see Ps 89) pushed this idea of the Davidic king's continuous universal sovereignty into the future as an eschatological hope. Though the NT does not quote Psalm 72, its use in Advent and Epiphany points to Jesus as a fulfillment of this hope (Mark 1:14-15).

---

4. Houston, "The King's Preferential Option," 343.

As a royal psalm, Psalm 72 views the king as the mediator of divine blessings and the manifestation of God's earthly rule (cp. royal Psalms 2, 21, 101, 110, 118, and 132). God's "justice" (משפתים) and "righteousness" (צדקה) undergird the king's reign; these qualities characterize God's reign in the enthronement psalms (Pss 96:13; 97:2, 6; 98:9; 99:4; 146:7). A chiasm in vv. 1-2 repeats these two terms in reverse order, thereby bracketing the "king's son" with what should define his rule. The result will be שלום ("wholeness," "prosperity") for people, land, and cosmos (vv. 3, 7, 16) as well as for "all nations" (v. 17b; cp. Gen 12:3). The agricultural images in vv. 6 and 16 are striking. As Ellen Davis argues, here "the land itself is the medium or even the agent through which we may experience life as divinely blessed."[5] Psalm 72 links this blessing to the king's justice. Davis notes the "ironic edge" to the association of Psalm 72 with Solomon, since "his empire building and the extravagance of his court placed an intolerable burden upon Israelite farmers (1 Kgs 12:3-4)."[6]

Carolyn Sharp argues that "irony often depends on hyperbole or understatement, [and] always exploits some sort of disjuncture" as a way to

Context of Prayer

Prayers, like any form of communication, are contextual. Where a prayer is spoken, who utters it, who hears it, and the circumstances of the prayer all influence the interpretation of its meaning. As a royal psalm, Psalm 72 is perhaps more public than most (used, as suggested above, in coronation ceremonies), making its context even more important to its meaning. If we imagine Psalm 72 in a different context, how might the rhetoric shift? For example, the bombastic language of Psalm 72 suggests a hoped-for utopia, while the utter opposite is the probable reality. If this is the case, perhaps the rhetoric of extreme hyperbole could be read sardonically. Imagine the king's subjects mocking the prayer in a pub-like context. The same hyperbolic language spoken tongue-in-cheek takes on an anti-imperial tone. How does Mother Bathsheba perform the prayer for her sisters, children, or grandchildren? Even the closing doxology now seems too saccharine. The inflection, tone, and context of the words are malleable, and their alteration shifts the rhetoric of the hyperbolic psalm.

Amy Beth Jones

5. Ellen F. Davis, *Scripture, Culture, and Agriculture: An Agrarian Reading of the Bible* (New York: Cambridge University Press, 2009), 104.

6. Ibid., 165.

destabilize the surface meaning of a text as "untrustworthy." Different readers will reject an unacceptable reading to different degrees.[7] Queen Mother Bathsheba would probably have noticed the idealistic hyperbole in this prayer at her son's coronation, which contradicted her own earlier experience of monarchy. As Queen Mother, Bathsheba ostensibly had power at court (1 Kgs 1), yet she was not treated justly by David or by the narrator of her story in 2 Samuel. She experiences David "as a consummate usurper—of kingdoms and of wives."[8] Desired by the king and "taken" in 2 Samuel 11, Bathsheba does not speak except to announce her pregnancy. "This narrative, by offering no possible access to Bathsheba's feelings or her perspective, presenting her instead through the sexualized lenses of David, denies Bathsheba her subjectivity, an act of textual violence."[9] She is simply one of many women (Michal, Abigail . . .) David uses to build his kingdom. She is widowed when David has her husband, Uriah, killed at the front, and she is "taken" again into the king's house after her period of mourning is over. David violates every aspect of "righteousness" in dealing with Bathsheba and Uriah. Walter Brueggemann defines righteousness within the context of covenant as "living generatively in the community in order to sustain and enhance the community's well-being"[10] and to contribute to the good ordering of creation that the Creator ordained. David's actions result in catastrophe for his entire family, as Nathan's judgment in 2 Samuel 12 anticipates. Did Bathsheba live to see her son Solomon also violate the expectations of royal righteousness by slaughtering his opponents to secure his kingship and instituting harsh policies of taxation and forced labor that oppressed the peasantry?

Those feminists who want to see Queen Mother Bathsheba as a "king-maker" need to realize that though she appears to be the main character, it is the prophet Nathan who takes center stage in 1 Kings 1–2. He approaches her and warns that Adonijah's enthronement puts her and her son Solomon in danger (together with himself, which he does not mention).

---

7. Carolyn J. Sharp, *Irony and Meaning in the Hebrew Bible* (Bloomington: Indiana University Press, 2009), 27, 23.

8. Jo Ann Hackett, "1 and 2 Samuel," in Newsom, Ringe, and Lapsley, *Women's Bible Commentary*, 159.

9. Ilse Müllner, "Books of Samuel: Women at the Center of Israel's Story," trans. Linda M. Maloney, in *Feminist Biblical Interpretation: A Compendium of Critical Commentary*, ed. Luise Schottroff and Marie-Theres Wacker (Grand Rapids, MI: Eerdmans, 2012), 140–52, at 147.

10. Walter Brueggemann, *Reverberations of Faith: A Theological Handbook of Old Testament Themes* (Louisville, KY: Westminster John Knox, 2002), 177.

Neither can Bathsheba be simply understood as a manipulative schemer or a street-smart lady who made the best of a bad situation. Nathan is firmly in charge. Luckily, David did listen to her as he was dying (1 Kgs 1) "but that does not make her a hero or a witch."[11] Perhaps Bathsheba brought Adonijah's request to Solomon that Abishag become his wife, not to ensure Adonijah's death (taking the royal harem meant taking the throne, 2 Sam 16), but rather because she took pity on her as another woman controlled by the men around her. Though she sits on a throne at Solomon's right hand (1 Kgs 2:19), Bathsheba is like most of the women in the books of Kings, a mother whose worth resides in her ability to produce a male heir.

The complexity of Bathsheba mirrors the complexity embodied in Psalm 72 itself. Verse 12, beginning with כי ("for," "because"), makes it clear that the king's justice for the poor and needy forms the foundation for his universal rule outlined in vv. 8-11. Kings will bow down to him because he will deliver the needy. Houston notes the striking emotional language employed by Psalm 72: the poor one "has no one to help" (v. 12b); the king "has pity on the weak" (v. 13a); "precious is their [the oppressed] blood in his sight" (v. 14b). In fact, the king acts as their גאל ("redeemer," v. 14a) because there is no one else. "This emotive heightening of the language underlines the seriousness of the king's concern."[12]

Yet Psalm 72 also prays for the king to "crush the oppressor" (v. 4) and receive tribute. Herein rests a contradiction: "tribute is oppressive"[13] and creates a heavy burden for the peasants. Since the Davidic king did not control other lands in the sense suggested by Psalm 72, tribute must come from the king's own territory, which was ruled by a state bureaucracy and its spheres of corruption. Consequently, it was "in the interests of the monarchy itself to repress the exploitation of the poor by wealthy local elites"[14] who threatened the king's power. Worse, the pathos-filled language "draws attention away from the interest of the king in controlling rival centres of power. And the king's own exploitative activities are displaced on to foreign nations, so that he appears exclusively beneficent to his own people."[15] Royal ideology is undermined by this less-than-ideal portrait. The king remains in control; no change in social structures or distribution of wealth is made.

---

11. Kyung Sook Lee, "Books of Kings: Images of Women without Women's Reality," in Schottroff and Wacker, *Feminist Biblical Interpretation*, 159–77, at 163.

12. Houston, "The King's Preferential Option," 348.

13. Ibid., 350.

14. Ibid., 359.

15. Ibid.

Book 3 of the Psalter

(Pss 73–89)

Psalm 73

Letting God Off the Hook?

As the first psalm in book 3 of the Psalter, Psalm 73 "tempers the optimism of Book I about the connection between character and its outcome."[1] Like Psalms 37 and 49, Psalm 73 questions whether or not a righteous life is lived in vain (v. 13) as it struggles with the success of the wicked. Also, the laments in book 1 are all individual in nature, and mostly so in book 2, while book 3 shifts toward communal lament, especially in the psalms attributed to Asaph (Pss 73–83; also Psalm 50), a Levite who led a guild of temple singers (Neh 7:44; 1 Chr 16:7, 25). These communal laments review Israel's history as a way to understand the failure of the Davidic monarchy to live up to the expectations sketched in Psalm 72. Book 3 ends with Psalm 89 and the destruction of Jerusalem; will Davidic kingship continue? Clearly, "the events of 587 highlight the corporate dimension of earlier portraits of the righteous individual."[2]

Interpreters make grand claims about Psalm 73. Walter Brueggemann, for example, declares that it "is central theologically as well as canonically"[3]

---

1. Daniel C. Owens, *Portraits of the Righteous in the Psalms* (Eugene, OR: Pickwick, 2013), 215.

2. Ibid., 218.

3. Walter Brueggemann, "Bounded by Obedience and Praise: The Psalms as Canon," *JSOT* 50 (1991): 63–92, at 81.

A Psalm of Asaph.

¹Truly God is good to the upright,
    to those who are pure in heart.
²But as for me, my feet had al-
        most stumbled;
    my steps had nearly slipped.
³For I was envious of the arrogant;
    I saw the prosperity of the
        wicked.

⁴For they have no pain;
    their bodies are sound and
        sleek.
⁵They are not in trouble as others
        are;
    they are not plagued like other
        people.
⁶Therefore pride is their necklace;
    violence covers them like a
        garment.
⁷Their eyes swell out with fatness;
    their hearts overflow with fol-
        lies.
⁸They scoff and speak with malice;
    loftily they threaten oppression.

⁹They set their mouths against
        heaven,
    and their tongues range over
        the earth.

¹⁰Therefore the people turn and
        praise them,
    and find no fault in them.
¹¹And they say, "How can God
        know?
    Is there knowledge in the Most
        High?"
¹²Such are the wicked;
    always at ease, they increase
        in riches.
¹³All in vain I have kept my heart
        clean
    and washed my hands in inno-
        cence.
¹⁴For all day long I have been
        plagued,
    and am punished every morn-
        ing.
¹⁵If I had said, "I will talk on in this
        way,"

in the structure of the entire Psalter, mirroring Israel's movement from the obedience of Psalm 1 through lament over failed kingship to doxology. Others idealize Psalm 73 as the model of "pilgrimage from doubt to faith,"[4] noting the psalm's logical progression from problem (theodicy, or the prosperity of the wicked, vv. 1-12), to turning point (the psalmist's

---

4. Leslie C. Allen, "Psalm 73: Pilgrimage from Doubt to Faith," *BBR* 7 (1997): 1–10. Similarly, Martin Buber, "The Heart Determines: Psalm 73," reprinted in *Theodicy in the Old Testament*, ed. James L. Crenshaw (Philadelphia: Fortress Press, 1983), 109–18.

I would have been untrue to the circle of your children.
[16]But when I thought how to understand this,
it seemed to me a wearisome task,
[17]until I went into the sanctuary of God;
then I perceived their end.
[18]Truly you set them in slippery places;
you make them fall to ruin.
[19]How they are destroyed in a moment,
swept away utterly by terrors!
[20]They are like a dream when one awakes;
on awaking you despise their phantoms.

[21]When my soul was embittered, when I was pricked in heart,
[22]I was stupid and ignorant;
I was like a brute beast toward you.

[23]Nevertheless I am continually with you;
you hold my right hand.
[24]You guide me with your counsel,
and afterward you will receive me with honor.
[25]Whom have I in heaven but you?
And there is nothing on earth that I desire other than you.
[26]My flesh and my heart may fail,
but God is the strength of my heart and my portion forever.

[27]Indeed, those who are far from you will perish;
you put an end to those who are false to you.
[28]But for me it is good to be near God;
I have made the LORD God my refuge,
to tell of all your works.

visit to the sanctuary, vv. 13-17), to resolution (a renewed sense of God's presence, vv. 21-28). The symmetry of the psalm's structure "highlights the reversal of the psalmist's perspective."[5] The whole is neatly tied together by the repetition of "good" in vv. 1 and 28; the psalm circles back at the end to affirm the declaration of v. 1 that was challenged by the success of the wicked.

5. J. Clinton McCann Jr., "The Book of Psalms," in *The New Interpreter's Bible*, vol. 4 (Nashville, TN: Abingdon Press, 1996), 639–1280, at 968.

Becoming Conscious

"But when I thought how to understand this, it seemed to me a wearisome task" (v. 16). This is the turning point of the psalm, which, as has already been pointed out in the body of this commentary, engages in ironic reversal. Yet it also speaks to the deep ambivalence of becoming conscious. Becoming conscious or thinking about how to understand what we are facing and what faces us is indeed a wearisome task. Becoming conscious draws us out of the stupor of our own dominant ways of living and seeing and asks us to suffer what we lack, have lost, never had to begin with, struggle to attain, and feel does not belong to us. Becoming conscious means looking at what has been, what we have done, and what has been done to us, facing these directly rather than tossing them to the side, burying them "six feet under," or pretentiously rising above them.

The psalmist courageously and vulnerably articulates the feelings of envy that arise when one looks upon others, those who seemingly live by standards other than those to which she holds herself, who are felt to have more or have what she feels she deserves. Envy, according to early Object Relations psychoanalyst Melanie Klein, "is the angry feeling that another person possesses and enjoys something desirable." This feeling is pervasive throughout the first half of the psalm as the psalmist confesses her envy of those who are prosperous, those who seem not to have any worries, those whose riches seem to increase with ease despite their perceived gossiping and prideful, haughty ways. Klein postulates that the envious impulse that results from the feeling of envy is to take away what the envied has and to spoil it. We notice this on the playground with our children when one child stares longingly at another who has a new bottle of bubbles and then impulsively reaches to take the bottle. After blowing a few bubbles, the child turns the bottle over, emptying it of its contents as if to say, "If I can't have these bubbles all to myself, no one can!" Here is an example from childhood, yet one we can all resonate with once we translate it into our various adult experiences.[6]

In Psalm 73 the envious impulse to take what the wealthy seem to have that the psalmist does not is read in the second half (vv. 17-18): "you make them fall to ruin . . . how they are destroyed in a moment, swept away utterly by terrors." We read in this psalm an

---

6. Melanie Klein, *Envy and Gratitude, and Other Works, 1946–1963* (London: The Hogarth Press and The Institute of Psycho-Analysis, 1975), 181.

articulation of envy and the utterances of the envious impulse that resonate deeply within. Still, there is a way forward at the end of the psalm. A confession of an embittered heart leads the psalmist to dwell not on what others have but on what she in fact has, the guidance and counsel of God, something that it may not be possible to see or quantify but that resides in her heart. Finally, at the very end, there is a recognition of what is good for the psalmist alone: "But for *me* it is good to be near God." While others may have riches and prestige, the psalmist declares what is good for her. It seems that, at some level, she begins consciously to suffer her own feelings of envy rather than remaining overwhelmed by unconscious suffering. In this way, for a moment, she steps away from the envious impulse and brings consciousness to the life she has chosen to live, for better or for worse, for she knows that for her it is good to be near God.

Tiffany Houck-Loomis

Other repetitions contribute to structural symmetry, including "heart" in vv. 1, 13, 21, and 26 and the particle אַךְ, which introduces each of the three psalm sections. Frequent reversals make clear the contrast between righteous and wicked. The psalmist had almost slipped (v. 2) while the wicked live securely (vv. 4-12), whereas in light of the new perspective gained in the sanctuary the wicked slip (vv. 18-20) while the psalmist finds refuge in God (v. 28). The wicked are "always at ease" (v. 12) while the psalmist has been "plagued all day long" (v. 14). The wicked are "destroyed in a moment" (v. 19) while the psalmist is "continually" with God (v. 24). However compelling these arguments, they risk oversimplifying the complexity of the psalm and obscure its powerful use of irony.

Other voices challenge these traditional interpretations. John Nordin, for example, notes that interpreters show a "strong tendency to turn away from the indictment made by the psalmist and focus on describing the writer as guilty: guilty of a lack of faith, guilty of envy, guilty of a failure to trust God." This tendency may make the reader feel better but, just as with Job's friends, it "reduces the cry for justice to personal psychology."[7]

---

7. John P. Nordin, " 'There Is Nothing on Earth That I Desire': A Commentary on Psalm 73," *CurTM* 29 (2002): 258–64, at 261.

This lets God off the hook and makes humans shoulder the blame for evil. As James L. Crenshaw notes, "Theodicy, therefore, has a twin— anthropodicy";[8] the former justifies God's actions while the latter indicts human actions in order to account for evil and innocent suffering in the world. The psalmist's quotation of the enemy in v. 11 stubbornly lingers: "And they say, 'How can God know?'" The quotation serves double duty as a complaint against the enemy and a complaint against God that the psalmist can express indirectly, without censure, through the mouths of others.[9]

Perhaps the most forceful challenge to traditional interpretations comes from Carolyn Sharp, who insists that "the closure in Ps 73 is a faux resolution"; the psalm engages instead in "doublespeak," that is, speech "that intends to mislead."[10] Linking Psalm 73 closely to Job and Qoheleth, Sharp contends that its pervasive irony, expressed especially in hyperbole, raises doubts and disrupts the surface meaning many have identified. Sharp suggests that irony invites the disoriented reader into the liminal space that Israel occupied during and after the exile. The argument over what kind of psalm 73 is—wisdom, thanksgiving, lament, or royal—reflects the destabilizing presence of this irony. Like Qoheleth, the psalmist finds that reflection on the contradictions between the theo- logical declaration in v. 1 and her own experience of the wicked (vv. 2-14) is עמל, "a wearisome task" (v. 16b). This task continues for the psalmist after her experience in the sanctuary in v. 17; she does not repudiate her earlier position as most interpreters claim. Her bitterness, envy, and feelings of abandonment continue throughout the psalm up to the final line, whose irony is "palpable" (v. 28). The king is "so consumed with pondering the epistemological dilemma that he has neither recounted all of God's works (v. 28) nor advocated for the powerless in his society."[11] His "narcissistic ranting" invites the audience either to join in the psalm- ist's doubts or to read further into other Asaph psalms that describe God's marvelous deeds on Israel's behalf.

8. James L. Crenshaw, *Defending God* (New York: Oxford University Press, 2005), 195.

9. Rolf A. Jacobson, *"Many Are Saying": The Function of Direct Discourse in the Hebrew Psalter*, JSOTSup 397 (Edinburgh: T & T Clark, 2004), 54, 58. Unlike Nordin, Jacobson insists that the psalmist avoids the temptation to speak like the wicked.

10. Carolyn J. Sharp, *Irony and Meaning in the Hebrew Bible* (Bloomington: Indiana University Press, 2009), 221, 225.

11. Ibid., 235.

TRANSLATION MATTERS

Sharp rejects the traditional view of the psalmist's spiritual transformation by noting three key semantic ambiguities within Psalm 73. First, the unexpected cohortative form in v. 17b that most translate as past tense reads literally "let me understand." This means that the psalmist's wrestling with theodicy continues; it is not confined to the past. Second, the particle אך, which most translate as an exclamation in v. 19a, is normally an interrogative: "how can it be that they have become a desolation?" referring not to the enemy but to Israel in exile. Third, Sharp translates the כי at the beginning of v. 21 not as a temporal, "*when* my soul was embittered," but rather as an asseverative: "*Indeed*, my [heart] is embittered," which reflects the ongoing state of the speaker.[12]

Finding Endurance

Reading Psalm 73 alongside the history of white privilege and black oppression, an African American reader can easily identify with the claims of the psalmist. From slavery to the Jim Crow South, there is no perceivable social or theological consequence for the ways in which black people have been used as tools to create wealth and status for white America. Moreover, in recent history we have borne witness to the lack of consequence for white aggression against black bodies when white sentiments of entitlement are seemingly challenged by the social progress of minoritized groups.

While Carolyn Sharp, focusing on the weariness in v. 16, might regard the resolution to Psalm 73 as shallow, for the African American reader, and perhaps for most oppressed people, resolution is not the aim. Hence the turn in v. 17 becomes crucial for survival. The psalmist's depiction of weariness—"until I went into the sanctuary of God"—resounds within black communities and congregations. The church, the Christian sanctuary, is not the place where black people find resolution for their pain and suffering; it is the place where they find endurance. Endurance is often predicated on the ability to understand the pitfalls of another's privilege. Such imagination requires the oppressed to exchange bitterness for grace through a realization that privilege built on oppression and entitlement deteriorates the inner being.

Yolanda Marie Norton

12. Ibid., 226–29.

Many interpreters posit the king as the speaker in Psalm 73. As noted above, with the shift to communal laments in book 3 the destinies of the monarch and the nation become intertwined, particularly following the failure of the monarch to live up to the expectations of Psalm 72. Also, v. 24 contains a motif widespread in the ancient Near East: a king being led by the hand of a deity (Isa 45:1, God and Cyrus).[13] Yet none of these suggestions is conclusive in terms of identifying the speaker. Several women in Tanakh could have prayed this psalm, Bathsheba among them. Second Samuel 11 suggests itself as intertext for Psalm 73 in several ways. First of all, both texts use the verb רחץ ("wash," "bathe"). The psalmist declares in v. 13a: "All in vain [אך, literally 'indeed,' 'truly'] I have kept my heart clean and washed [רחץ] my hands in innocence." In the psalm, hand-washing functions as a metaphor for righteous living; it is paralleled by "clean heart" in v. 13a. David from his roof spies Bathsheba literally "bathing" (רחץ) in 2 Samuel 11. Later in the text we learn that "she was purifying herself [קדש] after her period" (v. 4) as she is required to do by Leviticus 15:19. Bathsheba is attempting to follow Torah prescriptions for ritual purification; she is trying to live righteously. In doing so, however, she becomes the object of David's lust: "in vain" has she done the right thing. Her obedience to Torah results in her rape and pregnancy and raises the possibility of her death by stoning for adultery. Her pregnancy is a constant reminder of her trauma: "for all day long I have been plagued, and am punished every morning" (v. 14); perhaps she is experiencing morning sickness.

The story of Bathsheba's rape is bracketed by the larger context of the war against the Ammonites (2 Sam 10; 12:26-31). David was supposed to have been away from Jerusalem besieging the Ammonite capital, Rabbah, when he spied Bathsheba from his rooftop. Joab, the general who does all his dirty work, even chides David to come to Rabbah and carry out the final assault lest the people credit Joab with the victory (2 Sam 12:26-28). It is Joab who carries out David's order to expose Bathsheba's husband Uriah in the fiercest part of the battle against the Ammonites so that he may die. One can imagine that the violence of rape, murder, and war lead Bathsheba to pray with the psalmist: "violence covers them [David and Joab] like a garment" (v. 6b). Bathsheba barely had time to grieve her husband before David "removed her" (אסף—the

13. Frank-Lothar Hossfeld and Erich Zenger, *Psalms 2: A Commentary on Psalms 51–100*, trans. Linda M. Maloney, Hermeneia (Minneapolis: Fortress Press, 2005), 233.

NRSV translates with the less forceful phrase "brought her") to his house and she became his wife (v. 27). Both David and Joab operate with little fear of being caught—after all, David is the king, a man after God's own heart, and Bathsheba lacks the power to say no. The prophet Nathan alludes to this sense of entitlement in 2 Samuel 12: "your neighbor [a reference to Absalom and his future rebellion against his father] . . . shall lie with your wives in the sight of this very sun. For you did it secretly; but I will do this thing before all Israel, and before the sun" (2 Sam 12:11-12). One can imagine that Bathsheba would say with the psalmist: "And they [David and Joab] say, 'how can God know?'" (v. 11a). Her quotation functions not only as a complaint against David but also against God. It becomes her question as well, which she can offer up without being censured (see n. 8 above).

Who can blame Bathsheba for being "stirred up about the arrogant" (v. 3a)? Though the verb קָנָא is often translated as "be jealous," it involves more broadly the idea of stirred-up passions, whether they be jealousy, anger, or lust. Throughout the trauma of her pregnancy one can imagine Bathsheba consumed by anger and questions about what had happened to her. It was not until she "went into the sanctuary of God" (v. 17) that she came to understand that God does know: "But the thing that David had done displeased the LORD" (2 Sam 11:27); God sends Nathan to David. By telling the parable of the ewe lamb (2 Sam 12:1-6) Nathan tricks David into condemning himself. The punishment is retributive: "You have struck down Uriah the Hittite with the sword. . . . Now therefore the sword shall never depart from your house" (2 Sam 12:9-10). As Bathsheba learned in God's sanctuary, "truly you set them [David and his court] in slippery places; you make them fall to ruin" (v. 18).

Like the psalmist, however, Bathsheba does not let God off the hook because of her experience in the sanctuary. God did not protect her from being raped by David; the child born of that rape dies (2 Sam 12:15-19). Bathsheba will carry the memory of the death of her firstborn with her for the rest of her life. We hear nothing of her after the birth of Solomon; she resurfaces at the end of David's reign, when she and Nathan manipulate the now old and feeble king (1 Kgs 1). Perhaps it is only when Bathsheba's son Solomon becomes king that she can finally cleanse her heart of the bitterness she has carried for so long (Ps 73:21). We can imagine a new superscription for Psalm 73: "A prayer when Bathsheba discovered she was pregnant with David's child."

Psalm 74

Jerusalem as Woman

ike the other psalms of Asaph in book 3 of the Psalter (Pss 73–83), Psalm 74 concerns itself with theodicy, that is, why do the wicked escape punishment? Why does God not penalize those who destroyed Jerusalem and the temple instead of adopting "a Napoleonic pose with concealed hand (74:11)"?[1] Psalm 74 wrestles corporately with what Psalm 73 confronts individually: the triumph of the wicked; shared vocabulary ties the two psalms together. The community in Psalm 74 seems bewildered about why God's anger "smokes" (v. 1b; cp. Deut 29:20; Ps 80:4) against the sheep of God's pasture. In order to persuade God to act, Psalm 74 focuses on divine abandonment of the covenant relationship and reminds God about God's power in the past. Many interpreters posit the Babylonian destruction of 587 BCE as context for Psalm 74, although some have argued for the Maccabean period in the second century BCE.

Psalm 74 begins with an agonizing question about God's abandonment, typical of the laments: "why do you cast us off forever?" (cp. Pss 43:2; 44:9, 23; 60:1, 10; 88:14; 89:38). The question "why?" brackets the first section (vv. 1, 11: twice in each verse). Time expressions are numerous, articulating communal anxiety: "forever" (vv. 1, 3, 10, 19), "from of old"

---

1. James L. Crenshaw, *The Psalms: An Introduction* (Grand Rapids, MI: Eerdmans, 2001), 25.

Psalm 74:1-23

A Maskil of Asaph.

[1]O God, why do you cast us off
    forever?
Why does your anger smoke
    against the sheep of
    your pasture?
[2]Remember your congregation,
    which you acquired long ago,
which you redeemed to be the
    tribe of your heritage.
Remember Mount Zion, where
    you came to dwell.
[3]Direct your steps to the perpetual
    ruins;
the enemy has destroyed every-
    thing in the sanctuary.

[4]Your foes have roared within your
    holy place;
they set up their emblems
    there.
[5]At the upper entrance they hacked
    the wooden trellis with axes.

[6]And then, with hatchets and ham-
    mers,
    they smashed all its carved work.
[7]They set your sanctuary on fire;
    they desecrated the dwelling
        place of your name,
    bringing it to the ground.
[8]They said to themselves, "We will
    utterly subdue them";
    they burned all the meeting
        places of God in the land.

[9]We do not see our emblems;
    there is no longer any prophet,
    and there is no one among us
        who knows how long.
[10]How long, O God, is the foe to
    scoff?
    Is the enemy to revile your
        name forever?
[11]Why do you hold back your hand;
    why do you keep your hand in
        your bosom?

(v. 12), "all day long" (v. 22), and "continually" (v. 23).[2] The question "how long?" (v. 10; cp. Pss 79, 80, 82) underscores this anxiety. "The question is not *whether* God is powerful . . . but *when* God will show God's power."[3] The people are left wondering because there is no "sign" (NRSV: "emblem"), that is, no prophet (v. 9; cp. v. 4) who knows how long.

The quotation of the enemy (v. 8)—"we will utterly subdue them"—followed by the burning of all God's meeting places echoes in reverse the Holy War language of Deuteronomy. To destroy a sanctuary is to defeat its god. Section three, vv. 18-23, petitions God in a series of negative and positive imperatives ("remember," "do not forget"). These petitions remind God of God's covenant obligations and "show that not just

2. Konrad Schaefer, *Psalms*, Berit Olam (Collegeville, MN: Liturgical Press, 2001), 182.
3. J. Clinton McCann Jr., "The Book of Psalms," in *The New Interpreter's Bible*, vol. 4 (Nashville, TN: Abingdon Press, 1996), 639–1280, at 973.

¹²Yet God my King is from of old,
   working salvation in the earth.
¹³You divided the sea by your might;
   you broke the heads of the
      dragons in the waters.
¹⁴You crushed the heads of Leviathan;
   you gave him as food for the
      creatures of the wilder-
      ness.
¹⁵You cut openings for springs and
   torrents;
   you dried up ever-flowing
      streams.
¹⁶Yours is the day, yours also the
   night;
   you established the luminaries
      and the sun.
¹⁷You have fixed all the bounds of
   the earth;
   you made summer and winter.
¹⁸Remember this, O LORD, how the
   enemy scoffs,

and an impious people reviles
   your name.
¹⁹Do not deliver the soul of your
   dove to the wild animals;
   do not forget the life of your
      poor forever.

²⁰Have regard for your covenant,
   for the dark places of the land
      are full of the haunts of
      violence.
²¹Do not let the downtrodden be
   put to shame;
   let the poor and needy praise
      your name.
²²Rise up, O God, plead your
   cause;
   remember how the impious
      scoff at you all day long.
²³Do not forget the clamor of your
   foes,
   the uproar of your adversaries
      that goes up continually.

Israel but God has something at stake in Jerusalem's recovery."[4] This point is reinforced by the repetition of the possessive suffix "your" in vv. 18-23: "your name," "your poor," "your covenant," "your foes," "your adversaries." In this way the psalm makes clear that God also experiences the effects of war and invites God to respond to that experience; the psalmist seeks to touch a divine nerve.

Psalm 74 offers several types of motivations to pressure God into taking retributive action, including an emotional, detailed description of the destruction of the sanctuary (vv. 3-8); indictments of the enemy who "reviles God's name" (vv. 10, 18; cp. "scoffs," vv. 18, 22); and references to God's suffering people as "the poor" (עני, vv. 19, 21). The most powerful motivator, however, emerges in section two (vv. 12-17), which connects

4. Walter Brueggemann, *From Whom No Secrets Are Hid: Introducing the Psalms*, ed. Brent Strawn (Louisville, KY: Westminster John Knox, 2014), 83.

the complaints in part one with the petitions of part three. These verses emphasize God's sovereign power in history and intentionally create a contrast between Israel's memory (vv. 12-17) and the present situation. Many interpreters insist, however, that v. 14 ("You crushed the heads of Leviathan") reveals the presence of the combat myth (*Chaoskampf*) from the Mesopotamian creation myth Enuma Elish, with its violent defeat of personified chaos (Tiamat) by Marduk.

More convincingly, Rebecca Watson argues that this mythic language is used to describe God's salvific activity in the exodus and wilderness; citing saving history is common in the communal laments. Israel has transformed the content and significance of violent ancient Near Eastern creation myths in its new situation. "God's activity in nature is employed to convey political assurance"[5] in a time of great anxiety. From an ecological perspective the emphasis on the combat myth in Psalm 74 is deadly for the earth because it describes earth as hostile in creation and now a dead thing. The combat myth objectified the earth and models for us today "ecological slaughter and geographical destruction,"[6] since Tiamat's corpse was used to create the ordered cosmos. Nevertheless, because Zion "gives a central role to a *place*, not a battle"[7] in Psalm 74, earth has value.

God's Sanctuary on Fire	Expansive wildfires in the western United States are common now. While other factors play minor roles, human-caused climate change has raised temperatures, decreased precipitation, and dramatically increased insect infestation, turning our forests into tinderboxes. Fire now destroys more than six times more land
God hung out his rainbow cross the sky,	
And he said to Noah: That's my sign!	
No more will I judge the world by flood—	
Next time I'll rain down fire.[8]	

5. Rebecca S. Watson, *Chaos Uncreated: A Reassessment of the Theme of "Chaos" in the Hebrew Bible* (Berlin and New York: de Gruyter, 2005), 166.

6. Ibid., 30.

7. Peter L. Trudinger, "Friend or Foe? Earth, Sea and *Chaoskampf* in the Psalms," in *The Earth Story in the Psalms and the Prophets*, ed. Norman C. Habel (Sheffield: Sheffield Academic Press, 2001), 29–41, at 40.

8. James Weldon Johnson, *God's Trombones* (New York: Viking Penguin, 1927), 37.

annually than it did thirty years ago.[9] These fires are having disastrous impacts on human health and safety, economic stability, water and food supplies, not to mention their effect on wildlife. And, as usual, the least among us are bearing the worst of the burden.

Indeed, we have set God's sanctuary of creation on fire. We have desecrated God's dwelling place and brought it to the ground (v. 7). But what about the covenant—the covenant God made with Noah and every living thing that the earth would not be destroyed again (Gen 9:8-17)? "Have regard for your covenant," the people plead (v. 20). Why isn't God *doing* something? Why is God *letting* this happen?

The Noachic covenant is not a one-way promise from God that invites us to sit idly by while God takes care of things. God is doing more than God's part. Covenant calls for the community to respond and to order itself in a manner "in tune with God's ordering of the cosmos."[10] It is not God but we who have failed the covenant by continuing to maintain lives and lifestyles that are causing temperatures to rise to deadly levels.

When read through the lens of the Noachic covenant, Psalm 74 suggests that it might be we who are now God's foes—those who have "destroyed everything in the sanctuary" (v. 3). Could it also be we who "have roared within your holy place" of creation and "set up [our] emblems there" (v. 4)? In line with this reading, the psalm too begs God's response to us: "Have regard for your covenant, for the dark places of the land are full of the haunts of violence" (v. 20). "Rise up, O God, plead your cause" with us (v. 22).

Beth Norcross

For Watson, Psalm 74's center section logically continues the introductory pleas of vv. 1-2, which refer to the exodus. The verb קנה ("acquired") in v. 2, for example, appears in the Song of the Sea to refer to God's people (Exod 15:16; cp. Ps 78:54). God divides the sea in Psalm 74:13a, which alludes to Exodus 14:21. God's opening of springs and drying up of streams in v. 15 recalls both provision of water in the wilderness (Exod 17:6; Num 20:8; Ps 78:15, 16, 20) and entry into the promised land (Josh 3:16-17;

9. A. L. Westerling, H. G. Hidalgo, D. R. Cayan, and T. W. Swetnam, "Global Warming and Earlier Spring Increase Western U.S. Forest Wildfire Activity," *Science* 313 (August 2006): 940–43, accessed March 1, 2015, DOI: 10.1126/science.1128834.

10. Bruce Birch, Walter Brueggemann, Terence E. Fretheim, and David L. Petersen, *A Theological Introduction to the Old Testament* (Nashville, TN: Abingdon Press, 1999), 131.

4:23). Israel's memory of divine saving activity on Israel's behalf indicts God's present inactivity.

Shifting from the combat myth to God's salvific action in the exodus does not, however, benefit women. Unfortunately, the focus on "the Liberator-Warrior-God-for-Us"[11] in the exodus can be misused to legitimate the violence of empire against the marginalized, as history has made us painfully aware. As Susanne Scholz argues, the image of God in Exodus "does not liberate; it instills fear even in the Israelites (e.g., 20:19)" who no longer call to God directly but complain instead to Moses. Moses, rather than liberation, stands at the center of Exodus, and even exceptional women like Miriam and Zipporah remain on the margins.[12]

Cynthia Chapman on "the Jerusalem Complex"

Encouraging from a feminist standpoint is the resistance Psalm 74 shows to the gendered language of warfare. Cynthia Chapman argues that, in the military expansion of Assyria in the ninth to seventh centuries BCE, "gendered language expressed through military titles, taunts, and curses played an important role in the self-representation of the victor as masculine and in the projected representation of the conquered as feminine" (p. 1). In this connection "the Jerusalem Complex" comes into play, that is, the metaphors formed around the image of "Jerusalem-as-woman" (p. 60). The prophets used this complex "to dramatize the historical encounter with Assyria as they experienced and remembered it" (p. 61). Not only Amos and First Isaiah drew up this Complex to address the Assyrian threat, but later Jeremiah and Ezekiel did so as well. These prophets feminized Jerusalem as a whore who deserved punishment from her aggrieved divine husband. "Jerusalem-as-woman" is also called Zion, Daughter Zion, Daughter Jerusalem, Judah, Faithless Judah, Oholibah.

The use of this bundle of metaphors served several goals. Primarily, it "preserved the honor of Yahweh in the face of the defeat of his capital city and the ultimate destruction of his temple by placing the blame for the conquest on his headstrong

---

11. L. Juliana M. Claassens, *Mourner, Mother, Midwife: Reimagining God's Delivering Presence in the Old Testament* (Louisville, KY: Westminster John Knox, 2012), 2.

12. Susanne Scholz, "Exodus: The Meaning of Liberation from 'His' Perspective," in *Feminist Biblical Interpretation: A Compendium of Critical Commentary*, ed. Luise Schottroff and Marie-Theres Wacker (Grand Rapids, MI: Eerdmans, 2012), 33–50, at 47.

daughter/wife" (p. 65). Viewing military defeat as God's punishment of a whoring wife reduced the role of the victor to that of "an unwitting pawn in a domestic dispute" (p. 65). In this way asymmetrical relationships of power could be maintained on several levels.

Exile, however, began to "expose cracks" (p. 171) in the Jerusalem Complex. No longer is exile seen as the deserved punishment of a feminized Jerusalem who played the whore with Assyria and then Babylon. Second Isaiah, for example, proclaims that Israel has "paid double" for her sins (Isa 40:2) and that God had abandoned Israel and hidden God's face in wrath (54:7-8); Isaiah 51:9 seems to accuse God of sleeping on the job (Ps 44:23).[13]

Denise Dombkowski Hopkins

Perhaps Psalm 74 joins Second Isaiah in "exposing cracks" in the idea of Jerusalem-as-woman. These cracks appear even though v. 12 refers to God as "king from of old," which taps into the violent, masculine Divine Warrior image of God in the exodus (see Ps 44 for a discussion of God as king). Even though the people petition in v. 2c ("Remember Mount Zion, where you came to dwell"), ties to the Jerusalem Complex are severed. Why? Because the people do not confess sin or ask for forgiveness in Psalm 74. There is no hint that Zion, "where you came to dwell," deserves punishment. This disconnect puts even more pressure on God to respond.

13. Cynthia Chapman, *The Gendered Language of Warfare in the Israelite-Assyrian Encounter* (Winona Lake, IN: Eisenbrauns, 2004).

Psalm 75

The Earth Totters

In its canonical position Psalm 75 seems to respond to the complaints and questions of Psalm 74. Psalm 74:10 asks "How long?"
and Psalm 75:2 asserts, "At the set time [מוֹעֵד] that I appoint, I will judge
with equity." The word מוֹעֵד is also found in the plural in Psalm 74:4 as
"holy place" or "sanctuary." These two Asaph psalms need not be tied
together, however, since Psalm 75 expresses in a very general way the
theme of the Two Ways of Psalm 1 without providing any specifics about
the identity of the righteous or the wicked or the historical location of
God's judgment. The psalm opens with communal thanksgiving, joined
by a report of others telling of God's "wondrous deeds," a term found
in Exodus 3:20; 34:10 and in Joshua 3:5, evoking God's saving acts on
Israel's behalf. The "we" of community changes to the divine "I" in vv.
2-5 as God announces future judgment. The psalmist, perhaps speaking
on behalf of the community, interrupts God's speech in vv. 6-9, and God
speaks again in v. 10. These speaker changes point to a liturgical context
for this prayer.

The word "horn" (קֶרֶן) occupies center stage in Ps 75; it is repeated
four times, symbolizing arrogant power for the wicked who "lift up"
their horns in vv. 4-5 and 10a but victorious power for the righteous in
v. 10b. Coupled with the sixfold repetition of the verb רוּם ("lift up," vv.
4-5, 6b, 7b, 10), the psalm makes clear that only God can "execute

Psalm 75:1-10

To the leader: Do Not Destroy.
A Psalm of Asaph. A Song.

[1]We give thanks to you, O God;
we give thanks; your name is
near.
People tell of your wondrous
deeds.

[2]At the set time that I appoint
I will judge with equity.
[3]When the earth totters, with all its
inhabitants,

it is I who keep its pillars
steady.   *Selah*

[4]I say to the boastful, "Do not boast,"
and to the wicked, "Do not lift
up your horn;
[5]do not lift up your horn on high,
or speak with insolent neck."

[6]For not from the east or from the
west
and not from the wilderness
comes lifting up;

judgment" (v. 7a), "putting down one and lifting up another" (v. 7b) as the God of reversals. God makes the wicked drink from a foaming cup of wine (v. 8), a motif used often by the prophets to portray God's eschatological judgment (see Pss 11:6; 60:3; Isa 51:17; Jer 25:15-29; 48:12; Ezek 23:32-34; Hab 2:15-16). In v. 3 God insists that when the earth "totters" (cp. Ps 46:6) "it is I [emphatic אנכי] who keep its pillars steady." Israel shares here the ancient Near Eastern concept of the three-tiered universe, with the earth disk anchored in the chaos waters and the sky dome above. Clearly "the firmness of the earth epitomizes that which is established and immovable"[1] and suggests stability in the historical sphere. This stability has consequences for the wicked.

Two strong links suggest the Song of Hannah in 1 Samuel 2:1-10 as intertext for Psalm 75. Hannah's song is also a thanksgiving, ostensibly for the birth of her son, Samuel, who is mentioned only indirectly in v. 5. In reality this ancient text was inserted into the narrative later, since it mentions a king in v. 10, suggesting that Hannah's longing for a child symbolizes Israel's longing for a king. Hannah's story and the song do share the theme of the God who reverses injustice; this theme is prominent in Psalm 75. In Hannah's song "the text expands the individual experience of rescue and embeds it in the actions of the God who reverses unjust and oppressive social conditions. . . . Motherhood is grasped in

---

1. Rebecca S. Watson, *Chaos Uncreated: A Reassessment of the Theme of "Chaos" in the Hebrew Bible* (Berlin and New York: de Gruyter, 2005), 130.

⁷but it is God who executes judgment,
putting down one and lifting up another.
⁸For in the hand of the LORD there is a cup
with foaming wine, well mixed;
he will pour a draught from it,
and all the wicked of the earth shall drain it down to the dregs.
⁹But I will rejoice forever;
I will sing praises to the God of Jacob.

¹⁰All the horns of the wicked I will cut off,
but the horns of the righteous shall be exalted.

its social dimension"² (cp. Mary's Magnificat in Luke 1:46-56). In addition, the same verb, רום ("lift up"), found repeatedly in Psalm 75, occurs in 1 Samuel 2:8b—"He lifts the needy from the ash heap"—to express God's sovereign judgment as the reverser of situations. In 1 Samuel 2:6 the act of bringing down (ירד) and raising up (עלה) echoes God's actions in Psalm 75:7b (שפל and רום), though the verbs are synonymous, not identical. In Hannah's story her husband's other wife, Peninnah, certainly "lifted up" her "horn" (Ps 75:4b, 5) by "provoking" Hannah "severely" for her barrenness year after year (1 Sam 1:6, 7a). One imagines that Peninnah "boasted" (Ps 75:4a) about her children constantly to remind Hannah of her childlessness. The second link between Psalm 75 and the Song of Hannah occurs in 1 Samuel 2:8d: "for the pillars [מצוקי] of the earth are the Lord's." Just as in Psalm 75:3 (עמודים), God's activity in creation undergirds stability in the realm of history and politics. Again, the words for "pillars" in each text are not identical, but they are synonymous.

Though ecological concerns are not specifically a gender issue or a feminist concern, they do shape the quality of life for men, women, children, and all creatures on our planet. Psalm 75:3 speaks of God keeping the earth's pillars "steady" "when the earth totters." The metaphor of a tottering earth suggests an earthquake, which many today associate with oil and gas drilling across the globe. A recent newspaper article³

2. Ilse Müllner, "Books of Samuel: Women at the Center of Israel's Story," trans. Linda M. Maloney, in *Feminist Biblical Interpretation: A Compendium of Critical Commentary*, ed. Luise Schottroff and Marie-Theres Wacker (Grand Rapids, MI: Eerdmans, 2012), 140–52, at 142.

3. For what follows, see Lori Montgomery, "Oklahoma Worries over Its Swarm of Quakes," *The Washington Post*, Thursday, January 29, 2015, A1 and A12.

claims that, in 2014, 567 earthquakes of at least 3.0 magnitude hit the state of Kansas in the United States; before 2009, fewer than two quakes a year were felt. In November 2011 a quake measuring 5.6 happened in a town east of Oklahoma City; it was the largest recorded quake in the history of the state of Oklahoma. A quake of the same magnitude occurred in September 2016 near Pawnee, Oklahoma. In both cases some scientists pointed to the deep wastewater disposal wells dug by the oil and gas industry as the cause. Kansas depends on oil wealth: one in five jobs is linked to the oil industry, which accounts for one-third of the Kansan economy. These statistics contribute to the contentious debates that surround the issue. Further, the US Geological Survey and the Oklahoma Geological Survey note a "sharp uptick in seismic activity" in Texas, Colorado, Arkansas, Oklahoma, and Ohio. Perhaps one can hear the earth crying out for God's justice in the words of Psalm 75. Can we "sing praises to the God of Jacob" (v. 9) while we ravage God's earth?

Fracking and the Environment

Also known as hydrofracking, fracking, or hydrofracturing, hydraulic fracturing is an oil and gas well development process that involves injecting water under high pressure into a bedrock formation via the well. It is used to increase oil and/or gas flow to a well from petroleum-bearing rock formations and is seeing increased use across the country.

Energy development often requires substantial amounts of water, and hydraulic fracturing is no exception. Water is needed not only for the traditional drilling process but for the actual fracturing as well. Water is first mixed with chemicals and fine sands and then pumped at extremely high pressure into the shale rock to fracture it, forming pathways for the oil and gas to reach the well. The water is then recovered along with the oil and gas. The US Geological Survey (USGS) is conducting studies to assess the amount of water required for hydraulic fracturing as well as the impacts of withdrawing water from the local environment. On-the-ground projects are currently proposed or ongoing in more than fifteen states to establish baseline water quantity and quality measurements and assessments.

In addition, oil and gas formations themselves often contain significant amounts of water that come up with the petroleum: this is referred to as produced water. Produced waters contain dissolved trace minerals from their formations of origin. USGS is studying the impacts of produced waters on local environments such as might result from a variety of energy development techniques.

Concerns also exist regarding the potential contamination of fresh groundwater resources from oil and gas extraction wells that use hydraulic fracturing, either from the petroleum resource being produced or from the chemicals introduced in the fracturing process. USGS is studying well water quality in several states where hydraulic fracturing is being practiced, including Arkansas, New York, Pennsylvania, and Wyoming.

Hydraulic fracturing, directional drilling, and other advanced technologies have allowed the production of oil and gas from rock formations that previously could not be developed. As a result, so-called unconventional resources like shale gas and shale oil are among the fastest-growing energy sources in the United States. Unconventional gas now accounts for well over 60% of the US gas supply.

USGS has conducted research that associates deepwell fluid injection, a process sometimes used to dispose of produced waters or flowback waters from hydraulic fracturing and gas production, with the triggering of earthquakes. Deepwell fluid injection is a technique in which wastewater, typically produced waters from the petroleum formation and flowback from the fracking operation, is injected back into the Earth for storage. Earthquakes may occur when the injected fluid reaches a critically stressed fault. USGS is researching the factors that control the generation of injection-induced earthquakes and maintains a list of FAQs regarding the potential earthquake hazards associated with deepwell fluid injection.[4]

Denise Dombkowski Hopkins

4. US Geological Survey, http://www.usgs.gov/hydraulic_fracturing/, accessed January 30, 2015.

Psalm 76

Peace through Violence?

References to troops, anger, fear, judgment, rebuke, and tribute draw the reader of Psalm 76 into the world of men, war, and power and seem to leave little room for women and children. The toggling between third-person speech about God (vv. 1-3) and second-person direct address to God (vv. 4-10), with third-person address to the world's inhabitants (vv. 11-12), suggests a liturgical setting. Many classify Psalm 76 as a Zion hymn (Pss 46, 48, 84, 87, 122, and Ps 137:3—"sing us one of the songs of Zion") because of v. 2, which declares that Zion is God's "dwelling place." But Zion/Salem (an ancient name for Jerusalem; Gen 14:18) is not the focus of the psalm. Rather, Zion "functions as a symbol of God's sovereignty in all times and places."[1] God's choice of Zion appears in several psalms in book 3 that respond to the destruction described in Psalms 74; 78:68b; 89:38-45. Psalm 76 looks to the future to inspire hope among the exiles. "The warring enemies and their implements described in Ps 74:3-8 [2-7], will be smashed by the God who dwells in Zion (76:3, 4 [2, 3])."[2] From Zion, God will end warfare, as in Psalm 46:9-10.

---

1. J. Clinton McCann Jr., "The Book of Psalms," in *The New Interpreter's Bible*, vol. 4 (Nashville, TN: Abingdon Press, 1996), 639–1280, at 980.
2. Robert L. Cole, *The Shape and Message of Book III (Psalms 73–89)*, JSOTSup 307 (Sheffield: Sheffield Academic Press, 2000), 49.

Psalm 76:1-12

To the leader: with stringed instruments.
A Psalm of Asaph. A Song.

¹In Judah God is known,
　his name is great in Israel.
²His abode has been established
　in Salem,
　his dwelling place in Zion.
³There he broke the flashing ar-
　rows,
　the shield, the sword, and the
　weapons of war.   *Selah*

⁴Glorious are you, more majestic
　than the everlasting moun-
　tains.

⁵The stouthearted were stripped
　of their spoil;
　they sank into sleep;
none of the troops
　was able to lift a hand.
⁶At your rebuke, O God of Jacob,
　both rider and horse lay
　stunned.

⁷But you indeed are awesome!
　Who can stand before you
　when once your anger is
　roused?
⁸From the heavens you uttered
　judgment;
　the earth feared and was still

Ironically, other verses in this psalm suggest that this God who will end war is also a Divine Warrior. This ambiguity marks Israel's struggle with the trauma of exile, careening between violent desire for revenge and a war-weariness longing for peace. Verse 2 describes God's place in Zion as "his abode" (סכו) and "his dwelling place" (מעונתו), both of which suggest a lion's den or lair in other texts (e.g., Ps 10:9; Amos 3:4). These metaphors connect with v. 6, which mentions God's "rebuke" (literally: "blast"). Together, vv. 2 and 6 suggest that God roars like a lion in judgment (cp. Jer 25:30; Amos 1:2; Joel 3:16).

God may break (literally "shatter") arrows, shields, swords, "and the weapons of war" (v. 3), but the reference to "rider and horse" that lay "stunned" (v. 6b) expresses an exodus memory (Exod 15:1) of God's destructive power over the Egyptians at the Reed Sea. This victory "typifies all God's victories on the people's behalf."[3] God's power is reinforced by the repetition of the Niphal participle נורא from the root ירא ("fear") in vv. 4, 7, 11, and 12, which NRSV translates variously as "glorious," "awesome," or "be feared." Even "the earth feared" (v. 8b, root ירא) when God uttered judgments from the heavens; no one can stand before God's anger (v. 7). Interpreters have suggested the Assyrian invasion and the

---

3. Konrad Schaefer, *Psalms*, Berit Olam (Collegeville, MN: Liturgical Press, 2001), 188.

9when God rose up to establish
judgment,
to save all the oppressed of
the earth. *Selah*

10Human wrath serves only to
praise you,
when you bind the last bit of
your wrath around you.

11Make vows to the LORD your
God, and perform them;
let all who are around him
bring gifts
to the one who is awesome,
12who cuts off the spirit of princes,
who inspires fear in the kings
of the earth.

defeat of Sennacherib in 2 Kings 19:35 as context for this reference, but the entire psalm may have "an eschatological thrust"[4] that looks to future deliverance in light of Psalm 74.

Verses 11-12 assert God's universal sovereignty by commanding the performance of vows and the bringing of "gifts" to the "awesome" one. This suggestion of tribute undercuts the claim made in v. 9b that God's judgments are "to save all the oppressed of the earth." The burden of giving tribute falls most heavily on the peasantry and its family units, whose own subsistence is put at risk by extra demands (v. 12b); the demand for cash crops (grain, wine, and oil) to pay tribute wreaks havoc on necessarily more diversified peasant subsistence farming. Fear seems a shaky foundation here for the "pilgrimage of the nations"; in Isaiah 2:1-4 and Micah 4:1-3 this pilgrimage is rooted in Torah rather than fear. Just as in Psalm 46:10, peace is achieved in Psalm 76 through violence. Walter Wink terms this "the myth of redemptive violence,"[5] which has meant suffering for countless women and children through the centuries.

Several features of Psalm 76 suggest the story of Judith in the Apocrypha as intertext. Rather than challenge the violence of Psalm 76 as feminist interpreters might hope, however, Judith simply affirms it. Though Judith is one of only four women for whom a biblical book is named (along with Ruth, Esther, and Susanna), she assumes the role of female warrior, mimicking God as Divine Warrior. Armed with only her great beauty, she goes into the enemy camp and decapitates the foreign general, Holofernes, with his own sword. Before Judith leaves the safety

4. McCann, "The Book of Psalms," 979.

5. Walter Wink, *Engaging the Powers: Discernment and Resistance in a World of Domination* (Minneapolis: Augsburg Fortress Press, 1992), 13.

of her town to enter the enemy camp, she prays a lengthy prayer (9:1-14). "In her prayer, Judith holds in tension weakness (in emphasizing her status as a widow) and power (in calling for revenge). The God to whom she prays reflects this tension as refuge of the weak and warrior."[6] The same tension appears in Psalm 76: God judges in order "to save all the oppressed" (v. 9) and also "cuts off the spirit of princes" (v. 12). In her prayer, Judith echoes language in Psalm 76 when she describes the Assyrians as "priding themselves in their horses and riders" (Jdt 9:7; cp. Ps 76:6) and as "trusting in shield, and spear, in bow and sling" (Jdt 9:7; see the weapon list in Ps 76:3). She pleads: "Break their strength" (Jdt 9:8), just as God "breaks" (שבר, the prophetic perfect) the weapons of the enemies in Psalm 76:3. Judith's victory song back in Bethulia praises "the Lord . . . who crushes wars" (16:2; cp. 9:7), just as God "shatters" the weapons of war in Psalm 76:3. The God "who inspires fear in the kings of the earth" (Ps 76:12) also inspires fear in the retreating army of Holofernes (Jdt 15:2; cp. 16:11), but God shows mercy to those who "fear" (revere) the Lord (Jdt 16:15).

Wrath as Liturgical Act

The beauty and necessity of a text such as Psalm 76 is found in its ability to touch an oftentimes rejected and repressed aspect of modern civilized human experience, that of hate, rage, and aggression. Of course, we know from the violent religious wars around the globe and the atrocious hate crimes that continue to erupt that hate and aggression are wildly active, and yet we surround ourselves with positive psychology, self-help strategies, and prayers for peace that lack the aggression necessary to take real action. The psalmist here delights in the wrath of God and in his or her own wrath, the wrath of a community against the outrageous injustices they have endured. That the Hebrew Bible contains this text, which boasts of wrath as a form of praise, speaks to the complex nature of humanity and God and the relationship between these two parties. As a liturgical act, wrath enables us to face the evil that is and to find our way through it. It forces us to own our own evil, our own transgressive acts of

---

6. Denise Dombkowski Hopkins, "Judith," in *Women's Bible Commentary*, ed. Carol A. Newsom, Sharon H. Ringe, and Jacqueline E. Lapsley, 3rd ed. (Louisville, KY: Westminster John Knox, 2012), 383–90, at 388.

peace and justice in the service of honoring the hate that is alive and active in each of us. In owning this part of us we are able to link it with the good, with love, and with reconciliatory care.

Ann Ulanov, Jungian analyst and professor emerita of psychiatry and religion at Union Theological Seminary, differentiates between the matriarchal and patriarchal super-egos.[7] The patriarchal super-ego conjures images of Jiminy Cricket on one's shoulder, the voice of conscience steering one toward societal morality that is struggled for and taken in or imbibed from culture. The matriarchal super-ego, on the other hand, is not something one takes in from outside; rather, it develops from the inside out, from one's own instincts, from one's own intertwined love and hate. It is a both/and point of view that arises from a lived place of ambivalence, from the recognition of the good and bad within, the conflicting viewpoints that exist internally.[8] The matriarchal super-ego is not constituted on the basis of repression of one's instincts and the desires that are unacceptable to outer society; rather, it is based on an ability to hold opposing views—love and hate, a desire to build up and a desire to destroy, an ability to stand in reverent awe and praise and to include wrath as a vital and valid expression of such praise. The matriarchal super-ego is what allows us to pray such prayers when we are outside our own Zion, our place of rest, when some injustice has intruded or evil has come upon our community. To be able to hold an image of God as one who is loving and nurturing and one whose anger can be aroused enables us to contain our own experiences of nurturing love and wrathful anger. Holding this ambivalence allows us to live in conscious acknowledgment of our own instincts, permitting our wrath to move us to informed action rather than reactively acting unconsciously in outward deeds of aggression and hatred toward injustices experienced.

Tiffany Houck-Loomis

7. Ann and Barry Ulanov, *Religion and the Unconscious* (Philadelphia: Westminster Press, 1975), 145–55.

8. Ibid., 154.

Bloody Sunday

On March 7, 1965, Bloody Sunday, the world of men, war, and power collided with a peaceful crowd of African American women and men gathered in Selma, Alabama, endeavoring peaceably to cross the Edmund Pettus Bridge. Armed with hope, assured by God's promises, and comforted by Zion's hymns, marchers embarked on the first steps of their fifty-mile journey to Montgomery, Alabama, to secure their civil right to vote. They were led by Amelia Boynton, John Lewis, and other civil rights leaders.

Although women gained the right to vote in 1920 via the Nineteenth Amendment to the Constitution (though African American men had been legally endowed with that right by the Fifteenth Amendment in 1870) and African Americans gained the right effectively through the Civil Rights Act of 1964, only 2.1 percent of African Americans in Selma, Alabama, were allowed to register to vote. Tired of being denied, a determined and resilient people clinging to the hope that God's judgment would "save all the oppressed of the earth" exited Brown Chapel singing: "No matter what may be the test, God will take care of you! Lean, weary one, upon His breast, God will take care of you!" I contend that saving the oppressed of the earth also means equal opportunity and exercise of legal rights for the marginalized and disenfranchised.

In contrast to the "violently aggressive female warrior" images of Judith and Jael, here women engaged in nonviolent protest. The tear gas, police sticks, and fists of white male police officers brutalized them as they attempted to cross the bridge. On Bloody Sunday the beaten and bloodied bodies of women and men covered the bridge, crying out to God for refuge. Victory, however, was delayed but not denied. Fourteen days later, on March 21, the nonviolent marchers crossed the bridge and marched toward Montgomery.

While voting rights for all African Americans were eventually secured, due in large part to surviving Bloody Sunday, in the twenty-first century some women still cry out to Zion, hoping for a female president. Equal opportunity, saving the oppressed of the earth, O God, is still the prayer and hope.[9]

Audrey Coretta Price

---

9. See President Barack Obama's comments given on the Edmund Pettus Bridge before the fiftieth anniversary commemoration of the Selma to Montgomery march, https://www.whitehouse.gov/the-press-office/2015/03/07/remarks-president -50th-anniversary-selma-montgomery-marches; *Be Not Dismayed Whate'er Betide*, lyrics by Civilla Durfee Martin and music by Walter Stillman Martin.

As in the story of Jael (Judg 4:21; 5:26), the motif of a woman's hand occupies a prominent place in Judith (8:33; 9:10; 12:4; 13:4, 14, 15; 16:5) and provides a contrasting link to Psalm 76:5, which describes the rout of the enemy, literally: "none of the warriors were able to find their hands." NRSV translates "was able to lift a hand." The enemies were so stunned (or "stupified" in a deep sleep) by God's "rebuke" (v. 6a) that they could not reach for their weapons. Similarly, Holofernes drinks too much wine at the banquet at which he planned to seduce Judith and becomes "dead drunk" (Jdt 13:2). Standing over him beside his bed, Judith prays to God, "look . . . on the work of my hands for the exaltation of Jerusalem" (13:4), and cuts off his head. He cannot "find" his hands to defend himself against her in his drunken stupor. Judith, however, is quite able to "find" her hands. She grabs Holofernes's sword with one and the hair of his head with the other, and she decapitates him. "As a violently aggressive female warrior, Judith is censured because she identifies too closely with male traits and values, and lauded by others for shattering female stereotypes. . . . The complex ambiguity of Judith's character helped Israel to deal with its uncertain situation in the Greco-Roman world,"[10] just as Psalm 76 did.

---

10. Hopkins, "Judith," 389–90.

Psalm 77

Refusing to Be Comforted

Psalm 77 opens with deeply emotional, body-based complaint from one who speaks on behalf of Israel. At night the psalmist's "hand is stretched out without wearying" (v. 2b). She cannot sleep because of God: "you keep my eyelids from closing" (v. 4a). She is so "troubled" that neither can she "speak" any more (v. 4b). Memory seems to paralyze her, yet all she can do is remember. The verb זכר ("remember") appears at the beginning of vv. 3, 6, and 11, marking the three sections of the psalm. Many other synonyms for "remember" occur in vv. 3-12: moan, meditate, consider, call to mind, muse. Psalm 77 shares with other Asaph psalms (74–83) a focus on national suffering, perhaps in exile, and a collective memory of God's deliverance of Israel in the exodus. The verb used in 71:1, צעק ("to cry out"), for example, is used in Exodus 14:10 as the Israelites flee Pharaoh's army and face the Reed Sea (cp. Deut 26:7; Josh 24).

The psalmist's remembering is juxtaposed with the accusation of God's "forgetting" to be gracious (v. 9). The series of blunt rhetorical questions about God's inaction in the present situation of suffering (vv. 7-9) suggests that these "retrospective elements" function "to express the painful paradox of the contrast between Yahweh's former acts of salvation as set against his present inactivity, and yet also as the basis of its resolution in the hope of a renewal of his חסד [covenant loyalty] (Pss. 77:16-21

Psalm 77:1-20

To the leader: according to Jeduthun.
Of Asaph. A Psalm.

¹I cry aloud to God,
   aloud to God, that he may hear
      me.
²In the day of my trouble I seek
      the LORD;
   in the night my hand is
      stretched out without
      wearying;
   my soul refuses to be com-
      forted.
³I think of God, and I moan;
   I meditate, and my spirit
      faints.   *Selah*

⁴You keep my eyelids from closing;
   I am so troubled that I cannot
      speak.

⁵I consider the days of old,
   and remember the years of
      long ago.
⁶I commune with my heart in the
      night;
   I meditate and search my
      spirit:
⁷"Will the LORD spurn forever,
   and never again be favorable?
⁸Has his steadfast love ceased
      forever?
   Are his promises at an end for
      all time?
⁹Has God forgotten to be gracious?
   Has he in anger shut up his
      compassion?"   *Selah*
¹⁰And I say, "It is my grief
   that the right hand of the Most
      High has changed."

[15-20]; 74:12-17; 44:2-9 [1-8]."[1] Some interpreters suggest that all of this remembering forms part of the "congregational search for identity and security," which in its liturgical context proves to be "educative and honorific," enabling believers to "immerse themselves in the great hymnic sea."[2]

The hopelessness of the psalmist's rhetorical questions in vv. 7-9 is countered by more memories and the rhetorical question in v. 13: "What God is so great as our God?" (cp. Exod 15:11). The psalmist's vocabulary points to the exodus. God's "wonders" (v. 14a) are praised in the Song of the Sea (Exod 15:11). God's "strong arm" (77:15a) redeems the people (Exod 15:16; cp. Pss 48:2; 95:3; 96:6-7; 99:2-3). The language of vv. 16-20 draws from ancient Near Eastern storm theophany traditions. It also appears frequently in the exodus traditions with one difference: "The thunder and lightning are not here presented as the weaponry of God, but as

1. Rebecca S. Watson, *Chaos Uncreated: A Reassessment of the Theme of "Chaos" in the Hebrew Bible* (Berlin: deGruyter, 2005), 142.
2. Erhard S. Gerstenberger, *Psalms, Part 2, and Lamentations* (Grand Rapids, MI: Eerdmans, 2001), 91.

¹¹I will call to mind the deeds of
the LORD;
I will remember your wonders
of old.
¹²I will meditate on all your work,
and muse on your mighty deeds.
¹³Your way, O God, is holy.
What god is so great as our
God?
¹⁴You are the God who works
wonders;
you have displayed your might
among the peoples.
¹⁵With your strong arm you re-
deemed your people,
the descendants of Jacob and
Joseph.   *Selah*

¹⁶When the waters saw you, O God,

when the waters saw you, they
were afraid;
the very deep trembled.
¹⁷The clouds poured out water;
the skies thundered;
your arrows flashed on every
side.
¹⁸The crash of your thunder was in
the whirlwind;
your lightnings lit up the world;
the earth trembled and shook.
¹⁹Your way was through the sea,
your path, through the mighty
waters;
yet your footprints were unseen.
²⁰You led your people like a flock
by the hand of Moses and
Aaron.

manifestations of his [*sic*] awesome presence and as an indication of the magnitude of his [*sic*] redemptive action."[3] Unlike Exodus 15, the enemy is not mentioned in Psalm 77. The word תהום ("deep") in v. 16c is used when the waters are in their weakest state, "exposing them in their trembling vulnerability,"[4] rather than as an allusion to a primeval battle at creation against the mythological chaos Sea. The "waters" and the "deep" have no volition or agency but are treated as objects acted upon by God.[5] Clearly, the emphasis is on God's historical redemption in the past and a hoped-for new exodus in the present.

Perhaps these more specific memories beginning with 77:11 are meant as a pep-talk that the psalmist delivers to herself and the traumatized congregation. We are left wondering, however, whether or not this second round of remembering produced a different result, one of hope

3. Watson, *Chaos Uncreated*, 150.
4. Ibid., 151.
5. Peter L. Trudinger, "Friend or Foe? Earth, Sea and *Chaoskampf* in the Psalms," in *The Earth Story in the Psalms and the Prophets*, ed. Norman C. Habel (Sheffield: Sheffield Academic, 2001), 35.

rather than despair. Several interpreters have argued that it does, since God is finally addressed directly in v. 11 (though see v. 4, in which the psalmist accuses God directly of causing her sleeplessness). Yet the psalm ends abruptly with a look back to God's shepherd guidance in the wilderness (Exod 15:13; Ps 23:3; Ezek 34:12) through Moses and Aaron (v. 20), without an update on the psalmist's or congregation's spiritual condition. Does despair turn to hope, or does the memory of God's guidance serve only to exacerbate the pain of the present situation? One wonders if the psalmist's constant seeking of God and calling up of memories ultimately brings any comfort or security at all. Does she still "refuse to be comforted" as she declared back in v. 2c? Is the contrast between then and now simply too much for a traumatized people to navigate? This is the question with which the exiles struggled, as did those who were left behind in a devastated Jerusalem. The book of Lamentations, for example, ends with a question about God's lingering anger left unanswered (5:22); God does not respond.

Sex Trafficking

The "deeply emotional, body-based complaint" that opens Psalm 77 awakens the tormented, troubled and unheard cries of the million young girls, teenagers, and women victimized by the lucrative industry of sex trafficking, which has reached pandemic levels in the twenty-first century. Sex trafficking claims the bodies, innocence, and freedom of women and children, who suffer greatly. Young girls are sold into a horrific life of sexual, emotional, and physical abuse at the hands of their entrepreneurial "owners" who enjoy hedonistic financial profit. Stripped of their human agency, mired in hopelessness, victimization, and trembling vulnerability, how can these young women see, know, or experience the great God of Psalm 77? At the very least, will they be comforted or liberated by the hope of God's "strong arm" once again bringing about redemption?

I can imagine that many of these fragile young girls refuse or lack the capacity to be comforted in their loss of innocence, freedom, security, and voice. As the psalmist speaks on behalf of Israel, we must speak and work on behalf of those victimized by sex trafficking. I question, as the psalmist does, whether or not God's compassion has been shut up. Where is the divine anger over this rapidly growing industry? How many more lives will be lost as God's people turn a blind eye? The tormented plea

in 77:1-4 impels us to be agents
of God's compassion and
liberation. God's people must
wage war and battle this
pharaoh. The young girls'
exodus from sex slavery should
not be an abstract idea of mercy
and compassion. Instead, may
God's people be moved by the
cry in Psalm 77 and compelled to
action. Let us demand of the sex
trafficking pharaoh to let God's
people go!

Audrey Coretta Price

Several figures in Israel's history refuse to be comforted in their loss, among them Jacob mourning the "death" of Joseph at the hands of his jealous brothers (Gen 37:35) and the dead Rachel weeping for her children (Israel) deported or killed by the Babylonians (Jer 31:15-22). This Jeremiah text can serve as a powerful intertext for Psalm 77. It is not accidental that Jeremiah refers to Rachel in his address to the exiles. As Jacob's favorite wife and Joseph's mother, she reminds Jeremiah's listeners that Jacob and Joseph were the last patriarchs before the exodus; mention of Joseph is frequent in the Asaph psalms (see 78:66; 80:1; 81:5). Initially barren, she demanded of Jacob: "Give me children or I shall die" (Gen 30:1). She did die while giving birth to Benjamin, whom she named Ben-oni ("child of my sorrow") but whom Jacob renames Benjamin ("son of the right hand" or "son of fortune"). This name change reflects the tension that Israel itself experiences as it struggles with its future in exile; it must choose despair or hope. Though Genesis 35:16-21 locates Rachel's tomb on the road to Bethlehem, 1 Samuel 10:2 suggests it is on the road to Ramah (near today's Ramallah). According to Gen. Rab. 82:10, Jacob buried Rachel by the road because "he knew that his descendants would pass by as they went into exile,"[6] which would allow her to weep and intercede for them. "Through the sheer power of her yearning for her children, 'who are not' (lit., who are gone), and practiced by much longing for children, who were not, Rachel will bring them back into real, coherent being."[7] All of these associations support God's declaration of "a new thing in Israel" (v. 22), that is, a future beyond exile.

6. Marvin Sweeney, "Jeremiah" annotations, *The Jewish Study Bible* (Oxford: Oxford University Press, 2004), 989.

7. Avivah Gottlieb Zornberg, *The Beginning of Desire: Reflections on Genesis* (New York: Doubleday, 1995), 213.

Living in the Gap

Living in the gap can fill us with dread. The gap-living space, the space between what we know or have known and what we do not know but is coming nonetheless toward us and into our lives, is a most avoided place.[8] In this space the rules we once knew, the rules which once allowed us to live and perhaps even thrive, no longer hold true and the sense we seek to make eludes rather than clarifies. The poetry of Psalm 77 invites us into the gap experienced by Israel during the exile, the gap between Israel and God, between the Covenant and the decimation experienced, and provides a way to reflect on our own times living in the gap throughout our lives.

The exodus, an image alluded to in Psalm 77, was another gap-living moment, a moment of transition between what was known and what remained to be known, between slavery and the Promised Land. In that gap-living moment the wilderness had to be suffered before arrival into the new homeland was possible. The use of this imagery throughout the psalms, primarily those purportedly written during exile, speaks to its timeless applicability. In Psalm 77 we are brought into the affective experience of the gap, the sleepless nights, the fainting spirit, the endless questioning, the moans of the soul. We can resonate with the timeless questions: What has happened? Where am I now? Where am I going? Where are you, God? The gap, put simply, is the space between subject and object, between you and your lover, between you and your God, between you and your theology. But living, really living in this gap, is not so simple at all. When we withdraw our projections upon the other, whether it be our image of God, our religious institution, our ideals of the self, our family members, our history, our rules and morals and recognize that these others are not our own, this can be terrifying.[9] For then, how do we really know the other and what do we really know of ourselves? Ann Ulanov suggests imagination is the bridge between one and the other, between here and there, between what is known and what remains unknown.

When we are able to traverse this path, standing in the gap, resting there as opposed to racing across or turning the other way to avoid the pain, Ulanov suggests we do three things: "We let it happen. We see

---

8. Ann and Barry Ulanov, *The Healing Imagination* (Canada: DaimonVerlag, 1999), 20–37.

9. Marie-Louise von Franz, *Projection and Re-Collection in Jungian Psychology* (Chicago: Open Court, 1995), 9–19.

what happens. We reflect upon what happened."[10] The psalmist here is doing just this. She is letting what will happen happen. She is seeing what happens. And she is seeking to reflect on what is happening. In reflecting, a bridge begins to emerge, the bridge of imagination. But before the bridge, the gap must be suffered, experienced, felt, and lived, not avoided. When we truly suffer the gap we create space between our selves and our circumstances. Suffering the gap creates space to imagine new possibilities, new ways of being, and new ways of being in relationship to others around us.

Tiffany Houck-Loomis

The psalmist's "voice" (קוֹל) of pain and complaint in 77:1 is over-powered by the memory of the "voice" of the sky (v. 17) and of the thunder (v. 18) in God's exodus deliverance, but it is heard again in Rachel's "voice" in Jeremiah 31:15. In Psalm 77:9, the psalmist questions whether or not God's "compassion" has been "shut up" by the divine anger. The word for "compassion" is רחמים, the plural of רחם ("womb") with a third masculine singular possessive suffix. As a plural it expresses the abstract idea of mercy or compassion, but it is rooted in the life-giving part of a woman's body. In Jeremiah 31:20, "God's attachment to Rachel's son is as strong as the mother's own: 'I am deeply moved for him; I will surely have mercy on him.' "[11] This last phrase comes from the verbal root רחם, which means "to show womb love, compassion." God assumes Rachel's mother-role here; it is this mother love that the psalmist in 77 longs to experience and remembers repeatedly. This is the same womb-love that God proclaims as characteristic of God's self in Exodus 34:6—"a God merciful [רחום, used as an adjective from the root רחם] and gracious." Psalm 77 lives in the emotionally exhausting intersections between the memory of the exodus and Rachel crying for her children in Jeremiah 31. Psalm 77 wonders whether God will announce a "new thing" (Jer 31:22) for Israel. The answer is not certain, so the psalm ends in memory, just as Rachel does not respond to God's declaration.

10. Ibid., 20.

11. Kathleen M. O'Connor, "Jeremiah," in *Women's Bible Commentary*, ed. Carol A. Newsom, Sharon H. Ringe, and Jacqueline E. Lapsley, 3rd ed. (Louisville, KY: Westminster John Knox, 2012), 267–77, at 276.

Psalm 78

God's "Womb-Love" and Memory

With its seventy-two verses, Psalm 78 is the second-longest psalm in the Psalter, after Psalm 119. Because of its length, many readers avoid it. Their aversion is intensified by its categorization as a "historical psalm" (along with Pss 105, 106, 135, 136) that retells Israel's story in order to teach future generations. Clearly, many readers prefer prayer to a history lesson. The problem with this "historical" label for Psalm 78 is that it "flattens" events and encourages us to read them "statically" like a photograph rather than "dynamically" like a film; the psalmist, however, "practices memory, not to recount the past, but to prompt the kind of remembrance that leads to change."[1] Not only is the unfaithfulness of the ancestors exposed but so are God's actions on Israel's behalf during the exodus, wilderness wanderings, settlement, and establishment of the Davidic monarchy anchored in Zion. The psalmist terms these actions "wonders" (v. 4, from the root פלא, "do wondrously"; cp. Exod 3:20; 15:11). Consequently, reciting this history invites "participating in the ongoing legacy of God's wonders, which instills a distinct communal identity."[2]

---

1. Edward L. Greenstein, "Mixing Memory and Design: Reading Psalm 78," *Prooftexts* 10, no. 2 (May 1990): 197–218, at 198, 197.

2. Walter Brueggemann, *From Whom No Secrets Are Hid: Introducing the Psalms*, ed. Brent A. Strawn (Louisville, KY: Westminster John Knox, 2014), 138.

Psalm 78:1-72

A Maskil of Asaph.

¹Give ear, O my people, to my
   teaching;
   incline your ears to the words
      of my mouth.
²I will open my mouth in a parable;
   I will utter dark sayings from of
      old,
³things that we have heard and
   known,
   that our ancestors have told
      us.
⁴We will not hide them from their
   children;
   we will tell to the coming gen-
      eration
the glorious deeds of the Lord,
   and his might,
   and the wonders that he has
      done.

⁵He established a decree in
   Jacob,
   and appointed a law in Israel,
which he commanded our ancestors
   to teach to their children;
⁶that the next generation might
   know them,
   the children yet unborn,
and rise up and tell them to their
   children,
   ⁷so that they should set their
      hope in God,
and not forget the works of God,
   but keep his commandments;
⁸and that they should not be like
   their ancestors,
   a stubborn and rebellious gen-
      eration,
a generation whose heart was not
   steadfast,

whose spirit was not faithful to
   God.

⁹The Ephraimites, armed with the
   bow,
   turned back on the day of
      battle.
¹⁰They did not keep God's covenant,
   but refused to walk according
      to his law.
¹¹They forgot what he had done,
   and the miracles that he had
      shown them.
¹²In the sight of their ancestors he
   worked marvels
   in the land of Egypt, in the
      fields of Zoan.
¹³He divided the sea and let them
   pass through it,
   and made the waters stand
      like a heap.
¹⁴In the daytime he led them with
   a cloud,
   and all night long with a fiery
      light.
¹⁵He split rocks open in the wilderness,
   and gave them drink abun-
      dantly as from the deep.
¹⁶He made streams come out of
   the rock,
   and caused waters to flow
      down like rivers.

¹⁷Yet they sinned still more against
   him,
   rebelling against the Most High
      in the desert.
¹⁸They tested God in their heart
   by demanding the food they
      craved.
¹⁹They spoke against God, saying,

"Can God spread a table in the
wilderness?
²⁰Even though he struck the rock
so that water gushed out
and torrents overflowed,
can he also give bread,
or provide meat for his
people?"

²¹Therefore, when the LORD heard,
he was full of rage;
a fire was kindled against
Jacob,
his anger mounted against
Israel,
²²because they had no faith in
God,
and did not trust his saving
power.
²³Yet he commanded the skies
above,
and opened the doors of
heaven;
²⁴he rained down on them manna
to eat,
and gave them the grain of
heaven.
²⁵Mortals ate of the bread of
angels;
he sent them food in
abundance.
²⁶He caused the east wind to blow
in the heavens,
and by his power he led out
the south wind;
²⁷he rained flesh upon them like
dust,
winged birds like the sand of
the seas;
²⁸he let them fall within their camp,
all around their dwellings.
²⁹And they ate and were well filled,

for he gave them what they
craved.
³⁰But before they had satisfied
their craving,
while the food was still in their
mouths,
³¹the anger of God rose against
them
and he killed the strongest of
them,
and laid low the flower of Israel.

³²In spite of all this they still
sinned;
they did not believe in his
wonders.
³³So he made their days vanish
like a breath,
and their years in terror.
³⁴When he killed them, they
sought for him;
they repented and sought God
earnestly.
³⁵They remembered that God was
their rock,
the Most High God their
redeemer.
³⁶But they flattered him with their
mouths;
they lied to him with their
tongues.
³⁷Their heart was not steadfast
toward him;
they were not true to his
covenant.
³⁸Yet he, being compassionate,
forgave their iniquity,
and did not destroy them;
often he restrained his anger,
and did not stir up all his wrath.
³⁹He remembered that they were
but flesh,

a wind that passes and does not come again.

40How often they rebelled against him in the wilderness
and grieved him in the desert!

41They tested God again and again,
and provoked the Holy One of Israel.

42They did not keep in mind his power,
or the day when he redeemed them from the foe;

43when he displayed his signs in Egypt,
and his miracles in the fields of Zoan.

44He turned their rivers to blood,
so that they could not drink of their streams.

45He sent among them swarms of flies, which devoured them,
and frogs, which destroyed them.

46He gave their crops to the caterpillar,
and the fruit of their labor to the locust.

47He destroyed their vines with hail,
and their sycamores with frost.

48He gave over their cattle to the hail,
and their flocks to thunderbolts.

49He let loose on them his fierce anger,
wrath, indignation, and distress,
a company of destroying angels.

50He made a path for his anger;
he did not spare them from death,
but gave their lives over to the plague.

51He struck all the firstborn in Egypt,
the first issue of their strength in the tents of Ham.

52Then he led out his people like sheep,
and guided them in the wilderness like a flock.

53He led them in safety, so that they were not afraid;
but the sea overwhelmed their enemies.

54And he brought them to his holy hill,
to the mountain that his right hand had won.

55He drove out nations before them;
he apportioned them for a possession

These memories are both individual and communal, as illustrated by the shift from the "I" of the psalmist in vv. 1-2 to the "we" of the congregation in vv. 3-4. Since memory is socially constructed, it is also selective, as seen in the way in which Psalm 78 orders events: exodus and the wilderness wanderings are recalled first (vv. 12-31), and then the psalmist returns to Egypt before the exodus to remember the plagues, followed by the entry into Canaan (vv. 40-64). In addition, some of the plagues are omitted and the choice of Zion and David is reordered (vv. 68-72). Social memory in-

and settled the tribes of Israel
in their tents.

⁵⁶Yet they tested the Most High
God,
and rebelled against him.
They did not observe his decrees,
⁵⁷but turned away and were faithless like their ancestors;
they twisted like a treacherous
bow.
⁵⁸For they provoked him to anger
with their high places;
they moved him to jealousy
with their idols.
⁵⁹When God heard, he was full of
wrath,
and he utterly rejected Israel.
⁶⁰He abandoned his dwelling at
Shiloh,
the tent where he dwelt among
mortals,
⁶¹and delivered his power to captivity,
his glory to the hand of the foe.
⁶²He gave his people to the sword,
and vented his wrath on his
heritage.
⁶³Fire devoured their young men,
and their girls had no marriage
song.

⁶⁴Their priests fell by the sword,
and their widows made no
lamentation.
⁶⁵Then the LORD awoke as from
sleep,
like a warrior shouting because
of wine.
⁶⁶He put his adversaries to rout;
he put them to everlasting disgrace.

⁶⁷He rejected the tent of Joseph,
he did not choose the tribe of
Ephraim;
⁶⁸but he chose the tribe of Judah,
Mount Zion, which he loves.
⁶⁹He built his sanctuary like the
high heavens,
like the earth, which he has
founded forever.
⁷⁰He chose his servant David,
and took him from the sheepfolds;
⁷¹from tending the nursing ewes
he brought him
to be the shepherd of his
people Jacob,
of Israel, his inheritance.
⁷²With upright heart he tended
them,
and guided them with skillful
hand.

volves both shared and contested meanings; it is not a "thing, but a complex of culturally specific processes."[3] Consequently, Edward Greenstein
reads Psalm 78 "as a process of remembering. . . . The psalm is not
static—it moves,"[4] addressing the present to transform the future.

3. Athalya Brenner and Frank Polak, eds., *Performing Memory in Biblical Narrative
and Beyond* (Sheffield: Sheffield Phoenix Press, 2009), 4.
4. Greenstein, "Mixing Memory," 209.

Soul History

As a psychotherapist I can attest to the absolute necessity of storytelling as a way to grapple with daily life experiences that are inevitably informed and colored by personal and collective history. History too is a form of storytelling, a kind of creative nonfiction. As the late psychoanalyst and founder of archetypal psychology James Hillman argues, the case history is actually a *soul history*, a kind of healing fiction.[5] We could read Psalm 78 as a historical psalm or, in psychoanalytic jargon, as a case history. We can also read the "case history" of Psalm 78, however, as a healing fiction or soul history, a biography that concerns experience.[6] History making and telling is also a "mode of imagining . . . one of the ways the soul speaks about itself, as a case and with a history."[7] Hillman speaks of the case history as a digestive operation for soul making; it is a way we continue to understand ourselves. As he says, "history digests events, moving them from case material to subtle matter."[8]

One of the struggles we have in understanding "history" is that we forget the literary quality of history making; we approach history in a dualistic way, separating mind from body, inner from outer, the world of external events from the inner life of the soul. Hillman concludes that if we remain locked in this old mechanical duality we neglect to "see the inner necessity of historical events, out there, in the events themselves, where 'inner' no longer means private and owned by a self or a soul or an ego, where inner is not a literalized place inside a subject, but the subjectivity in events and that attitude which interiorizes those events, goes into them in search of psychological depths."[9] This is how I read Psalm 78: as a healing fiction, a digestive process, a way in which the psalmist is working to make sense of the events that have transpired within his or her community. It is clear that the writer's perspective is rooted in southern and potentially Deuteronomistic propaganda, as can be read in vv. 67-68 ("He rejected the tent of Joseph; he did not choose the tribe of Ephraim, but he chose the tribe of Judah, Mount Zion, which he loves") and v. 70 ("He chose David his servant . . . to shepherd Jacob"). We read a

5. James Hillman, *Healing Fiction* (Putnam, CT: Spring Publications, 1994).

6. James Hillman, *Suicide and the Soul* (Dallas, TX: Spring Publishing, 1978), 77–79.

7. Hillman, *Healing Fiction*, 26.

8. Ibid., 27.

9. Ibid., 26.

concretized account of events leading up through the beginning of Israel's demise at the hand of God, who intentionally forsook God's dwelling place in Shiloh (in the North) and went to strengthen and support the work of the enemy as a consequence of Israel's leaders having forsaken God's instructions.

While we might be able to discern this from the text, it is the work of history telling as a literary art that enables individuals and communities to digest events and to continue to experience the events in a lived way; history telling allows one to slow down and find one's own way through. This art of story making and storytelling provides individuals and communities alike a place to hang their experiences, hurts, and trauma suffered and survived. Finding an enemy to blame also constructs a place to put the bad, the evil of which one has been the recipient. Writing it down, making it into history allows one to experience catastrophic events in a digestive way, in order to see again and experience in a new way, and eventually to withdraw the projection and slow down the parade of history.

Tiffany Houck-Loomis

Israel's continuous process of remembering in Psalm 78 is underscored by the repeated use of "ancestors" (vv. 3, 5, 8, 12, 57), "children" (vv. 4, 5, 6), and "generation" (referring to the coming generation in vv. 4 and 6 and to the ancestors' generation in v. 8). Israel's relationship with God has endured; to forget (שכח, vv. 7, 11) that relationship is akin to being unfaithful, as Moses reminds the people in Deuteronomy (4:9, 23, 31; 6:12; 7:18-19). Perhaps these memories are meant to respond to the laments of Psalms 74 and 77 by reminding the people of God's "pattern of gracious persistence"[10] in order to cultivate hope in exile, though interpreters date Psalm 78 anywhere from the time of Solomon in the tenth century BCE to King Hezekiah in the eighth century, or even to the exilic and postexilic periods.

---

10. Richard J. Clifford, *Psalms 73–150* (Nashville, TN: Abingdon Press, 2003), 46.

Memory as Hope

African Americans have found special cultural interaction with the Hebrew Bible as it traces and retraces moments and issues surrounding bondage, exile, and journey that parallel the history of black people in America. To that end, Cornel West asserts that "Afro-American thought must take seriously the most influential and enduring intellectual tradition in its experience: evangelical and pietistic Christianity. This tradition began the moment that African slaves, laboring in sweltering heat on plantations . . . tried to understand their lives and servitude in the light of biblical texts."[11] West makes clear the reality that black thought is rooted in a cultural memory that is inextricably linked to the biblical narrative. Regardless of whether or not individuals or communities of African Americans subscribe to Christian thought, our collective identity is shaped in response to the native narrative of Christianity—the Bible.

West and others have drawn particular attention to the importance of prophetic literature and the exodus narrative in relating the black religious experience. But it is crucial that we give voice to the relevance of the Psalter in African American spiritual existence. The psalms are interwoven with the "history" of Exodus and the prophets; they tell the story of Israel's past. The songs of Zion—the hymns, spirituals, and anthems rooted in black religious experiences—serve the same function as the psalms of Israel. They are a poetic, rhythmic expression of the lived reality of a people. They give life to the social and emotional evolution of a people whose story is grounded in trauma and turmoil. William McClain suggests that "to understand the religious history of a people is to know their social habits, their politics, their hopes and aspirations, their fears, their failures, their understanding of who they are and what they value most."[12] In the psalms and spirituals we find the life of generations of those oppressed by chattel slavery, Jim Crow, the prison industrial complex, and myriad other systemic realities.

The "psalms" of Africa, much like the psalms of Israel, tell an intergenerational story that calls on interactions between God and our ancestors. Further, these hymns "demand participatory imagination"; they require the

---

11. Cornel West, *Prophesy Deliverance! An Afro-American Revolutionary Christianity* (Louisville, KY: Westminster John Knox, 2002), 15.

12. William McClain, *Come Sunday: The Liturgy of Zion* (Nashville, TN: Abingdon Press, 1990), 22.

hearer to recollect the history of our struggles in order to recall God's deliverance so that we might have hope in the midst of the troubles we face in our present era. Much as in Psalm 78, the dominant rhetoric in black communities has traditionally been a hope that God will remember us again.

Yolanda Marie Norton

Many interpreters have noted the didactic/wisdom elements in Psalm 78, especially in the introduction (vv. 1-11). The psalmist opens with a formula that introduces instruction: "Give ear, O my people, to my teaching" (תורתי; cp. Prov 1:8b). This formula calls to mind as intertexts both Woman Wisdom in Proverbs and Judith in the Apocrypha. Like the psalmist, Woman Wisdom demands that all pay attention to her instruction: "in the squares she raises her voice" (Prov 1:20), declaring to passersby: "Listen to me: happy are those who keep my ways. Hear instruction and be wise" (Prov 8:32-33; cp.1:8, 20-21, 23; 8:6). Judith[13] seems to wrap herself in the mantle of Woman Wisdom. The leader of Bethulia speaks of Judith's wisdom (8:29) and Holofernes calls her "wise" (11:21, 23). Three times Judith proclaims "listen to me": in 8:11 when addressing the rulers of Bethulia to rebuke them; in 8:32 when she responds to the suggestion after her rebuke that she pray for rain with a declaration that she is about to do something "that will go down through all generations"; and in 14:1, after she returns from the enemy camp with Holofernes's head and gives instructions about how to take advantage of the Assyrian panic when they find his head missing. She boldly tells the elders that their declaration of imminent surrender "is not right" (8:11); like Lady Wisdom, *she* speaks what is right (Prov 8:6). The psalmist, Lady Wisdom, and Judith all seem to be speaking with authority, perhaps in the name of God in the manner of the prophets or in the tradition of Moses instructing the people before they enter the Promised Land (Deut 29:1–30:20; 32:1-43). Unlike Moses, however, the psalmist does not exhort the people directly but rather "by example," setting "a model of remembering by

13. For what follows, see Denise Dombkowski Hopkins, "Judith," in *Women's Bible Commentary*, ed. Carol A. Newsom, Sharon H. Ringe, and Jacqueline E. Lapsley, 3rd ed. (Louisville, KY: Westminster John Knox, 2012), 383–90.

engaging himself [*sic*] in a sophisticated exercise of memory."[14] Judith exercises her memory in her prayer to God in 9:1-6.

The psalmist uses more wisdom language in v. 2a: "I will open my mouth in a parable" (משל, literally "comparison"; cp. Prov 1:6), which demands participatory imagination. This invitation to remember together is reinforced by the use of חידות ("dark sayings," "riddles"; cp. Prov 1:6) in v. 2b. The people are to compare themselves to the ancestors so as to avoid their mistakes of "forgetting" (vv. 7, 11, 42; cp. Deut 4:9, 23, 31; 6:12) and repeated sinning (see the refrain in Ps 78:17, 32, 40, 56). Judith's conversations with Holofernes approximate riddles because they teem with double meanings (e.g., 12:14, in which "my lord" may refer to Holofernes or to God; cp. Jdt 11:5, 6; 12:18, etc.). She also exhorts the elders of her town by comparing their status with that of the ancestors: "For never in our generation, nor in these present days has there been any[one] . . . that worships gods made with hands, as was done in days gone by. That was why our ancestors were handed over to the sword and to pillage" (Jdt 8:18-19). The comparison is clear: do not become like the ancestors in this moment of crisis, but trust in God.

The theme of testing also links Judith with Psalm 78 and invites a comparison with Exodus 17:1-6, in which the people test God by asking whether God will provide water (Num 14:24). The people of Bethulia are fainting from thirst because their town is under siege (Jdt 7:19-22). Psalm 78:15-16 alludes to God's providential care in Exodus 17: "God split rocks open in the wilderness and gave them drink." These allusions suggest Judith's (and the psalmist's?) role as a leader like Moses. In her rebuke of the elders of Bethulia who plan to surrender if God does not intervene in five days, Judith demands: "who are you to put God to the test today?" (8:12; see also 8:13). She concludes that "you will never learn anything," that is, acquire wisdom (8:13). Psalm 78 notes how the ancestors "tested" God (vv. 18, 41); "they tested God again and again and provoked the Holy One of Israel" (v. 56). Judith and Psalm 78 also refer to God's wrath or anger (Jdt 8:14; 9:9; Ps 78:21, 31, 41, 49, 50, 58, 59, 62).

God is described as "compassionate" in both Judith and Psalm 78. In Psalm 78:38 (as in Exod 33:19; 34:6), the word describing God comes from the noun for a female body part: רחם ("womb"). God shows compassion by forgiving iniquity and restraining the divine anger in the wilderness. Why? Because God "remembered [זכר] that they were but flesh" (v. 39).

---

14. Greenstein, "Mixing Memory," 201.

This verse stands at the center of Psalm 78. Memory is essential to the covenant relationship for both sides. God's memory is motherly, rooted in the womb. In her prayer before leaving the safety of her town to go to the enemy camp, Judith presumes upon God's compassion twice (9:4, 9) by stressing her widowhood as a special reason for God to grant her prayer for success against Holofernes. She reminds God that God is the God "of the lowly, helper of the oppressed, upholder of the weak, protector of the forsaken" (9:11). In her victory prayer she notes that these same oppressed people cried out to God, who turned back the enemy (16:11). The metaphor of God's "womb love" is extended in Psalm 78 by the pairing of "young men" devoured by the fire of battle and "girls" who "had no marriage song" in v. 63. The pairing indicates "the destruction of Israel's posterity (compare Deut 32:25)"; in their prime, these young people carry "the promise of fertility and virility,"[15] but that promise is snuffed out by God's angry response to the people's testing. Consequently, the widows of the priests "made no lamentation" (v. 64) because they and their husbands were also killed. This verse alludes to the specialized role of women in ancient Israel in communal keening or lamentation.

In Psalm 78, God remembers the people again after the rejection of Shiloh as the central sanctuary in the Northern Kingdom by choosing Zion and the Davidic dynasty (vv. 60, 67-72). Both Shiloh and the northern people continue in Zion and Judah.[16] For Erhard Gerstenberger "the fundamental issue" here is "who is being privileged," underscored by the verbs בחר ("elect," vv. 68, 70) and מאס ("reject," vv. 59, 67). Ideology is clearly at work in an attempt to unify the people behind God's choice of the Davidic dynasty in the face of crisis. The book of Judith also privileges Jerusalem in Judith's warning to the elders not to give up and allow the city to fall (Jdt 8:21), in victory remarks from the high priest (16:9), as well as in the description of the three-month victory celebration in Jerusalem (16:20). Whereas the Ephraimites instruct hearers how not to act (Ps 78:9-11) and the wilderness generation offers a negative role model for speaking—"Can God spread a table in the wilderness?" (Ps 78:19)[17]— the psalmist models appropriate behavior and speech. Judith as intertext concretizes that behavior and speech for the audience in crisis.

---

15. Carol Meyers, "Pss 78:63; 148:12—Young Women (and Young Men)," in *Women in Scripture*, ed. Carol Meyers (Boston: Houghton Mifflin, 2000), 300.

16. Clifford, *Psalms 73–150*, 45.

17. Rolf A. Jacobson, *"Many Are Saying": The Function of Direct Discourse in the Hebrew Psalter*, JSOTSup 397 (Edinburgh: T & T Clark, 2004), 58.

Psalm 79

Redirected Anger

Ruins, unburied bodies scavenged by birds of prey, blood poured out like water—these images jolt the readers of lament psalm 79. As is the case in other Asaph psalms, the description of the destruction of Jerusalem is meant to invite God's sympathetic response to the psalmist's petitions for retribution against the enemy, presumably Babylon (vv. 6, 10, 12). Psalm 79 challenges the memory of a glorious Zion/ Jerusalem, "the epicenter of God's ordering of the world," in "Songs of Zion" such as Psalm 46; as one of the "Sad Songs of Zion" (along with Ps 74) it grieves rather than celebrates.[1] The tension inherent in these two different Zion images is amplified by God's choice of Zion and David at the end of Psalm 78 (vv. 67-72); this choice is immediately destabilized at the beginning of Psalm 79 by the image of Jerusalem in ruins (cp. Jer 26:18; Mic 3:12). The word "inheritance" in each psalm also shares in this tension (78:71; 79:1).

Psalm 79 seems to be shaped by the Babylonian exile, as are many of the communal laments in book 3 of the Psalter (see Pss 80, 83–85, 89). The suggestion of God as shepherd in 79:13 (the word "shepherd" is not used, but the people self-refer as "the flock of your pasture"), links the

---

1. Walter Brueggemann, *From Whom No Secrets Are Hid: Introducing the Psalms*, ed. Brent Strawn (Louisville, KY: Westminster John Knox, 2014), 82–83.

A Psalm of Asaph.

¹O God, the nations have come
    into your inheritance;
  they have defiled your holy
      temple;
  they have laid Jerusalem in
      ruins.
²They have given the bodies of
    your servants
  to the birds of the air for food,
  the flesh of your faithful to the
      wild animals of the earth.
³They have poured out their blood
    like water
  all around Jerusalem,
  and there was no one to bury
    them.
⁴We have become a taunt to our
    neighbors,
  mocked and derided by those
    around us.

⁵How long, O LORD? Will you be
    angry forever?
  Will your jealous wrath burn
    like fire?
⁶Pour out your anger on the
    nations
    that do not know you,
  and on the kingdoms
    that do not call on your name.
⁷For they have devoured Jacob

and laid waste his habitation.
⁸Do not remember against us the
      iniquities of our ancestors;
  let your compassion come
        speedily to meet us,
  for we are brought very low.
⁹Help us, O God of our salvation,
    for the glory of your name;
  deliver us, and forgive our sins,
    for your name's sake.
¹⁰Why should the nations say,
    "Where is their God?"
  Let the avenging of the outpoured
      blood of your servants
    be known among the nations
      before our eyes.

¹¹Let the groans of the prisoners
      come before you;
  according to your great power
        preserve those doomed
      to die.
¹²Return sevenfold into the bosom
    of our neighbors
  the taunts with which they
        taunted you, O LORD!
¹³Then we your people, the flock
    of your pasture,
  will give thanks to you forever;
  from generation to generation
      we will recount your
      praise.

psalm both to Psalm 78 (vv. 52-53) and to Psalm 80 (v. 1). In Psalm 79 the people anticipate praise for the shepherd who will rescue them from the "wild animals" who are currently preying upon them (v. 2). This psalm is recited at the Western Wall in Jerusalem on Friday evenings and on the ninth of Av (Tisha B'Av), which liturgically commemorates the destruction of the two Jerusalem temples and other disasters that befell the Jewish people; it is a day of mourning and fasting.

Black Lives Matter

The idea that the "flesh of the faithful [has been given] to the wild animals of the earth" in v. 2 upsets the ecological balance outlined in creation. Such images paired with Hopkins's synthesis of Jacqueline Grant's assertions about black female servanthood conjure the gender dynamics of the Black Lives Matter movement. This movement largely rests on the shoulders of black women who are unwilling to tolerate the destruction of black lives. The collective conscience of this swelling of political activism is grounded by the bodies of black servants that have been offered up to a society that refuses to acknowledge us as a part of the ecological system of creation, believing that our existence holds no import. Reading v. 2, one can't help but see the lifeless body of Michael Brown Jr. left on the street in Ferguson, Missouri, for hours, with no concern for his humanity or dignity.

Michael Brown Jr.'s body is just one of the many offered up; their blood has been "poured out like water" (v. 3). All over the United States the blood flowing from black people stains the ground and the conscience of this country. Yet, while black women fight for the humane treatment of all black lives, their personhood is largely ignored. Black female bodies become inconsequential sacrifices to buttress black male sacred identity. We know Jordan Davis, and we know Tamir Rice and Freddie Gray, but little lasting attention is paid to the bodies of Sandra Bland or Tanisha Anderson. They, like Ezekiel's wife, become forgotten casualties in the wake of devastating destruction.

Yolanda Marie Norton

Two standard lament questions mark the sections of Psalm 79: "how long?" (v. 5; cp. Pss 74:10; 80:5; 89:6: Jer 47:6) and "why?" (v. 10; cp. Pss 43:2; 44:24-25; 74:1, 11; 80:13; 88:15; Lam 5:20). Like communal lament Psalms 74 and 83, Psalm 79 raises the agonizing theological question: has God been defeated by foreign gods? Psalm 79 assumes that the conflict between Israel and its enemy (Babylon) is a conflict between the gods of each nation (cp. Exod 7:5, in which God declares that the purpose of the plagues is so that "the Egyptians shall know that I am the LORD"). The enemy taunt quotation in v. 10—"Why should the nations say, 'Where is their God?'"—drives home the god/nation link (see also Pss 42:3, 10 and 115:2; cp. Isa 10:9-10; 36:18b-20; Mic 7:10; Joel 2:17; 1 Kgs 18:27). This "taunt" (חרפה) is "the major reason that the psalmist gives for why God should answer the prayer."[2] The psalmist "reperforms" the enemy taunt for God as a motivation for divine action on Israel's behalf. Verses 4 and 12 reinforce v. 10. The psalmist complains that "we have become a taunt to our neighbors" (v. 4) and then demands retribution in v. 12: "return sevenfold . . . the taunts with which they taunted you, O Lord!" (see "taunt" in Pss 22:6; 31:11; 69:7; 44:13; 89:41). The people's humiliation is also God's humiliation.

The repeated use of the second-person masculine singular possessive suffix "your" emphasizes the point that Judah's loss is God's loss:[3] the nations have entered "your inheritance" and defiled "your holy temple" (v. 1); they have left unburied "your servants" (vv. 2-3), which is an act of humiliation in warfare (see Deut 21:23; 28:26; Josh 10:27; Jer 7:33; 8:2; 14:16). Because God's reputation is at stake, God must act for the "glory" and "sake" of "your name" (v. 9); conversely, God must punish the nations who "do not call on your name" (v. 6). Psalm 79 is the only communal lament that confesses sin (v. 9); this confession offers another motivation for God to act, as well as "exonerates the God whom the laments would indict."[4] The people plead "not that God cool down but rather redirect the anger from the people to the offensive nations."[5] How ironic that this petition is supported by an appeal to God's "compassion" (רחמים), which is anchored in the female body part that is the womb (רחם), site of nurturing, tenderness, and life.

The Sin of Servitude

Though "servant" (עבד) frequently appears in the psalms as a synonym for the psalmist as faithful one, and the plural "servants" (עבדים) for the faithful community who call on God's name (Ps 79:2, 6, 10), Jacquelyn Grant argues that these terms need to be reevaluated in light of black women's experience. She asks: "Could it be that women in general are believed to be, by nature, servants of men, and in the context of women's community, Black women are

---

2. Rolf A. Jacobson, *"Many Are Saying": The Function of Direct Discourse in the Hebrew Psalter*, JSOTSup 397 (Edinburgh: T & T Clark, 2004), 43.

3. Konrad Schaefer, *Psalms*, Berit Olam (Collegeville, MN: Liturgical Press, 2001), 195.

4. Richard J. Bautch, "Lament Regained in Trito-Isaiah's Penitential Prayer," in *Seeking the Favor of God: The Origins of Penitential Prayer in Second Temple Judaism*, ed. Mark Boda, Daniel Falk, and Rodney Werline (Atlanta, GA: Society of Biblical Literature, 2006), 98.

5. Ibid., 195.

seen primarily as servants to all?" (p. 199). She points out that terms like "servant" "are customarily used to relegate certain victimized peoples— those on the underside of history—to the lower rung of society. . . . In fact, African-American women have been the 'servants of the servants.' . . . Servanthood in this country [USA], in effect, has been servitude," especially in light of slavery and domestic service work. Grant asks: "Why are the real servants overwhelmingly poor, Black, and Third World?" In light of her observations, Grant postulates that "perhaps Christians, in the interest of fairness and justice, need to reconsider the servant language, for it has been this language that has undergirded much of the human structures causing pain and suffering for many oppressed peoples."

Given the fact that "some people are more servant than others," Grant asks whether these "servant" people have been empowered for "partnership" with God or simply forced into resigned suffering. The abolition of slavery left the basic oppressor/oppressed relationship between white and black women intact, mirroring the domination of blacks by whites in larger society. "Because Black women were really not women, but property (or better still, animals), they could be used to further protect white women from the drudgeries of daily existence." Subject to economic exploitation, this system of servitude "has led not only to the suffering of Black women, but also of the Black family." This system has also created a theological dilemma, one of "overspiritualization," in which promise of the next world is used "to undergird the status quo." Grant urges us to "resist the tendency of using language to camouflage oppressive reality, rather than eliminating the oppressive reality itself." Such resistance will also lead to reexamination of traditional interpretations of "sin." The sin of pride, for example, "is not the sin of women. . . . [F]or women of color, the sin is not the lack of humility, but the sin is too much humility. Further, for women of color, the sin is not the lack of service, but too much service." Grant concludes that "the church does not need servants, as oppressively conceived of and experienced by many; the church needs followers of Christ—disciples."[6]

Denise Dombkowski Hopkins

6. Jacquelyn Grant, "The Sin of Servanthood and the Deliverance of Discipleship," in *A Troubling in My Soul: Womanist Perspectives on Evil and Suffering*, ed. Emilie M. Townes (Maryknoll, NY: Orbis Books, 1993), 199–218.

The mention of blood "poured out like water" in 79:3 and "outpoured blood" of God's "servants" in 79:10 connects us to the practice of sacrifice in ancient Israelite worship. When sacrifices are offered at the temple or when meat is eaten, Deuteronomy 12:23-27 stipulates that "the blood is the life. . . . You shall not eat it; you shall pour it out on the ground like water" (cp. Lev 17:10-14). In this context "Judah was a sacrifice whose blood was poured out."[7] Because the enemy poured out Judah's blood, the psalm petitions God for a reversal: "pour out" divine anger on the enemy (v. 6). Blood also defiles, as does the entrance of the nations (גוים) into the temple (v. 1). The concern with sacrifice and ritual holiness suggests a connection with Ezekiel, who was a priest among the exiles in Babylon; he received his prophetic call there. Just as the people have become a "taunt" to the neighboring people in Psalm 79:4, Ezekiel declares that they will become a "taunt" to the nations because of God's anger (5:15). If the exilic community is looking at Jerusalem "from a distance," as Erhard Gerstenberger argues,[8] then Ezekiel's priestly circle—"prisoners," who are "doomed to die" apart from the temple (v. 11)—may have prayed this psalm. This group is mourning not only the loss of the temple but also their own loss of identity.

This circle would have included Ezekiel's unnamed wife, who makes "a cameo appearance"[9] in Ezekiel 24:15-27 at the end of a lengthy judgment section. This passage can serve as intertext for Psalm 79. God describes the wife of Ezekiel as "the delight of your eyes" (v. 16), just as the temple is "the delight of your eyes" for the people (v. 21). God prohibits Ezekiel from mourning his wife's death as a model or sign-action for the people, who will not be allowed to mourn the destruction of the temple. Ezekiel's wife dies that very night (v. 18). Rather than "sigh, but not aloud" (v. 17) as Ezekiel is instructed to do, his wife, having learned that her death was imminent, may have prayed Psalm 79. Knowing that she would be separated from her husband whose identity would be eradicated by the destruction of the temple, she mourns for Jerusalem and the temple on behalf of her husband and herself. In effect, she gives voice to one of the

---

7. *The Jewish Study Bible*, ed. Adele Berlin and Marc Zvi Brettler (Oxford: Oxford University Press, 2004), 1371.

8. Erhard S. Gerstenberger, *Psalms, Part 2, and Lamentations* (Grand Rapids, MI: Eerdmans, 2001), 101.

9. Jacqueline E. Lapsley, "Ezekiel" in *Women's Bible Commentary*, ed. Carol A. Newsom, Sharon H. Ringe, and Jacqueline E. Lapsley, 3rd ed. (Louisville, KY: Westminster John Knox, 2012), 289.

"sad songs of Zion" that her husband is forbidden from uttering. In doing so, she creates a space that acknowledges Ezekiel's loss of identity wrapped up in the temple and her own loss of identity as the wife of a priest as well. Despite the fact that women[10] "did not figure prominently" in the world of priests and that Ezekiel uses metaphorical "negative and highly sexualized images of women" to feminize the male elites whom he was addressing (Ezek 16:23), Ezekiel does not accuse his wife of infidelity as the analogy with the profaned temple would require. In the book of Ezekiel, "real" women are the victims of male sexual aggression rather than the perpetrators of it; Ezekiel treats metaphorical women differently. Consequently, this prayerful act of loyalty on the part of his wife can make sense and help us enter into the suffering of the exiles.

Bearing Suffering

I work with the suffering of the human soul day in and day out. What presents itself in my consulting room is the set of symptoms from which one suffers. Rarely does one begin psychoanalytic treatment with a desire to understand the symptom but rather with the desire to medicate the symptom or, at the very least, find a solution or trick that may help keep the symptom under control or at bay. This desire is a product of our modern culture, a culture that seeks less pain and quick fixes and lives primarily in virtual realities where we can choose how we present ourselves to the world. Take, for instance, when a woman is in labor at a hospital. The first thing she is offered is an epidural. "Why feel pain," the doctors and staff inquire, "when you have the option of laboring without it?" One may wonder how it is possible to labor without pain when the etymology of the word labor is toil, hardship, and pain? Many choose to labor without the unpleasant side effects of the pain that brings forth new life, and why not?

This relatively benign yet prevalent example elucidates how we have lost an important perspective on suffering. The etymology of the word *suffer* clarifies this lost perspective: it is to bear something from below. To suffer something, a crisis or a trauma, a symptom we would rather medicate away, or some newness that is beginning to emerge, means to bear that which is emerging, that which is coming from below. If we become identified with our suffering we suffer only from the ego perspective and we say, "I

---

10. For what follows, see ibid., 289–90.

am suffering." When we say this, we have become identified with the suffering as if we are it and it is us; there is no separation. When we are identified with suffering we are unable to see a way through, unable to suffer what has come upon us, and we rush to get rid of its annoying and sometimes disastrous presence. A mentor of mine once commented that the reason we can't bear suffering is because we turn our face away from it, refuse to look at it and into it for what it may have to show us and teach us. Carl Jung says, "In the case of psychological suffering, which always isolates the individual from the herd of so-called normal people, it is also of the greatest importance to understand that the conflict is not a personal failure only, but at the same time a suffering common to all and a problem with which the whole epoch is burdened. This general point of view lifts the individual out of himself and connects him with humanity."[11]

Psalm 79 is a communal lament that seeks to suffer the reality of the trauma of exile and in this way address the epoch of exilic Israel. It speaks of the decimation in their midst, the shame experienced, and the longing for God to come and see, to join them in their suffering, to answer their plea for salvation. Not evading the suffering but naming it, allowing it to live— this is how one turns one's face toward suffering in order to bear what comes out of it and through it. As Ann Ulanov reminds us, "If we try merely to get past the trauma, to get over it, we may succeed but at the cost of turning down the volume of our living, or amputating our sexuality, or stifling our aggression."[12] To suffer a trauma, a symptom, harm done to you or harm you have done to someone else, gives something back to the collective, to the world. To suffer something, though isolating on the one hand, eventually connects one with the suffering of humanity. Suffering or bearing what comes moves it along out of stagnation and makes something out of it.

Tiffany Houck-Loomis

---

11. Carl G. Jung, *The Collected Works*, vol. 18, ed. and trans. Gerhard Adler and R. F. C. Hull (Princeton, NJ: Princeton University Press, 1980), par. 232.

12. Ann Ulanov, *Knots and Their Untying: Essays on Psychological Dilemmas* (New Orleans: Spring Journal, 2014), 35.

Psalm 80

Covenant Expectations Met and Unmet

Standing in dialogical tension with the psalms that come before and after it, Psalm 80 claims that God is responsible for the people's suffering. It does this by reversing traditional vine imagery that both expresses God's commitment to Israel and points out Israel's failure to reciprocate that commitment (see Isa 5:1-7; Jer 2:21; 6:9; Ezek 17:1-10; 19:10-14; Hos 10:1; 14:7). Normally the vine metaphor suggests that God the gardener engages in "careful planning, preparation, and patient nurturing, which makes possible growth and fruitfulness"[1] for Israel, the vine (Exod 15:17; Ps 44:2; John 15:4-5). Psalm 80 notes God's care in v. 9a: "you cleared the ground for it." God did such a good job that the vine "took deep root and filled the land" (v. 9). The psalmist asks God directly why (v. 12a) a careful gardener would put so much effort into transplanting the vine from Egypt (v. 8, a reference to the exodus) only to abandon it to destruction (vv. 12b-13). This question turns the vine metaphor on its head. "In fact, Psalm 80 is the only case in the Old

---

1. J. Clinton McCann Jr., "The Book of Psalms," in *The New Interpreter's Bible*, vol. 4 (Nashville, TN: Abingdon Press, 1996), 639–1280, at 1000.

Psalm 80:1-19

To the leader: on Lilies, a Covenant.
Of Asaph. A Psalm.

¹Give ear, O Shepherd of Israel,
  you who lead Joseph like a flock!
You who are enthroned upon the
  cherubim, shine forth
²before Ephraim and Benjamin
  and Manasseh.
Stir up your might,
  and come to save us!

³Restore us, O God;
  let your face shine, that we
  may be saved.

⁴O Lᴏʀᴅ God of hosts,
  how long will you be angry with
  your people's prayers?

⁵You have fed them with the bread
  of tears,
and given them tears to drink
  in full measure.
⁶You make us the scorn of our
  neighbors;
our enemies laugh among
  themselves.

⁷Restore us, O God of hosts;
  let your face shine, that we
  may be saved.
⁸You brought a vine out of Egypt;
  you drove out the nations and
  planted it.
⁹You cleared the ground for it;
  it took deep root and filled the
  land.

Testament/Hebrew Bible where this vine imagery is used for the purpose of critiquing God's unfaithfulness."[2]

In this way the vine metaphor functions as a motivation to support the plea for God to intervene. As Patrick Miller puts it, "God may not be coerced, but God can be persuaded."[3] A good look at the pitiful state of God's vine—"look down from heaven and see" (v. 14b)—ought to be enough to spur God to action, especially since the verb ראה ("see") is the same verb used in Exodus 3:7 in God's self-revelation at the burning bush: "I have observed." This compassionate God has seen the oppression of the Hebrew slaves and is determined to "come down" to deliver them.

Verses 8 and 15 remind God of past divine actions on Israel's behalf—the exodus and settlement in the land of Canaan—as most of the Asaph psalms do. Psalms 78, 79, and 81 make it clear, however, that the people have brought their suffering upon their own heads by testing God (Ps

---

2. Hee Suk Kim, "A Critique against God? Reading Psalm 80 in the Context of Vindication," in *Why? . . How Long? Studies on Voice(s) of Lamentation Rooted in Hebrew Poetry*, ed. LeAnn Snow Flesher, Mark Boda, and Carol Dempsey (New York: Bloomsbury, 2013), 100–114, at 105.

3. Patrick D. Miller, *They Cried to the Lord: The Form and Theology of Biblical Prayer* (Minneapolis: Augsburg Fortress Press, 1994), 125.

¹⁰The mountains were covered
with its shade,
the mighty cedars with its
branches;
¹¹it sent out its branches to the sea,
and its shoots to the River.
¹²Why then have you broken down
its walls,
so that all who pass along the
way pluck its fruit?
¹³The boar from the forest
ravages it,
and all that move in the field
feed on it.

¹⁴Turn again, O God of hosts;
look down from heaven, and see;
have regard for this vine,

¹⁵the stock that your right hand
planted.
¹⁶They have burned it with fire,
they have cut it down;
may they perish at the rebuke
of your countenance.
¹⁷But let your hand be upon the
one at your right hand,
the one whom you made
strong for yourself.
¹⁸Then we will never turn back
from you;
give us life, and we will call on
your name.

¹⁹Restore us, O Lᴏʀᴅ God of hosts;
let your face shine, that we
may be saved.

78:18, 41, 56), sinning (79:9), and not listening to God (Ps 81:8, 11, 13). The tension created by Psalm 80 among these psalms is intensified by the shared image of God as shepherd who feeds the flock (Israel; see 78:52; 79:13; 80:5; 81:16). This linking image does not allow the reader to escape the tension inherent in Israel's grappling with theodicy (literally, "God's justice"). Along with Psalm 80, Psalms 74 (vv. 1, 10, 11), 79 (vv. 5, 10), and 82 (v. 2) ask the primary theodicy questions: "why?" and "how long?" The focus on theodicy runs like a thread through the Asaph psalms, but these psalms offer different responses. Though the divine epithet "Lᴏʀᴅ God of hosts" is used four times in Psalm 80 (vv. 4, 7, 14, 19), the use of the shepherd image in v. 1 "adds pathos to the sense of abandonment"[4] Israel is experiencing. Though the metaphors are very different, both express the people's expectations about the nurturing and protective activity of God. God must claim the power of the "Lord of hosts" who is "enthroned upon the cherubim" (v. 1b), a reference connected with the ark of the covenant on which God is invisibly enthroned (1 Sam 4:4; Ps 99:1; 1 Kgs 6:23-28; 8:6-7). The power of this warrior God must be directed not at Israel but rather at the enemy (vv. 12b-13; 16b).

4. James L. Crenshaw, *The Psalms: An Introduction* (Grand Rapids, MI: Eerdmans, 2001), 24.

Yearning for God

O LORD God of hosts, where are you?! Wake up, give ear, come save us, let your face shine! O LORD God of hosts, hear the cry of the marginalized, oppressed, fearful yet faithful African American people in the United States! The first half of the second decade of the twenty-first century has been a particularly painful time for African Americans in the United States. More than fifty years after the civil rights movement, racially motivated violence reminiscent of acts perpetrated in the Jim Crow and segregated South once again haunt the black community. In 2012 a seventeen-year-old black male youth[5] was murdered while walking home because he made the fateful decision to transit a white neighborhood. The murderer and resident found his presence in the neighborhood suspicious; this resulted in the young man's death. His murder is a somber and disheartening reminder of the brutal beating and lynching of Emmett Till in 1955 because he looked and whistled at a white woman during his first visit to the South.

In 2014 and 2015, the black community lived through several cases in which African American males died at the hands of police officers, either gunned down in the street,[6] choked to death during an arrest,[7] or dying of injuries sustained while being taken into custody.[8] While the community was trying to make sense of and heal from these hateful acts, the unthinkable happened in June 2015. A white male entered Emanuel African Methodist Episcopal Church, joined the evening Bible study, and then savagely gunned down nine members[9] of the church, including the pastor. "The church is the center of African American life. . . . [It is] a foundation stone for liberty and

---

5. Trayvon Martin was shot and killed by George Zimmerman while walking through Zimmerman's neighborhood. Martin was coming from the convenience store where he had purchased candy and a soft drink he was carrying when approached by Zimmerman. Zimmerman appealed to Florida's "Stand Your Ground" law and said he shot unarmed Martin in self-defense. Although Zimmerman was indicted and tried for murder, a jury found Zimmerman not guilty and acquitted him of all charges related to the murder of Trayvon Martin.

6. Michael Brown in Ferguson, MO; Laquan McDonald in Chicago; how many more?

7. Eric Garner in Staten Island, NY.

8. Freddie Gray in Baltimore, MD.

9. The victims of this act of terror/hate were The Rev. Clementa C. Pinckney, Cynthia Marie Graham Hurd, The Rev. Sharonda Coleman-Singleton, Tywanza Sanders, Ethel Lee Lance, Susie Jackson, Depayne Middleton Doctor, The Rev. Daniel Simmons, and Myra Thompson.

justice, for that's what the [black] church means."[10] Slain in their "sanctuary," they were a bitter reminder of the four African American girls killed when a bomb exploded in their church in Birmingham, Alabama, as the girls were on their way to Sunday School.[11]

Where is the God of Exodus 3:7 who has observed, heard, and known the suffering of the oppressed and decides to "come down" and deliver them? The African American community yearns and hopes for "the nurturing and protective activity of God" to cease this revisiting of oppression, dehumanization, and assassination on African American persons and personhood.

Audrey Coretta Price

Psalm 80 not only stands in tension with its surrounding psalms but also expresses tension within itself, particularly in the images of God it presents. The opening imperatives of Psalm 80 signal the urgency of the people's situation: "give ear" (v. 1); "stir up [literally, 'wake up'; Ps 44:23] and come to save us!" (v. 2); "let your face shine" (v. 3, a reference to God's theophany or presence, intertwined with solar imagery; the opposite would be the "hiding" of God's face). These verbs strongly suggest that the people experience God as "inattentive, inactive, absent," yet ironically "even if God is the problem, nonetheless God is the solution."[12] God is invoked as the "shepherd of Israel" (v. 1) because God is supposed to find food and water for the flock that is Israel. "Shepherd" was also a title for kings in the ancient Near East (see 2 Sam 7:7; Ezek 34:1-16; Ps 78:70-72).

10. President Barack Obama's eulogy on June 26, 2015, at The Reverend Clementa Pinckney's funeral. Rev. Pinckney was the pastor of Mother Emanuel AME Church and one of the nine slain by the gunman who terrorized the Bible study and shot and killed nine members in attendance.

11. On September 15, 1963, a bomb exploded during Sunday morning services in the Sixteenth Street Baptist Church in Birmingham, Alabama, killing four young girls. The church served as a meeting place for civil rights leaders, including Martin Luther King Jr. This was the third church bombing in Birmingham in eleven days after a federal order was issued to integrate Alabama's school system. The bombing killed fourteen-year-olds Cynthia Wesley, Carole Robertson, and Addie Mae Collins and eleven-year-old Denise McNair. While it was determined that the bombing was an act of hatred committed by the Ku Klux Klan, no one was found guilty of the crime. See history.com, "This Day in History: September 15."

12. McCann, "The Book of Psalms," 999.

The psalmist notes instead that God has "fed them with the bread of tears" and "given them tears to drink" (v. 5; cp. Pss 42:3; 102:9; Job 3:24; Jer 23:15). Further, the shepherd is supposed to protect the flock from animal predators (see 1 Sam 17:34-35; Isa 31:4; Amos 3:12; Mic 5:8; John 10:12), but in anger God (v. 4a) has broken down the walls of the sheepfold (v. 12a) so that "the boar from the forest ravages it, and all that move in the field feed on it" (v. 13). The use of the root רעה (literally "graze") for the action of the predators in v. 13 is juxtaposed with the noun from the same root, "shepherd," in v. 1 and underscores the disappointment of the people's covenantal expectations in terms of God's behavior.

Ambiguity and intentional juxtaposition also undergird the use of the verb שׁוב ("turn, return, repent") in the petitions functioning as refrains. In vv. 3, 6, and 19 the verb is in the *hiphil* masculine singular imperative form with a first common plural suffix: literally "cause us to return," in the sense of "save" or "rescue." The verb is often used of God bringing the people back from exile (1 Kgs 8:34; Jer 27:22). In v. 14, a modified refrain that stands at the theological center of Psalm 80, however, the verb changes to the Qal imperative and means literally: "you turn, O God of hosts." Rather than confessing sin, the people demand that God change; God must forego the divine anger that literally "smokes against" them (v. 4) and instead "have regard" (v. 14b) for Israel, God's vine. This reading argues against seeing v. 18 as an implicit admission of sin: "then we will never turn back (the verb is סוג, not שׁוב here) from you." If God changes, then the people will not be forced to turn away from a God who does not shepherd the flock or tend the vine that is Israel. Human shepherds have failed, but God must be the reliable shepherd and the persistent gardener.

Return and Change

In the woman-focused book of Ruth, שׁוב ("turn, return") takes on different shades of socio-political meaning. The book of Ruth features two female characters. Naomi is a Bethlehemite woman who seeks refuge in Moab during famine and is subsequently widowed after the death of her husband and sons in Moab. Ruth, Naomi's Moabite daughter-in-law, is also widowed when Naomi's son (Ruth's husband) dies. When it seems Naomi has exhausted her options in Moab and food becomes available back home, she decides to return to Bethlehem, and Ruth insists on accompanying her.

The downbeat of the book of Ruth is *return*. Twelve times in the first chapter we read שׁוב as the narrator introduces us to Naomi and Ruth. Alongside the steady pulse of *return* is *foreignness*, as the narrator finds it necessary to remind us repeatedly that Ruth is a *Moabite*. Much ambiguity lurks around themes of return and foreignness in the book of Ruth, but the two together make one thing clear: it is impossible to return to the same place one left. Places change. People change. "Call me no longer Naomi, call me Mara, for the Almighty has dealt bitterly with me," Naomi says (Ruth 1:20-21). Naomi has changed since she left Bethlehem. Return has also changed Ruth, who is reduced to little more than her ethnicity. The community at Bethlehem is changed by the presence of the duo. The accommodation of the two widows requires special consideration.

Ruth challenges us to remember that שוב, (re)turn, means change. Psalm 80 read alongside the book of Ruth invites the possibility that the restored community will be racially, ethnically, economically, socially, and politically different from before. When God turns, whom will God see? Will those on God's right hand include foreigners? Moabites? And who will see God? Will they recognize God?

Amy Beth Jones

The ambiguity in the use of the verb שוב in Psalm 80 suggests a link to Isaiah 7:1-9 as intertext. The main connection rests with Isaiah's son, Shear-jashub, whose name means literally "a remnant shall return (שוב)." God has commanded Isaiah to go out with his son to meet King Ahaz of Judah, who was inspecting Jerusalem's water supply in preparation for a siege. The son's name, a prophetic sign-action that concretizes the divine word of coming judgment and hope, is filled with ambiguity. One wonders what the boy was thinking as his father confronted the king with him in tow, or for that matter, what the boy thought of the name his father had given him. Shear-jashub joins Hosea's unfortunate children birthed by Gomer (Hos 1) in bearing the weight of names that embodied the divine word. The Septuagint adds to the superscription of Psalm 80 the words "concerning the Assyrians," which provides another link to Isaiah 7, since the historical situation facing King Ahaz involved pressure from Syria and the northern kingdom Israel to join their alliance against the encroaching power of the Assyrian empire (ca. 734 BCE; see 2 Kgs 16:1-20). These two neighboring nations threatened to overthrow King Ahaz if he did not join them (7:5-6). Shear-jashub's name perhaps conveyed to the king a promise and/or a threat: the bad news is that only a remnant will be left (see Isa 10:20-23); the good news is that a remnant will be left after the approaching disaster. It might also mean that only a remnant of those threatening Judah will survive. Isaiah urges the king to trust God and not enter into the alliance (7:9b).

Perhaps Shear-jashub prayed Psalm 80 while watching his father confront the king. Enigmatic v. 17 may have had special meaning for the boy, since it petitions God to "let your hand be upon the one at your right hand, the one whom you made strong for yourself." Did he connect this verse with his father, the prophet? Isaiah was strengthened for his prophetic task by being cleansed with a burning coal touched to his lips during his call (Isa 6:6-7) and by learning that the message he was to deliver would lead not to repentance but rather to the certainty of God's punishment (6:9-13). Shear-jashub learned early on through his name that prophecy was costly for the prophet. Perhaps his praying of Psalm 80 was meant to jolt God into action on behalf of his father so that his words might be heeded. As Jacqueline Lapsley notes, it is no accident that Isaiah's son embodies the divine word. Rather than "a form of creepy instrumentalism," Shear-jashub expresses "the importance of children in God's economy." The children in Isaiah (see also "Immanuel, God with us" and Maher-shalal-hash-baz, "pillage hastens; looting speeds") not only convey the message; "they themselves are part of the message: children, children, children . . . essential to salvation. . . . How children are treated, both in the present and in the future, is essential to the divine vision of what God would have for Israel."[13]

13. Jacqueline E. Lapsley, " 'Look! The Children and I Are as Signs and Portents in Israel': Children in Isaiah," in *The Child in the Bible*, ed. Marcia J. Bunge, et al. (Grand Rapids, MI: Eerdmans, 2008), 82–102, at 102.

Children in Ancient Israel

"In the central highland villages of the early Iron Age, all children were valued for the contributions that they could make to the economic success of their parents' households . . . but the biblical writers do not offer much information about the specific activities, duties and expectations of a young girl. . . . The actual period of childhood in ancient Israel is hard to define because different cultures see this social category differently. . . . Contrary to our Western view that childhood is biologically defined . . . many cultures do not emphasize chronological age but, rather, maturity" and the work a child can do.

"[L]ike women, children are often believed to be associated with private space rather than public space, which accounts for their perceived invisibility. . . . Children carried water, looked after goats, sheep and poultry, and helped at harvest time by threshing, winnowing, picking fruit and olives and gleaning." Carol Meyers notes that in the Iron Age "the household was the only arena in which children could learn basic social and technical skills as well as the cultural patterns of their household and community. . . . A child acquired most technical expertise simply by experience. Children in traditional societies are an integral part of the household labor force. Toddlers perform a few simple tasks and have some regular assignments by the age of six, and children older than ten are often like adults in their contributions to household work. Biblical texts mention the labor of children: for example, helping with harvest (Prov 10:5) and gathering firewood (Jer 7:18). Younger children of both genders tend to stay with their mothers and gain a rudimentary knowledge of her tasks, and older children accompany and work with the same-gender parent. And as they work, they learn. . . . [W]omen tend to have the primary role in managing the pool of child labor, assigning tasks to both girls and boys even when the latter are dispatched to work with their fathers."[14]

Denise Dombkowski Hopkins

14. Jennie E. Ebeling, *Women's Lives in Biblical Times* (London and New York: T & T Clark, 2010), 45–46; Carol Meyers, *Rediscovering Eve: Ancient Israelite Women in Context* (Oxford: Oxford University Press, 2013), 136–37.

Psalm 81

Time for Decision— Whose Voice Is Heard?

Unlike Psalm 80, which blames God's unfaithfulness for Israel's current suffering, Psalm 81 focuses on Israel's inability to "listen" to God as the cause of its situation. Such are the conflicted prayers of a people traumatized by exile or by some other disaster in the history of Israel. Yet the first three verses of Psalm 81 seem far removed from any trauma since they point to a liturgical setting of celebration. Multiple imperatives spoken by the psalmist in the hymnic introduction urge Israel to "sing aloud," "shout for joy," "raise a song" (cp. Exod 15:2), play the tambourine, lyre, and harp, and "blow the trumpet" on this "festal day," which was appointed by God (vv. 4-5). This language, along with the mention of "new moon" (v. 3), suggests a setting during one of the major festivals in the seventh month (see Lev 23:23-36; Num 29:1-39), perhaps Tabernacles, also called the feast of Booths or Sukkoth.

Verse 5c seems to interrupt the celebration, as the psalmist declares: "I hear a voice [literally 'lip' or 'language'] I had not known." After this interruption God starts speaking directly in v. 6 with the divine "I" and continues speaking until the end of the psalm in v. 16. Many interpreters suggest that the speaker in Psalm 81 may be a prophet, whose interruption in v. 5c seems to function much like the messenger

Psalm 81:1-16

To the leader: according to The Gittith.
Of Asaph.

[1]Sing aloud to God our strength;
shout for joy to the God of
Jacob.
[2]Raise a song, sound the tambourine,
the sweet lyre with the harp.
[3]Blow the trumpet at the new
moon,
at the full moon, on our festal
day.
[4]For it is a statute for Israel,
an ordinance of the God of
Jacob.
[5]He made it a decree in Joseph,
when he went out over the
land of Egypt.

I hear a voice I had not known:
[6]"I relieved your shoulder of the
burden;
your hands were freed from
the basket.
[7]In distress you called, and I rescued you;
I answered you in the secret
place of thunder;
I tested you at the waters of
Meribah.   *Selah*
[8]Hear, O my people, while I admonish you;
O Israel, if you would but listen
to me!
[9]There shall be no strange god
among you;
you shall not bow down to a
foreign god.

formula in prophetic oracles—"this is what the Lord says"—distin-
guishing the divine words that follow from those spoken previously
by the prophet.

In a liturgical psalm such as Psalm 81 (e.g., liturgical or festival Pss 50,
75, and 95, which also contain God quotations), however, "a God quotation that is repeated numerous times in the liturgy will not imply a present
communication from God."[1] Instead, this God quotation functions "to
admonish and teach the gathered community" and to support an encounter with God in worship.[2] Like the other liturgical psalms, Psalm 81 contains within its quotation a reference to the Decalogue; it offers in v. 9 the
most direct reference to the first commandment: "you shall have no other
gods before me" (Exod 20:3; Deut 5:7). God's self-identification follows
in v. 9b—"I am the LORD your God, who brought you up out of the land
of Egypt"—known as the prologue to the Decalogue in the Christian
tradition; it is the first commandment in the Jewish tradition. These ref-

1. Rolf A. Jacobson, *"Many Are Saying": The Function of Direct Discourse in the Hebrew
Psalter*, JSOTSup 397 (Edinburgh: T & T Clark, 2004), 92.
2. Ibid., 110.

> [10]I am the LORD your God,
>   who brought you up out of the
>   land of Egypt.
>   Open your mouth wide and I
>   will fill it.
>
> [11]"But my people did not listen to
>   my voice;
>   Israel would not submit to
>   me.
> [12]So I gave them over to their
>   stubborn hearts,
>   to follow their own counsels.
> [13]O that my people would listen to
>   me,

> that Israel would walk in my
>   ways!
> [14]Then I would quickly subdue
>   their enemies,
>   and turn my hand against their
>   foes.
> [15]Those who hate the LORD would
>   cringe before him,
>   and their doom would last for-
>   ever.
> [16]I would feed you with the finest
>   of the wheat,
>   and with honey from the rock I
>   would satisfy you."

erences illuminate another function of the God quotation: "to connect the liturgical and ethical dimensions of life"[3] by drawing on God's words communicated in the past in the Decalogue.

In the two-part liturgical sermon that quotes God's words from the past in 81:6-16, God calls Israel to "listen," and in vv. 11-16 the people respond to God's call. The repeated verb שמע ("hear," "listen") links the first five verses with the two parts of the sermon. The psalmist "hears" God's voice (v. 5c), God calls the people to "hear" the divine admonishment (v. 8a), God wistfully desires that Israel "listen" (v. 8b), the people do not "listen" (v. 11a), and God again wistfully hopes that they will (v. 13a). Clearly, "the essence of Israel's identity as God's people is found in the ability to listen."[4] These repeated imperatives to "hear" echo Moses' exhortations in the Deuteronomic tradition (Deut 4:1; 5:1; 9:1), particularly in the Shema in Deuteronomy 6:4: "Hear, O Israel: the LORD is our God, the LORD alone." As with Moses, listening and obedience are intertwined in Psalm 81 (vv. 11, 13), framed by the Sinai/Horeb tradition.

God reviews the divine history with Israel, beginning with the memory of the exodus in v. 6, as the basis for the right to "admonish" (literally "witness against") the people in v. 8c (cp. Ps 50:7). The word "burden"

---

3. Ibid.

4. Konrad Schaefer, *Psalms*, Berit Olam (Collegeville, MN: Liturgical Press, 2001), 200.

(v. 6a) occurs in Exodus 1:11; 2;11; 5:4-5; 6:6, and the word "basket" (v. 6b) suggests the slave labor of the Israelites under the Egyptians as they made and carried bricks for Pharaoh's building projects (Exod 1:11, 14). In addition, "the place of thunder" (v. 7b) alludes to God's theophany on Sinai (Exod 19:16-20). God reminds the people that God delivers those who cry out in distress (v. 7ab). The reference to Meribah (v. 7c) ties the psalm to God's deliverance in the wilderness wanderings, though here the tradition is turned around and God speaks of testing Israel instead of Israel testing God (as in Exod 17:7; Num 20:13). "Since God had heard the people's cries for deliverance in Egypt (Exod 3:7), it is reasonable that now they obey the command to hear God (see Deut 6:4; Ps 95:7). . . . The choice belongs to the people."[5] God notes in v. 11 that the people chose not to obey: "But my people did not listen to my voice" (cp. Deut 9:23; 18:19; 28:1, 15; Judg 2:2, 17, 20; 1 Sam 15:19; 2 Kgs 17:14). All of Deuteronomic theology "revolves around the concepts of 'listening and obeying the word of Yahweh' and the dreadful opposite: 'rejecting or disobeying the word' "[6] (cp. Deut 30:15-19).

The story of Huldah the prophet in 2 Kings 22:11-20 (2 Chr 34:22-28) suggests itself as intertext for Psalm 81. Huldah "is the only woman prophet of the royal era known by name,"[7] appearing in a book that often treats foreign women with hostility and concerns itself with other women only in their capacities as mothers. In 622 BCE the "book of the law" (*torah*) was "discovered" during repairs to the Jerusalem temple (2 Kgs 22:3-10). When this book was read aloud to King Josiah he "tore his clothes," a traditional sign of lamentation (v. 11), and then commanded a group, including the High Priest Hilkiah, to "go, inquire of the LORD for me . . . concerning the words of this book." They go to Huldah, who does not live in the city center but rather in a newer section of Jerusalem, the Second Quarter. She "sits" (יֹשֶׁבֶת) there to carry out her duties, just as Deborah "used to sit under the palm of Deborah" in Judges 4:5; perhaps this verb indicates her workplace. This description suggests that she is

5. J. Clinton McCann Jr., "The Book of Psalms," in *The New Interpreter's Bible*, vol. 4 (Nashville, TN: Abingdon Press, 1996), 639–1280, at 1004.

6. Erhard Gerstenberger, *Psalms, Part 2, and Lamentations* (Grand Rapids, MI: Eerdmans, 2001), 110.

7. Kyung Sook Lee, "Books of Kings: Images of Women without Women's Reality," in *Feminist Biblical Interpretation: A Compendium of Critical Commentary*, ed. Luise Schottroff and Marie-Theres Wacker (Grand Rapids, MI: Eerdmans, 2012), 159–77, at 174.

"not directly associated" with the temple cult; instead, "this could indicate that she is a court prophet, consulted at her home."[8] Huldah's status as prophet is also supported by the idiom דרש את יהוה, which means "to seek a divine oracle that will be spoken through a human agent,"[9] usually a prophet (1 Sam 9:9; 1 Kgs 14:5; 22:8, 18).

Critiquing the Norm from the Periphery

If we read 2 Kings 22 and the story of Huldah as intertext with Psalm 81 we must first understand the potential importance of Huldah's presence in the Bible to black women. Regardless of her social status as court prophet, Huldah is still peripheral because of her gender. Her presence in the text is functional. The narrative is not overwhelmingly concerned with her history but only with her role in the ideological evolution of Israel. Huldah stands counter to most women in the text, however, because she is able to cultivate social importance that is not wrapped up in maternal identity. The Israelite community actively engages her for wisdom in the midst of transition. Huldah stands apart from Ruth and Hagar, who are acknowledged for their wombs. She is different from Jezebel who is evaluated as violent, aggressive, and sexualized. Huldah, the outsider, is important because of her insights. We do not know much about Huldah's story, but we can imagine that her position as outsider would have come with some isolation, and yet she finds herself in a moment in history in which she has serious influence on the theological course of Israel. She is the new voice for God and thus offers new potential for the importance of foreign women in the biblical narrative and black women in contemporary society.

Emilie Townes suggests that to understand a womanist perspective on suffering we must realize that living and working "through pain acknowledges our human ability to effect change in individual lives and the lives of others. We must learn to move from the reactive position of suffering to that of the transforming power of pain, to use it as a critical stance and

8. Cameron B. R. Howard, "1 and 2 Kings," in *Women's Bible Commentary*, ed. Carol A. Newsom, Sharon H. Ringe, and Jacqueline E. Lapsley, 3rd ed. (Louisville, KY: Westminster John Knox, 2012), 164–79, at 178.

9. Diana Edelman, "Huldah the Prophet—of Yahweh or Asherah?," in *A Feminist Companion to Samuel and Kings*, ed. Athalya Brenner (Sheffield: Sheffield Academic Press, 1994), 231–50, at 232.

refuse to accept the 'facts' handed to us. . . . Pain allows the victim to examine her or his situation and make a plan for a healthy future."[10] Consequently, the previous struggle and trauma of black women is not to be viewed as a positive; our suffering is not an enactment of God's divine plan. Instead, these experiences become the backdrop for our ability to listen and to alter the norms of value and wisdom. Stereotypes perpetuated of black women as welfare queens and mammies do not limit our possibilities in society, and these wounds of subjugation and relegation to the periphery should not be uplifted as salvific honors. Instead, we understand that these moments and realities in which we have been relegated to the periphery provide a historical backdrop from which we offer a critique of normative values and allow our epistemological privilege to give us language to change societal norms and influence the future.

Yolanda Marie Norton

King Josiah's emotional reaction to the "discovery" of the "book of the Torah" (some form of Deuteronomy) was prompted by his belief that God's wrath was kindled against Israel "because our ancestors did not obey the words of this book" (2 Kgs 22:13). Huldah authenticates the book and declares that because Josiah heard how God spoke against "this place" and wept about it, Josiah will not see the coming disaster (v. 19). Instead, he will be given a proper ritual burial (v. 20), unlike his successors who will be buried in foreign lands. Five times the verb שׁמע ("hear, listen, obey") is used in the Huldah story (vv. 11, 13, 18, 19 twice), connecting her to Psalm 81 and its repetition of the same root. Given Josiah's death at the hand of the Egyptians in 609 BCE at Megiddo, the link between Huldah and Psalm 81 is strengthened by the "iconography of the blow" in v. 14b—"I will rear back my hand above their foes"—that reminds the people that God "has supplanted the pharaoh in his position of dominance" during the exodus and can now take on any enemy oppressing Israel,[11] whether it be Egypt again or Babylonia. The image of

10. Emilie M. Townes, "Living in the New Jerusalem: The Rhetoric and Movement of Liberation in the House of Evil," in *A Troubling in My Soul: Womanist Perspectives on Evil and Suffering*, ed. Emilie M. Townes (Maryknoll, NY: Orbis Books, 1993), 78–91, at 84.

11. Joel M. LeMon, "YHWH's Hand and the Iconography of the Blow in Psalm 81:14-16," *JBL* 132 (2013): 865–82, at 865 (abstract).

the "smiting posture" suggested by this verse originated in Egyptian art to symbolize the pharaoh's power over enemies; this image is found on scarab seals in Syria-Palestine.

The image is reinforced by v. 15: "those who hate the LORD will cringe before him," which echoes the "iconographic principle of hierarchy of scale"; God dominates the enemies spatially.[12] The psalm pictures the moment before the blow, a moment of expectation. Just as God delivered the Hebrew slaves from Egypt, God will avenge the death of good king Josiah once Israel "listens" and "walks" in God's "ways" (v. 13). In addition, Huldah's word from God mentions that the people have "abandoned" God and "have made offerings to other gods" (v. 17), which connects to Psalm 81:9 and its restatement of the first commandment. The adjectives modifying "gods" (אחרים in 2 Kgs 22:17; זר and נכר in Ps 81:9) are not the same but synonymous.

Diana Edelman[13] argues that Huldah was a prophet of Asherah, God's consort. Asherah, like many female deities, had a role as intercessor in patriarchal pantheons, which made her a logical deity to consult in 2 Kings 22 to avoid the risk of angering God by asking God directly about the ignored "book of the torah." As Asherah's prophet, Huldah would be the logical one to authenticate the scroll and diffuse God's anger. She may have been co-opted by a later editor who wrote Asherah and other gods and goddesses out of the national religion of Israel (see 2 Kgs 23:4-6). Whether she was God's or Asherah's prophet, it may be that Huldah interrupted the people's festal celebration in the temple or in a local sanctuary by praying Psalm 81 during the time of chaos following Josiah's death. Second Kings does not say what happened to Huldah after she authenticated the scroll brought to her, but she helps us to imagine a different superscription for Psalm 81: "According to the Gittith. Of Huldah, after good king Josiah was killed."

---

12. Ibid., 876. LeMon translates "cringe" as "shrink."
13. Edelman, "Huldah the Prophet," 231, 247–48.

Psalm 82

God's Hiddenness

Psalm 82 joins the other Asaph psalms (50, 73–81, 83) in raising the urgent question of theodicy, perhaps in response to Babylonian exile. Though these psalms perceive God's absence, "divine speech is imagined, nonetheless"[1] (cp. 50:7-15, 16b-21; 75:3-4, 11; 81:6-16). God quotations are not confined to the Asaph psalms; eighteen psalms include quotations from God, and these quotations function in different ways. In Psalm 82 the God quotation pushes God to grant the closing petition in v. 8 instead of warning or instructing the congregation as in Psalms 50, 75, 81, 95.[2] In Psalm 82, vv. 1 and 8 are spoken by the psalmist and bracket the God quotation in vv. 2-7. Paying attention to how the psalmist dialogues with God's speech in Psalm 82 "by framing it with his own" reveals that the psalmist quotes the divine voice "in order to quarrel with it."[3]

1. James L. Crenshaw, *The Psalms: An Introduction* (Grand Rapids, MI: Eerdmans, 2001), 26.

2. Rolf A. Jacobson, *"Many Are Saying": The Function of Direct Discourse in the Hebrew Psalter*, JSOTSup 397 (Edinburgh: T & T Clark, 2004), 114.

3. Herbert J. Levine, *Sing unto God a New Song: A Contemporary Reading of the Psalms* (Bloomington: Indiana University Press, 1995), 113.

Psalm 82:1-8

A Psalm of Asaph.

[1]God has taken his place in the divine council;
in the midst of the gods he holds judgment:
[2]"How long will you judge unjustly and show partiality to the wicked?   *Selah*
[3]Give justice to the weak and the orphan;
maintain the right of the lowly and the destitute.
[4]Rescue the weak and the needy;
deliver them from the hand of the wicked."

[5]They have neither knowledge nor understanding,
they walk around in darkness;
all the foundations of the earth are shaken.

[6]I say, "You are gods, children of the Most High, all of you;
[7]nevertheless, you shall die like mortals,
and fall like any prince."
[8]Rise up, O God, judge the earth;
for all the nations belong to you!

This view challenges many interpretations of Psalm 82 that focus instead on how the psalm declares an end to polytheism in Israel's thinking and asserts monotheism in the final verse. These different foci are connected to debates over the translation of the word אלהים in vv. 1 and 6. Translated as "gods" in the NRSV, this word has been understood to refer variously to human judges, oppressive foreign rulers, or, most often, deities in a pantheon of gods. As reference to gods in a pantheon the word connotes something like Second Isaiah's idols in Isaiah 44:9-20; Israel's God renders these divine beings "impotent and totally powerless," in effect declaring "the death of the gods."[4] In addition, the phrase עדת אל in v. 1 ("the divine council," literally "the council of El") is understood as a reference to the heavenly assembly of high gods common in ancient Near Eastern thought and taken as the frame for understanding Psalm 82.

One interpreter, however, rightly challenges the prevailing view, which he deems "almost irresistible," by looking more closely at v. 1.[5] The Hebrew word אל can refer generically to any god or specifically to the personal name of the Canaanite high god El. In addition, "children of the Most High" in verse 6 is literally "sons of Elyon"; Elyon is a typical

4. Patrick D. Miller, "When the Gods Meet: Psalm 82 and the Issue of Justice," *Journal for Preachers* 9 (1986): 2–5, at 4.
5. James M. Trotter, "Death of the אלהים in Psalm 82," *JBL* 131 (2012): 221–39, at 231.

epithet for El. Recognizing the ambiguity in translation means recognizing also that Israel's God can either be presiding over the divine council or standing with these gods in the assembly with El presiding. The verb נצב in v. 1 is usually taken to mean "take [his] place" or "preside" in reference to Israel's God, but in this light it can mean that Israel's God is standing with the other gods "to indicate the position of the inferior relative to the superior,"[6] who would be the seated El. This hierarchical spatial relationship of seated/standing is prevalent in ancient Near Eastern literature and iconography. Israel's God in the midst of this assembly raises a question about the justice dispensed by these other beings and declares in v. 7 that they "shall die like mortals." If the אלהים are human judges this would make no sense, since humans are already mortal. Humans do not possess both divinity and immortality; "the only two groups believed to possess these attributes in the ancient Near East were gods and divine kings."[7] Since most of the gods in the ancient Near East had limited spheres of influence, and not all of them were responsible for justice, human kings with divine status would be the specific group Israel's God accuses in El's assembly. God uses כאדם ("like a human") sarcastically to put these divine kings in their place.[8]

The rhetorical question God poses in v. 2 functions as an accusation against these divine kings, and the imperatives in vv. 3-4 flesh out the nature of their wrongdoing: they pervert justice by failing to protect the "weak," "orphan," "lowly," "destitute," and "needy," groups that warrant royal empathy and action. Certainly Israel viewed its kings as responsible for overseeing justice (Pss 45:6b-7a; 72:1-4, 12-14; 2 Sam 15:2-6; Isa 9:2-7; 11:1-5; Mic 3:9-12). Verses 2 and 4b bracket the list of the marginalized with the word "wicked," suggesting that the vulnerable are always under attack by the powerful because the powerful show partiality in judgment. Tanakh warns often against such partiality (e.g., Lev 19:9-10, 15, 34; Deut 1:16-17; 16:19; 24:17-18). God describes these divine kings who pervert justice as having "neither knowledge nor understanding" (cp. Ps 92:6); they "walk around in darkness" (v. 5ab). Lack of knowledge and darkness symbolize the absence of order in the world; indeed, God asserts that "all the foundations of the earth are shaken" (v. 5c) because of these divine kings without understanding. Verse 5 switches from the direct

6. Ibid., 226.
7. Ibid., 230.
8. See kings who thought themselves divine in Ezek 28:1-10 (the king of Tyre); Isa 14:3-12 (the king of Babylon); Dan 11:36-39 (Antiochus IV Epiphanes).

second-person address in vv. 2-4 to a third-person description, which is "a typical feature of a vision report, an interjection"[9] (cp. 1 Kgs 22; Job 1–2; and Zech 3:1–6:8). This interjection serves to emphasize that justice is "the cornerstone of the universe."[10] Psalm 82 defines justice as protecting the weak. Without justice, the world slips into chaos (Pss 75:22-23; 96:10; Hos 4:1-3; Isa 24:1-6; Jer 4:23-26; Gen 6). Given this emphasis, it is not surprising that the verb שׁפט ("judge, rule") occurs four times in Psalm 82, in vv. 1, 2, 3, and 8. The chiastic structure of the psalm also makes this point about the centrality of justice:[11]

A 1: God stands and judges (שׁפט)
    B 2-4: divine kings confronted
        C 5: chaos
    B' 6-7: divine kings confronted
A' 8: God petitioned to rise (קום) and judge (שׁפט)

Chaos, not justice, stands at the center. That is what demands redress.

Critique of Kings

Humans and God have always had an intertwined relationship. Humans are the apex of creation in Genesis 1. Psalm 8 beautifully describes humans as little less than gods. "What are human beings that you are mindful of them, mortals that you care for them? Yet you have made them little lower than God" (Ps 8:4-5). Made in the image of God, humans are reflections of the divine, and the social hierarchy of the ancient world puts kings at the top of the social pyramid, with even greater proximity to the divine.

With this in mind, we may perhaps perceive Psalm 82 as using the voice of God to critique the ignoble actions of kings. By this reading, the object of Psalm 82 is kings who refuse to acknowledge the injustice around them. Verses 6-7 take on a mocking tone, poking fun at the mortal human kings who imagine themselves as high and mighty gods but accomplish little more than their own opulence.

The spatial aspects of the psalm also align with a tongue-in-cheek interpretation. Though kings have constructed

---

9. Trotter, "Death," 236.

10. Miller, "When the Gods Meet," 4.

11. Lowell K. Handy, "Sounds, Words and Meanings in Psalm 82," *JSOT* 47 (1990): 51–66, at 63. Where Handy sees "gods" confronted, I have substituted "divine kings," in line with Trotter.

themselves as deities, it is God who holds judgment amid this "divine council." God sits above mortal kings, who only pretend to be immortal. Their reign is impermanent, as "all the nations belong to you [God]" (82:8). Ultimately, kings are like any common regent. They rise and fall; they die like everyone else.

As a cipher for the critique of kings, the psalm gives a voice to those who must live with the decisions kings make. It is a call to action for those who have all the necessary power and resources to solve injustices but continue to ignore the social and economic problems of the people they are charged to serve.

Amy Beth Jones

Herbert J. Levine persuasively suggests that the speaker hurls a bold challenge at God in v. 8. God is "the ultimate addressee" who "does not speak performatively but rather fictively, in a representation of how God might speak in a divine tribunal if we humans were privileged to overhear it."[12] More to the point, the doing of justice that God demands of the divine kings in vv. 2-4 "is precisely what the psalmist demands of God on earth" in v. 8: "judge [שפט]!" Within the poem's inner dialogue, God's accusation is understood through the lens of v. 8, "so that the whole poem becomes charged with irony."[13] The final line represents "a redressive action, an attempt to remedy a breach between human reality and divine rhetoric."[14] Like Psalms 79 and 80, Psalm 82 critiques God's unfaithfulness. None of these three psalms lets God off the hook when raising the theodicy question. God's response to the critique in both cases is not recorded, but it will determine the future of the relationship between God and Israel, a relationship that has been badly ruptured.

Levine notes that Martin Buber termed v. 8 of Psalm 82 a cry uttered in the time of "God's hiddenness."[15] God's hiddenness suggests the story of Esther as intertext for Psalm 82. The book of Esther, whose name comes from the root סתר ("hide"), does not mention the name of God, whose complete absence from the canonical story is remedied by the Greek

---

12. Levine, *Sing unto God*, 116. Note that Levine also argues for "gods" to mean "divine beings" and points out the ambiguity of the same word being used also for Israel's God.

13. Ibid., 117.

14. Ibid., 118.

15. Ibid., 215.

Additions to Esther in the Apocrypha. Esther hides her own Jewish identity at the request of Mordecai. Esther is an orphan; Esther 2:7 tells us that "she had neither father nor mother" and that her uncle Mordecai "adopted her as his own daughter." Both Mordecai and Esther are Diaspora Jews in the midst of the Persian Empire ruled by the powerful but unstable King Ahasuerus; they are clearly marginalized, and it is only her beauty and his chance overhearing of a plot against the king that help them to survive in this unstable sociopolitical environment. Esther's powerlessness is emphasized by the use of the verb לָקַח ("take" in the Niphal) in 2:8: "Esther also was taken into the king's palace and put in custody of Hegai, who had charge of the women." Esther was one of many young beauties who were being evaluated as possible replacements for the proud Queen Vashti, who had refused the king's command to be ogled at a drunken banquet. Later, Haman, a descendant of Agag and himself a foreigner at Ahasuerus's court, tricks the king into decreeing a pogrom against all of the Jews in the kingdom by insisting that the Jews "do not keep the king's law" (3:8). Thus Esther, Mordecai, and all the Jews in the Persian Empire need protection; they can count themselves among the orphan, lowly, and weak mentioned in Psalm 82:3-4. Esther notes their precarious position when she learns of Haman's treacherous maneuvers: "we have been sold, I and my people, to be destroyed, to be killed and to be annihilated" (Esth 7:4; cp. 8:6 and Ps 44:4; Jdt 7:25).

Though Esther does not pray, practice dietary laws, or mention God's name in the Hebrew book that bears her name, we can imagine that she privately prayed Psalm 82 at the end of chapter 8, after Mordecai has warned her that she will not escape the king's decree to annihilate the Jews. After she decides to risk death by approaching the king without being summoned (Esth 8:16), we can imagine that she challenges God to come out of hiding and assume the role of God of all the nations, even of Persia (or Greece or Rome): "Rise up, O God, judge the earth; for all the nations belong to you!" (Ps 82:8). The word כל is repeated in Psalm 82:5c, 6b, and 8c to emphasize the desired universal power of Israel's God. Bold enough to risk death by appearing unsummoned before the king (Esth 2:11; 5:1-2) and to trick the wily Haman (5:8; 7:1-8), Esther is certainly bold enough to challenge God with God's own words in Psalm 82. The bold Esther of the Hebrew text who would pray Psalm 82 is not the Esther of the Greek Additions who faints when she approaches the king unbidden and whose prayer evokes God's sympathy for her and her sinful people's precarious position.

Esther sees that King Ahasuerus challenges Israel's God by acting like a divine king. The first chapter of Esther flaunts the king's power and excessive wealth and notes the extent of his vast empire and its complex administrative machine. His government is portrayed throughout the book as "virtually omnipotent" yet is critiqued at the same time; this critique "reinforces those in power as Other and not to be trusted by insiders."[16] The pairing of wicked/lowly and gods/God in Psalm 82 echoes the pairing of Haman/Mordecai, Haman/Esther, and King Ahasuerus/Israel's hidden God; these pairings underscore the sense of Us versus Them. They also undergird the irony that infuses the Esther novella. "Esther is a female Jewish orphan, the least powerful member (orphan) of the less powerful gender (female) of a powerless people (Jews) in the mighty Persian Empire. Yet she reaches the heights of power, and the powerful man who attempted to slaughter her and her people ends up dead himself"[17] on the gallows he had originally erected for Mordecai. In Psalm 82 irony also resides in the fact that Israel's God calls for justice from divine kings while apparently not ensuring justice for God's own people and remaining hidden on earth.

Esther boldly prays for a reversal of this situation in the words of Psalm 82 and comes to experience such reversal. The king's decree in Esther 8:11 allows the Jews to defend themselves and "annihilate" (7:4) anyone who attacks them. The Jews rejoice and another reversal occurs: "many peoples of the country professed to be Jews, because the fear of the Jews had fallen upon them" (8:17; cp. 9:2, 3). The marginalized are now the feared. The notion of justice as protecting the marginalized is found in the practices of the festival of Purim, which celebrates the victory of the Jews over their enemies. Gifts of food are exchanged and sent to the poor (Esth 9:22; 10:3). An imagined superscription for Psalm 82 might be: "A psalm, when Esther learned that her people would be annihilated."

16. Jean-Daniel Macchi, "Denial, Deception, or Force: How to Deal with Powerful Others in the Book of Esther," in *Imagining the Other and Constructing Israelite Identity in the Early Second Temple Period*, ed. Ehud Ben Zvi and Diana V. Edelman (London: Bloomsbury, 2014), 219–29, at 220, 223.

17. Sidnie White Crawford, "Esther," in *Women's Bible Commentary*, ed. Carol A. Newsom, Sharon H. Ringe, and Jacqueline E. Lapsley, 3rd ed. (Louisville, KY: Westminster John Knox, 2012), 201–7, at 203.

Psalm 83

Corrupting Retributive Violence

Another communal lament and the last of the Asaph psalms, Psalm 83 opens with a petition (v. 1) that contrasts God's silence with the threatening speech of the enemies in vv. 4 and 12. These enemy quotations emphasize the theological problem Psalm 83 addresses: the seeming absence of God in the midst of peril. While God holds God's peace and keeps "still" (v. 1b), God's enemies are laying "crafty plans" (v. 3), conspiring together (v. 5) against God's people, and uttering public threats. The contrast functions to persuade or shame God to take action. The urgency of the community's plea is underscored by the repetition of God's name at the beginning and end of v. 1 as well as by the clear link to the first of the Asaph psalms, 50:3 (cp. Isa 62:1-2, 6-7; 42:14), which asserts: "Our God comes and does not keep silence."

The threat described in vv. 2-8 seems overwhelming. The enemies are "in tumult" (v. 2; cp. Ps 46:6; Jer 6:22) and are ganging up against God's people (v. 5). The use of the second-person masculine singular possessive suffix "your" in vv. 2a, 3a, and 3b makes it clear that the people's enemies are also God's enemies (cp. Exod 23:22), which offers another motivation for God to grant the people's petition. The enemies are referred to as "those who hate you" (v. 2b). They plan nothing less than to "wipe out" Israel as a nation (v. 4a); the verb כחד in the Hiphil means literally "make disappear; destroy." They also plan to take possession of "the dwellings

315

Psalm 83:1-18

A Song. A Psalm of Asaph.

[1]O God, do not keep silence;
    do not hold your peace or be
        still, O God!
[2]Even now your enemies are in tu-
    mult;
    those who hate you have
        raised their heads.
[3]They lay crafty plans against your
    people;
    they consult together against
        those you protect.
[4]They say, "Come, let us wipe
    them out as a nation;
    let the name of Israel be re-
        membered no more."

[5]They conspire with one accord;
    against you they make a
        covenant—
[6]the tents of Edom and the
    Ishmaelites,
    Moab and the Hagrites,
[7]Gebal and Ammon and Amalek,
    Philistia with the inhabitants of
        Tyre;
[8]Assyria also has joined them;
    they are the strong arm of the
        children of Lot.   *Selah*

[9]Do to them as you did to
    Midian,
    as to Sisera and Jabin at the
        Wadi Kishon,

of God" (v. 12). The NRSV translates "pastures of God," but the feminine plural construct noun נאות can mean either "pastures" or "abode, residence." Perhaps this noun is intentionally ambivalent. The wiping out of a whole people means that their land, a gift from God, is now available for the aggressors to take. It also suggests that the God of this people and land is powerless to intervene and unfaithful to those who call upon God and that such a God will be defeated.[1]

The strange list in vv. 6-8 of enemy peoples involved in conspiring against God and God's people is not seen elsewhere, and most of those listed never joined together in a coalition. If Psalm 83 responds to exile, it is striking that Babylon is not among the list. Most interpreters view the list as hyperbolic and stereotypical; it is probably a "cultic list" developed for worship rather than a historical catalogue; its roots may be in ancient Egyptian execration rituals.[2] The petition in v. 9a demands that God "do to them as you did to Midian" and is followed in vv. 9b-11 by examples of enemy leaders defeated by God during the conquest of Canaan: Sisera

1. Rolf A. Jacobson, *"Many Are Saying": The Function of Direct Discourse in the Hebrew Psalter*, JSOTSup 397 (Edinburgh: T & T Clark, 2004), 48.
2. Erhard Gerstenberger, *Psalms, Part 2, and Lamentations* (Grand Rapids, MI: Eerdmans, 2001), 119.

¹⁰who were destroyed at En-dor,
who became dung for the
ground.
¹¹Make their nobles like Oreb and
Zeeb,
all their princes like Zebah and
Zalmunna,
¹²who said, "Let us take the pastures of God
for our own possession."

¹³O my God, make them like whirl-
ing dust,
like chaff before the wind.
¹⁴As fire consumes the forest,
as the flame sets the mountains ablaze,
¹⁵so pursue them with your tempest
and terrify them with your hurricane.
¹⁶Fill their faces with shame,
so that they may seek your
name, O LORD.
¹⁷Let them be put to shame and
dismayed forever;
let them perish in disgrace.
¹⁸Let them know that you alone,
whose name is the LORD,
are the Most High over all the
earth.

and Jabin (Judg 4–5) and Oreb, Zeeb, Zebah, Zalmunna (Midianite chief-tains defeated by Gideon in Judg 7–8). Marc Zvi Brettler[3] suggests that God as Warrior is the central image of vv. 9-11, even though the word "warrior" and its related terms are not used. Israel urges God to act as God has acted in the past against enemies (Pss 44, 77, 80).

Where Is Jael?

Where is Jael? Psalm 83:9 mentions Sisera's death but says nothing of Jael's role in his demise. The failure to remember female characters is endemic to the Hebrew Bible, but the sting of rejection ripples through the experience of women into the present. With one swipe of the pen, Jael's story is forgotten. Even so, deep within the sharpness of Jael's neglect is relief that Psalm 83 spares Jael the trauma of reliving Sisera's gruesome death. The story is grisly. Sisera flees from Barak and his army and finds refuge in Jael's tent. She welcomes him, offering him sanctuary, a place to rest, a blanket, and even milk. Jael mothers the unwitting Sisera to death just as he drifts to slumber. Lifting a tent peg, she drives it through Sisera's skull. The scene has sexual overtones,

---

3. Marc Zvi Brettler, "Images of YHWH the Warrior in Psalms," *Semeia* 61 (1993): 135–65.

maternal threads, and a violent ending.

Intoxicated by the power Jael displays in abruptly murdering the enemy, the reader cheers at her courage, but the authors of *Soul Repair*,[4] Rita Nakashima Brock and Gabriella Lettini, caution us to consider the full impact the act of killing has on an individual as they describe the moral effect of war. Killing takes the life of one and the humanity of the other. For those trained to kill, or for those for whom killing is a reflex, the moral and spiritual injury is serious and sometimes fatal. It causes a crisis of conscience and endangers the soul. Should Jael be celebrated as a hero, or does such recognition diminish the strong possibility that her murder of Sisera unraveled her humanity? Perhaps it is a kindness to Jael that the deity takes responsibility for Sisera's life and death in this psalm, freeing her from any moral responsibility.

In the final lines of Psalm 83 creation is reversed (cp. Jer 4:23-26). People return to dust, plants are reduced to ashes, mountains are set ablaze, and the waters become untamed. It is as though the soul-crushing moral injury of murder is externalized. What was once "very good" is decimated; it reverts to the primal void (Gen 1:2). War extinguishes light, life, and hope.

Amy Beth Jones

God as Warrior uses meteorological weapons (Ps 11:6) to vanquish the enemy: wind (v. 13; cp. Pss 1:4; 35:5; Job 21:18; Isa 17:13), fire and flame (v. 14), tempest and hurricane (v. 15); these weapons show God's "superlative power." The psalmist wants the enemy consumed "as fire consumes the forest" (v. 14a) as retribution for the enemy's declaration that Israel is to be "wiped out" as a nation (v. 4a). Do to *them* what they planned to do to *us*; they are Other and must be destroyed as well as shamed (vv. 16a, 17a). As much as the community wants the enemies destroyed, it also wants them to "seek your name, O Lord" (v. 16b) and recognize that God alone, "whose name is the Lord," is the Most High (v. 18). Here again Israel demands retribution for the enemy declaration in verse 4: "let the name of Israel be remembered no more," which by implication means blotting out the name of Israel's God as well.

---

4. Rita Nakashima Brock and Gabriella Lettini, *Soul Repair: Recovering from Moral Injury after War* (Boston: Beacon Press, 2012).

The Other as Threat

How to talk about the animosity, hatred, and vengeance sought, perhaps deservedly so, in the utterance of these verses from Psalm 83? This is the hard question—particularly in light of the current state of affairs between Israel and Palestine over land and the daily loss of innocent lives caught in the conflict over whose land, whose God, whose right. The question from the psychoanalytic point of view is "Can *I* exist if the *Other* remains?" By Other here I am referring to both internal others—images and perspectives from within that arise to meet our ego-conscious perspective and press in on us to see and hear in different ways—and external others, those with whom we are confronted who hold opposing views, political persuasions, and religious convictions. What we often neglect to account for is how much the internal others are projected on these external others around us, those that challenge our way of living, being, and seeing (or not seeing) our own selves in the world. When we can stay in dialogue with our internal others, those that threaten our conventional life, our conscious way of living, we can begin to withdraw their projections from the external others. It is only then that I can start to hear the Other as a true other with her own point of view that does not have to threaten mine.

The plea in Psalm 83 is essentially one of self- or communal validation. The feeling here is that if Israel's enemy were to win, Israel would no longer exist, would be made to disappear. So the question remains: "Can I exist if the Other exists?" If the one who is my opposite, the one who worships a different God, who does not honor my God's name, who lives, eats, and celebrates differently from me is allowed to exist, how can I exist alongside them? If the two of us remain side by side, in the same land, in the same territory, does that nullify my God? My belief? My perspective? Me?

Ruth Stein, a psychoanalyst in New York City, explains that the religious quest, while felt to be a search for meaning, is at the same time a "series of transformations of fear." The fear is related to the fear of death, of human finitude, and also of the "other's existence, of the force of the other's own intentions and aims." She surmises:

> The desire to put an end to these threats leads to the search for radical solutions, such as fundamentalism. The fundamentalist mind-set . . . would then be the quest to rid oneself of one's fears and finitude and loss of identity and self-valida-tion. Such a mindset aims at liquidating the necessity to surrender and depend on

other human beings; it wants to destroy its own fears of dependency and of fear and the helplessness, humiliation, and rage they engender. The transcendence of fear and rage can be accomplished through processes of idealization and purification, which are meant to oppose destruction of the self even as they enact destruction on another level.[5]

Therefore the urge to annihilate, or the plea for God to annihilate, is related to the deep-seated anxiety that two opposing views cannot exist together without one nullifying the other. This has important ramifications for how we engage in our own quest for meaning. It also has implications for interreligious dialogue and offers a new lens for understanding religious violence across the globe. In our personal and often collective responses to the numinous, to what is supremely other, there lies a fear that another's response or engagement with this numinous will eradicate our own experience. Psalm 83 leaves room for articulating such a fear residing in the human experience. At the same time it creates space for us to reflect on why we experience the Other as a threat to our own personal existence.

Tiffany Houck-Loomis

Psalms 82 and 83 are linked by use of אליון ("Most High," 82:6 and 83:18) and "earth" (82:8 and 83:18). Thus it makes sense that the story of Esther presents itself as intertext for Psalm 83 as it did for Psalm 82. Psalm 83 and the story of Esther share violent, retributive language. Just as Haman tricked the king into issuing an irrevocable decree "to destroy, to kill, and to annihilate [אבד] all Jews" in the Persian Empire (Esth 3:13), Esther tricks him into a second decree that allows for defensive vengeance: "the king allowed the Jews who were in every city to assemble and defend their lives, to destroy, to kill, and to annihilate [אבד] any armed force of any people or province that might attack them" (Esth 8:11). Annihilation of the enemies is what the psalmist demands in 83:17: "let them perish [אבד] in disgrace"; tit for tat. The terror Israel experienced because of the enemy threats will now be experienced by the enemy: "terrify [בהל] them with your hurricane" (83:15b). Similarly, in the book of Esther the king's first

---

5. Ruth Stein, *For the Love of the Father: A Psychoanalytic Study of Religious Terrorism* (Stanford, CA: Stanford University Press, 2010), 45–46.

decree about destroying the Jews is met with great mourning and lamenting by Mordecai and the Jews of the Empire (4:1-4), while the king's second edict causes "many of the peoples of the country" to profess "to be Jews, because the fear [פחד, 'terror'] of the Jews had fallen upon them" (Esth 8:17; 9:2); terror is reversed, just as it is in Psalm 83. An imagined superscription for Psalm 83 might be: "A lament, when Esther and the Jews of Persia learned that they would be annihilated."

The story of Judith also suggests itself as intertext for Psalm 83, for some of the same reasons that Esther does, particularly the violence of Holofernes's decapitation at Judith's hand (Jdt 13:6-10) and the slaughter of his retreating, terrified army (15:1-7). Just as the might of the Persian Empire in Esther established "a relationship of alterity between those who exercise power and those who perceive power as a constraint imposed on them,"[6] so too in Judith the awesome power of Holofernes's Assyrian army described in chapters 1–3 also creates an Other who is destroyed "by the hand of a woman" (Jdt 9:10; 16:5). Psalm 83 and the books of Judith and Esther all resist this Other through the strategy of violence. In Esther, however, "the act of war is a last resort" that prompts "a reflection over the legitimacy of the use of force more than it glorifies violence."[7] Similar tension appears in Judith's prayer to God before she leaves Bethulia for the Assyrian camp. She declares that the Assyrians "do not know that you are the Lord who crushes wars. . . . Break their strength by your might . . . . For your strength does not depend on numbers, nor your might on the powerful. But you are the God of the lowly, helper of the oppressed, upholder of the weak" (Jdt 9:7-8, 11). God ends war by Judith's hand, which is not the way of the Assyrian generals. "It is not by male and military dominance that Yhwh unfolds his power, but through female beauty that can paralyze men"; by reinforcing male and female stereotypes "the construction of femininity has a positive value, while male forms of rule and behavior (strength, use of violence in war) are rejected. At this point there is a glimpse of a critical perspective toward patriarchal forms of rule and forms of rule that are

---

6. Jean-Daniel Macchi, "Denial, Deception, or Force: How to Deal with Powerful Others in the Book of Esther," in *Imagining the Other and Constructing Israelite Identity in the Early Second Temple Period*, ed. Ehud Ben Zvi and Diana V. Edelman (London: Bloomsbury, 2014), 219–29, at 219.

7. Ibid., 226.

understood as male, such as war and imperialism."[8] The stories of these two women as intertexts help us to recognize the seeming contradiction in Psalm 83 between a God who destroys Israel's enemies (vv. 13-15) and a God who shames them "so that they may seek your name, O LORD" (vv. 16-18). The interplay of these texts prompts deep reflection about violence in the midst of our violently conflicted world today.

8. Claudia Rakel, "Judith: About a Beauty Who Is Not What She Pretends to Be," in *Feminist Biblical Interpretation: A Compendium of Critical Commentary*, ed. Luise Schottroff and Marie-Theres Wacker (Grand Rapids, MI: Eerdmans, 2012), 515–30, at 518.

Psalm 84

Unrequited Love

After the intense pain, questions, petitions, and challenges expressed in Asaph Psalms 74, 77, 79, 80, 82, and 83, Psalm 84 washes over the reader much like a soothing balm, at least on the surface. A closer look at the psalm, however, confirms that the painful intensity of the previous psalms continues, albeit in a different way. Psalm 84 introduces a group of Korah psalms (84, 85, 87, 88), and like Psalm 42:1-2, which begins an earlier Korah collection (Pss 42–49), it expresses longing for God.[1] The opening words, מה ידידות ("how lovely!"), convey "a virtually erotic intensity in the speaker's longing for the temple on Mount Zion."[2] Interpreters make several connections between "lovely" and the root דוד: in terms of "love" or "beloved," as in the superscription of Psalm 45 ("a love song"; also see Isa 5:1); David's name; God's "beloved" in Psalms 60:7; 127:2; and Solomon's special name, Jedidiah (2 Sam 12:24-25; cp. Benjamin in Deut 33:12). "In a word, the poet is in love with the temple."[3]

---

1. Erhard Gerstenberger, *Psalms, Part 2, and Lamentations* (Grand Rapids, MI: Eerdmans, 2001), 123.

2. Robert Alter, *The Book of Psalms* (New York: Norton, 2007), 297.

3. Konrad Schaefer, *Psalms*, Berit Olam (Collegeville, MN: Liturgical Press, 2001), 209.

Psalm 84:1-12

To the leader: according to the Gittith.
Of the Korahites. A Psalm.

¹How lovely is your dwelling place,
O LORD of hosts!
²My soul longs, indeed it faints
for the courts of the LORD;
my heart and my flesh sing for joy
to the living God.

³Even the sparrow finds a home,
and the swallow a nest for herself,
where she may lay her young,
at your altars, O LORD of hosts,

my King and my God.
⁴Happy are those who live in your
house,
ever singing your praise.   *Selah*

⁵Happy are those whose strength
is in you,
in whose heart are the high-
ways to Zion.
⁶As they go through the valley of
Baca
they make it a place of springs;
the early rain also covers it
with pools.

The intensity of this love, expressed in hyperbolic language, surpasses what is found in other Zion psalms (46, 48, 76, 87, 122). We must ask, however, whether this intense emotion is a pilgrim's expression of delight upon finally reaching the temple or a cry of searing, unrequited love. Many interpreters assume that Psalm 84 offers a "happy image." Could this psalm, like Psalm 42–43, express instead a taunting memory of past experience of temple worship that is not now available to the psalmist? Since Scripture does not come with stage directions, how might we modulate our voice in speaking Psalm 84? What emotions might we convey in the speaking of the psalm?

The words of Psalm 84 give us mixed signals in this regard. In v. 2 the psalmist's נפש ("being," "throat") "longs" and "faints" for the Lord's courts, while her "heart" and "flesh" "sing for joy." The whole person of the speaker is absolutely caught up in thoughts and images of the temple, but in what sense? The word כסף ("longs" in the Niphal) is found in only a few places in Tanakh: Psalm 17:12; Genesis 31:30; Zephaniah 2:1; Job 14:15. This is a singular emotion, unlike any other. The word כלה (NRSV: "faints" means literally "end, be finished"). The juxtaposition of longing and fainting with singing for joy is intentionally jarring and should cause us to linger over these words. Another mixed signal comes from the image of sparrows nesting in the temple (vv. 3-4). Birds as a metaphor for the psalmist occur several times in the Psalter. In Psalm 11:1, for example, friends of the speaker urge her to "flee like a bird to the mountains" to escape the wicked. In Psalm 55:6 the psalmist wishes to "fly away" like

⁷They go from strength to
strength;
the God of gods will be seen in
Zion.

⁸O Lᴏʀᴅ God of hosts, hear my
prayer;
give ear, O God of
Jacob!   *Selah*
⁹Behold our shield, O God;
look on the face of your
anointed.

¹⁰For a day in your courts is better
than a thousand elsewhere.

I would rather be a doorkeeper in
the house of my God
than live in the tents of wickedness.
¹¹For the Lᴏʀᴅ God is a sun and
shield;
he bestows favor and honor.
No good thing does the Lord withhold
from those who walk uprightly.
¹²O Lᴏʀᴅ of hosts,
happy is everyone who trusts
in you.

a dove from the horror that overwhelms her in the city, and in Psalm 102:6-7 she is "a lonely bird" and an "owl of the wilderness" in her suffering. In each case birds symbolize the vulnerability, defenselessness, and suffering of the psalmist. These are not "happy" images.

Many interpreters take delight in the image of sparrows flitting about in God's house and point to the sense of security and protection the metaphor conveys. Herbert J. Levine, however, hears "plaintive tones" in vv. 1-3 that "convey the pilgrimage experience from the point of view of those who cannot participate." That the birds have a home in the temple "points to the speaker's homelessness." Rather than a delightful image, the sparrows suggest that "the state of being cut off from the holy pilgrimage community makes one something less than human."[4] Both Psalms 42–43 and 84 use animal imagery to express the depth of the psalmists' suffering. That an animal can find a place close to God while the psalmist cannot simply intensifies the psalmist's pain. The psalmist is looking for the safety the sparrow finally "finds" (v. 3a) but the psalmist has not yet experienced. Psalm 84 may be a Zion psalm, "but it is a Zion longed for rather than possessed."[5]

Much has been written about the "beatitudes" found in Psalm 84:4, 5, 12: "happy are those. . . ." These אשרי sayings occur twenty-five times in

4. Herbert J. Levine, *Sing unto God a New Song: A Contemporary Reading of the Psalms* (Bloomington: Indiana University Press, 1995), 74–75.
5. Richard J. Clifford, *Psalms 73–150* (Nashville, TN: Abingdon Press, 2003), 74.

the Psalter (e.g., Pss 40:4; 41:1; 119:1-2), three times more often than in Proverbs. The very first verse of Psalm 1 begins with a beatitude, which suggests that the rest of the Psalms concern the nature of happiness or blessedness. Those deemed "happy" in Psalm 84 include "those who live in your house" (v. 4; cp. Pss 65:4; 91:1-10), which refers back to the sparrows of v. 3 and to the temple personnel; "those whose strength is in you" (v. 5); and "everyone who trusts in you" (v. 12). The psalm moves from the specific to the more general and all-encompassing, which is uncommon in poetry. The canonical arrangement of the Psalms, from a preponderance of laments to hymns of praise and thanksgiving, suggests "a dynamic of happiness that finds a way *through* misery rather than around it."[6]

Psalm 84, however, yearns for happiness rather than celebrating happiness achieved. The psalmist also recognizes that happiness is a gift from God that requires human effort, particularly in terms of trust (v. 12; cp. Ps 40:4) and walking "uprightly" (v. 11; cp. Pss 15:1-2; 89:15). Verses 5-7 describe the pilgrimage through the dry Valley of Baca, a place unknown, on the way to Zion. The valley is transformed by springs and pools of water (v. 6). Second Isaiah also describes this transformation of the land (Isa 35:6-7; 41:18). Lack of water and its miraculous provision also figure prominently in the wilderness stories (Exod 16–17; Num 11; 14). Many interpreters suggest Psalm 84 is connected with the fall festival of Sukkoth, which occurs before the early rains. The Septuagint version of Psalm 84's superscription—"for the wine-presser"—strengthens this connection. Verses 8-9 offer intercession for "our shield" and "your anointed" (v. 9), either the king (Pss 2:2; cp. 61:6-7) or the high priest if this psalm emerged out of exile, when a king was not possible under Persian rule. God is often called "shield" (Pss 3:3; 18:2; 28:7). Following the intercession the psalmist returns to longing for the temple (vv. 10-12). A final beatitude closes the psalm.

The repeated use of the epithet "LORD of Hosts" for God in vv. 1, 3, 8, 12 (see Pss 24, 46, 48, 59, 69, 80, 84, 89), reinforced by "my King" in v. 3d, suggests the image of God as Divine Warrior who leads Israel's army and the heavenly armies (see 1 Kgs 22:19). Taking this together with the bird imagery that implies the psalmist's homelessness and suffering, one can imagine the psalmist in a situation of war, separated from the safety and protection of God's presence in the temple and desperately longing for it. This probable setting invites as intertext the story of the unnamed Israelite serving girl in 2 Kings 5. As "a young girl captive" (v. 2), this little girl is

6. William P. Brown, "Happiness and Its Discontents in the Psalms," in *The Bible and the Pursuit of Happiness*, ed. Brent A. Strawn (Oxford: Oxford University Press, 2012), 95–116, at 108.

truly homeless, plucked from her family in the land of Israel to serve the wife of the commander of the Syrian (Aramean) army, Naaman. Syria was a constant threat to Israel in the ninth century BCE. The little girl's "marginality as a child captive in enemy territory represents the weakness of the northern kingdom of Israel, which was unable to protect her and no doubt many others like her in time of war."[7] Unfortunately, many interpreters romanticize this little girl by focusing on her wish in 2 Kings 5:3: "If only my lord were with the prophet who is in Samaria," which they take as evidence of her compassionate choice to love rather than hate her enemy. Like Rahab in Joshua 2, she becomes a paradigm for healing in the midst of war and death. This expectation of her is perhaps more than her tiny shoulders can bear and does not accord with the stories of many children traumatized by war today or in the ancient world.

The text does not tell us why the little captive girl suggests a cure for Naaman. Perhaps she seeks revenge by sending Naaman back into Israelite territory where resentment lingers after his victory. Perhaps the hidden transcript here suggests that her voice has been co-opted by later editors of the Deuteronomistic History to make a theological point about God's sovereignty over all political power. Like Rahab in Joshua 2, she tells the exiles what they want and need to hear: that God works across national boundaries for restoration and peace. What gets overlooked in this interpretation is the reality of war. Women and children experience the brutality of war in ways that drown out hope, as the stories of Jael and Sisera's mother in Judges 4–5 make clear (cp. Lam 4:2, 4, 10; 5:11). Modern examples from Mali, the Sudan, the former Yugoslavia, and Syria horrify us: children are forced to serve in the army (e.g., the "Lost Boys" of the Sudan) and young girls are sexually abused by the soldiers who have abducted them (e.g., the victims of Boko Haram in Nigeria).

As Erhard Gerstenberger notes, Psalm 84 describes a "spiritual pilgrimage" in the imagination of the psalmist.[8] One can imagine the little servant girl making this pilgrimage in her mind to keep up her ties with her people and reinforce her identity amid her captors (see 1 Kgs 8:46-53). She clings to the northern kingdom's sanctuaries at Dan and Bethel as idealized memory and symbol of God's presence in her loneliness.

7. Esther M. Menn, "Child Characters in Biblical Narratives: The Young David (1 Samuel 16–17) and the Little Israelite Servant Girl (2 Kings 5:1-19)," in *The Child in the Bible*, ed. Marcia J. Bunge, et al. (Grand Rapids, MI: Eerdmans, 2008), 324–52, at 343.

8. Gerstenberger, *Psalms*, 125.

Space and Power

Social and cultural theorist Thomas Tweed argues that one of the roles of religion is to help people move through space and find a place. He writes: "Religious women and men make meaning and negotiate power as they appeal to contested historical traditions of storytelling, object making, and ritual performance in order to make homes (*dwelling*) and cross boundaries (*crossing*)."[9] The carefully arranged and thoughtfully chosen words of Ps 84 do more than simply describe a place. They transport the psalmist and her audience to Zion, to the divine court, the temple, enveloped in the presence of God. The words of the psalm orient devotees in time and space, appealing to religious traditions and spaces to help negotiate power.

It is clear from the psalm that the place described is not the place from which the psalmist writes but a place the psalmist longs to be. The mixed metaphors of Psalm 84 are a subtle commentary on the psalmist's situation. She dreams of idyllic Zion but the shadow side of her imagined paradise is an ugly reality. Her psalm is a subversive condemnation of her situation. The words of the psalm provide a cognitive "map" for those who want little more than to flee.

Amy Beth Jones

As the little slave girl prays Psalm 84 in her captivity she fills it with the pathos of her situation far from home. Like the sparrow, she hopes to nest in God's house someday; she prays that she too will "find" (v. 3a) a home there. She dares to imagine being "happy," that is, trusting in God. She constantly addresses God as "Lord of hosts," which reminds God of God's power as Divine Warrior to save her. This title for God expresses core testimony about the way God is supposed to act and implicitly critiques God's absence in her situation. God must act like "the God of gods" (v. 7b) whom Psalm 82 goads into appearing. The little girl also petitions God to "look on the face of your anointed," the face of the king. She calls the king "our shield" (v. 9a). In this phrase the first-person plural suffix expresses her solidarity with her people. The word "shield" connotes the king's role as God's instrument of her rescue. God is also her "shield" who will not withhold "one good thing" (v. 11). Again, core testimony intends to remind God of who God is and prompt God to action. Her

9. Thomas A. Tweed, *Crossing and Dwelling: A Theory of Religion* (Cambridge, MA: Harvard University Press, 2009), 74.

longing for God is painful and deep. God's name is invoked repeatedly: the word "God" appears seven times, the word "Lord" seven times, and the phrase "Lord of hosts" four times. Where else can she turn? Let us imagine a new superscription for Psalm 84: "To the leader. A Psalm. When the little servant girl was taken away captive to Syria."

Psalm 85

Promises to Keep

Powered by some of the most imaginative and evocative metaphors in the Bible, Psalm 85 counters our world of anxiety, scarcity, self-sufficiency, denial, amnesia, and despair with hope rooted in "God the Promise Keeper."[1] In vv. 1-13 the attributes of God are personified (cp. Ps 43:3), creating a remarkable image: חסד ("steadfast love" or "covenant loyalty") and "faithfulness" meet, and צדק ("righteousness") and שלום ("peace," "wholeness") kiss each other (v. 10). In Tanakh a kiss often expresses a greeting (Gen 29:11, 13; 33:4; 45:15; 48:10; Exod 4:27) or friendship (1 Sam 20:41; 2 Sam 15:5; 19:39). It is a sign of hospitality and welcome. "Faithfulness" is used twice, and "righteousness" three times in vv. 10-13. This repetition emphasizes a transformed future different from what is experienced in the present.

Energy infuses this transformation: faithfulness "will spring up from the ground" (v. 11a) and righteousness "will look down from the sky," joining heaven and earth. "Here the entire vocabulary of fidelity is thrown toward the future," toward the "not yet." Psalm 85 asserts that God is not finished: "The Lord will give" stands at the center of this

---

1. Walter Brueggemann, *From Whom No Secrets Are Hid: Introducing the Psalms*, ed. Brent Strawn (Louisville, KY: Westminster John Knox, 2014), 32.

Psalm 85:1-13

To the leader. Of the Korahites.
A Psalm.

¹Lᴏʀᴅ, you were favorable to your
land;
you restored the fortunes of
Jacob.
²You forgave the iniquity of your
people;
you pardoned all their
sin.   *Selah*
³You withdrew all your wrath;
you turned from your hot
anger.

⁴Restore us again, O God of our
salvation,
and put away your indignation
toward us.
⁵Will you be angry with us forever?
Will you prolong your anger to
all generations?
⁶Will you not revive us again,
so that your people may rejoice in you?
⁷Show us your steadfast love, O
Lᴏʀᴅ,
and grant us your salvation.

section (v. 12a).² In v. 13 the metaphor of pathway is offered from the
standpoint of God: righteousness "will make a path for [God's] steps."
"Pathway" is one of the two most prominent metaphors in the Psalter,
along with "refuge"; usually it signifies the path through life that
people must follow in order to reach God as refuge,³ but here God is
described as the one on the move; God's "glory" is coming to dwell in
the land (v. 9b). "God continues to open a path and move into the
future."⁴

What has prompted these delightful metaphors of divine movement
and personified attributes? Psalm 85 opens with a grateful review of
God's past acts of deliverance on Israel's behalf (vv. 1-3): "you were
favorable," "you restored," "you forgave," "you pardoned," "you withdrew your wrath," "you turned from anger." The heaping up of ways
to describe God's forgiveness in the past suggests that all is not well in
the present. God needs to be reminded about how God has acted and
should be acting toward Israel, God's people. No specific historical situations are mentioned, although "restore the fortunes" is a phrase often
used for Israel's return from exile (Jer 30:3, 18; 31:23; 33:7, 11; Ezek 39:25;

2. Ibid.

3. William P. Brown, *Seeing the Psalms: A Theology of Metaphor* (Louisville, KY:
Westminster John Knox, 2002), 42.

4. Konrad Schaefer, *Psalms*, Berit Olam (Collegeville, MN: Liturgical Press, 2001),
210.

⁸Let me hear what God the LORD will speak,
for he will speak peace to his people,
to his faithful, to those who turn to him in their hearts.
⁹Surely his salvation is at hand for those who fear him,
that his glory may dwell in our land.

¹⁰Steadfast love and faithfulness will meet;
righteousness and peace will kiss each other.
¹¹Faithfulness will spring up from the ground,
and righteousness will look down from the sky.
¹²The LORD will give what is good,
and our land will yield its increase.
¹³Righteousness will go before him,
and will make a path for his steps.

Job 42:10). The verb שׁוב ("turn, return, restore") brackets this opening section: "restored" (v. 1b) and "turned from" (v. 3b). This verb also ties vv. 1-3 to the complaint and petitions in vv. 4-7. Verse 4 begins with the petition "restore us again" (שׁוב; cp. Ps 126:1, 4). This linking verb makes it clear that the preceding look back is meant to motivate God to act now. This second section also ends with a petition; it is bracketed by the word "salvation," again pointing to the disparity between past and present (vv. 4a, 7b; also v. 9a).

A series of rhetorical questions in vv. 5-6 (cp. Ps 77:7-9) is sandwiched between the opening and closing petitions. The verb שׁוב appears again here in v. 6: "will you not revive us again?" These questions function to contrast God's past and present behaviors. They are full of reproach and pleading, reminding God about God's nature: "show us your חסד" (see v. 10a; Exod 34:6-7). Covenant loyalty challenges the notion that God could be angry at Israel "forever" (v. 5a). The psalm offers core testimony about who God is in the midst of lived counter-testimony about who God is not at the moment. Psalm 85 does not try to cover over this tension. The independent personal pronoun "you" in v. 6 lays responsibility for salvation squarely on God, the divine patron who must protect the dependent client.

Verses 8-13 seem to present some kind of oracle. The promise of the oracle shifts the tone of the psalm: אך ("surely") "[God's] salvation is at hand." The ties to God are reaffirmed—"his people," "his faithful" (v. 8bc)—yet the people have their own work to do. God's people are those who are "faithful," who "turn" (שוב; vv. 1, 3, 4, 6) to him in their hearts, who "fear him" (cp. Pss 61:5; 112:1-2). This good news communicates both hope and challenge and underscores the tension between the present and the not yet, which is ultimately up to God. The psalm ends with God on the way, moving from the anger Israel is currently experiencing to the now-hoped-for forgiveness experienced in the past.

The repetition of the word ארץ ("land") in vv. 1, 9, 11, and 12 suggests that "the problem reflected in the lament of verses 5-8 [4-7] has to do with the failure of the land to yield its expected produce."[5] If Israel lives its life in fear of the Lord, then "the LORD will give what is good," and the land "will yield its increase" (v. 12). In concrete terms, "good things" means a good harvest. Land is the source of life (Ps 25). This understanding concretizes the metaphor in v. 11a; faithfulness springing up from the ground connotes harvest. Similarly, in v. 11b righteousness looking down from the sky conjures the rain sent by God. God's judgment has meant that the land has not produced (cp. 1 Kgs 8:35-37). Psalm 85 pleads with God to reverse (שוב) that judgment. Similarly, the prophets often link the produce of the land with salvation (Amos 9:13; Isa 30:23-25; 32:15-18; 45:8; 55:10; 61:11).

The importance of land and harvest in the book of Ruth suggests the story of Ruth and Naomi as intertext for Psalm 85. The book of Ruth begins with a flight from famine in Bethlehem, the "house of bread," to Moab, where Naomi's husband and both of her sons (who have married Moabite women) die. In Ruth 1:6, Naomi learns that God has given her starving people food, and she resolves to return home, which she does at the beginning of the barley harvest (1:22). One can imagine Naomi hopefully praying Psalm 85 while living in Moab all those years, waiting for fertility to return to her land. The harvest motif continues in chapter 2, when Ruth gleans in Boaz's fields, and in chapter 3, when she asks him on the threshing floor to marry her. Also linking psalm and story is the repetition of the verb שוב in Ruth 1:6-18. Ruth's insistence on returning with Naomi to Bethlehem matches the instance of the psalmist that God turn back to God's people. Both psalm and story are concerned with relationship, security, and identity.

---

5. Patrick D. Miller, "The Land in the Psalms," in *The Land of Israel in Bible, History, and Theology: Studies in Honour of Ed Noort*, ed. Jacques van Ruiten and J. Cornelis DeVos (Leiden: Brill, 2009), 183–96, at 193.

Hope and Challenge

In contrast to Psalm 65, in which the rains have finally come and crops are flourishing, Psalm 85 is a plea for better times in the midst of difficult times. While God had returned the Israelites to their homeland, all is not well. The land is not producing. The people are hungry and anxious. Hopkins notes that the women and children, who played a significant role in the agricultural labor force, were particularly affected.

For many, in the intervening three thousand years since the psalm was probably written, little has changed. "Women are the backbone of the development of rural and national economies. . . . Despite the important roles they play in agricultural economies, rural women in Africa suffer from the highest illiteracy rates and are the most visible face of poverty."[6] Psalm 85 asks of God: "Will you be angry with us forever?" (v. 5). It would seem so.

Yet, later wisdom literature questioned the "just desserts" theology reflected in the psalm (e.g., Job and Ecclesiastes) and affirmed that the righteous often are punished unjustly. More often than not, it seems, it is human behavior that separates the poor and marginalized from enjoying God's bounty, rather than God's wrath. Consider the impact of First World carbon output that has warmed the planet and brought extended droughts, water, and food shortages to vulnerable populations worldwide, including Africa.[7] Consider the impact of First World resource extraction that has left vast South American forests denuded and local villages compromised.[8] Closer to home, consider the impact of providing energy to increasingly bigger homes and churches by removing whole mountaintops to extract coal in

---

6. Saquina Mucavele, "The Role of Rural Women in Agriculture," *World Farmers' Organization,* accessed July 1, 2015: http://www.wfo-oma.com/women-in-agriculture/articles/the-role-of-rural-women-in-agriculture.html.

7. Munir A. Hanjraa and M. Ejaz Qureshib, "Global Water Crisis and Future Food Security in an Era of Climate Change," *Food Policy* 35, no. 5 (October 2010): 365–77, accessed August 10, 2015: http://bwl.univie.ac.at/fileadmin/user_upload/lehrstuhl_ind_en_uw/lehre/ss11/Sem_Yuri/Water-food.pdf.

8. David S. Hammond, Valéry Gond, Benoit de Thoisy, Pierre-Michel Forget, and Bart P. E. DeDijn, "Causes and Consequences of a Tropical Forest Gold Rush in the Guiana Shield, South America," *AMBIO: A Journal of the Human Environment* 36, no. 8 (2007): 661–70, accessed August 10, 2015: http://www.jstor.org/stable/25547834?seq=1#page_scan_tab_contents.

rural West Virginia, causing toxins to accumulate in rural water supplies.[9]

And yet, Psalm 85 is a psalm of trust—not a psalm of thanks *after* the rains and the harvest, but rather a psalm expressing trust that they *will* come. And why do the people trust? Because they remember. They recall the times not only when God was "favorable to your land" (v. 1) but also when God "forgave the iniquity of your people . . . and pardoned their sin" (v. 2). Inherent in that forgiveness is recognition by the people of their sinfulness and a commitment to turn themselves around. The promise in v. 12 that God will "give what is good" is premised on righteousness going before God (v. 13)—a righteousness in which we are invited to participate so that all might enjoy God's bounty.

Beth Norcross

The importance of land and harvest in Psalm 85 also points to "Everywoman Eve" as one who might have prayed Psalm 85. "Everywoman Eve" is "every woman who lived in ancient Israel, or at least every ordinary woman. . . . The reality of daily life in ancient Israel informs the reality biblical Eve faces as she leaves the garden."[10] Despite being known as "a land flowing with milk and honey" (this phrase is used twenty times in Tanakh), studies show that "the imagery of a bountiful land reflects an ideal more than the reality"[11] in the face of numerous environmental constraints that supported only labor-intensive subsistence farming at a minimal level of self-sufficiency. "Women (and children too) were thus a vital part of the labor force of Israelite households, especially at harvest time"[12] in addition to their regular daily household maintenance tasks such as grinding and textile making. Food shortages caused by inadequate rainfall, war, or locusts meant chronic hunger and poor nutrition and interfered with the reproductive process. Women needed to produce children to meet labor needs for the survival of the household.

9. M. A. Palmer et al., "Mountaintop Mining Consequences," *Science* 327, no. 5962 (January 20, 2010): 148–49, accessed August 10, 2015: http://www.sciencemag.org /content/327/5962/148.

10. Carol Meyers, *Rediscovering Eve: Ancient Israelite Women in Context* (Oxford: Oxford University Press, 2013), 3.

11. Ibid., 43.

12. Ibid., 51.

In addition, food processing was mostly women's work in ancient Israel (see Lev 26:6; Jer 7:18), as it is in most cultures. Carol Meyers argues that "religious activities of Israelite households, carried out mainly by women and dealing with health issues, reproductive concerns, and agrarian fertility, would have been considered critical for [the household's] well-being."[13] These women knew the high stakes involved in their household religious practices (see Jer 44:15-19, 25). That Everywoman Eve embraced and prayed the hope of Psalm 85 for God's favor expressed in a bountiful harvest is not surprising.

Food Insufficiency Today

Both migration in time of famine and gleaning are short-term solutions to the problem of food insufficiency. As the ancient Near East's "breadbasket," Egypt was the destination for Abram and Sarai fleeing famine (Gen 12:10) and for Jacob's sons (Gen 42–43; 46). The United Nations World Food Programme[14] reports that 795 million people in the world are without enough food to lead a healthy, active life; that means one in nine people. Asia has the largest numbers of hungry people, fully two-thirds of the total. One in four people in sub-Saharan Africa are undernourished. Poor nutrition causes 45 percent of the deaths in children under five, a total of 3.1 million children per year. The Food and Agriculture Organization of the United Nations[15] reports that three-quarters of all the world's hungry live in rural areas, especially in the villages of Asia and Africa. They depend on agriculture, farming marginal land that is prone to flood or drought, and have no alternative income. Many migrate to shanty towns on the edge of cities. Perhaps Psalm 85 can help us to create the space to imagine ways in which we can help God move along a path of righteousness that creates food for all who are hungry.

Denise Dombkowski Hopkins

13. Ibid., 169.

14. http://wfpusa.org/; accessed February 5, 2016.

15. http://www.fao.org/home/en/; accessed February 5, 2016.

Psalm 86

Need and Devotion

With its puzzling placement as one of only two individual laments in the midst of the communal laments in book 3 of the Psalter (Ps 88 is the other), Psalm 86 grabs our attention. Interpreters have described it rather simply as an "anthology" or "collage" of borrowings from other texts; for example, compare v. 1a and Psalm 102:2b.[1] These "borrowings" are combined, however, in a powerful way in Psalm 86 and deserve a second look. The superscription, "A prayer of David," is the only David attribution in book 3. This superscription begs reassignment, since the psalm opens with a twofold petition to God supported by the motivation "for I am poor and needy" (v. 1b), hardly a descriptor of the future second king of Israel who is the resourceful son of the well-off Jesse of Bethlehem. The word אביון ("poor") denotes "one lacking material goods, honor, and power."[2] The psalmist counts herself

1. For other parallels, see v. 1b and Ps 40:17a; v. 2 and Ps 25:50; v. 4b and Ps 25:1; v. 8 and 2 Sam 7:22; 1 Kgs 8:23; and Jer 10:6-7; v. 10a, "you are great," and Deut 10:17; Jer 10:6; Pss 48:1; 95:3; 147:5; v. 10b, "you alone are God," and 2 Kgs 19:19; Pss 72:18; 83:18; 136:4; 148:13; v. 11a and Ps 27:11a; v. 14 and Ps 54:3; vv. 5 and 15 with Ps 103:8 and Exod 34:6; v. 16a and Ps 25:16a.

2. Patrick J. Hartin, "Poor," in *Eerdmans Dictionary of the Bible*, ed. David Noel Freedman (Grand Rapids, MI: Eerdmans, 2000), 1070–71, at 1070.

Psalm 86:1-17

A Prayer of David.

¹Incline your ear, O LORD, and answer me,
for I am poor and needy.
²Preserve my life, for I am devoted to you;
save your servant who trusts in you.
You are my God; ³be gracious to me, O LORD,
for to you do I cry all day long.
⁴Gladden the soul of your servant,
for to you, O LORD, I lift up my soul.
⁵For you, O LORD, are good and forgiving,
abounding in steadfast love to all who call on you.

⁶Give ear, O LORD, to my prayer;
listen to my cry of supplication.
⁷In the day of my trouble I call on you,
for you will answer me.

⁸There is none like you among the gods, O LORD,
nor are there any works like yours.
⁹All the nations you have made shall come
and bow down before you, O LORD,
and shall glorify your name.
¹⁰For you are great and do wondrous things;
you alone are God.
¹¹Teach me your way, O LORD,

among the most vulnerable in Israel: widows, orphans, and strangers/ aliens (Exod 23:6, 9; Deut 24:17-18; Prov 31:9; Pss 10:2; 82:3; Isa 32:7; Job 24). In her vulnerability she seeks God's protection in vv. 1-2 (cp. Pss 40:17; 70:5; 109:22) because God cares especially for the needy (Pss 9:18; 10:12; 35:10; 82:3-4; 138:6).

Clinging to God, the psalmist describes herself as God's "servant" three times, in vv. 2b, 4a, and 16b, using the possessive suffix "your" each time to claim relationship. In v. 16c the psalmist petitions God: "save the child of your serving girl." Most interpreters understand this request as another way to describe the male psalmist (along with "your servant") and gain God's sympathy by connecting him to his marginalized mother. The mother of the psalmist is mentioned in eleven psalms. In Psalms 86:16 and 116:16 "the mother is mentioned in the second part of a verse, parallel to a male in the first part."[3] Though the psalms are edited by a male elite and not specifically composed by and for women, one can imagine that women in ancient Israel reclaimed the masculine singular

---

3. Marc Zvi Brettler, "Mother of Psalmist (God's Serving Girl)," in *Women in Scripture*, ed. Carol Meyers (Boston: Houghton Mifflin, 2000), 296–97, at 297.

that I may walk in your truth;
give me an undivided heart to
revere your name.
¹²I give thanks to you, O LORD my
God, with my whole heart,
and I will glorify your name
forever.
¹³For great is your steadfast love
toward me;
you have delivered my soul
from the depths of
Sheol.

¹⁴O God, the insolent rise up
against me;
a band of ruffians seeks my
life,
and they do not set you before
them.

¹⁵But you, O LORD, are a God merciful and gracious,
slow to anger and abounding
in steadfast love and
faithfulness.
¹⁶Turn to me and be gracious to
me;
give your strength to your
servant;
save the child of your serving
girl.
¹⁷Show me a sign of your favor,
so that those who hate me
may see it and be put to
shame,
because you, LORD, have
helped me and com-
forted me.

word "servant" for their own situations. As one interpreter notes, v. 16c "refers to one who has been born into life-long servitude."[4]

The story of the mother of Moses and Miriam comes to mind in this connection as intertext for Psalm 86 (see Exod 2:1-10). Her people are enslaved and vulnerable at the beginning of the book of Exodus, oppressed by a pharaoh "who did not know Joseph" (Exod 1:8-14). A Levite woman married to a man from the house of Levi (Exod 2:1), she can readily be identified with "your serving girl" in Psalm 86, petitioning God in v. 16c to save her child, Moses. In order to escape Pharaoh's command that all newborn Hebrew boys be thrown into the Nile (Exod 1:22), she puts her son in a papyrus basket when he is three months old (Exod 2:2-4). One can imagine Moses' mother praying Psalm 86 as she places him tenderly in the basket. Pharaoh's daughter spots the basket while bathing and adopts Moses as her own (Exod 2:5-6); his mother's prayer is answered.

Moses' mother, identified as Jochebed in Exodus 6:20, combines in her petition a description of her social/economic vulnerability as "poor and

4. Konrad Schaefer, *Psalms*, Berit Olam (Collegeville, MN: Liturgical Press, 2001), 211.

needy" with an aspect of her character: "I am devoted to you; save your servant who trusts in you" (v. 2). She contends that devotion and trust mark her relationship with God; her self-descriptions function to motivate God to grant her petitions. In Psalm 86 "the speaker combines both desperate need and covenantal devotion, both of which place God under some obligation."[5] Though the psalmist-God relationship is a vertical one, the "loyalty language" used in Psalm 86 and other laments signifies "mutual interdependence, personal connection, and solidarity." Loyalty language figures prominently in patronage relationships in the ancient world; the patron is obligated to protect the client and the client is entitled to that protection. This loyalty language "endows the psalmist with relational power."[6] Just as she had defied the pharaoh's order, Jochebed dares to claim her relational power with God on behalf of her son. She connects her expectation of deliverance with "God's enhanced social reputation and honor." In v. 11 she promises that she "will glorify" (כבד) God's name forever, and in v. 9 she insists that "all the nations . . . shall glorify" (כבד) God's name if God grants her petition for deliverance. "In essence, the psalmist promises increasing numbers of clients who know and acclaim God's power and ability to deliver. . . . Public, demonstrable events are the means of maintaining honor."[7] In the mouth of the mother of Moses, these words point forward to the exodus event.

During all these years of enslavement Jochebed had kept alive the distant memory of God's promises to her ancestors—Abraham and Sarah, Isaac and Rebekah, Jacob and Leah. Her devotion and need join with appeals to God's character in vv. 5 and 15, anticipating the description of God in Exodus 34:6-7 and Numbers 14:18. God is "good and forgiving, abounding in חסד ['steadfast love,' better: 'covenant loyalty']" (v. 5) and "merciful and gracious" (v. 15a), "abounding in חסד and faithfulness" (v. 15b; cp. Ps 145:8). God's quality of mercy (רחום) is connected to the word רחם ("womb"); a woman's body part serves as the basis for God's characteristic compassion (cp. Exod 34:6; Deut 4:31; Ps 103:8). This point is underlined by the fact that Jochebed has recently given birth to Moses. As a new mother, she viscerally understands womb-love and expects it of God. She reminds God about who God is supposed to be

---

5. Walter Brueggemann, *From Whom No Secrets Are Hid: Introducing the Psalms*, ed. Brent Strawn (Louisville, KY: Westminster John Knox, 2014), 90.

6. Amy C. Cottrill, *Language, Power, and Identity in the Lament Psalms of the Individual* (New York and London: T & T Clark, 2008), 122.

7. Ibid., 130.

and how God is supposed to act in the covenant relationship. Moses' mother presses the expectation of divine obligation and fidelity by using the independent personal pronoun אני ("I") twice, in vv. 1b and 2a, and the second-person masculine singular independent personal pronoun אתה ("you") seven times (vv. 2b, 5a, 10ab, 12, 15a, 17). The contrast between "I" and "you" is also meant to propel God into action on behalf of her and her son, both of whom represent the whole group of enslaved Hebrews. This message would certainly resonate later on with Jews in exile or in an imperial context.

Soul-Crushing Demands

Pharaoh orders midwives Shiphrah and Puah to kill all Hebrew baby boys at birth (Exod 1:15), which is tantamount to asking them to forfeit their humanity. It is a grisly demand: snapping the neck of the infant as he exits his mother's body, terminating his life before his mother could even deliver her placenta and before he could ever know the security of his mother's arms or the warmth of the milk from her breast. Pharaoh puts the midwives in a position to choose between the moral fiber that makes them human and obedience.

The implications of the command are wide reaching too, because anyone who discovers a Hebrew baby is instructed to abduct him and drown him in the Nile. Pharaoh's insidious decree asks a whole society to sacrifice their moral conscience.

Psalm 86 is a prayer of the poor, those without economic and material wealth, but it is also a prayer of those in positions that compromise their humanity. It is a prayer of those forced to drown a baby. It is a prayer of those seeking the courage to subvert soul-crushing demands. It is not only a prayer of the powerless but also a prayer of those with *just enough* power to incite a band of ruffians to make a break for freedom.

Amy Beth Jones

Mothers and Children

Recently I saw a piercing and heartbreaking image online. It was a collage of three photos, two in black and white and one in color. All three communicated a singular, painful reality. While staring at this collage, a plethora of emotions stirring in me, I imagined from the hollow depths of the hearts and spirit of the adult women subjects their lament: "Incline Your ear, O LORD, and answer me; For I am afflicted and needy. . . . O You my God, save Your [*serving girl*] who trusts in You. For to You I cry all day long" (Ps 86:1, 2b, and 3b).

The collage contained photos taken at three funerals, each a close-up of a mother hugging her young children while they sat at their husbands' and fathers' funerals—three mothers and twelve children *captured* in this profound moment of history.

The mothers were Betty Shabazz,[8] Coretta Scott King,[9] and Jennifer Pinckney,[10] and the children of slain civil rights advocates Malcolm X, Rev. Dr. Martin Luther King Jr., and Rev. Clementa Pinckney, frozen for a moment in time. Three prophetic voices assassinated at a young age—Martin and Malcolm at thirty-nine, Pinckney at forty-four—because of their commitment to social justice and civil rights for all of God's children. Because of their devotion to love and their enemies' devotion to hate, violence, and racism, these men left three widows. One can imagine the three at that funeral moment identifying with the serving girl Hopkins lifts up in Ps 86. In order to persevere in and after that moment, Betty, Coretta, and Jennifer must have "combined both desperate need and covenantal devotion, both of

---

8. Betty Shabazz, wife of Malcolm X. At the time of his death they had four children aged two to seven, and Betty was pregnant with twins. For biographical information, see http://www.biography.com/people/malcolm-x-9396195; accessed August 7, 2015.

9. Coretta Scott King, wife of Rev. Dr. Martin Luther King Jr. At the time of his death the couple had four children aged five to twelve. None of the King children married or had children. For biographical information, see http://www.biography.com/people/martin-luther-king-jr-9365086; accessed August 7, 2015.

10. Jennifer Pinckney, wife of Rev. Clementa Carlos "Clem" Pinckney. At the time of his death the couple had two children aged six and eleven. Pinckney was a Democratic member of the South Carolina Senate, representing the forty-fifth district from 2000 until his death. He was previously a member of the South Carolina House of Representatives from 1997 through 2000. Pinckney was an African Methodist Episcopal minister and a vocal advocate for social justice. He was assassinated in June 2015 while conducting Bible study at his church.

which place God under some obligation." Hopkins's powerful treatment of the serving girl in lament Psalm 86 and the witness of God's faithfulness to these three widows serve as a comfort and hope to suffering African American women that we too can survive circumstances that break us down to deep levels of need and desperation, because God will heed our cries.

Audrey Coretta Price

Several interpreters have noted the chiastic (inverted or reversed) structure of Psalm 86 in which complaints and petitions surround a declaration of praise in the middle of the psalm. The psalm begins and ends with "your servant" (vv. 1-2, 16-17). God is reminded of God's חסד (vv. 5-6, 16), and the psalmist complains (vv. 7, 14). The hymnic praise in the center verses, 8-13, begins with the declaration "there is none like you among the gods, O LORD" (v. 8; cp. 1 Kgs 8:23; Jer 10:1-16, and the rhetorical question that asserts the same in Exod 15:11; Pss 35:10; 113:5; Mic 7:18-20). God's incomparability is mentioned again in v. 10b: "you alone are God," so that it surrounds "all the nations" in v. 9, who "shall come and bow down before you, O Lord, and shall glorify your name." One can imagine Moses' mother asserting God's sovereignty over Pharaoh and the gods and goddesses of Egypt as she fights for the life of her son doomed by Pharaoh's decree.

God's "name" is mentioned three times, in vv. 9, 11, and 12. It is bound up with God's reputation and character. When Moses' mother prays these words she anticipates the purpose of the plagues: "The Egyptians shall know that I am the LORD" (Exod 7:5; cp. 9:14). Jochebed herself seeks to learn more about this God on whom she depends for the safety of her son. Thus in v. 11 she pleads: "teach me your way." Along with deliverance for her son and her people she demands a reversal characteristic of laments: she will receive a "sign" of God's favor, while her enemies (the Egyptians enforcing Pharaoh's command) will be "put to shame" (v. 17). One can understand her declarations in vv. 13b and 17c as confessions of trust in anticipation of the deliverance she expects but that has not yet occurred. Such is the faith of a mother enslaved in Egypt. We can imagine a new superscription for Psalm 86: "A prayer of Jochebed when she places her son in the basket in the Nile."

Psalm 87

Mother Zion

Although Psalm 87 presupposes the other Songs of Zion among which it is usually classified (Pss 46, 48, 76, 84, 122), it moves beyond them to a remarkable alternative vision of the future in which Zion unites all peoples as their universal mother. Psalm 87 shares with these other Songs of Zion God's "love" for Zion (v. 2), which is expressed in God's choice of Zion as God's residence on earth (Pss 46:4-5; 48:2, 8, 9; 76:2; 122:1; cp. 132:13). God rules from the city as "Most High" in Psalms 87:5; 46:4; and 48:8. Also, Jerusalem is called "the city of God" in Psalms 87:3b; 46:4; 48:1, 8, for God has "established" it (Pss 87:4; 48:8). Zion is blessed by "springs" (87:7) that connect it to the idea of the primal world-mountain and mountain of paradise with its life-giving waters in Psalm 46:4 (cp. Gen 2:10-14 and the four rivers flowing from Eden). "All Zion songs draw a visionary image of Jerusalem that cannot be equated with its topography or its political status."[1]

What Psalm 87 does not share with these other psalms is the idea of Zion as the place of God's victory over the nations (cp. Pss 47:2-3; 48:4-7; 76:3-9) or Zion as inviolable refuge and secure stronghold (Pss 46:1, 5, 7, 11; 48:3; 84:11; 122:3, 7). Psalm 87:7 hints at Zion as the center of the pilgrimage

---

1. Christl M. Maier, "Psalm 87 as a Reappraisal of the Zion Tradition and Its Reception in Galatians 4:26," *CBQ* 69 (2007): 473–86, at 477.

Psalm 87:1-7

Of the Korahites. A Psalm. A Song.

¹On the holy mount stands the city
he founded;
²the LORD loves the gates of
Zion
more than all the dwellings of
Jacob.
³Glorious things are spoken of you,
O city of God.   *Selah*

⁴Among those who know me I men-
tion Rahab and Babylon;
Philistia too, and Tyre, with
Ethiopia—

"This one was born there,"
they say.

⁵And of Zion it shall be said,
"This one and that one were
born in it";
for the Most High himself will
establish it.
⁶The LORD records, as he registers
the peoples,
"This one was born
there."   *Selah*

⁷Singers and dancers alike say,
"All my springs are in you."

of the nations (Ps 76:11), a theme that is amplified in and imported from prophetic texts (Isa 55:4-5; 56:6-8; 60:11, 14; Zeph 3:6-10). But in Psalm 87 these are not defeated nations coming to pay submissive homage to God; instead, they are kin to Israel, metaphorically birthed in Zion.

That the extraordinary vision of Psalm 87 is ignored, resisted, or explained away by many interpreters disappointing and that the personification of Zion as female is often overlooked even more so. Several interpreters note the abruptness of the psalm's short lines and lack of transition between different speakers; they consequently suggest unnecessary extensive rearrangements of the Hebrew text. The structure of Psalm 87 appears to be fairly simple. The first two verses assert that God "loves," more than any other, the city of Jerusalem, which God "founded" (v. 1; cp. Pss 78:68-69; 132:13) "on the holy mount" (Zion). The psalm then unfolds in a chiastic arrangement, that is, in concentric or mirroring order, ABA, with female Zion clearly in the spotlight at the center. Repetition of feminine singular prepositional suffixes structures this mirroring and ties the psalm together: בך ("of/in you," v. 3), בה ("in her," v. 5), and בך ("in you," v. 7). "Her" in v. 5 is surrounded by שם ("there") in vv. 4 and 6.[2] "All of the pronouns point to feminine Zion, the city of God, and what takes place 'there.'"[3]

2. Mark S. Smith, "The Structure of Psalm LXXXVII," *VT* 38 (1988): 357–58.
3. Johanna W. H. VanWijk-Bos, "Psalm 87," *Int* 47 (1993): 281–85, at 283.

Different voices in the psalm make it very dynamic and suggest a liturgical setting. Since this is a psalm of Korah (a temple guild singer/musician), perhaps a Korahite speaks *about* Zion in vv. 1, 2, and 7 and directly *to* Zion personified in v. 3: "glorious things are spoken of you, O city of God." Most interpreters argue that God speaks in v. 4 and the people in the congregation speak in vv. 5 and 6. A shift in speakers is supported by the term "Selah" (perhaps an indicator of some pause in the liturgy for silence, dance, or music) after vv. 3 and 6, though the speakers are not identified.

The ambiguity of the speakers in vv. 4-6 invites a second look. Even those interpreters who recognize the female personification of Zion in Psalm 87 suppose that God, and not Zion, speaks in these verses. As is common in West Semitic tradition, cities are grammatically feminine and are given metaphorical titles such as "mistress," "virgin," "widow," "daughter," etc. "Such a metaphorical use of female roles helps to express the various relationships among the city, its ruler, and its inhabitants. The city might be conquered like a daughter and embraced like a royal bride by its ruler. It offers shelter and food to its inhabitants like a mother."[4] In the postexilic period the poet of Psalm 87 certainly knew of the frequent use of "Daughter Zion" in the prophets (e.g., Isa 1:8; Jer 4:31) and in the book of Lamentations (e.g., 1:6; 2:1, 4, 8, 10, 13, 15; 4:21, 22). Given this usage, it is strange that the city remains voiceless for so many interpreters of Psalm 87. If the psalm pushes toward a radically different vision of the future, it makes sense that female Zion speaks in vv. 4-6. She speaks to claim a new identity and a different future. No more the wife divorced by her husband and "put away" (Isa 50:1), or the mother bereft of her children (Isa 49:21; Jer 10:20; Lam 2:19; 4:4, 10), or the widow sitting alone (Lam 1:1), or a spoil of war raped by the enemy (Lam 5:11), female Zion reclaims her dignity. No longer a victim, she boldly claims her place in God's ordering activity in the tradition of Lady Wisdom in Proverbs 1–9 (see especially Prov 8). In her, the universal mother, all the peoples of the earth are born.

---

4. Maier, "Psalm 87," 479.

Zion as Embodied Space

It is interesting to note the personification of Zion as female in Psalm 87, especially when we consider all that Zion represents both here and elsewhere in the Psalter. Zion, as Hopkins mentions, is God's residence on earth; it is the space God establishes as refuge. Zion is the site of pilgrimage, of holy journey toward the sacred. During slavery, Zion became central to black Christianity as African descendants attempted to imagine a place of refuge in the midst of exile in torturous situations. Zion has been used to represent various countries in Africa, or the continent as a whole, or has been used to speak of Jerusalem as the holy epicenter for Christian life.

Given the complicated social and political environment of Israel in contemporary society, however, it would be difficult to imagine it as a place of refuge for marginalized black people. Further, when we consider Africa as Zion we must contend with the very painful legacy of colonialism and apartheid. If we as black people cannot draw meaningful solace and safety from Africa, and we as Christians have a complicated relationship with Israel as a space of divine peace, what is Zion?

Engaging the female personification of Zion in the text, it is fruitful to imagine the possibility that Zion is not a geographical site but an embodied space represented in the very being of black womanhood. For better or worse, black women have been the site of solace, comfort, and redemption for the black community. From our actual and proverbial wombs the church has continued to be the site of emerging social and political change and a place of refuge for the discarded and disenfranchised. Furthermore, much like Jerusalem, we too have been pillaged and have fallen victims to empire and war.

The experience of black women mirrors the multivalent description of the city as feminine. One cannot help but read Christl Maier's assertion[5] that "the city might be conquered like a daughter and embraced like a royal bride by its ruler. It offers shelter and food to its inhabitants like a mother" and recall the daunting history of black women in the United States. Black women were conquered as slaves, both as laborers and sexual objects. Similarly, they were asked to serve as domestics in white households, feeding and clothing white families in order to feed and clothe their own children. Meanwhile, they gave life to

5. Ibid.

abolition movements as runners for the Underground Railroad and started anti-lynching and voting rights campaigns in the Jim Crow South. Black women sat on buses and at lunch counters not intended for them as a means to provide grace, humanity, and hospitality for future generations. Through it all, black women maintain a sacred spring from which flows life. Absent from the picture is the social embrace of black women with the honor of "royal bride."

Yolanda Marie Norton

In Psalm 87:4, Lady Zion speaks of "those who know me," who will say: "This one was born there," that is, in her, in Zion; this latter phrase is repeated exactly in v. 6. She includes traditional enemies of Israel, Rahab (a mythical name for Egypt; see Isa 30:7), and Babylon, two great oppressive empires that precipitated the exodus and exile. She also names Philistia, Tyre, and Ethiopia (Cush in Hebrew). This is meant to be a representative rather than an exhaustive list, indicating the whole world. It covers the four points of the compass with Israel in the center. All nations will come to "know" Jerusalem/Zion and its God, who is inextricably entwined with the city. This knowledge of Zion and God, however, will not come as a consequence of defeat or punishment as it did for Egypt through the plagues (Exod 14:4; cp. Pss 46:10; 59:13; 100:3), or as it did for Babylon at the hands of God's "anointed one," Cyrus of Persia (Isa 14:1-2; 44:28; 45:1, 14). This future does not embrace the pilgrimage to Jerusalem of humbled, defeated nations bearing tribute (Ps 47:3, 8; Isa 14:1-3). It does not, as some have suggested, stand in the tradition of Zechariah 2:11 with its Day of the Lord as a day of defeat of Israel's enemies, when "many nations shall join themselves to the Lord on that day." Instead, this future embraces "full citizenship" for the world's inhabitants; "the psalmist strips them of their foreign status and, shockingly, makes them naturalized citizens,"[6] brothers and sisters. The female Zion observes that the universal God who is called "the Most High" (v. 5), records all people in the divine birth register (v. 6) to secure the birthright of each one. No longer does Zion function in Psalm 87 "as the center of the world, not even primarily as God's dwelling place, but as the place of the peoples' belonging, the peoples' dwelling place. . . .

---

6. Konrad Schaefer, *Psalms*, Berit Olam (Collegeville, MN: Liturgical Press, 2001), 213.

Here the peoples do not come to Zion either to assault it or to do homage; they *belong* there in all their differences, with all their failings, from far and near."[7] Why? Zion is their mother.

TRANSLATION MATTERS

Verse 5 stands at the center of the chiastic or mirrored structure in vv. 3-6. As said above, "her" occurs twice in v. 5 and is encompassed by "there" in vv. 4 and 6, pointing to Zion. That all people can claim their birthright in Zion is reinforced by the phrase in v. 5b, the middle of three lines of poetry, איש ואיש ילד־בה, is translated literally: "a man and a man are born in her." The repetition of איש suggests the distributive sense of the phrase, "each or every man [person] is born in her," or the idea of entirety, "all people are born in her," former enemies included.

In a sense Psalm 87 engages postexilic Israel in addressing its "moral injury," that is, "the hidden wound of war" that is "the result of reflection on memories of war or other extreme traumatic conditions. It comes from having transgressed one's basic moral identity and violated core moral beliefs."[8] These wounds generate fear and reinforce difference. Communal laments in book 3 of the Psalter repeatedly dehumanize and demonize Israel's enemies, as do the individual laments in books 2 and 3. Enemies viciously destroyed the temple and reviled God's name (Pss 74:3-8, 10, 18; 79:1-3, 10; 83:4). This enemy behavior justifies Israel's pleas for equally brutal retributive justice (e.g., in Pss 79:6, 12; 83:13-18). These petitions are expressions of moral injury.

What female Zion engages in is nothing less than "soul repair."[9] She rejects the "collective false forgiveness" that requires a demonizing of the enemy to justify violence against it, followed by "imperialist nostalgia" that demands "that those who have been harmed assuage the guilt of their conquerors."[10] This "nostalgia" can be seen in Psalms 47:3-4; 48:4-7; 66:5-8; 68:21, 29-32; 76:11-12. The defeated enemy kings will come to Jerusalem bearing gifts. Psalm 47 instructs "all you peoples" to "shout to God with loud songs of joy" (v. 1) because God as king has "subdued peoples under us [Israel]" (v. 4). Incredibly, these subdued peoples are

---

7. VanWijk-Bos, "Psalm 87," 285.

8. Rita Nakashima Brock and Gabriella Lettini, *Soul Repair: Recovering from Moral Injury after War* (Boston: Beacon Press, 2012), xv, xiv.

9. Ibid., 115.

10. Ibid., 103, 104, 115.

supposed to be grateful for being conquered; Israel shows no empathy for the trauma the enemies experienced. In the midst of this retributive mind-set, soul repair occurs in Psalm 87 as it seeks a connection with the Other. The psalm attempts to reclaim the moral conscience of the Israelite people, who are kin to all nations born of Mother Zion. The LXX makes this universal motherhood explicit by calling Zion "mother" in v. 5. The humanity of all is embraced in this universal kinship.

Resistance to this interpretation is expressed by those who argue that Psalm 87 deals only with proselytes from foreign nations. For them, Psalm 87 is a pilgrimage psalm for proselytes, since universal salvation comes only with the crucifixion and death of Jesus. Others argue that this is a nationalistic psalm meant to encourage Diaspora Jews to maintain a strong relationship with Zion/Jerusalem. For them, God is literally tied to a particular place and people; Zion loses its metaphorical quality as the center from which God dispenses blessings to all of creation. As Frank-Lothar Hossfeld and Erich Zenger argue, however, Psalm 87 "presents a postexilic new version of the preexilic Zion theology," showing "an astonishing openness in which it sees the relationship of the nations to Israel."[11] In contrast to Psalm 83, the final psalm of the Asaph collection (Pss 50, 73–83) that speaks of God conquering the nations who attacked Israel and forcing them to acknowledge God's rule, here in Psalm 87 the nations join together with Israel in celebration, reversing the point of view of Psalms 45–48. "Now it is no longer a matter of the salvation of Zion, but of the salvation of the nations through Zion/starting from Zion: 'all the springs' of life are to be found in Zion."[12] Psalm 87 takes seriously God's future plans for Zion expressed in Isaiah 2:1-4; 11:1-10; and Micah 4, and it anticipates Galatians 4:26.

Who better to embrace and pray the vision of Psalm 87 than the foreign wives divorced by their Jewish husbands in Ezra–Nehemiah? In fact, God's recording of names in the birth register of Psalm 87:6 "may be related historically to the list of the members of the postexilic community mentioned in Ezra and Nehemiah, especially as the term 'document' (כתב) in Psalm 87:6 is also used in Ezra 2:62 and Neh 7:64."[13] In the period of return from Babylonian exile, issues of survival, identity, and communal boundaries became paramount and controversial. The book of Ruth and Isaiah 56:1-8 can be viewed as inclusive of foreigners, in

---

11. Frank-Lothar Hossfeld and Erich Zenger, *Psalms 2: A Commentary on Psalms 51–100*, trans. Linda M. Maloney, Hermeneia (Minneapolis: Fortress Press, 2005), 382.

12. Ibid., 386–87.

13. Maier, "Psalm 87," 478.

opposition to Ezra–Nehemiah, which emphasized ethnic purity and prohibited intermarriage (Ezra 9–10). Foreign female spouses (or perhaps Jewish women who had not gone into exile but remained behind and were not recognized as Jews by the returning elite) threatened religious purity but also posed an economic threat; communal land could be lost to them when their husbands died. In fact, "uniquely in Ezra–Nehemiah, the verb that most translations render as 'married' (Ezra 10:2, 10, 14, 17; Neh 13:23-24) means in fact 'settle' or 'dwell.' Such terminology underscores the preoccupation with the fate of the land as a reason for opposition."[14] The reaction of these foreign women to their expulsion is not recorded. One can imagine they prayed Psalm 87, reminding the community of their shared kinship through Mother Zion.

Stories and Identity

Psalm 87 begs for a story: a story about "this one," a story about origins, a story about birthplaces and families—stories about fratricide; stories about half-blooded brothers, incestuous fathers, a Hebrew baby raised by Egyptian royalty; stories of marriage, pregnancy, and death; stories about annihilation, torture, and rape. These are the stories of the Israelite people. The essence of identity emerges in the story that is created, assigned, or assumed to moments of rupture and trauma.

"The truth about stories is that that's all we are," writes North American novelist Thomas King. Psalm 87 invites us to a new narrative. We are urged to acknowledge the humanity of each person, to see beyond the ethnicity of the Other to behold the similarities: familiar family features. The Other is an easily discarded object, but the stories of the Kenite, the Egyptian, the Edomite, the Moabite, and the Midianite intertwine with Israel's story—they are family. Stories are not just all we have. Stories are all we are.

Amy Beth Jones

---

14. Tamara Cohn Eskenazi, "Ezra–Nehemiah," in *Women's Bible Commentary*, ed. Carol A. Newsom, Sharon H. Ringe, and Jacqueline E. Lapsley, 3rd ed. (Louisville, KY: Westminster John Knox, 2012), 192–200, at 194.

Psalm 88

Meaningless Suffering?

The contrast between Psalms 87 and 88 jolts the reader. From Psalm 87's uplifting eschatological vision of all peoples united by their metaphorical birth in Zion, the universal mother, we are plunged into the isolation of Sheol and the realm of the dead in individual lament Psalm 88. Walter Brueggemann calls Psalm 88 "our best script for praying to a wall" in the sense of experiencing God's absence and silence; the psalm offers "a model for unanswered prayer."[1] Even Job received an "answer"—albeit an unsatisfactory one—to his complaints: God bellows at him in the speeches from the whirlwind (Job 38–41). The supplicant in Psalm 88, however, hears nothing at all from God; the psalm literally begins and ends in darkness. One can imagine that Psalm 88 is like a telephone call to 911—"incline your ear to my cry" (v. 2b)—during which the operator puts the caller on endless hold. Unlike most individual laments, Psalm 88 contains no shift in tone from complaint to protestation of innocence (e.g., Ps 17:3-5), declaration of trust (e.g., Ps 13:5), or vow of praise (e.g., Ps 59:16-17); the psalmist confesses no sin (as in Ps 51). Instead, Psalm 88 presents one long complaint and aims its accusations against God instead of earthly enemies. Its uniqueness makes

---

1. Walter Brueggemann, *From Whom No Secrets Are Hid: Introducing the Psalms*, ed. Brent Strawn (Louisville, KY: Westminster John Knox, 2014), 113.

Psalm 88:1-18

A Song. A Psalm of the Korahites.
To the leader: according to
Mahalath Leannoth.
A Maskil of Heman the Ezrahite.

¹O Lᴏʀᴅ, God of my salvation,
   when, at night, I cry out in your
      presence,
²let my prayer come before you;
   incline your ear to my cry.

³For my soul is full of troubles,
   and my life draws near to Sheol.
⁴I am counted among those who
      go down to the Pit;
   I am like those who have no
      help,
⁵like those forsaken among the
      dead,
   like the slain that lie in the
      grave,

like those whom you remember
   no more,
for they are cut off from your
   hand.
⁶You have put me in the depths of
      the Pit,
   in the regions dark and deep.
⁷Your wrath lies heavy upon me,
   and you overwhelm me with all
      your waves.   *Selah*

⁸You have caused my companions
      to shun me;
   you have made me a thing of
      horror to them.
I am shut in so that I cannot escape;
   ⁹my eye grows dim through
      sorrow.
Every day I call on you, O Lᴏʀᴅ;
   I spread out my hands to you.

many interpreters uncomfortable; they call it "gloomy" or "the least hopeful lament." Many simplify the complexity and limit the scope of Psalm 88 by suggesting that it is a plea from one who is gravely ill and facing death, but by doing so they reduce the metaphors about death to literal descriptions and undercut the visceral power of the psalm. Others suggest that Psalm 88 offers a model for Christ's suffering that can enhance our appreciation of the resurrection. These arguments sidestep the central theological questions with which Psalm 88 struggles.

The psalm unfolds in three major sections. The two outer sections contain emotionally charged descriptions of the psalmist's suffering (vv. 1-9a, 13-18). These two sections parallel one another in their structure; each speaks metaphorically of God's wrath (vv. 7, 16) and of the destructive power of water (vv. 7, 17), and each ends with the psalmist's experience of being shunned by companions (vv. 8, 18). The word נפש (NRSV: "soul," literally "being," "person") also ties the two together (vv. 3, 14); the whole person is suffering. The outer sections surround a center section of confrontational rhetorical questions hurled at God (vv. 9b-12). Each of the three sections begins with a different verb for "cry" or

¹⁰Do you work wonders for the
 dead?
 Do the shades rise up to
  praise you? *Selah*
¹¹Is your steadfast love declared in
 the grave,
 or your faithfulness in Abaddon?
¹²Are your wonders known in the
 darkness,
 or your saving help in the land
  of forgetfulness?

¹³But I, O LORD, cry out to you;
 in the morning my prayer
  comes before you.
¹⁴O LORD, why do you cast me off?

Why do you hide your face
 from me?
¹⁵Wretched and close to death
 from my youth up,
 I suffer your terrors; I am desperate.
¹⁶Your wrath has swept over me;
 your dread assaults destroy me.
¹⁷They surround me like a flood all
 day long;
 from all sides they close in on
  me.
¹⁸You have caused friend and
 neighbor to shun me;
 my companions are in darkness.

"call"—vv. 1 (צעק), 9b (קרא), and 13 (שוע)—"as if to indicate that the psalmist has exhausted every approach."[2] The psalmist's cries come in the night (v. 1; the Hebrew actually says "day and night"), every day (v. 9b), and in the morning (v. 13); her prayer is urgent and unceasing, but God does not answer. Darkness haunts each section: vv. 6 ("regions dark and deep"), 9b (her "eyes grow dim"), 12 ("darkness"), 18 ("dark place"). The psalm ends abruptly: its very last word is מחשך ("darkness" or "dark place"). This word occurs only five times in Tanakh, perhaps indicating how extraordinarily painful and terrifying the psalmist's experience is.

Though the psalmist begins by addressing God as "God of my salvation" (v. 1a), perhaps interpreters are too quick to credit this as an expression of trust based on memories of God's favorable responses to those who cried out (e.g., Exod 3:7; Pss 9:12; 77:1). Given the pervasiveness of darkness in Psalm 88, one wonders how the psalmist can pray at all, let alone embrace any core testimony (normative speech about the characteristic nature and activity of God expressed by such verbs as delivers, creates, forgives, judges). Instead, the psalmist seems immersed in counter testimony, that is, a cross-examination of core testimony prompted

2. J. Clinton McCann Jr., "The Book of Psalms," in *The New Interpreter's Bible*, vol. 4 (Nashville, TN: Abingdon Press, 1996), 639–1280, at 1027.

by questions emerging out of the lived experience of God's absence.[3] An immediate insistence on core testimony in v. 1 blunts the overwhelming force of the counter-testimony that pervades Psalm 88; at most, the echoes of core testimony found in vv. 10-12 serve as a foil and magnifying glass for the psalmist's present agony. The myriad metaphors for death in vv. 3-7 virtually swallow the reader: troubles, Sheol, Pit, without help, dead, grave, forsaken, not remembered, cut off, depths, regions dark and deep, overwhelming waves. The concluding section in vv. 9b-18 also piles up terms for death: dim eyes, dead, shades, grave, Abaddon (from the Hebrew verb "perish," or "be lost"; another name for Sheol), darkness, land of forgetfulness.

The Hebrew word for "Pit" in v. 4 is בור, literally "cistern." It is used as a name for the abode of the dead here (also in Isa 14:15); sometimes it represents a prison (see Gen 37:20-29 where Joseph's brothers throw him into a pit). This nuance of pit as prison operates in Psalm 88. The psalmist feels as if there is no escape; she is as good as dead, as vv. 4-5 suggest: "I am *like* the slain that lie in the grave." The psalmist's words in v. 3 are experienced viscerally: "For my נפש is full of troubles and my life draws near to Sheol." The verb used for "full of," שבע, usually means "be satisfied," "be satiated" in terms of food and other good things (e.g., Pss 63:5; 65:4), but here it takes on the negative sense of "too much of." The psalmist has had enough and can take no more of trouble; she is so full of and weighted down by her troubles that she is sinking toward Sheol. As one interpreter puts it, "the tug of gravity is real."[4]

The psalmist's speech is raw because she is fighting not only for her life but also "for the divinity of [her] God."[5] Not surprisingly, then, the psalmist moves toward direct accusation of God, because "the unity of that God *of the supplicant's faith* and this God *of personal suffering* can no longer be maintained. . . . What remains is the *gulf between faith and experience*."[6] The unity of these God images is broken and the psalmist will not mend it at the expense of her own innocence. Instead, she holds God accountable for her suffering: "*You* have put me in the depths of the Pit. . . . *You* overwhelm me with all *your* waves. . . . *You* have caused my companions to shun me" (vv. 6a, 7b, 8a); "why do *you* cast me off . . . and hide *your* face from me?" (v. 14); "*your* wrath has swept over me; *your* dread assaults

3. Walter Brueggemann, *Theology of the Old Testament* (Minneapolis: Fortress Press, 1997), 117–44, 317–32.

4. Konrad Schaefer, *Psalms*, Berit Olam (Collegeville, MN: Liturgical Press, 2001), 215.

5. Ibid., 222.

6. Ibid., 228.

destroy me" (v. 16); "*you* have caused friend and neighbor to shun me" (v. 18). God is clearly the psalmist's enemy. God's inexplicable wrath has "above all, thrust him [the psalmist] into social death" (vv. 8, 18).[7] She is shunned, isolated, and pushed farther toward Sheol and away from God.

TRANSLATION MATTERS

There are several words in Hebrew that the psalmist uses to describe her experience of feeling as good as dead. In v. 4b, "I am like those who have no help" reads literally in the Hebrew: "I am like a גבר ['warrior,' 'strong man'] with no strength." This condition defies explanation and adds to the psalmist's terror. In v. 5a, "like those forsaken among the dead" in Hebrew is literally: "Like one set free among the dead." The Hebrew verb is חפש, an adjective meaning "freed," usually from slavery (Exod 21:5 and many times in Exodus), from taxes (1 Sam 17:25), or from violence (Isa 58:6). This verb refers to the "release of a legally responsible subject from an obligation," which means that the psalmist "can offer no further service to God" and is no longer subject to God's power or tied to God or to the living. The psalmist is in freefall, untethered; the closer she draws to Sheol, the farther she moves from God. Also, in v. 5d, the psalmist likens herself to the dead who "are cut off from your hand." The Hebrew word גזר ("cut off") is used in 2 Chronicles 26:21 to describe being separated from the house of God and thus from God's presence (see Ps 31:22) and in Isaiah 53:8 to convey being cut off from life or from the land of the living. If the Servant Songs in Second Isaiah aim to make sense of Israel's suffering in exile (the Servant may represent the people), then "cut off" also has political and covenantal connections in Psalm 88 (see Ezek 37:11). The psalmist would represent the exiles who feel they have no future in the Lord.[8]

The middle section of Psalm 88, vv. 10-12, makes clear what is at stake for both God and the psalmist in a series of rhetorical questions with the obvious answer "no": no, the shades do not rise up to praise you (v. 10b); no, your steadfast love is not declared in the grave (v. 11a; cp. Ps 6:5); no, your wonders are not known in the darkness. That God does not remember the psalmist any longer (v. 5c) will have consequences for God: "in such a way he [*sic*] too vanishes from memory. The terrifying image of a 'land of forgetting' [v. 12b] . . . which is meant to move Yhwh to a saving intervention, is a threatening possibility for God himself!"[9]

7. Frank-Lothar Hossfeld and Erich Zenger, *Psalms 2: A Commentary on Psalms 51–100*, trans. Linda M. Maloney, Hermeneia (Minneapolis: Fortress Press, 2005), 395.

8. Bernd Janowski, *Arguing With God* (Louisville, KY: Westminster John Knox, 2013), 218, 224.

9. Hossfeld and Zenger, *Psalms 2*, 396.

Perhaps, however, the psalmist has given up on God intervening at all; her pain is too great. These rhetorical questions suggest that God desires (needs?) our praise and thanks, but if God allows the psalmist to go down to Sheol, giving such praise and thanks will not be possible. Undergirding these rhetorical questions is the idea of the "public relations value of the psalmist";[10] that is, the psalmist is valued as one who praises God and bolsters God's reputation and prestige, countering the wicked who question God's power and presence (as in Pss 10:13; 53:1; 59:7; 64:5-6; 71:11; 73:11; 75:10; etc.). These rhetorical questions also list positive attributes of God: wonders (twice), steadfast love, faithfulness, saving help. The questions in a sense mock core testimony, which at this point seems like a distant memory or pure fantasy for the suffering psalmist.

Carleen Mandolfo, "Psalm 88 and the Holocaust: Lament in Search of a Divine Response"

Mandolfo calls Psalm 88 "an ideal biblical prayer for a post-Holocaust world" (abstract, p. 152). She notes that several laments are "double-voiced," that is, they show interaction between "two consciousnesses," a supplicant in the first person and a didactic voice in the third person that interrupts the supplicant with "a theological corrective to their [the supplications'] implicit complaint" (p. 153). Psalm 7:6-11 provides a good example of this typical lament shifting; it produces a theological result "akin to a quarrel between faith and experience, the former defending a retributive theology along the lines of Deuteronomistic thinking . . . and the latter challenging YHWH's justice or *hesed*" (p. 154). Psalm 88, however, privileges experience; it is "uniquely single-voiced" (ibid.).

If much of Christian and Jewish theodicy is "about answers and justifications" (p. 157) and making sense of crushing suffering, then Psalm 88 models what Zachary Braiterman terms "antitheodicy,"[11] that is, a refusal to let God off the hook in the covenant relationship or to make meaning out of suffering. Consequently, the didactic voice is absent from Psalm 88. For Mandolfo, "in a post-Shoah age the silence of the didactic voice

---

10. Denise Dombkowski Hopkins, *Journey through the Psalms* (St. Louis, MO: Chalice Press, 2002), 103–4.

11. Zachary Braiterman, *God After Auschwitz: Tradition and Change in Post-Holocaust Jewish Thought* (Princeton, NJ: Princeton University Press, 1998), 4.

'says' all we need, or dare, hear." The role of the didactic voice is to make meaningful the torment of the supplicant into whose prayer it is inserted. Mandolfo notes that Jewish scholars Richard Rubenstein and Emil Fackenheim have emphatically insisted, however, that the search for meaning in a post-Shoah age "is not only futile, it is an insult to the victims" (p. 168). Though we may want an answer, at present "there is no answer. Maybe there never will be. . . . The former answers, represented by the didactic voice of other lament psalms, are unacceptable" (pp. 168–69). God does not answer in Psalm 88, perhaps because God recognizes the enormity of the supplicant's suffering and respects it. It may be that God is sitting *shiva* with God's people.[12]

Denise Dombkowski Hopkins

Beth LaNeel Tanner, "Psalm 88 and the Concubine of the Book of Judges: Sometimes the Story Does Not End Happily Ever After"

Tanner notes that reading Judges 19 as intertext for Psalm 88 means that we can no longer fix or soften the psalm or ignore the brutalization of the Levite's concubine. The two texts stand together in their brutality and "find victims of violence where they are. The abandonment voiced is their reality" (p. 176). Tanner sees an echo between Psalm 88:9—"I call on you, O LORD; I spread out my hands to you"—and Judges 19:27, which describes the gang-raped concubine "lying at the door of the house, with her hands on the threshold." "This unsettling image of her hands on the threshold of safety, and her body left broken in the street seemed to sound the same note of unresolved sorrow as does the psalm" (p. 167). Also, just as the psalmist cries day, night, and morning, "the concubine's ordeal was long and drawn out, lasting from evening into the next morning. This is no quick act of violence, but like the psalmist's cry represents a long period of suffering" (pp. 166–67). "Finally the psalm ends with the person praying being rejected by 'friend and neighbor.' The woman was betrayed and thrown into the street by the very people she thought would provide her with safety on her journey. She, like the psalmist, is rejected by those close to her. . . . These haunting texts of abandonment share the theme of a hand stretched out toward safety and of safety

---

12. Carleen Mandolfo, "Psalm 88 and the Holocaust: Lament in Search of a Divine Response," *BibInt* 15 (2007): 151–70. For more on "double-voiced" laments, see Mandolfo's *God in the Dock: Dialogic Tension in the Psalms of Lament*, JSOTSup 357 (Sheffield: Sheffield Academic Press, 2002).

undelivered. . . . Each text asks difficult questions of God. Where is God and how could God allow such an act to happen? Each story ends with death. . . . This is not the God of our childhood Sunday School and this is not the God of most American churches or classrooms" (p. 168).

What makes both Psalm 88 and Judges 19 more painful is that a similar version of the concubine's story was presented in Genesis 19. In Sodom, Lot offered his daughters up to the mob to save himself and his two guests, but all were saved by God's intervention through these visitors, who strike the mob blind and help Lot and his group escape. In Judges 19, however, the concubine "is the sacrificial lamb, a suffering servant. The one without even a name. The one who never utters a word. She is as silent as God. The only statement she makes is her outstretched hands on the threshold" (pp. 169–70). "The point of transformation, of hope if you will, is that the psalm is only about God and the suffering human. Consider that the enemies are a missing element for a reason other than that this psalm is about sickness and that petitions for salvation and the assurance of being heard are missing for a reason. . . . To whom does one lift a cry when the hate in the eyes of your attacker tells you there will be no rescue? . . . You know that the story will end there and not happily. There is only one place left to turn, only God to cry out to, begging to be heard. . . . In the end there is only God and victim. Cries of deliverance will not do any good; there is no tomorrow. . . . For like our world, there are places in the biblical text that are not made right. . . . God does not fix it . . . [b]ut even in the darkness, God is there, not in the superman form we had hoped, but in hearing the cries of the broken and dying" (pp. 172–73).

"Psalm 88 ends so abruptly that we want to fix it. . . . Yet the text invites us or maybe even forces us to hang here suspended. . . . So ultimately, we are the ones left to write the end of the psalm. We know the worst has happened and we can allow the evil of the humans to be the last word, or like the psalmist turn to God . . . in the midst of suffering and violence. . . . The questions at the end of life lie with God, not humans, even if those questions are ones of dismay and sorrow brought on by other humans or by sickness" (p. 174). The words of Psalm 88 and Judges 19 are "an indictment of a world where violence against women is still a reality . . . a call to action on behalf of the ones placed in the position where she feels abandoned by everyone" (p. 175).[13]

Denise Dombkowski Hopkins

---

13. Beth LaNeel Tanner, *The Book of Psalms through the Lens of Intertextuality*, StBib-Lit 26 (New York: Peter Lang, 2001).

The radicality of Psalm 88 demands an equally radical text as intertext: the gang rape of the Levite's concubine and the subsequent hacking of her body to pieces to incite tribal civil war in Judges 21. Her brutally violent treatment at the hands of the men around her demands images of the depths and dark places of Psalm 88. Core testimony cannot be expressed in the presence of the concubine's mutilated body. Yes, Psalm 88 read intertextually with the rape and mutilation of the Levite's concubine can give voice to her and to those women today who have suffered abuse, as Tanner argues. In fact, some feminist interpreters have given names to the concubine as "an act of insubordination to the text," since no name means "no narrative power."[14] Yet despite Tanner's insistence that the God of Judges 19 and Psalm 88 is "not the God of our Sunday schools," that is, the God of core testimony, her intertextual exploration ends up with exactly that kind of God: the God who "suffers with."[15] God is again "let off the hook" at human expense in a corollary of traditional theodicy. The question of God's responsibility in covenant is sidestepped. Is this an adequate understanding for today's post-Shoah world? The rape of the concubine embodies the voice of the psalmist in Psalm 88 but also limits her voice and actually softens her rhetorical questions.

The question that will not go away is this: why did God *not* intervene? As my sexually abused students tell me repeatedly, God may not have actually carried out their abuse, but because God allowed it and did not stop it, God is culpable, whether or not God suffers with them. As David Blumenthal argues, "The innocence of the victim, not the depth of the suffering or the cruelty of the perpetrator, is what makes abusive behavior 'abusive.' . . . Abusive behavior is abusive; it is inexcusable, in all circumstances."[16] Motive and intent are irrelevant to the victim. Psalm 88, alone among all the psalms, pushes us to consider Blumenthal's shocking argument: "To have faith in God in a post-holocaust, abuse-sensitive world, we must (1) acknowledge the awful truth of God's abusing behavior; (2) adopt a theology of protest and sustained suspicion; (3) develop the religious affections of distrust and unrelenting challenge; (4) engage the process of renewed spiritual healing with all

14. Mieke Bal, "Dealing/With/Women: Daughters in the Book of Judges," in *The Book and the Text: The Bible and Literary Theory*, ed. Regina M. Schwartz (Oxford: Basil Blackwell, 1990), 16–39.

15. Terence E. Fretheim, *The Suffering of God: An Old Testament Perspective* (Minneapolis: Fortress Press, 1984), 127–37.

16. David Blumenthal, *Facing the Abusing God: A Theology of Protest* (Louisville, KY: Westminster John Knox, 1993), 248.

that entails of confrontation, mourning, and empowerment; (5) resist all evil mightily, supporting resistance to abuse wherever it is found; (6) open ourselves to the good side of God . . . and (7) we must turn to address God, face to Face, presence to Presence."[17]

17. Ibid., 259.

Psalm 89

We Told You So

Psalm 89 ends book 3 of the Psalter with a jarring juxtaposition of hymn and lament. It begins with traditional claims about God's character, actions, and promises and ends with accusations emerging out of present suffering that challenge those claims. As Walter Brueggemann notes, this kind of juxtaposition is "unremarkable" in Tanakh; core and counter-testimony about God are often, as in Psalm 89, "left to stand together, in tension, unresolved and without comment," permitting "no single 'final' say."[1] If Psalm 89 emerged in response to exile or Persian imperialism, as many of the psalms in book 3 perhaps do, this juxtaposition makes sense. Trauma produces varied, conflicted responses. More striking is that the order of the contrast between hymn and lament is reversed in Psalm 89. Most lament psalms move from complaint to a vow to praise God in anticipation of deliverance, but this psalm begins with praise. "Apparently Psalm 89 intends a sharpening of the contrast between praise and lament"[2] by reversing expectations attached to communal complaints.

---

1. Walter Brueggemann, "A Fissure Always Uncontained," in *Strange Fire: Reading the Bible after the Holocaust*, ed. Tod Linafelt (New York: New York University Press, 2000), 62–75, at 66–67.

2. Frank-Lothar Hossfeld and Erich Zenger, *Psalms 2: A Commentary on Psalms 51–100*, trans. Linda M. Maloney, Hermeneia (Minneapolis: Fortress Press, 2005), 404.

Psalm 89:1-52

A Maskil of Ethan the Ezrahite.

¹I will sing of your steadfast love,
O Lord, forever;
with my mouth I will proclaim
your faithfulness to all
generations.
²I declare that your steadfast love
is established forever;
your faithfulness is as firm as
the heavens.

³You said, "I have made a covenant with my chosen one,
I have sworn to my servant
David:
⁴'I will establish your descendants
forever,
and build your throne for all
generations.'"   *Selah*

⁵Let the heavens praise your wonders, O Lord,
your faithfulness in the assembly of the holy ones.
⁶For who in the skies can be compared to the Lord?
Who among the heavenly
beings is like the Lord,
⁷a God feared in the council of the
holy ones,
great and awesome above all
that are around him?
⁸O Lord God of hosts,
who is as mighty as you, O Lord?
Your faithfulness surrounds
you.
⁹You rule the raging of the sea;
when its waves rise, you still
them.
¹⁰You crushed Rahab like a carcass;
you scattered your enemies
with your mighty arm.

¹¹The heavens are yours, the
earth also is yours;
the world and all that is in it—
you have founded them.
¹²The north and the south—you
created them;
Tabor and Hermon joyously
praise your name.
¹³You have a mighty arm;
strong is your hand, high your
right hand.
¹⁴Righteousness and justice are
the foundation of your
throne;
steadfast love and faithfulness
go before you.
¹⁵Happy are the people who know
the festal shout,
who walk, O Lord, in the light
of your countenance;
¹⁶they exult in your name all day
long,
and extol your righteousness.
¹⁷For you are the glory of their
strength;
by your favor our horn is
exalted.
¹⁸For our shield belongs to the
Lord,
our king to the Holy One of Israel.

¹⁹Then you spoke in a vision to
your faithful one, and said:
"I have set the crown on one
who is mighty,
I have exalted one chosen
from the people.
²⁰I have found my servant David;
with my holy oil I have
anointed him;
²¹my hand shall always remain
with him;

my arm also shall strengthen
him.
²²The enemy shall not outwit him,
the wicked shall not humble
him.
²³I will crush his foes before him
and strike down those who
hate him.
²⁴My faithfulness and steadfast
love shall be with him;
and in my name his horn shall
be exalted.
²⁵I will set his hand on the sea
and his right hand on the rivers.
²⁶He shall cry to me, 'You are my
Father,
my God, and the Rock of my
salvation!'
²⁷I will make him the firstborn,
the highest of the kings of the
earth.
²⁸Forever I will keep my steadfast
love for him,
and my covenant with him will
stand firm.
²⁹I will establish his line forever,
and his throne as long as the
heavens endure.
³⁰If his children forsake my law
and do not walk according to
my ordinances,
³¹if they violate my statutes
and do not keep my commandments,
³²then I will punish their transgression with the rod
and their iniquity with
scourges;
³³but I will not remove from him
my steadfast love,
or be false to my faithfulness.
³⁴I will not violate my covenant,

or alter the word that went
forth from my lips.
³⁵Once and for all I have sworn by
my holiness;
I will not lie to David.
³⁶His line shall continue forever,
and his throne endure before
me like the sun.
³⁷It shall be established forever
like the moon,
an enduring witness in the
skies."   *Selah*

³⁸But now you have spurned and
rejected him;
you are full of wrath against
your anointed.
³⁹You have renounced the covenant with your servant;
you have defiled his crown in
the dust.
⁴⁰You have broken through all his
walls;
you have laid his strongholds
in ruins.
⁴¹All who pass by plunder him;
he has become the scorn of
his neighbors.
⁴²You have exalted the right hand
of his foes;
you have made all his enemies
rejoice.
⁴³Moreover, you have turned back
the edge of his sword,
and you have not supported
him in battle.
⁴⁴You have removed the scepter
from his hand,
and hurled his throne to the
ground.
⁴⁵You have cut short the days of
his youth;

Psalm 89:1-52 (cont.)

you have covered him with
    shame.   *Selah*

[46]How long, O LORD? Will you hide
    yourself forever?
How long will your wrath burn
    like fire?
[47]Remember how short my time
    is—
for what vanity you have
    created all mortals!
[48]Who can live and never see
    death?
Who can escape the power of
    Sheol?   *Selah*

[49]LORD, where is your steadfast
    love of old,
which by your faithfulness you
    swore to David?
[50]Remember, O LORD, how your
    servant is taunted;
how I bear in my bosom the
    insults of the peoples,
[51]with which your enemies taunt,
    O LORD,
with which they taunted the
    footsteps of your
    anointed.
[52]Blessed be the LORD forever.
    Amen and Amen.

Unfortunately, many interpreters of Psalm 89 have been unable to live with such a reversal. They have raised questions about the unity of the psalm, argued that certain verses are later insertions, and engaged in what has been called "expository denial."[3] Some argue that the questions posed in Psalm 89 about the apparent end of the Davidic dynasty are answered by books 4 and 5 of the Psalter, which assert God's universal sovereignty and shift to an eschatological hope. Perhaps so, but this view must remain a provisional one. We as readers must dwell a while with Israel in the abyss of jumbled thoughts; we are called to experience Israel's pain rather than rush to explain it away.

The uncomfortable juxtaposition of the belief in God's presence and power (core testimony) and the questions that arise out of the lived experience of God's absence (counter-testimony) cannot be avoided when one compares the three sections of Psalm 89 (1-18, 19-37, and 38-51). The first section, vv. 1-18, offers a hymn of praise to God: "I will sing [cp. Exod 15:1; Isa 5:1; Pss 13:6; 59:16; 101:1; 104:33; etc.] of your חסד ['covenant loyalty'], O LORD." Core testimony saturates this section. God's "covenant loyalty" ("steadfast love" in the NRSV) and "faithfulness" are paired seven times in Psalm 89; they frame the psalm (vv. 1, 2, 49) and also tie sections together (vv. 14b, 24, 28, 33). In vv. 3-4, God's covenant promise

3. Ibid., 67.

to David (2 Sam 7) is quoted as another piece of core testimony, introduced by "you said," spoken by the psalmist in v. 3a. Royal Psalms 2, 89, 110, and 132 also quote God about promises to the Davidic monarchy. God is quoted as using the first-person divine "I" three times in vv. 3-4: "I have made a covenant," "I have sworn," and "I will establish your descendants forever" (v. 4a; cp. 2 Sam 7:13, 16).

Verses 5-8 shift to a direct address to God as Lord of Hosts, sovereign over all other gods. Two rhetorical questions (vv. 6, 8)—"who . . . can be compared to the LORD?" and "who is as mighty as you?"—are answered by v. 7: no one, no other god, can be compared to Israel's God. Second Isaiah, in exile, also stresses God's incomparability (Isa 40:18; cp. Pss 18:31 and 77:13) amid the competition of other gods. In vv. 9-14 the repeated use of the second-person masculine singular pronoun אתה ("you") in vv. 9 (twice), 10, 11b, and 12a emphasizes God's power and sovereignty as creator of the cosmos: "you," "you," "you." People respond to God's sovereignty with worship (vv. 16-17). The hymnic section ends as it began, with the Davidic king (vv. 17-18) who is given the royal titles "our horn" and "our shield."

A second, extended divine speech about God's promise to David is quoted in the second section, vv. 19-37. It is introduced by "then you spoke . . . and said." The word אז ("then") also introduces a God quotation about David in Psalm 2:5. The God quotations in both psalms (and in Pss 110 and 132) draw on a past oracle from God rather than a present revelation in worship: they "are bearing the authority of the theological tradition."[4] The psalmist will use the power of God's authority in the third section to challenge God and remind God of the divine promises so that God may act in the present situation of distress.[5] In vv. 19-20 David is God's "chosen one" (2 Sam 7:8; 16:18; 1 Kgs 11:34; Ps 78:70) and "servant" (Isa 42:1; 45:4), whom God elevates (1 Kgs 14:7; 16:2) and anoints. The verb משׁח ("anoint") links Psalm 89 to the story of Samuel's anointing of David in 1 Samuel 16. These links make clear that Davidic power comes from God; this core belief will be turned against God as accusation in section three of the psalm.

Throughout this extended quotation in vv. 19-37, God's attributes praised in section one are applied to the king. God rules the sea and crushes Rahab (vv. 9-10) and God sets the king's hand on the sea (v. 25).

---

4. Rolf A. Jacobson, *"Many Are Saying": The Function of Direct Discourse in the Hebrew Psalter*, JSOTSup 397 (Edinburgh: T & T Clark, 2004), 125.

5. Ibid., 126.

God is above all the other gods, incomparable (vv. 6-7), and God makes the king "the highest [אֶלְיוֹן] of the kings of the earth" (v. 27). The title Elyon ("highest") is used for God in Genesis 14:19, 20; Deuteronomy 32:8; Psalms 47:2; 82:6, and is here transferred to the king. God has a mighty arm and strong right hand (v. 13, an extension of exodus language; cp. Ps 44:2-3 in the context of the conquest of the promised land), and God's hand "shall always remain" with the king and God's arm "shall strengthen him" (v. 21; also vv. 14 and 17 with v. 24). David's sovereignty depends on God's sovereignty. The close relationship between God and king is underscored by v. 26: "he shall cry to me, 'You are my Father'" (cp. 2 Sam 7:14; Pss 2:7; 110:1). God/king kinship is a common motif in the ancient Near East. The king will be God's firstborn (v. 27), with special privilege.

The second section of the psalm goes beyond 2 Samuel 7 in describing God's promises to David. God calls the divine promise a "covenant" in vv. 28 and 34 (cp. vv. 3, 39; see also 2 Sam 23:5: Isa 55:3; Jer 33:21; 2 Chr 13:5; 21:7, all late texts). In addition, God declares with the divine "I" that "I have sworn [שבע in the Niphal] to my servant David" in vv. 3 and 35. Rolf Jacobson suggests that God's swearing "performed" a contractual speech to David that made specific commitments. The verb שבע ("swear") is "a legally binding word that God spoke and that committed God to the covenant"[6] with David ("the Lord has sworn" in Pss 110:4 and 132:11). The divine commitments include giving the king victory in battle (vv. 22-23; Ps 2:1-3), adopting the king as God's son (v. 26), and responding to the king when he calls to God (v. 26). The "language of permanence" pervades the first two sections and tempers the conditionality of the covenant in vv. 30-32. Davidic descendants who do not obey God's commandments will be punished, but the Davidic covenant will not be ended (vv. 33-37). The word "forever" and its synonyms are repeated in vv. 1, 4, 21a, 28, 29, 36, 37, contributing to the sense of permanence. The Davidic line will be "established forever like the moon" (v. 37); it is part of the cosmic order.

In stark contrast to the "then" of v. 19 that introduces a second God quotation of Davidic promises, "but now" in v. 38 abruptly switches gears to lament (vv. 38-51). The phrase jars the community away from core testimony wrapped in past promises to the present reality of counter-testimony in the midst of suffering. "Everything said and sung so far in

6. Ibid.

this impressive psalm is turned upside down, brought to nothing."[7] This is where the psalm forces us to sit with Israel's pain, just as Psalm 44 does. Imitating the style of the first section with a repetition of the second-person independent personal pronoun "you," the psalmist makes it clear that God is the cause of the present suffering. God becomes the object of complaint instead of praise.

"You" (God) have "spurned" and "rejected" the king (v. 38), "renounced the covenant with your servant" (v. 39a), "defiled his [the king's] crown in the dust" (v. 39b), "laid his [the king's] stronghold in ruins" (v. 40b), "exalted the right hand of his [the king's] foes" (v. 42a; cp. v. 25), "have not supported him [the king] in battle" (v. 43b), "hurled his [the king's] throne to the ground" (v. 44b), and "covered him [the king] with shame" (v. 45b)—"you," "you," "you." The Davidic king represents the whole people in this long list; they become the bearers of God's promises in the exilic period.

The idea of permanence is challenged in vv. 46-48: the psalmist asks "how long?": how long will this suffering continue? This is a typical lament question that reflects concern with the transitory nature of life: "who can escape the power of Sheol?" (note the connection with Ps 88 here). God's חסד ("covenant loyalty") praised in the first two sections of the psalm is now nowhere in evidence: the psalmist demands "where is your חסד of old?" (v. 49a). The only two petitions offered are for God to "remember" (vv. 47a, 50a). The implication is that God has forgotten or purposely broken God's promises to David and the people have suffered for it. God has allowed the highest of kings (v. 27b) to be humiliated; there has been no victory in battle. If God remembers, perhaps God will save.

Book 3 of the Psalter closes with the reality of God's absence. The doxology in v. 52 that ends book 3 jars the reader, following as it does the repetition of the word "taunt" in v. 51. The king is no longer the highest of kings (v. 27b) but the object of derision and so, correspondingly, are the king's people, the community in exile. The closing doxology sharpens the contrast between core (vv. 1-37) and counter-testimony (vv. 38-51) presented in Psalm 89. The Davidic king no longer sits on the throne. The promises of God have not been kept. God's faithfulness is in question. In reading Psalm 89 one cannot escape the haunting presence of Michal, Abigail, Bathsheba, and Abishag, hovering perhaps with an "I told you

---

7. Erhard Gerstenberger, *Psalms, Part 2, and Lamentations* (Grand Rapids, MI: Eerdmans, 2001), 153.

so" on their lips. Who better to evaluate the assertions about Davidic monarchy than these four women so intimately connected with the founder of the dynasty with whom God has entered into covenant? These women experienced firsthand the pitfalls of God's promises to David. As Adele Berlin has suggested, "There is a correspondence between the public and private stages in David's life in terms of his responses to his wives";[8] aspects of his character that shape the kingship of those who follow in his line are revealed in his interaction with these women, as we see below. The core testimony of Psalm 89 that transfers God's attributes to the king would certainly be suspect in their eyes. They can only shake their heads as they listen to exiled Israel pray Psalm 89: they saw it coming.

Adele Berlin on David's Wives

Michal is forced into an unfeminine role in the narrative in 1 and 2 Samuel. She is never called beautiful, as most women connected to the king are. It is recorded twice that she loved David (1 Sam 18:20, 28), but to David she was merely a political pawn. As King Saul's daughter, she could cement David's claim to the throne: "it pleased David to be the king's son-in-law" (1 Sam 18:26). Any love or tenderness David might have shown to Michal is "reserved for Jonathan" (p. 71), Saul's son (1 Sam 20:41; 2 Sam 1:26: "you have been very pleasing to me— more wonderful was your love to me than the love of women"). Michal's criticism of David's procession with the ark of the covenant into Jerusalem (2 Sam 6:20) leads to her being written out of the story by the Deuteronomistic editor: she had no children to the day of her death (2 Sam 6:23). Childless, she "never filled a female role" (p. 72). David's interactions with Michal demonstrate "the cold, calculated gaining of power" (p. 70) that marks David's kingship and those of his followers, leading eventually to exile.

Abigail (1 Sam 25) functions as a type in David's story; both she and her husband Nabal ("fool") are "exaggerated stereotypes" (p. 77). He is a stubborn and boorish drunk; she is "a model wife and modest woman" who prevents David from committing murder and tainting his future kingship. In the "mirror" story of David and Bathsheba, he commits murder (killing Uriah) because of a woman. As Berlin insists, "The Abigail story, no less than the Saul stories, is a strong endorsement of David's destiny

---

8. Adele Berlin, "Characterization in Biblical Narrative: David's Wives," *JSOT* 23 (1982): 69–85, at 79.

to reign as the chosen favorite of God" (p. 77). Abigail's declaration in 1 Samuel 25:29-30 dovetails with the core testimony about God's promises to David in Psalm 89:1-37. Abigail illumines David's "self-assurance as a popular leader" (p. 79), the kind of self-assurance that leads him and his descendants into trouble.

Bathsheba, "taken" (2 Sam 11:4) as Samuel had warned the people a king would do (1 Sam 8), "enters the story as a passive object, someone seen from a rooftop" (p. 72). The narrator says nothing regarding Bathsheba's feelings about the murder of her husband Uriah or the death of her illegitimate son. Berlin argues that "she is not even a minor character, but simply part of the plot" (p. 73). Though Berlin thinks she becomes a "real" person in 1 Kings 1–2 when she works to secure the throne for her son, Solomon, she is actually manipulated by the prophet Nathan, who tells her what to do, including tricking the old and frail David into believing that he had already promised the throne to her son. David's interactions with Bathsheba illustrate his "desire to increase his holdings, [and] expand his empire" (p. 79).

Again, grasping for more will mark the reigns of David's descendants on the throne.

Abishag, introduced in 1 Kings 1:4, "provides a contrast to David—her youth and beauty offset his age and feebleness" (p. 74). In 1 Kings 1:15 we are reminded again of Abishag's presence with the king when Bathsheba enters the king's chambers. Why? "It is Bathsheba who is now noticing the presence of Abishag as she enters the room. Bathsheba, who was once young and attractive like Abishag, is herself now aging, and has been, in a sense, replaced by Abishag, just as she comes for the purpose of replacing David with Solomon" (p. 74). Jealousy may be at play here, though both Abishag and Bathsheba are simply "agents," that is, functions of the plot. When Bathsheba agrees to take to Solomon the request of David's son Adonijah to be given his father's concubine, it causes Adonijah's death; his request is the equivalent of a claim to the throne. David's encounter with Abishag illustrates "his loss of control of the kingship" (p. 79).[9]

Denise Dombkowski Hopkins

9. Ibid., 69–85.

Works Cited

Abraham, Dulcie. "Rizpah's Story: II Samuel 21:1-14." In *Women of Courage: Asian Women Reading the Bible*, edited by Lee Oo Chung, et al. SaDang Publishing House, 1992.

Adams, Samuel L. *Social and Economic Life in Second Temple Judea*. Louisville, KY: Westminster John Knox, 2014.

Allen, Leslie C. "Psalm 73: Pilgrimage from Doubt to Faith." *BBR* 7 (1997): 1–10.

Alter, Robert. *The Art of Biblical Poetry*. New York: Basic Books, 1985.

———. *The Book of Psalms*. New York: Norton, 2007.

Anderson, Gary A. "King David and the Psalms of Imprecation." *ProEccl* 15 (2006): 267–80.

Avrahami, Yael. "בוש in the Psalms—Shame or Disappointment?" *JSOT* 34 (2010): 259–313.

Bach, Alice. "The Pleasure of Her Text." *USQR* 43 (1989): 41–58.

Bail, Ulrike. "'O God, Hear My Prayer': Psalm 55 and Violence against Women." In *A Feminist Companion to Wisdom and Psalms*, edited by Athalya Brenner and Carol Fontaine, 242–63. FCB 2nd ser. Sheffield: Sheffield Academic Press, 1998.

Bal, Mieke. "Dealing/With/Women: Daughters in the Book of Judges." In *The Book and the Text: The Bible and Literary Theory*, edited by Regina M. Schwartz, 16–39. Oxford: Basil Blackwell, 1990.

Barré, Michael. "The Seven Epithets of Zion in Ps 48, 2-3." *Bib* 69 (1988): 558–60.

Bautch, Richard J. "Lament Regained in Trito-Isaiah's Penitential Prayer." In *Seeking the Favor of God: The Origins of Penitential Prayer in Second Temple Judaism*, edited by Mark Boda, Daniel Falk, and Rodney Werline. Atlanta, GA: SBL, 2006.

Beal, Timothy. "Ideology and Intertextuality: Surplus of Meaning and Controlling the Means of Production." In *Reading Between Texts: Intertextuality and the Hebrew Bible*, edited by Dana Nolan Fewell, 27–39. Louisville, KY: Westminster John Knox, 1992.

Bellinger, W. H. *A Hermeneutic of Curiosity and Readings of Psalm 61*. Studies in Old Testament Interpretation. Macon, GA: Mercer University Press, 1995.

Berlin, Adele. "Characterization in Biblical Narrative: David's Wives." *JSOT* 23 (1982): 69–85.

———. "On Reading Biblical Poetry: The Role of Metaphor." In *Congress Volume*, 25–36. Leiden: Brill, 1997.

———. "Psalms and the Literature of Exile: Psalms 137, 44, 69, and 78." In *The Book of Psalms: Composition and Reception*, edited by Peter W. Flint and Patrick D. Miller, 65–86. Leiden: Brill, 2005.

Berquist, Jon L. *Judaism in Persia's Shadow: A Social and Historical Approach*. Minneapolis: Fortress Press 1995.

Beyerlin, Walter. *Im Licht der Traditionen: Psalm LXVII and CXV: ein Entwicklungszusammenhang*. VTSup 45. Leiden: Brill, 1992.

Birch, Bruce, Walter Brueggemann, Terence E. Fretheim, and David L. Petersen. *A Theological Introduction to the Old Testament*. Nashville, TN: Abingdon Press, 1999.

Bland, Dave, and David Fleer, eds. *Performing the Psalms*. St. Louis, MO: Chalice Press, 2005.

Blumenthal, David. *Facing the Abusing God: A Theology of Protest*. Louisville, KY: Westminster John Knox, 1993.

Boda, Mark. "The Daughter's Joy." In *Daughter Zion: Her Portrait, Her Response*, edited by Mark Boda, Carol J. Dempsey, LeAnn Snow Flesher, 321–42. Atlanta, GA: SBL, 2012.

Bodner, Keith. "The 'Embarrassing Syntax' of Ps. 47:10: A (Pro)Vocative Option." *JTS* (2003): 50–75.

Bos, Johanna W. H. "Oh When the Saints: A Consideration of the Meaning of Psalm 50." *JSOT* 24 (1982): 65–77.

Bosworth, David. "Weeping in the Psalms." *VT* 62 (2013): 36–46.

Botha, Philippus J. " 'I Am Like a Green Olive Tree': The Wisdom Context of Psalm 52." *HTS* 69 (2013).

———. "Psalm 54: The Power of Positive Patterning." *SK* 21 (2000): 504–16.

———. "The Textual Strategy and Social Background of Psalm 64 as Keys to Its Interpretation." *JSem* 11 (2002): 64–82.

Bowen, Nancy R. "A Fairy Tale Wedding? A Feminist Intertextual Reading of Psalm 45." In *A God So Near: Essays on Old Testament Theology in Honor of Patrick D. Miller*, edited by Brent Strawn and Nancy Bowen, 53–71. Winona Lake, IN: Eisenbrauns, 2003.

Braiterman, Zachary. *God after Auschwitz: Tradition and Change in Post-Holocaust Jewish Thought*. Princeton, NJ: Princeton University Press, 1998.

Braude, William G. *The Midrash on Psalms.* Vol. 1. New Haven, CT: Yale University Press, 1954.

Braun, Joachim. *Music in Ancient Israel/Palestine: Archaeological, Written, and Comparative Sources.* Grand Rapids, MI: Eerdmans, 2002.

Brenner, Athalya, and Fokkelien Van Dijk-Hemmes. *On Gendering Texts: Female and Male Voices in the Hebrew Bible.* Leiden: Brill, 1993.

Brenner, Athalya, and Frank Polak, eds. *Performing Memory in Biblical Narrative and Beyond.* Sheffield: Sheffield Phoenix Press, 2009.

Brettler, Marc Zvi. "Images of YHWH the Warrior in Psalms." *Semia* 61 (1993): 135–65.

———. "Mother of Psalmist (God's Serving Girl)." In *Women in Scripture*, edited by Carol Meyers, 296–97. Boston: Houghton Mifflin, 2000.

———. "Women and Psalms: Toward an Understanding of the Role of Women's Prayer in the Israelite Cult." In *Gender and Law in the Hebrew Bible and the Ancient Near East*, edited by Victor Matthews, Bernard Levinson, and Tikva Frymer-Kensky, 25–56. JSOTSup 262. Sheffield: Sheffield Academic Press, 1998.

Brock, Rita Nakashima, and Gabriella Lettini. *Soul Repair: Recovering from Moral Injury after War.* Boston: Beacon Press, 2012.

Brown, William P. "Happiness and Its Discontents in the Psalms." In *The Bible and the Pursuit of Happiness: What the Old and New Testaments Teach Us about the Good Life*, edited by Brent A. Strawn, 95–116. Oxford: Oxford University Press, 2012.

———. "The Psalms and 'I': The Dialogical Self and the Disappearing Psalmist." In *Diachronic and Synchronic: reading the Psalms in Real Time*, Proceedings of the Baylor Symposium on the Book of Psalms, edited by Joel Burnett, W. H. Bellinger, and W. Dennis Tucker, 26–44. Edinburgh: T & T Clark, 2007.

———. *Seeing the Psalms: A Theology of Metaphor.* Louisville, KY: Westminster John Knox, 2002.

Brown Douglas, Kelly. *Sexuality and the Black Church: A Womanist Perspective.* Maryknoll, NY: Orbis Books, 1999.

Brueggemann, Walter. "Bounded by Obedience and Praise: The Psalms as Canon." *JSOT* 50 (1991): 63–92.

———. "A Fissure Always Uncontained." In *Strange Fire: Reading the Bible after the Holocaust*, edited by Tod Linafelt, 62–75. New York: New York University Press, 2000.

———. *From Whom No Secrets Are Hid: Introducing the Psalms.* Edited by Brent Strawn. Louisville, KY: Westminster John Knox, 2014.

———. *The Message of the Psalms.* Minneapolis: Augsburg, 1984.

———. "Psychological Criticism: Exploring the Self in the Text." In *Method Matters: Essays on the Interpretation of the Hebrew Bible in Honor of David L. Petersen*, edited by Joel LeMon and Kent Harold Richards, 213–32. Atlanta, GA: SBL, 2009.

———. *Reverberations of Faith: A Theological Handbook of Old Testament Themes.* Louisville, KY: Westminster John Knox, 2002.

———. *Theology of the Old Testament: Testimony, Dispute, Advocacy.* Minneapolis: Fortress Press, 1997.

Buber, Martin. "The Heart Determines: Psalm 73." In *Theodicy in the Old Testament*, edited by James L. Crenshaw, 109–18. Philadelphia: Fortress Press, 1983.

Burgh, Theodore. *Listening to the Artifacts: Music Culture in Ancient Palestine.* New York: T & T Clark, 2006.

Camp, Claudia. "The Wise Women of 2 Samuel: A Role Model for Women in Early Israel?" *CBQ* 43 (1981): 14–29.

Cannon, Katie G. *Black Womanist Ethics.* Atlanta, GA: Scholars Press, 1988.

Carter, Warren. "Postcolonial Biblical Criticism." In *New Meanings for Ancient Texts*, edited by Steven L. McKenzie and John Kaltner, 97–116. Louisville, KY: Westminster John Knox, 2013.

Cartledge, Tony W. "Conditional Vows in the Psalms of Lament: A New Approach to an Old Problem." In *The Listening Heart: Essays in Wisdom and the Psalms in Honor of Roland E. Murphy*, edited by Kenneth G. Hoglund, 77–94. Sheffield: JSOT Press, 1987.

Chalmers, Aaron. " 'There Is No Deliverer (From My Hand)'—A Formula Analysis." *VT* 55 (2005): 287–92.

Chapman, Cynthia. *The Gendered Language of Warfare in the Israelite-Assyrian Encounter.* Winona Lake, IN: Eisenbrauns, 2004.

Claassens, L. Juliana M. *Mourner, Mother, Midwife: Reimagining God's Delivering Presence in the Old Testament.* Louisville, KY: Westminster John Knox, 2012.

Clifford, Richard. *Psalms 1–72.* Nashville, TN: Abingdon Press, 2002.

———. *Psalms 73–150.* Nashville, TN: Abingdon Press, 2003.

Cohn Eskenazi, Tamara. "Ezra–Nehemiah." In *Women's Bible Commentary*, edited by Carol A. Newsom, Sharon H. Ringe, and Jacqueline E. Lapsley, 192–200. 3rd ed. Louisville, KY: Westminster John Knox, 2012.

Cole, Robert L. *The Shape and Message of Book III (Psalms 73–89).* JSOTSup 307. Sheffield: Sheffield Academic Press, 2000.

Cone, James H. *God of the Oppressed.* Maryknoll, NY: Orbis Books, 1997.

Coogan, Michael D. *The Old Testament: A Historical and Literary Introduction to the Hebrew Scriptures.* Oxford: Oxford University Press, 2006.

Cooper-White, Pamela. "Com/plicated Woman: Multiplicity and Relationality across Gender and Culture." In *Women Out of Order: Risking Change and Creating Care in a Multicultural World*, edited by Jeanne Stevenson-Moessner and Teresa Snorton, 7–21. Minneapolis: Fortress Press, 2010.

Coote, Robert B. " 'Let This House Be Healed' (Psalm 51)." In *Religion und Krankheit*, edited by Gregor Etzelmüller and Annette Weissenrieder, 217–30. Darmstadt: Wissenschaftliche Buchgesellschaft, 2010.

Copeland, M. Shawn. *Enfleshing Freedom: Body, Race, and Being.* Minneapolis: Fortress Press, 2010.

Cottrill, Amy C. *Language, Power, and Identity in the Lament Psalms of the Individual.* New York and London: T & T Clark, 2008.

Craigie, Peter. *Psalms 1–50.* Waco, TX: Word Books, 1983.

Creach, Jerome F. D. "Psalm 70." *Int* 60 (2006): 64–66.

Crenshaw, James L. *Defending God.* New York: Oxford University Press, 2005.

———. *The Psalms: An Introduction.* Grand Rapids, MI: Eerdmans, 2001.

Crow, Loren. "The Rhetoric of Psalm 44." *ZAW* 104 (1992): 394–401.

Davis, Ellen. *Scripture, Culture, and Agriculture: An Agrarian Reading of the Bible.* Cambridge: Cambridge University Press, 2009.

Davison, Lisa W. " 'My Soul Is Like the Weaned Child That Is with Me': The Psalms and the Feminine Voice." *HBT* 23 (2001): 155–67.

Day, Linda. "Rhetoric and Domestic Violence in Ezekiel 16." *BibInt* 8 (2000): 205–30.

deClaissé-Walford, Nancy. "Psalm 44: O God, Why Do You Hide Your Face?" *RevExp* 104 (Fall 2007): 745–59.

———. "Psalms." In *Women's Bible Commentary,* edited by Carol A. Newsom, Sharon H. Ringe, and Jacqueline E. Lapsley, 221–31. 3rd ed. Louisville, KY: Westminster John Knox, 2012.

Dell, Katharine J. " 'I Will Solve My Riddle to the Music of the Lyre' (Psalm XLIX 4 [5]): A Cultic Setting for Wisdom Psalms?," *VT* 54 (2004): 445–58.

Dever, William G. *Did God Have a Wife? Archaeology and Folk Religion in Ancient Israel.* Grand Rapids, MI: Eerdmans, 2005.

Dillard, Annie. *Teaching a Stone to Talk.* New York: HarperCollins, 1982.

Dombkowski Hopkins, Denise. *Journey through the Psalms.* St. Louis, MO: Chalice Press, 2002.

———. "Judith." In *Women's Bible Commentary,* edited by Carol A. Newsom, Sharon H. Ringe, and Jacqueline E. Lapsley, 383–90. 3rd ed. Louisville, KY: Westminster John Knox, 2012.

Dombkowski Hopkins, Denise, and Michael S. Koppel. *Grounded in the Living Word: The Old Testament and Pastoral Care Practices.* Grand Rapids, MI: Eerdmans, 2010.

Doyle, Brian. "Howling Like Dogs: Metaphorical Language in Psalm LIX." *VT* 54 (2004): 61–82.

———. "Where Is God When You Need Him Most? The Divine Metaphor of Absence and Presence as a Binding Element in the Composition of the Book of Psalms." In *The Composition of the Book of Psalms,* edited by Erich Zenger, 277–90. Leuven: Peeters, 2010.

Dube, Musa. *Postcolonial Feminist Interpretation of the Bible.* St. Louis, MO: Chalice Press, 2000.

Dykstra, Laurel A. *Set Them Free: The Other Side of Exodus.* Maryknoll, NY: Orbis Books, 2002.

Ebeling, Jennie E. *Women's Lives in Biblical Times.* London and New York: T & T Clark, 2010.

Edelman, Diana. "Huldah the Prophet—of Yahweh or Asherah?" In *A Feminist Companion to Samuel and Kings*, edited by Athalya Brenner, 231–50. Sheffield: Sheffield Academic Press, 1994.

Eidevall, Goeran. "Images of God, Self, and the Enemy in the Psalms: On the Role of Metaphor in Identity Construction." In *Metaphor in the Hebrew Bible*, edited by Pierre van Hecke, 55–65. Leuven: University Press, 2005.

Estes, David J. "Poetic Artistry in the Expression of Fear in Psalm 49." *BSac* 161 (2004): 55–71.

Exum, J. Cheryl. *Fragmented Women: Feminist (Sub)versions of Biblical Narratives.* Valley Forge, PA: Trinity Press International, 1993.

———. "Murder They Wrote: Ideology and the Manipulation of Female Presence in Biblical Narrative." In *The Pleasure of Her Text: Feminist Readings of Biblical and Historical Texts*, edited by Alice Bach, 45–68. Philadelphia: Trinity Press International, 1990.

Fewell, Danna Nolan. *The Children of Israel: Reading the Bible for the Sake of Our Children.* Nashville, TN: Abingdon Press, 2003.

von Franz, Marie-Louise. *Projection and Re-Collection in Jungian Psychology.* Chicago: Open Court, 1995.

Fretheim, Terence E. "God, Creation, and the Pursuit of Happiness." In *The Bible and the Pursuit of Happiness: What the Old and New Testaments Teach Us about the Good Life*, edited by Brent A. Strawn, 33–56. Oxford: Oxford University Press, 2012.

———. *The Suffering of God: An Old Testament Perspective.* Minneapolis: Fortress Press, 1984.

Frymer-Kensky, Tikva. "Reading Rahab." In *Tehillah le-Moshe: Biblical and Judaic Studies in Honor of Moshe Greenberg*, edited by Mordechai Cogan, Barry L. Eichler, and Jeffrey H. Tigay, 57–76. Winona Lake, IN: Eisenbrauns, 1997.

Fuchs, Esther. "The Literary Characterization of Mothers and Sexual Politics in the Hebrew Bible." In *Women in the Hebrew Bible: A Reader*, edited by Alice Bach, 127–40. New York: Routledge, 1999.

Gafney, Wilda C. *Daughters of Miriam: Women Prophets in Ancient Israel.* Minneapolis: Fortress Press, 2008.

Gaiser, Frederick. "'I Will Tell You What God Has Done for Me' (Psalm 66:16): A Place for 'Testimony' in Lutheran Worship?" *WW* 26 (Spring 2006): 138–48.

Gallares, Judette A. *Images of Faith: Spirituality of Women in the Old Testament.* Maryknoll, NY: Orbis Books, 1992.

Gerstenberger, Erhard. *Psalms, Part 2, and Lamentations.* Grand Rapids, MI: Eerdmans, 2001.

Gillingham, Susan. "New Wine and Old Wineskins: Three Approaches to Prophecy and Psalmody." In *Prophecy and Prophets in Ancient Israel: Proceedings of the Oxford Old Testament Seminar*, edited by John Day, 370–90. New York: T & T Clark, 2010.

Gillmayr-Bucher, Susanne. "Body Images in the Psalms." *JSOT* 28 (2004): 301–26.

Goldingay, John. *Psalms*. Vol. 2. Grand Rapids, MI: Baker Academic, 2007.

Gordon, Pamela, and Harold C. Washington. "Rape as a Military Metaphor in the Hebrew Bible." In *A Feminist Companion to the Latter Prophets*, edited by Athalya Brenner, 308–25. Sheffield: Sheffield Academic Press, 1995.

Gordon, Robert P. *Holy Land, Holy City: Sacred Geography and the Interpretation of the Bible*. Waynesboro, GA: Paternoster Press, 2004.

Grant, Jacqueline. "The Sin of Servanthood and the Deliverance of Discipleship." In *A Troubling in My Soul: Womanist Perspectives on Evil and Suffering*, edited by Emilie M. Townes, 199–218. Maryknoll, NY: Orbis Books, 1993.

Greenstein, Edward L. "Mixing Memory and Design: Reading Psalm 78." *Prooftexts* 10, no. 2 (May 1990): 197–218.

van Grol, Harm. "War and Peace in the Psalms: Some Compositional Explorations." In *Deuterocanonical and Cognate Literature Yearbook 2010: Visions of Peace and Tales of War*, edited by Jan Liesen and Pancratius Beentjes, 173–206. Berlin and New York: de Gruyter, 2010.

Hackett, Jo Ann. "1 and 2 Samuel." In *Women's Bible Commentary*, edited by Carol A. Newsom, Sharon H. Ringe, and Jacqueline E. Lapsley, 150–63. 3rd ed. Louisville, KY: Westminster John Knox, 2012.

Handy, Lowell K. "Sounds, Words and Meanings in Psalm 82." *JSOT* 47 (1990): 51–66.

Hartin, Patrick J. "Poor." In *Eerdmans Dictionary of the Bible*, edited by David Noel Freedman, 1070–71. Grand Rapids, MI: Eerdmans, 2000.

Heard, R. Christopher. "Penitent to a Fault: The Characterization of David in Psalm 51." In *The Fate of King David: The Past and Present of a Biblical Icon*, edited by Tod Linafelt, Claudia Camp, and Timothy Beal, 163–74. New York: T & T Clark, 2010.

Hendel, Ronald. "Cultural Memory and the Hebrew Bible." *The Bible and Interpretation*. www.bibleinterp.com. July 2011.

Hilber, J. W. *Cultic Prophecy in the Psalms*. BZAW 352. Berlin: de Gruyter, 2005.

Hillman, James. *Healing Fiction*. Putnam, CT: Spring Publications, 1994.

———. *Suicide and the Soul*. Dallas, TX: Spring Publishing, 1978.

Hobbins, John H. "Zion's Plea That God See Her as She Sees Herself: Unanswered Prayer in Lamentations 1–2." In *Daughter Zion: Her Portrait, Her Response*, edited by Mark Boda, Carol J. Dempsey, and LeAnn Snow Flesher, 149–76. Atlanta, GA: SBL, 2012.

hooks, bell. *Yearning: Race, Gender, and Cultural Politics*. Boston: South End Press, 1990.

Horsley, Richard A. *Covenant Economics*. Louisville, KY: Westminster John Knox, 2009.

Hossfeld, Frank-Lothar, and Erich Zenger. *Psalms 2: A Commentary on Psalms 51–100*. Translated by Linda M. Maloney. Hermeneia. Minneapolis: Fortress Press, 2005.

Houston, Walter. "The King's Preferential Option for the Poor: Rhetoric, Ideology and Ethics in Psalm 72." *BibInt* 7 (1999): 341–67.

Howard, Cameron B. R. "1 and 2 Kings." In *Women's Bible Commentary*, edited by Carol A. Newsom, Sharon H. Ringe, and Jacqueline E. Lapsley. 3rd ed. Louisville, KY: Westminster John Knox, 2012.

Hundley, Michael. *Gods in Dwellings: Temples and Divine Presence in the Ancient Near East*. Atlanta, GA: SBL, 2013.

Hunter, Alastair G. "Inside Outside Psalm 55: How Jonah Grew Out of a Psalmist's Conceit." In *Psalms and Prayers*. OtSt 55. Leiden: Brill Academic Publishers, 2006.

Jacobson, Rolf A. " 'The Altar of Certitude': Reflections on 'Setting' and the Rhetorical Interpretation of the Psalms." In *My Words Are Lovely: Studies in the Rhetoric of the Psalms*, edited by Robert L. Foster and David M. Howard, 3–18. New York: T & T Clark, 2008.

———. *"Many Are Saying": The Function of Direct Discourse in the Hebrew Psalter*. JSOTSup 397. Edinburgh: T & T Clark, 2004.

Janowski, Bernd. *Arguing with God: A Theological Anthropology of the Psalms*. Translated by Armin Siedlecki. Louisville, KY: Westminster John Knox, 2013.

The Jewish Study Bible, Tanakh Translation. Edited by Adele Berlin and Marc Zvi Brettler. Oxford: Oxford University Press, 2004.

Johnson, James Weldon. *God's Trombones*. New York: Viking Penguin, 1927.

Johnson, Vivian L. *David in Distress: His Portrait through the Historical Psalms*. New York and London: T & T Clark, 2009.

Jung, Carl G. *The Collected Works*. Vol. 18. Edited and Translated by Gerhard Adler and R. F. C. Hull. Princeton, NJ: Princeton University Press, 1980.

Kalmanofsky, Amy. "Their Heart Cried Out to God: Gender and Prayer in the Book of Lamentations." In *A Question of Sex? Gender and Difference in the Hebrew Bible and Beyond*, ed. Deborah Rooke, 53–65. Sheffield: Sheffield Phoenix Press, 2007.

Kaminsky, Joel. *Yet I Loved Jacob: Reclaiming the Biblical Concept of Election*. Nashville, TN: Abingdon Press, 2007.

Keefe, Alice A. "Rapes of Women/Wars of Men." *Semeia* 61 (1993): 79–93.

Kim, Hee Suk. "A Critique against God? Reading Psalm 80 in the Context of Vindication." In *Why? . . . How Long? Studies on Voice(s) of Lamentation Rooted in Hebrew Poetry*, edited by LeAnn Snow Flesher, Mark Boda, and Carol J. Dempsey, 100–114. New York: Bloomsbury, 2013.

Kim, Simone Sunghae. "A Korean Feminist Perspective on God Representation." *Pastoral Psychology* 55 (2006): 35–45.

King, Philip J., and Lawrence E. Stager. *Life in Biblical Israel*. Louisville, KY: Westminster John Knox, 2001.

Klein, Melanie. *Envy and Gratitude, and Other Works, 1946–1963*. London: The Hogarth Press and The Institute of Psycho-Analysis, 1975.

Knohl, Israel. "Between Voice and Silence: The Relationship between Prayer and the Temple Cult." *JBL* 115 (1996): 17–30.

Kraus, Hans-Joachim. *Psalms 1–59: A Commentary*. Translated by Hilton C. Oswald. Minneapolis: Fortress Press, 1989.

Kselman, John S., and Michael L. Barré. "A Note on ʾelem in Psalm LVIII 2." *VT* 54 (2004): 400–402.

———. "Psalm 55: Problems and Proposals." *CBQ* 60 (1998): 440–62.

Kyung, Chung Hyun. *Struggle to Be the Sun Again*. Maryknoll, NY: Orbis Books, 1990.

Lapsley, Jacqueline E. "Ezekiel." In *Women's Bible Commentary*, edited by Carol A. Newsom, Sharon H. Ringe, and Jacqueline E. Lapsley. 3rd ed. Louisville, KY: Westminster John Knox, 2012.

———. "'Look! The Children and I Are as Signs and Portents in Israel': Children in Isaiah." In *The Child in the Bible*, edited by Marcia J. Bunge et al., 82–102. Grand Rapids, MI: Eerdmans, 2008.

———. *Whispering the Word: Hearing Women's Stories in the Old Testament*. Louisville, KY: Westminster John Knox, 2005.

Lawrence, Beatrice. "Gender Analysis: Gender and Method in Biblical Studies." In *Method Matters: Essays on the Interpretation of the Hebrew Bible in Honor of David L. Petersen*, edited by Joel LeMon and Kent Harold Richards, 333–48. Atlanta, GA: SBL, 2009.

Lee, Kyung Sook. "Books of Kings: Images of Women without Women's Reality." In *Feminist Biblical Interpretation: A Compendium of Critical Commentary*, edited by Luise Schottroff and Marie-Theres Wacker, 159–77. Grand Rapids, MI: Eerdmans, 2012.

LeMon, Joel M. *Yahweh's Winged Form in the Psalms: Exploring Congruent Iconography and Texts*. Fribourg: Academic Press; Göttingen: Vandenhoeck & Ruprecht, 2010.

———. "YHWH's Hand and the Iconography of the Blow in Psalm 81:14-16." *JBL* 132 (2013): 865–82.

Levine, Herbert J. *Sing unto God a New Song: A Contemporary Reading of the Psalms*. Bloomington: Indiana University Press, 1995.

Little, Deborah. "Theology of the Poor." In *Handbook of U.S. Theologies of Liberation*, edited by Miguel De La Torre, 274–80. St. Louis, MO: Chalice Press, 2004.

Lorde, Audre. "The Master's Tools Will Never Dismantle the Master's House." In *Sister Outsider: Essays and Speeches*. Berkeley, CA: Crossing Press, 2007.

Maathai, Wangari. *Replenishing the Earth: Spiritual Values for Healing Ourselves and the World*. New York: Doubleday, 2010.

Macchi, Jean-Daniel. "Denial, Deception, or Force: How to Deal with Powerful Others in the Book of Esther." In *Imagining the Other and Constructing Israelite Identity in the Early Second Temple Period*, edited by Ehud Ben Zvi and Diana V. Edelman, 219–29. London: Bloomsbury, 2014.

MacDonald, Nathan. *Not Bread Alone: The Uses of Food in the Old Testament*. Oxford: Oxford University Press, 2008.

Maier, Christl M. "Psalm 87 as a Reappraisal of the Zion Tradition and Its Reception in Galations 4:26." *CBQ* 69 (2007): 473–86.

Mandolfo, Carleen. *God in the Dock: Dialogic Tension in the Psalms of Lament*. JSOTSup 357. Sheffield: Sheffield Academic Press, 2002.

———. "Psalm 88 and the Holocaust: Lament in Search of a Divine Response." *BibInt* 15 (2007): 151–70.

McCann, J. Clinton, Jr. "The Book of Psalms." In *The New Interpreter's Bible*, 639–1280. Vol. 4. Nashville, TN: Abingdon Press, 1996.

———. "Preaching the Psalms, Ps 68:1-10, 32-35, Ascension Sunday." *Journal for Preachers* 31 (Easter 2008): 17–20.

McClain, William. *Come Sunday: The Liturgy of Zion*. Nashville, TN: Abingdon Press, 1990.

McKinlay, Judith E. *Reframing Her: Biblical Women in Postcolonial Focus*. Sheffield: Sheffield Phoenix Press, 2004.

Menn, Esther M. "Child Characters in Biblical Narratives: The Young David (1 Samuel 16–17) and the Little Israelite Servant Girl (2 Kings 5:1-19)." In *The Child in the Bible*, edited by Marcia J. Bunge et al., 324–52. Grand Rapids, MI: Eerdmans, 2008.

Meyers, Carol. "Contesting the Notion of Patriarchy: Anthropology and the Theorizing of Gender in Ancient Israel." In *A Question of Sex? Gender and Difference in the Hebrew Bible and Beyond*, ed. Deborah Rooke, 83–105. Sheffield: Sheffield Phoenix Press, 2007.

———. "The Function of Feasts: An Anthropological Perspective on Israelite Religious Festivals." In *Social Theory and the Study of Israelite Religion: Essays in Retrospect and Prospect*, edited by Saul M. Olyan, 141–68. Atlanta, GA: SBL 2012.

———. "Gender Imagery in the Song of Songs." In *A Feminist Companion to the Song of Songs*, edited by Athalya Brenner and Carole R. Fontaine, 197–212. Sheffield: Sheffield Academic Press, 1993.

———. "Ps 48:7, Woman in Labor." In *Women in Scripture: A Dictionary of Named and Unnamed Women in the Hebrew Bible, the Apocryphal/Deuterocanonical Books, and the New Testament*, edited by Carol Meyers and Toni Craven, 298–99. Boston: Houghton Mifflin, 2000.

———. "Pss 78:63; 148:12—Young Women (and Young Men)." In *Women in Scripture*, edited by Carol Meyers. Boston: Houghton Mifflin, 2000.

———. *Rediscovering Eve: Ancient Israelite Women in Context*. New York: Oxford University Press, 2013.

———. "Women Dividing the Spoil, Ps 68:12." In *Women in Scripture*, edited by Carol Meyers. Boston: Houghton Mifflin, 2000.

———. "Women's Religious Life in Ancient Israel." In *Women's Bible Commentary*, edited by Carol A. Newsom, Sharon H. Ringe, and Jacqueline E. Lapsley, 354–60. 3rd ed. Louisville, KY: Westminster John Knox, 2012.

Miller, Patrick D. "The Land in the Psalms." In *The Land of Israel in Bible, History, and Theology: Studies in Honour of Ed Noort*, edited by Jacques van Ruiten and J. Cornelis DeVos, 183–96. Leiden: Brill, 2009.

———. *They Cried to the Lord: The Form and Theology of Biblical Prayer*. Minneapolis: Fortress Press, 1994.

———. "When the Gods Meet: Psalm 82 and the Issue of Justice." *Journal for Preachers* 9 (1986): 2–5.

Miller, Robert D. "The Origin of the Zion Hymns." In *The Composition of the Book of Psalms*, edited by Erich Zenger, 667–76. Leuven: Peeters, 2010.

Mitchell, Kenneth R., and Herbert Anderson. *All Our Losses, All Our Griefs: Resources for Pastoral Care*. Louisville, KY: Westminster John Knox, 1983.

Moore, Anne. *Moving Beyond Symbol and Myth: Understanding the Kingship of God of the Hebrew Bible through Metaphor*. New York: Peter Lang, 2006.

Morton, Nelle. *The Journey Is Home*. Boston: Beacon Press, 1985.

Muilenburg, James. "Psalm 47." *JBL* 63 (1944): 235–57.

Müllner, Ilse. "Books of Samuel: Women at the Center of Israel's Story," translated by Linda M. Maloney. In *Feminist Biblical Interpretation: A Compendium of Critical Commentary*, edited by Luise Schottroff and Marie-Theres Wacker, 140–52. Grand Rapids, MI: Eerdmans, 2012.

Murphy, Roland. "The Faith of the Psalmist." *Int* 34 (1980): 229–39.

Neher, Andre. *The Exile of the Word: From the Silence of the Bible to the Silence of Auschwitz*. Translated by David Maisel. Philadelphia: Jewish Publication Society of America, 1981.

Nelson, Judith Kay. *Seeing through Tears*. New York: Routledge, 2005.

Neumann, Erich. *Depth Psychology and a New Ethic*. Translated by Eugene Rolfe. Boston and London: Shambhala, 1990.

Newsom, Carol A. "Job." In *Women's Bible Commentary*, edited by Carol A. Newsom, Sharon H. Ringe, and Jacqueline E. Lapsley, 208–15. 3rd ed. Louisville, KY: Westminster John Knox, 2012.

Niditch, Susan. "Defining and Controlling Others Within: Hair, Identity, and the Nazirite Vow in a Second Temple Context." In *The "Other" in Second Temple Judaism: Essays in Honor of John J. Collins*, edited by Daniel C. Harlow, Karina Martin Hogan, Matthew Goff, and Joel S. Kaminsky, 67–85. Grand Rapids, MI: Eerdmans, 2011.

Nielsen, Kirsten. "Poetic Analysis: Psalm 121." In *Method Matters: Essays on the Interpretation of the Hebrew Bible in Honor of David L. Petersen*, edited by Joel LeMon and Kent Harold Richards, 293–309. Atlanta, GA: SBL, 2009.

———. *Ruth*. OTL. Louisville, KY: Westminster John Knox, 1997.

Nordin, John P. " 'There Is Nothing on Earth That I Desire': A Commentary on Psalm 73." *CurTM* 29 (2002): 258–64.

Obinwa, Ignatius M. C. *Yahweh My Refuge: A Critical Analysis of Psalm 71*. Frankfurt: Peter Lang, 2006.

O'Brien, Julia M. "Because God Heard My Voice: The Individual Thanksgiving Psalm and Vow-Fulfillment." In *The Listening Heart: Essays in Wisdom and the Psalms in Honor of Roland E. Murphy*, edited by Kenneth G. Hoglund, 281–98. Sheffield: JSOT Press, 1987.

———. *Challenging Prophetic Metaphor: Theology and Ideology in the Prophets*. Louisville, KY: Westminster John Knox 2008.

O'Connor, Kathleen. *Jeremiah: Pain and Promise*. Minneapolis: Fortress Press, 2011.

———. "Jeremiah." In *Women's Bible Commentary*, edited by Carol A. Newsom, Sharon H. Ringe, and Jacqueline E. Lapsley, 267–77. 3rd ed. Louisville, KY: Westminster John Knox, 2012.

Ogden, Graham S. "Psalm 60: Its Rhetoric, Form, and Function." *JSOT* 31 (1985): 83–94.

Owens, Daniel C. *Portraits of the Righteous in the Psalms*. Eugene, OR: Pickwick, 2013.

Pleins, J. David. *The Psalms: Songs of Tragedy, Hope, and Justice*. Maryknoll, NY: Orbis Books, 1993.

———. *The Social Vision of the Hebrew Bible: A Theological Introduction*. Louisville, KY: Westminster John Knox, 2001.

Potgieter, Johan Hendrik. "The Profile of the Rich Antagonist and the Pious Protagonist in Psalm 52." *HTS* 69 (2013).

Propp, William Henry. "Is Psalm 45 an Erotic Poem?" *BRev* 20 (2004): 33–37, 42.

Pui-lan, Kwok. "Sexual Morality and National Politics: Reading Biblical 'Loose Women.'" In *Engaging the Bible: Critical Readings from Contemporary Women*, edited by Choi Hee An and Kathryn Pfisterer Darr, 21–46. Minneapolis: Fortress, Press, 2006.

Rakel, Claudia. "Judith: About a Beauty Who Is Not What She Pretends to Be." In *Feminist Biblical Interpretation: A Compendium of Critical Commentary*, edited by Luise Schottroff and Marie-Theres Wacker, 515–30. Grand Rapids, MI: Eerdmans, 2012.

Rigby, Cynthia L. "All God, and Us: Double Agency and Reconciliation in Psalms 22 and 51." In *Psalms and Practice: Worship, Virtue, and Authority*. Collegeville, MN: Liturgical Press, 2001.

Roberts, Kathryn L. "My Tongue Will Sing Aloud of Your Deliverance: Praise and Sacrifice in the Psalms." In *Psalms and Practice: Worship, Virtue, and Authority*. Collegeville, MN: Liturgical Press, 2001.

Rom-Shiloni, Dalit. "Psalm 44: The Powers of Protest." *CBQ* 70 (2008): 683–98.

Rosenblit, Barbara Ellison. "David, Bat Sheva, and the Fifty-First Psalm." *Cross Currents* (Fall 1995): 326–40.

Sakenfeld, Katharine Doob. *Just Wives? Stories of Power and Survival in the Old Testament and Today*. Louisville, KY: Westminster John Knox, 2003.

———. *The Meaning of Hesed in the Hebrew Bible*. HSM 17. Missoula, MT: Scholars Press, 1978.

———. "Numbers." In *Women's Bible Commentary*, edited by Carol A. Newsom, Sharon H. Ringe, and Jacqueline E. Lapsley, 79–87. 3rd ed. Louisville, KY: Westminster John Knox, 2012.

————. *Ruth*. Louisville, KY: Westminster John Knox, 1999.

Schaefer, Konrad. *Psalms*. Berit Olam. Collegeville, MN: Liturgical Press, 2001.

Schökel, Luis Alonso. "The Poetic Structure of Psalm 42–43." *JSOT* 1 (19776): 4–21

Scholz, Susanne. "Exodus: The Meaning of Liberation from 'His' Perspective." In *Feminist Biblical Interpretation: A Compendium of Critical Commentary*, edited by Luise Schottroff and Marie-Theres Wacker, 33–50. Grand Rapids, MI: Eerdmans, 2012.

————. "Judges." In *Women's Bible Commentary*, edited by Carol A. Newsom, Sharon H. Ringe, and Jacqueline E. Lapsley, 113–27. 3rd ed. Louisville, KY: Westminster John Knox, 2012.

Schroer, Silvia. " 'Under the Shadow of Your Wings': The Metaphor of God's Wings in the Psalms, Exodus 19.4, Deuteronomy 32.11 and Malachi 3.20, as Seen Through the Perspectives of Feminism and History of Religion." In *A Feminist Companion to Wisdom and Psalms*, edited by Athalya Brenner and Carol Fontaine, 264–82. FCB 2nd ser. Sheffield: Sheffield Academic Press, 1998.

Seibert, Eric. *The Violence of Scripture: Overcoming the Old Testament's Troubling Legacy*. Minneapolis: Fortress Press, 2012.

Sharp, Carolyn J. *Irony and Meaning in the Hebrew Bible*. Bloomington: Indiana University Press, 2009.

Sheppard, Gerald T. " 'Enemies' and the Politics of Prayer in the Book of Psalms." In *The Bible and the Politics of Exegesis*, edited by David Jobling, Peggy Day, and Gerald T. Sheppard, 61–82. Cleveland, OH: Pilgrim Press, 1991.

Smith, Mark S. "El." In *Eerdmans Dictionary of the Bible*, edited by David Noel Freedman, 384–86. Grand Rapids, MI: Eerdmans, 2000.

————. "The Structure of Psalm LXXXVII." *VT* 38 (1988): 357–58.

Smith-Christopher, Daniel. *Jonah, Jesus, and Other Good Coyotes: Speaking Peace to Power in the Bible*. Nashville, TN: Abingdon Press, 2007.

Soskice, Janet Martin. *Metaphor and Religious Language*. Oxford: Clarendon Press; New York: Oxford University Press, 1985.

Stein, Ruth. *For the Love of the Father: A Psychoanalytic Study of Religious Terrorism*. Stanford, CA: Stanford University Press, 2010.

Steussy, Marti J. *Psalms*. St. Louis, MO: Chalice Press, 2004.

Tanner, Beth LaNeel. *The Book of Psalms through the Lens of Intertextuality*. StBibLit 26. New York: Peter Lang, 2001.

————. "Preaching the Penitential Psalms." *WW* 27 (Winter 2007): 88–98.

Tate, Marvin E. *Psalms 51–100*. Dallas, TX: Word Books, 1990.

Tilford, Nicole. "The Greek Book of Daniel." In *Women's Bible Commentary*, edited by Carol A. Newsom, Sharon H. Ringe, and Jacqueline E. Lapsley, 426–31. 3rd ed. Louisville, KY: Westminster John Knox, 2012.

De La Torre, Miguel. Guest Lecture in Liberation Social Ethics. Vanderbilt University. Nashville, TN. November 19, 2013.

Tournay, Raymond. *Seeing and Hearing God with the Psalms: The Prophetic Liturgy of the Second Temple in Jerusalem*. Translated by J. Edward Crowley. JSOTSupp 118. Sheffield: Sheffield Academic Press, 1991.

Townes, Emilie. *In a Blaze of Glory: Womanist Spirituality as Social Witness*. Nashville, TN: Abingdon Press, 1995.

———. "Living in the New Jerusalem: The Rhetoric and Movement of Liberation in the House of Evil." In *A Troubling in My Soul: Womanist Perspectives on Evil and Suffering*, edited by Emilie M. Townes, 78–91. Maryknoll, NY: Orbis Books, 1993.

Townsend Gilkes, Cheryl. "Go and Tell Mary and Martha: The Spirituals, Biblical Options for Women, and Cultural Tensions in the African American Religious Experience." In *Womanist Theological Ethics: A Reader*, edited by Katie G. Cannon, Emilie M. Townes, and Angela D. Sims, 217–36. Louisville, KY: Westminster John Knox, 2011.

———. "'Mother to the Motherless, Father to the Fatherless': Power, Gender, and Community in an Afrocentric Biblical Tradition." *Semeia* 47 (1989): 57–85.

Trible, Phyllis. *God and the Rhetoric of Sexuality*. Philadelphia: Fortress Press, 1978.

Trotter, James M. "Death of the אלהים in Psalm 82." *JBL* 131 (2012): 221–39.

———. "The Genre and Setting of Psalm 45." *ABR* 57 (2009): 34–46.

Trudinger, Peter L. "Friend or Foe? Earth, Sea and *Chaoskampf* in the Psalms." In *The Earth Story in the Psalms and the Prophets*, edited by Norman C. Habel, 29–41. Sheffield: Sheffield Academic Press, 2001.

Tucker, W. Dennis. "Is Shame a Matter of Patronage in the Communal Laments?" *JSOT* 31 (2007): 465–80.

Tweed, Thomas A. *Crossing and Dwelling: A Theory of Religion*. Cambridge, MA: Harvard University Press, 2009.

Ulanov, Ann. *Knots and Their Untying: Essays on Psychological Dilemmas*. New Orleans: Spring Journal, 2014.

Ulanov, Ann, and Barry Ulanov. *The Healing Imagination*. Canada: Diamon Verlag, 1999.

———. *Religion and the Unconscious*. Philadelphia: Westminster Press, 1975.

VanWijk-Bos, Johanna W. H. "Psalm 87." *Int* 47 (1993): 281–85.

Vassar, John. *Recalling a Story Once Told: An Intertextual Reading of the Psalter and the Pentateuch*. Macon, GA: Mercer University Press, 2007.

Villanueva, Frederico G. *The 'Uncertainty of a Hearing': A Study of the Sudden Change of Mood in the Psalms of Lament*. Leiden: Brill, 2008.

Vonk Brooks, Claire. "Psalm 51." *Int* 49 (1995): 62–66.

Walker, Alice. *The Color Purple*. New York: Harcourt Brace Jovanovich, 1982.

———. *In Search of Our Mothers' Gardens: Womanist Prose*. San Diego, CA: Harvest Books: 1983.

Wallace, Beverly. "A Womanist Legacy of Trauma, Grief, and Loss: Reframing the Notion of the Strong Black Woman Icon." In *Women Out of Order: Risking Change and Creating Care in a Multicultural World*, 43–56. Minneapolis: Fortress Press, 2010.

Wallace, Howard N. "*Jubilate Deo omnis terra*: God and Earth in Psalm 65." In *The Earth Story in the Psalms and the Prophets*, edited by Norman C. Habel, 51–64. Cleveland, OH: Pilgrim Press; Sheffield: Sheffield Academic Press, 2001.

Warrior, Robert. "A Native American Perspective: Canaanites, Cowboys, and Indians." In *Voices from the Margin: Interpreting the Bible in the Third World*, edited by R. S. Sugirtharajah, 277–85. Maryknoll, NY: Orbis Books, 1995.

Watson, Rebecca. *Chaos Uncreated: A Reassessment of the Theme of "Chaos" in the Hebrew Bible*. Berlin: de Gruyter, 2005.

Watts, James W. *Psalm and Story: Inset Hymns in Hebrew Narrative*. Sheffield: Sheffield Academic Press, 1992.

Weems, Renita J. *Battered Love: Marriage, Sex, and Violence in the Hebrew Prophets*. Minneapolis: Fortress Press, 1995.

———. "A Mistress, a Maid, and No Mercy." In *Just a Sister Away*. Philadelphia: Innisfree Press, 1988.

Wenham, Gordon J. *Psalms as Torah: Reading Biblical Song Ethically*. Grand Rapids, MI: Baker Academic, 2012.

West, Cornel. *Prophesy Deliverance! An Afro-American Revolutionary Christianity*. Louisville, KY: Westminster John Knox, 2002.

White Crawford, Sidnie. "Esther." In *Women's Bible Commentary*, edited by Carol A. Newsom, Sharon H. Ringe, and Jacqueline E. Lapsley, 201–7. 3rd ed. Louisville, KY: Westminster John Knox, 2012.

Whitekettle, Richard. "Forensic Zoology: Animal Taxonomy and Rhetorical Persuasion in Psalm 1." *VT* 58 (2008): 404–19.

Williams, Ronald J. *Williams' Hebrew Syntax*. 3rd ed. Revised and expanded by John Beckman. Toronto: University of Toronto Press, 2010.

Williamson, H. G. M. "Prophetesses in the Hebrew Bible." In *Prophecy and Prophets in Ancient Israel: Proceedings of the Oxford Old Testament Seminar*, edited by John Day, 65–80. New York: T & T Clark, 2010.

Wilson Costa, Melva. *African American Christian Worship*. Nashville, TN: Abingdon Press, 2007.

Wink, Walter. *Engaging the Powers: Discernment and Resistance in a World of Domination*. Minneapolis: Augsburg Fortress Press, 1992.

Winnicott, Donald W. *Playing and Reality*. London: Routledge Classics, 2005.

Wolde, Ellen van. "Sentiments as Culturally Constructed Emotions: Anger and Love in the Hebrew Bible." *BibInt* 16 (2008): 1–24.

Wren, Brian. *What Language Shall I Borrow? God-Talk in Worship; A Male Response to Feminist Theology*. New York: Crossroad, 1989.

Yoder, Christine Roy. "Proverbs." In *Women's Bible Commentary*, edited by Carol A. Newsom, Sharon H. Ringe, and Jacqueline E. Lapsley, 232–43. 3rd ed. Louisville, KY: Westminster John Knox, 2012.

Zornberg, Avivah Gottlieb. *The Beginning of Desire: Reflections on Genesis*. New York: Doubleday, 1995.

Index of Scripture References

Genesis		23:2	111	Exodus	
1	11, 36, 75,	28:20-22	181		43, 46n,
	174, 310	29:11	112		66, 68, 100,
1:2	318	29:13	331		174, 244,
1:22	186	29:14-30	242, 118		276, 341,
2	35n	30:1	265		359, 370
2:7	75	30:10	74	1	219
2:10-14	38, 175,	30:38-39	74	1:8–2:10	xxx, 341
	347	31:13	181	1:4	134
2:24	160	33:30	324	1:11	121, 302
4:19-20	370	33:4	9, 112,	1:14	134, 302
5:24	59		199, 331	1:15	343
6	310	34	124	1:22	341
7:6	72	35:16-21	265	2	23–25
7:22	75	37:20-29	358	2:1-10	341
8	101n	37:35	265	2:1	341
8:21	74n	42–43	337	2:5-6	341
9:8-17	243	42:24	9, 199	2:11	302
12:1-3	188	43:30	9, 74, 199,	3:7	290, 302,
12:3	47, 224		204		357
12:7	135	46	337	3:20	247, 269
12:10	337	45:2	9, 199	4:27	331
14:18	253	45:15	331	5:4-5	302
16	152	48:10	331	6:6	302
18:25	124	49:10	135	6:9	134
19	100, 362			6:20	342
20:14	74	**Gen. Rab**		7:5	283, 345
21:16	111	82:10	265	9:14	345

Index of Subjects

General Editor

Barbara E. Reid, OP, is a Dominican Sister of Grand Rapids, Michigan. She holds a PhD in biblical studies from The Catholic University of America and is vice president and academic dean and professor of New Testament studies at Catholic Theological Union, Chicago. Her most recent publications are *Wisdom's Feast: An Invitation to Feminist Interpretation of the Scriptures* (2016) and *Abiding Word: Sunday Reflections on Year A, B, C* (3 vols.; 2011, 2012, 2013). She served as president of the Catholic Biblical Association in 2014–2015.

Volume Editor

Linda M. Maloney, PhD, ThD, is a native of Houston, Texas. She studied at St. Louis University (BA, MA, PhD), the University of South Carolina (MIBS), and Eberhard-Karls-Universität Tübingen, where she earned her ThD in New Testament in 1990 under the direction of Prof. Gerhard Lohfink. She has taught at public and private colleges, universities, and seminaries in the United States and was academic editor at Liturgical Press from 1995 to 2005. She is a priest of the Episcopal Church (USA) and lives in Vermont and California.

Author

Denise Dombkowski Hopkins is Woodrow and Mildred Miller Professor of Biblical Theology and Hebrew Bible at Wesley Theological Seminary in Washington, DC. She has authored *Journey through the Psalms* (Chalice Press, 2002) and (with Michael Koppel) *Grounded in the Living Word: The Old Testament and Pastoral Care Practices* (Eerdmans, 2010). She and Michael Koppel have co-chaired the Bible and Practical Theology section in the Society of Biblical Literature for six years. The mother of two, she holds PhD and MA degrees from Vanderbilt University and a BA from Syracuse University.